HISTORICAL DICTIONARIES OF U.S. HISTORICAL ERAS
Jon Woronoff, Series Editor

1. *From the Great War to the Great Depression*, by Neil A. Wynn, 2003.
2. *Civil War and Reconstruction*, by William L. Richter, 2004.
3. *Revolutionary America*, by Terry M. Mays, 2005.

Historical Dictionary of Revolutionary America

Terry M. Mays

Historical Dictionaries of U.S. Historical Eras, No. 3

The Scarecrow Press, Inc.
Lanham, Maryland • Toronto • Oxford
2005

SCARECROW PRESS, INC.

Published in the United States of America
by Scarecrow Press, Inc.
A wholly owned subsidiary of
The Rowman & Littlefield Publishing Group, Inc.
4501 Forbes Boulevard, Suite 200, Lanham, Maryland 20706
www.scarecrowpress.com

PO Box 317
Oxford
OX2 9RU, UK

British Library Cataloguing in Publication Information Available

Library of Congress Cataloging-in-Publication Data

Mays, Terry M.
Historical dictionary of Revolutionary America / Terry M. Mays.
p. cm. — (Historical dictionaries of U.S. historical eras ; no. 3)
Includes bibliographical references.
ISBN 0-8108-5389-2 (hardcover : alk. paper)
1. United States—History—Revolution, 1775–1783—Dictionaries. 2. United States—History—Colonial period, ca. 1600–1775—Dictionaries. 3. United States—History—Confederation, 1783–1789—Dictionaries. I. Title. II. Series.

E209.M356 2005
973.2'5'03—dc22

2005002271

∞™ The paper used in this publication meets the minimum requirements of American National Standard for Information Sciences—Permanence of Paper for Printed Library Materials, ANSI/NISO Z39.48-1992.
Manufactured in the United States of America.

For Richard Reis,
a friend

Contents

Editor's Foreword

This volume on Revolutionary America covers three basic periods, all of them important, but quite different in nature. The most decisive, obviously, was the actual war that was fought to throw off the tyranny of the British Crown, and which accomplished this unprecedented challenge with some difficulty. But it should not, and here does not, overshadow the intriguing period, somewhat arbitrarily fixed as starting in about 1763, when the American colonists as a whole began to feel that this "tyranny," which many of them could have managed to live with, was sufficiently intolerable that a war should be fought. But the period that is most momentous actually followed the war, when the American colonies had to determine both how to govern themselves individually and whether to remain united as one country, this choice being relatively simple, and how to govern an already vast and variegated nation, which required considerably more thought and effort. This period was particularly momentous for the United States of America, because it determined the basis on which the Americans would have to live with one another henceforth. And it was the first time in world history that anything quite like this had been done. No wonder the debate was complex and divisive and it took until 1787 for the Constitution to be framed, and finally ratified two years later.

Historical Dictionary of Revolutionary America covers all three periods, although much of the details of the actual war appear in a companion volume. This book takes a closer look at the causes and the consequences. It includes entries on the various unwise measures imposed by the Crown, the reactions of the colonists, the sparks that ignited the war, and the crucial battles. Especially, it has entries on the assemblies that presided over the creation of the Constitution, the persons who played a significant role in framing it, many of whom soon moved on to governing the country. The complexity of the times becomes somewhat clearer by including entries on the thirteen colonies that eventually became the original thirteen states. The overall process is described more generally in the introduction and traced more precisely in the chronology. Given the impact of the revolutionary era, not only for subsequent American history but also more broadly, there is no lack of books that have been written on the period, but the problem of any bibliography is not to produce a long list of titles but rather to limit them to those that provide adequate coverage of the period as a whole and its various aspects.

This volume was fortunately written by the author of the *Historical Dictionary of the American Revolution*, Terry M. Mays. That makes it much easier for the two to cover the period, the first stressing the military side, the current one dealing more with the economic, social, and especially political aspects. Dr. Mays, who is presently associate professor of political science at the Citadel, teaches and writes on history with some emphasis on the revolutionary era. But his interests are considerably broader, having also written the *Historical Dictionary of Multinational Peacekeeping* and the *Historical Dictionary of International Organizations in Sub-Saharan Africa*. He obviously likes this approach, and has become accustomed to it, which is an advantage to those reading this latest addition to the series of Historical Dictionaries of U.S. Historical Eras.

Jon Woronoff
Series Editor

Acknowledgments

Many individuals and organizations deserve thanks for assisting with this project. The illustrations in this book are included courtesy of Dover Publishing Company (*The American Revolution: A Picture Source Book*, edited by John Grafton). Librarians and library staff at the Citadel, College of Charleston, and the University of South Carolina were very helpful during the preparation of the book. As usual, Jon Woronoff and Kim Tabor have proven to be a great editorial team with whom to work. The Citadel Foundation funded a research trip to gather information for this book. Last, but certainly not least, my wife, Leslee, provided the moral support required to complete this project.

Chronology

1733 **17 May:** Molasses Act passed.

1751 **June 10:** Currency Act of 1751 passed by parliament.

1754 **19 June–10 July:** Albany Congress.

1758 **October:** Treaty of Easton.

1761 **November:** Mohawk Valley Report is released.

1763 **10 February:** Treaty of Paris. **7 May:** Pontiac's War begins. **5 August:** Battle of Edgehill. **6 August:** Battle of Bushy Run. **7 October:** Proclamation of 1763. **November:** Augusta Conference of 1763. **16 November:** General Gage arrives in New York City.

1764 **5 April:** Sugar Act passed. **19 April:** Currency Act passed. **30 June:** Americans arrest the captain of the British vessel *Saint John*. **9 July:** Americans fire upon the *Saint John*.

1765 **22 March:** Stamp Act passed. **29 May:** Virginia Resolves passed in Virginia. **14 August:** First use of a "Liberty Tree" to hang British officials in effigy. **7–24 October:** Stamp Act Congress. **14 October:** Stamp Act Congress approves the Declaration of Rights and Grievances (1765). **1 November:** Effective date for implementation of the Stamp Act.

1766 **17 March:** Parliament repeals the Stamp Act and passes the Declaratory Act. **24 July:** End of Pontiac's War. Treaty of Oswego.

1767 **29 June:** Townshend Acts passed. **5 November:** American Board of Customs Commissioners arrives in the colonies. **20 November:** Effective date for the Townshend Revenue Act.

1768 **10 June:** British customs officials seize the *Liberty*. **30 June:** Massachusetts Assembly refused to repeal the Massachusetts Circular

Letter. **1 August:** Nonimportation Agreements established in Boston. **1 October:** British soldiers arrive in Boston. **November:** First Treaty of Fort Stanwix.

1769 16 May: Virginia Resolves passed. **18 May:** Passage of the Virginia Association.

1770 19 January: Confrontation on Golden Hill. **5 March:** Boston Massacre. **12 April:** Parliament repeals the Townshend Revenue Act.

1771 16 May: Battle of the Alamance.

1772 9 June: Americans burn the *Gaspée*.

1773 10 May: Parliament passes the Tea Act. **14 October:** British cargo burned at Annapolis. **28 November:** The first British tea ship, the *Dartmouth*, arrives in the Colonies following the Tea Act of 1773. **2 December:** Tea ship *Eleanor* arrives in Boston. **16 December:** Boston Tea Party.

1774 25 March: Parliament passes the Boston Port Bill. **19 May:** Farmington Resolves adopted. **20 May:** Parliament passes the Administration of Justice Act, the Massachusetts Government Act, and the Quebec Act. **1 June:** Boston Port Act becomes effective. **2 June:** Quartering Act passed. **1 September:** British seize gunpowder stored in Charleston. **5 September:** First Continental Congress convenes. **9 September:** Passage of the Suffolk Resolves. **28 September:** Galloway Plan of Union is proposed to Congress. **10 October:** Battle of Point Pleasant. **14 October:** Congress approves the Statement of Rights and Grievances. **19 October:** *Peggy Stewart* incident. **20 October:** Congress approves the Continental Association. **26 October:** First Continental Congress adjourns. **26 October:** Massachusetts Acts are adopted. **9 December:** Ordnance seized in Newport. **14 December:** Ordnance seized from Fort William and Mary in Portsmouth. **27 December:** Charleston Tea Party.

1775 26 February: British raid Salem. **27 February:** Parliament passes the Conciliatory Resolution. **23 March:** Patrick Henry delivers his "Give Me Liberty, or Give Me Death" speech. **19 April:** Battle of Lexington-Concord. **10 May:** Second Continental Congress convenes. **31 May:** Passage of the Mecklenburg Resolves. **14 June:** Congress establishes the Continental Army. **30 June:** Congress adopts the Continental Articles of War. **3 July:** George Washington assumes command of the Continental Army. **5 July:** Congress adopts the Olive Branch Petition. **6 July:** Congress adopts the Declaration of the Causes and Necessities of Taking Up Arms. **3 September:** Grand Union Flag adopted. **13 October:** Congress authorizes a navy. **30 October:** Congress establishes the Naval Committee. **7 November:** Congress amends the Continental Articles of War. **29 November:** Congress establishes the Committee of Secret Correspondence. **13 December:** Congress authorizes the Naval Construction Act of 1775. **22 December:** Parliament passes the American Prohibitory Act.

1776 10 January: *Common Sense* is published. **23 March:** Congress authorizes privateering. **2 May:** France authorizes secret aid to the Americans. **13 June:** Congress establishes the Board of War and Ordnance. **4 July:** American colonies declare their independence from Great Britain. **19 December:** *Crisis* is published. **20 December:** Congress reconvenes in Baltimore. **21 December:** Benjamin Franklin arrives in Paris.

1777 23 January: Congress passes the Naval Construction Act of 1777. **17 April:** Committee of Secret Correspondence renamed the Committee on Foreign Affairs. **17 April:** Congress establishes the Navy Board of the Eastern Department. **14 June:** Congress adopts the Stars and Stripes. **27 September:** Congress reconvenes in Lancaster after evacuating Philadelphia. **17 October:** Board of War and Ordnance reorganized as the Board of War. **15 November:** Articles of Confederation signed.

1778 6 February: Franco-American alliance signed. **2 July:** Congress reconvenes in Philadelphia. **29 October:** Congress reorganizes the Board of War.

1779 21 June: Spain declares war on Great Britain. **28 October:** Congress establishes the Board of Admiralty.

1780 29 February: Russia proposes the establishment of the Neutrality League. **20–22 September:** Hartford Conference.

1781 6 January: Committee of Foreign Affairs transformed into the Executive Secretary of Foreign Affairs. **7 February:** Department of War replaces the Board of War. **7 March:** Final ratification of the Articles of Confederation. **3 March:** Second Continental Congress becomes the United States in Congress Assembled (Congress of the Confederation). **31 December:** Congress establishes the Bank of North America.

1782 19 April: Netherlands officially recognizes the independence of the United States.

1783 11 April: Congress proclaims the end of the American Revolution. **13 May:** Society of the Cincinnati formed. **3 September:** Treaty of Paris is signed.

1784 23 April: Ordinance of 1784 is passed. **October:** Second Treaty of Fort Stanwix. **November:** Treaty of Augusta.

1785 January: Treaty of Fort McIntosh. **27 January:** University of Georgia becomes the first public, nondenominational state university in the United States. **March:** Alexandria convention. **May:** Treaty of Dumplin Creek. **November:** Treaty of Galphinton.

1786 January: Treaty of Fort Finney. **February:** John Adams meets with the Tripoli ambassador to Great Britain. **1 March:** Ohio Company is organized. **August:** Shays's Rebellion begins. **September:** Annapolis convention.

1787 2 February: Shays's Rebellion ends. **25 May:** Constitutional Convention opens. **17 September:** Delegates complete the Constitution. **7 December:** Delaware ratifies the Constitution. **12 December:** Pennsylvania ratifies the Constitution. **18 December:** New Jersey ratifies the Constitution.

1788 2 January: Georgia ratifies the Constitution. **9 January:** Connecticut ratifies the Constitution. **6 February:** Massachusetts ratifies the Constitution. **12 April:** Doctors' Mob attacks a New York hospital. **28 April:** Maryland ratifies the Constitution. **23 May:** South Carolina ratifies the Constitution. **21 June:** The Constitution becomes effective with its ratification by New Hampshire. **25 June:** Virginia ratifies the Constitution. **21 July–2 August:** Hillsborough convention. **26 October:** New York ratifies the Constitution.

1789 4 March: Congress of the United States of America replaces the Congress of the Confederation. **6 April:** Electors select George Washington as the first president of the United States. **21 November:** Fayetteville convention concludes and North Carolina ratifies the Constitution.

1790 29 May: Rhode Island ratifies the Constitution.

Introduction

Many authors have prepared research books on the Revolutionary War—a conflict that secured American independence. The bold American stand on independence opened the door for the country to rise and become the greatest economic and political power on the globe in less than 200 years after that hot July day in 1776 when representatives of each of the 13 colonies penned their names to the Declaration of Independence. While the vast majority of the research works concentrate on the American reaction to British taxation policies and the military aspects of the conflict, what about the other political as well as economic and social events of the era?

The years 1763 to 1789 represented the most pivotal period in American history until the Civil War. Between 1763 and 1776, the colonies evolved to challenge British taxation, form a new confederation based on Enlightenment principles, and then declare themselves free from the mother country. From 1776 to 1782, this new political entity struggled to remain in existence as it fought one of the greatest military powers in the world while engaged in a near civil war at home over independence and desperately seeking other countries that would pledge military and/or economic support to its cause. The United States swayed precariously between being dissolved or strengthening itself between 1783 and 1789 as the 13 states acted more like 13 sovereign countries than a single united country.

Historical Dictionary of Revolutionary America examines the political, economic, and social issues facing Americans between 1763 and 1789. While military issues are mentioned in this book, it is intended as a companion volume to *Historical Dictionary of the American Revolution* (Scarecrow Press, 1999), which concentrates on the military issues of the Revolutionary War. Together, these two books should provide general readers and students a concise snapshot of the issues, people, and events confronting the United States during its Revolutionary period.

Readers will notice many interesting things about the Revolutionary period. Americans in the 21st century often make comments about political dynasties such as the Kennedy and Bush families. Family dynasties are not unique to current American politics because many statesmen were related to each other during the Revolutionary period as well. For example, John and Samuel Adams were cousins. John would become president of the United States and then be followed in the same position later by his son, John Quincy Adams. Benjamin and Jonathan Austin were brothers; Daniel and John Carroll were brothers as well as the cousins of Charles Carroll; Richard Dana was the father of Francis Dana; Benjamin Harrison's son, William Henry Harrison, and great-grandson, Benjamin Harrison, would each become president of the United States; Allen and Willie Jones were brothers; John and Woodbury Langdon were brothers; Henry Laurens was the father of John Laurens; Arthur, Francis, Richard Henry, and William Lee were brothers and related to Henry (Light Horse Harry) Lee, the father of Robert E. Lee of Civil War fame; Philip and William Livingston were brothers and the cousins of Robert Livingston; Thomas Lynch Sr. was the father of Thomas Lynch Jr.; George Mason was the uncle of Stevens Mason; Henry Middleton was the father of Arthur Middleton; Gouverneur Morris was the half-brother of Lewis and Robert Morris; Charles Pinckney was the cousin of brothers Charles Cotesworth Pinckney and Thomas Pinckney; Caesar Rodney was the father of Thomas Rodney; and Edward and John Rutledge were brothers. Many other statesmen of the period were also related.

Many Americans in the 18th century moved between states although not as frequently as those of the 21st century. William Few sat in Congress for Georgia while Rufus King served in Congress for Massachusetts. Later, both men became U.S. senators from New York. Thomas McKean served as a congressional representative from Delaware and later became governor of Pennsylvania. John Mercer was elected to serve in Congress for Virginia and later signed the U.S. Constitution for Maryland and became governor of that state.

Americans faced various social issues between 1763 and 1789 that would divide the population and not be solved until later centuries. Many Americans, such as John Bacon, questioned the morality of slavery and its place in a society founded under Enlightenment principles. Despite the slavery issue, African Americans made important contributions to Revolutionary America. Many fought for American independence and others emerged as leaders in other fields. Phillis Wheatley became a great American poet of the era while Richard Allen is known for his social work with other African Americans. John Bacon and others also stood up for the rights of Native Americans and the treatment they received as Americans pushed ever westward into their lands. Women like Abigail Adams began to question the issues related to women's rights. Adams reminded her husband, John, to not forget the role of women when he and the other Founding Fathers were debating the core documents related to American government. Despite the widening gaps between various opponents of social issues, Revolutionary America witnessed the budding international recognition of American art and science with men such as Benjamin Franklin, cousins John Bartram and Humphrey Marshall, and William Bartram, the son of John.

The American economy, based on the colonial development of agriculture, fishing/whaling, and the lumber-related industries, was export driven. Economics and taxation played major roles in the growing tensions between the American colonies and Great Britain that would lead to the development of the United States. After independence, the United States found itself adrift with few locations willing to trade on favorable terms with the new country. Perseverance and American diplomacy would slowly erode these barriers. Printing also proved to be an important element of the American economy. The large number of American printers can be seen as an important element in uniting Americans to oppose British taxation policies and then promoting the development of democracy in the newly established United States.

The survival of the United States hung in the balance during the Revolutionary period. Americans were often divided in the direction and strength of a national government. The inhabitants of Kentucky, Tennessee, and Vermont threatened to declare the establishment of their own independent countries or become provinces of the colonial holdings of European countries if not admitted as states to the United States. The completion of the U.S. Constitution in 1787 followed bitter debates between state representatives over slavery, representation in Congress, and other issues. Rhode Island balked at ratifying the U.S. Constitution until May 1790. Today, the U.S. Constitution is the oldest written constitution in current use by a sovereign country. Despite all of the differences and challenges, the United States emerged and survived to grow into the economic and political power that it has become in the 21st century. The collection of entries in *Historical Dictionary of Revolutionary America* presents this story.

The Dictionary

– A –

ADAIR, JAMES (c.1709–c.1783). James Adair, a trader, is noted for his written descriptions of **Native Americans** in the southeast during the Revolutionary period. In 1775, Adair wrote *The History of the American Indian*. Although Adair falsely believed and claimed that Native Americans were descended from the Jews, his book is a classic for its description of southeast Native American culture in the mid to late 18th century.

ADAMS, ABIGAIL (1744–1818). Abigail Adams, the wife of President **John Adams** and mother of President John Quincy Adams, demonstrated the stamina exhibited by many **women** during the Revolutionary period. While her husband served in **Congress** and later as the American minister to **France**, Abigail Adams assumed the responsibility of managing the family farm and overseeing family affairs. After the **Revolutionary War**, she joined her husband in France. She is well known today as a writer and produced a considerable correspondence that described her life and that of her husband as well as general conditions during the Revolutionary period of American history.

ADAMS, ANDREW (1736–1797). Andrew Adams, a lawyer and judge, served in the **Connecticut** legislature. He accepted an appointment as a colonel in the **militia** and became a member of the Council of Safety. He represented Connecticut in the **Second Continental Congress** from 1777–1779 and signed the **Articles of Confederation**. Adams, after departing Congress, returned to the state legislature and then became chief justice of the Connecticut Supreme Court.

ADAMS, HANNAH (1755–1837). Hannah Adams, a distant cousin of **John Adams**, emerged as a successful historian in Revolutionary America. Although she wrote many books, her 1784 work on the history of religious groups and sects is the most famous.

ADAMS, JOHN (1735–1826). John Adams was one of the greatest individuals to rise to prominence during the Revolutionary period. Adams, a cousin of **Samuel Adams**, was born in **Massachusetts** and became one of the best lawyers in that colony. Adams emerged as a major political leader following the imposition of the **Stamp Act of 1765** by **Great Britain**. He opposed the act along with other attempts at British **taxation** of the **colonies**. However, he refused to stand by and permit any unfair persecution of the British soldiers involved in the **Boston Massacre**. Adams defended the soldiers against murder charges although two did receive manslaughter convictions. The popularity of Adams resulted in his selection to serve in the colonial legislature in 1771 alongside his cousin Samuel. John Adams continued to oppose British taxation policies and applauded the **Boston Tea Party**, an event probably orchestrated by his cousin.

The legislature chose Adams as one of its four delegates to the **First Continental Congress** in 1774 and then the **Second Continental Congress** from 1775–1777. When **Richard Henry Lee** introduced a resolution declaring the colonies an independent country, Adams seconded the motion and became a member of the committee that drafted what is now known as the **Declaration of Independence**. **Thomas Jefferson** later credited Adams as one of the greatest defenders of the Declaration during the congressional debate over its adoption. In 1778, Congress dispatched Adams to Paris where he replaced **Silas Deane** and worked with **Benjamin Franklin** and **Arthur Lee** to represent the new country in **France**. Adams warned Congress of the friction between Franklin and Lee resulting in that body designating Franklin as the chief representative of the United States. Adams returned home in 1779 where he proved to be instrumental in developing a constitution for his home state. In 1780, Adams returned to France and then traveled to the **Netherlands** to negotiate treaties between that country and the United States. After much hard work, he did secure Dutch recognition of the United

States in 1782, after the former had entered the war against Great Britain. He also obtained a Dutch loan for the American government.

In 1782, Adams returned to France and helped negotiate the **Treaty of Paris** with which Great Britain recognized American independence. He remained in Europe to negotiate another treaty with the Dutch as well as a commercial treaty with France. Congress named Adams as minister to Great Britain in 1785. However, after three years of unsuccessful attempts to negotiate commercial and **trade** treaties with the British government, Adams requested to be replaced and returned home in 1788. Adams became the first vice president of the United States under the **Constitution** and later the country's second president from 1797–1801. His son, John Quincy Adams, served as president of the United States from 1825–1829. *See also* ADAMS, ABIGAIL.

ADAMS, SAMUEL (1722–1803). Samuel Adams of **Massachusetts**, a cousin of **John Adams**, emerged as one of the most important American political agitators prior to the commencement of armed hostilities with **Great Britain** in 1775. Adams, an unsuccessful businessman, became a leading spokesman in **Boston** against the various **taxation** plans imposed by the British. He served in the colonial legislature between 1765 and 1775, during which he corresponded with individuals in other **colonies** about British political and economic aims in North America. He has been credited with much of the political agitation that resulted in the **Boston Massacre** in 1770. Adams helped form the **Sons of Liberty** and the **Nonimportation Association,** wrote the **Massachusetts Circular Letter**, and was active in preparing the **Suffolk Resolves**. Adams is often cited as the political leader behind the **Boston Tea Party** in 1773. When the British retaliated with the **Intolerable Acts**, he called for unified colonial resistance. His actions were partially responsible for the convening of the **First Continental Congress** in 1774. The British attempted to arrest Adams in 1775, leading to the clash of arms at the **Battle of Lexington-Concord**. Adams served in the First Continental Congress and **Second Continental Congress** from 1774–1781. He signed the **Articles of Confederation**. Adams provided important support for the ratification of the **Constitution** and later served as the governor of Massachusetts.

ADAMS, THOMAS (1730–1788). Thomas Adams served in the **Virginia** legislature. Between 1777 and 1788, he represented Virginia in the **Second Continental Congress** and signed the **Articles of Confederation**. He was elected later to the Virginia Senate.

ADMINISTRATION OF JUSTICE ACT OF 1774. Following the **Boston Tea Party**, the British government enacted the four **Intolerable Acts** in retaliation against **Boston** and **Massachusetts**. Passed on May 20, 1774, the Administration of Justice Act, also known as the Impartial Administration of Justice Act, was one of these four Intolerable Acts. This act declared that royal officials, including magistrates and customs collectors, charged with breaking a law while carrying out an act of the British Parliament or attempting to halt a riot by the populace could face trial in another colony or England. The British government believed that such officials might not be able to receive fair trials in Massachusetts. Witnesses were to be given free transportation to the place of trial and remain free from any arrest while testifying at the trial. The act, along with the other Intolerable Acts, served to anger the inhabitants of Massachusetts and helped to solidify the opposition of the American **colonies** against **Great Britain**.

ADMIRALTY COURTS. Admiralty Courts, also known as Vice-Admiralty Courts, handled court cases dealing with maritime issues. In the American **colonies**, local civil courts usually tried maritime cases until 1696 when the Admiralty Courts assumed this responsibility. The British extended the jurisdiction of these courts in the **Townshend Revenue Act of 1767** and established Admiralty Courts in **Boston**, **Charleston**, **Halifax**, and **Philadelphia**. Halifax was designated as the senior or supreme Admiralty Court since it was located outside of the 13 American colonies. British officials felt that its location would make it more difficult for American smugglers to influence the judges who were royal appointees. The colonists despised the Admiralty Courts because they operated without juries and tried cases resulting from enforcement of the various **taxation** acts passed by Parliament. Colonists also viewed the system as one in which the accused individual was presumed guilty and then had to prove innocence. Even if cleared of the charges, the accused could not claim or sue for damages or the expenses associated with the trial.

AFRICAN AMERICANS AND REVOLUTIONARY AMERICA. The term "African American" is utilized in this book to refer to individuals of African origin who were living in the American **colonies** or the independent United States. The vast majority of the African Americans living in Revolutionary America were slaves. However, a minority of African Americans were free and could be found in nearly every **colony**, if not every colony. **Slavery** existed in every colony prior to the Revolution. There were even free African Americans living in the **southern colonies** where slavery was more prevalent. Some of the latter were forced to wear special tags to identify themselves and prevent confusion with slaves. While some free African Americans lived comfortable lives as social equals with others in the general population, many others faced prejudice and social persecution. Free African Americans could be found in many professions, including sailors and soldiers during the **Revolutionary War**. In 1787, **Richard Allen** formed the Free African Society as an organization to assist in meeting the needs of free African Americans. Prominent African Americans during the Revolutionary America period include **Crispus Attucks**, **Paul Cuffee**, **Prince Hall**, **Jupiter Hammon**, **Peter Salem**, and **Phillis Wheatley**. *See also* BACON, JOHN; BOWDOIN, JAMES; FRANCHISE.

AGENT OF THE MARINE. The **Second Continental Congress** transferred oversight of the **Continental Navy** from the **American Board of Admiralty** to the Agent of the Marine on August 29, 1781. Congress appointed **Robert Morris** to this position in addition to his regular duties as the superintendent of finances. The one-man, part-time organization oversaw the Continental Navy until 1784. One reason for the transfer of duties from a seven-man committee to a single individual can be understood when realizing that by the close of 1781, the Continental Navy consisted of only two operational vessels, the *Alliance* and the *Deane*.

AGRICULTURE. Farming was the most important profession in Revolutionary America. Estimates place 90 percent of the American population as farmers through 1787. The majority of the farmers produced food for personal consumption but many did harvest a surplus for sale to others, including those living in towns. The agricultural conditions were most difficult in **New England** where the soil was often rocky and poor for many crops. The harsh winters of the area and shortened summers also affected agriculture in the area. As a result, many New Englanders made their living from the sea and others fished on a part-time basis to supplement their poor agricultural harvests. New England farms tended to be subsistence only and crops included corn, oats, rye, barley, buckwheat, fruits, and vegetables. Individual farmers worked their own land or hired free workers to assist them.

The **middle colonies** had more fertile soil and a longer growing season than New England. This permitted the production of different crops such as **wheat** and potatoes as well as barley, oats, and rye. Many scholars refer to the area as the "colonial breadbasket" because of the wheat production. Farms tended to be larger than those in New England, leading to the export of some crops such as wheat, which was **traded** with the British West Indies. Labor included landowners, free workers hired as assistants, and some **slavery**.

Farming in the **southern colonies** naturally included subsistence but also a much greater number of large-scale plantations producing crops intended for export rather than the local market. Export crops included **indigo**, **rice**, and **tobacco** that were worked via the slavery system. Crops for local consumption included corn, fruit, and vegetables.

During the **Revolutionary War**, the agricultural export industry declined but many American products still found their way to British markets by means of transshipping through neutral ports. Despite the war, up to one-third of pre-Revolution tobacco exports still arrived in **Great Britain**. Immediately after the Revolution, the Europeans imposed tariffs on American goods and the British refused to negotiate a commercial treaty with the United States. These difficulties continued to keep American agricultural exports below their pre-Revolution levels.

AITKEN BIBLE. *See* AITKEN, ROBERT.

AITKEN, ROBERT (1734–1802). Robert Aitken, a printer and publisher, immigrated to **Philadelphia** from Scotland in 1771. He printed the New Testament in 1777 after the British embargo prevented the importation of testaments and Bibles from **Great Britain**. Aitken is perhaps best known for his "Aitken Bible" of 1782, which became the first English-language Bible printed in the United States.

ALAMANCE, BATTLE OF THE. The Battle of the Alamance, fought on May 16, 1771, between the **regulators** and the government of **North Carolina**, ended what is sometimes referred to as the War of the Regulation. The engagement occurred at Alamance Creek near the modern cities Greensboro and Burlington, North Carolina. In March 1771, the Superior Court of Hillsborough reported that its members could not conduct business due to fears of regulator interference. In response, Governor **William Tryon** called out the **militia** and ordered General Hugh Waddell to march with a second militia contingent from the Cape Fear area to the western frontier. A small group of regulators attacked and destroyed a gunpowder convoy dispatched from **South Carolina**. The regulators also confronted General Waddell and his 284-man force at the Yadkin River. Due to overwhelming odds and the concern that his men would not fire upon the regulators, Waddell ordered his militia unit to withdraw to Salisbury.

Meanwhile, Governor Tryon, commanding approximately 1,100 militia, camped near the Alamance Creek while the regulators, numbering approximately 2,000, moved to block Tryon's advance. At this point many of the regulators still hoped to avoid a clash with the militia. Governor Tryon ordered the regulators to submit and disperse. When they refused the order, Tryon ordered the militia to fire upon the regulators. The militia hesitated but commenced firing following the continued demands of Governor Tryon. Many of the regulators returned fire, leading to a battle that lasted two hours. Although a few regulators held their ground against the militia and even managed to capture an artillery piece, the majority of the group departed the battlefield. Reportedly, the militia suffered nine deaths and 61 wounded while the regulators had nine killed and an undetermined number of wounded. Fifteen regulators were captured. One was executed on the spot and six others were executed later.

The engagement demonstrates the frustrations of the North Carolina colonists living on the frontier with the government along the eastern seaboard. The frontiersmen would demonstrate a unique independence throughout the upcoming **Revolutionary War** and prove to be key elements in the battles of Moore's Creek in North Carolina and King's Mountain in South Carolina.

ALARM. *Alarm* was the name given to a series of **newspaper** articles in **New York City** during 1773 protesting the British intent to allow the **East India Company** to import chests of tea into **Boston**, **Charleston**, **New York City**, and **Philadelphia** under the **Tea Act**. The articles added tension to the economic situation over **taxation** and helped fuel the popular opposition that led to the **Boston Tea Party**. *See also* HAMPDEN.

ALARM RIDERS. The **Massachusetts** Provincial Congress established the alarm riders after the British imposed the **Intolerable Acts** in 1774. The riders would ride throughout the countryside warning the inhabitants whenever the British troops marched from **Boston**. **Paul Revere** and **William Dawes** are the best known of the alarm riders due to their attempt to alert the local **militia** units prior to the **Battle of Lexington-Concord**.

ALBANY CONGRESS. In 1754, **Great Britain** called a conference between the **Iroquois** Confederation and the American **colonies** located north of **North Carolina**. The British invited **Maryland**, **Massachusetts**, **Pennsylvania**, **New Hampshire**, **New Jersey**, **New York**, and **Virginia**. New Jersey opted not to participate and Virginia requested that **James DeLancey**, the lieutenant governor of New York, represent it at the meeting. Although not invited, **Connecticut** and **Rhode Island** sent delegates to the gathering. The seven colonies in attendance sent a total of 23 delegates under the leadership of **Benjamin Franklin**, **William Johnson**, and **Thomas Hutchinson** to the meeting. The conference, held from June 19 to July 10, 1754, aimed at securing a peace treaty with the Iroquois during the opening of hostilities between the French and British in the **French and Indian War**. The delegates met with approximately 150 Iroquois chiefs and attempted to persuade them to form an alliance against the French.

The Iroquois leaders rejected the arguments and bribes of the colonists and in turn delivered a series of complaints against them. During the war most of the Iroquois did side with the English colonies due to French and other **Native American** attacks on their settlements. The meeting failed to complete a treaty with the Iroquois but did result in the never-ratified **Albany Plan of Union**.

ALBANY PLAN OF UNION. The colonial delegates at the **Albany Congress** in 1754, at the urging of **Benjamin Franklin** and others, developed the Albany Plan of Union. The document called for a loose union of all the North American **colonies** except Nova Scotia and **Georgia**. Some have argued that Franklin developed the plan after observing the **Iroquois** Confederation. The Union would have a president general appointed by **Great Britain** who would serve as the chief executive of the government. The legislative branch, the grand council, would consist of delegates from all of the American colonies except **Delaware** and Georgia. Colonies would have varied representation in the legislature based on their size and wealth. The powers of the legislature would include raising a colonial army, purchasing **Native American** lands in the name of the British Crown, establishing taxes, and enacting colonial-wide laws. None of the colonies ratified the plan, to the relief of Great Britain, which felt wary of a colonial unification scheme in North America. The plan is significant in that it set a precedent for establishing a union that would materialize with the **First Continental Congress** and the **Second Continental Congress**.

ALCOHOL. American gentry tended to consume imported alcoholic beverages while poorer Americans frequently turned to locally brewed drinks. Sherry and Madeira wine were favorites of the wealthy while most Americans consumed large quantities of ale, beer, or rum brewed from West Indies molasses. Other alcoholic beverages included cider, whiskey, and brandy and were made from local ingredients. The domestic consumption of alcohol was frequently controlled on Sundays through the introduction of "blue laws." The **Sugar Act of 1764** was a British attempt to restrict **trade**, especially sugar and molasses, from the West Indies and led to considerable **smuggling** by American merchants and traders. Madeira wines were also smuggled into Revolutionary America to avoid British trade restrictions. *See also* PUNCH.

ALEXANDRIA CONVENTION. Poor economic conditions in the post-Revolution United States and the weakness of the government under the **Articles of Confederation** to solve them resulted in near anarchy in many states. **Shays's Rebellion** in 1786 **Massachusetts** stands out as one of the most visible and potentially violent confrontations. In March 1785, **Maryland** and **Virginia** recognized that they needed to do something within their particular states. The states shared a common border yet had different commercial regulations and faced similar problems with potentially lawless groups of residents. Representatives of the two states met in 1785 to examine their mutual problems and moved their discussions to Mount Vernon, the home of **George Washington**, at the latter's request. The representatives completed an agreement and sent the document to **Congress** for ratification. At the same time, Maryland suggested calling a convention on commercial issues and invited **Delaware** and **Pennsylvania** to join itself and Virginia in the negotiations. The state of Virginia agreed with the suggestion but added that the meeting should include representatives of all 13 states. This particular meeting, known as the **Annapolis Convention**, met in September 1786. The Alexandria and Annapolis Conventions are forerunners to the **Constitutional Convention of 1787**.

ALGIERS AND REVOLUTIONARY AMERICA. *See* BARBARY STATES AND REVOLUTIONARY AMERICA.

ALLEN, ANDREW (1740–1825). Andrew Allen, a lawyer, was elected to the **Committee of Safety** for **Pennsylvania** in 1775 and then the **Second Continental Congress** in 1776. He opposed the **Declaration of Independence** that had been signed just prior to his arrival in Congress and resigned from that body after serving for only one month. Allen sought British protection and became the lieutenant governor of Pennsylvania during the British occupation of **Philadelphia**. He departed the city with the British army and left the United States. After the **Revolutionary War**, Pennsylvania pardoned Allen. However, he chose to live permanently in **Great Britain** and died there in 1825.

ALLEN, ETHAN (1737–1789). Ethan Allen, the brother of **Ira Allen**, is best known as a soldier during the **Revolutionary War** and the leader of the Green Mountain Boys. Allen and his brother opened negotiations with Quebec when **Congress** balked at granting statehood to **Vermont**. Historians are not sure today if the move was serious or just a ploy to persuade others to act in favor of admitting Vermont to the country as a state.

ALLEN, IRA (1751–1814). Ira Allen, the brother of **Ethan Allen**, served as a soldier during the **Revolutionary War**. Along with his brother, Allen is known for the negotiations with Quebec following the refusal of **Congress** to grant statehood to **Vermont**. Historians are not sure today if the move was serious or just a ploy to persuade others to act in favor of admitting Vermont to the country as a state.

ALLEN, RICHARD (1760–1831). Richard Allen, a former slave in **Delaware**, purchased his freedom in 1786. Allen moved to **Philadelphia** and in 1787 helped establish the Free African Society, an organization that assisted free **African Americans** during the Revolutionary period. He later founded the African Methodist Episcopal Church (A.M.E.). *See also* SLAVERY.

ALLEN, WILLIAM (1704–1780). William Allen, a merchant and jurist, proved to be influential in the protest against British **taxation** policies prior to the **Revolutionary War**. In 1763, Allen, in **Great Britain**, persuaded the British government to postpone the new sugar duties. He also assisted **Benjamin Franklin** to secure the repeal of the **Stamp Act of 1765**. Allen believed in reconciliation and compromise between the American **colonies** and Great Britain. He chose to remain in Great Britain but returned to **Philadelphia** in 1779 in order to free his slaves.

ALMANACS. *See* PUBLICATIONS.

AMERICAN BOARD OF ADMIRALTY. The **Second Continental Congress** transformed the **Marine Committee** into the American Board of Admiralty on October 28, 1779. The Marine Committee, which oversaw the operations of the **Continental Navy**, exhibited many internal problems and proved unable to oversee American ships at sea. The American Board of Admiralty consisted of two congressmen and three individuals not serving in Congress. The latter three were expected to have knowledge of naval affairs. The establishment of the board was an attempt to reorganize oversight of the Continental Navy by duplicating the British method for controlling their navy. Additional problems led to a second reorganization with the transformation of the board to the **Agent of the Marine** in the late summer of 1781.

AMERICAN BOARD OF CUSTOMS COMMISSIONERS. The **Townshend Acts of 1767**, enacted by **Charles Townshend**, included the establishment of the American Board of Customs Commissioners in 1767. Before this period, the British government utilized a tax-collection system for the **colonies** employing commissioners. These individuals received their commissions and usually remained at home in **Great Britain**. The commissioners would hire other individuals to travel to the colonies and carry out the duties of collecting import taxes. Townshend, Chancellor of the Exchequer, opted to tighten this system by establishing the American Board of Customs Commissioners. The board consisted of five commissioners actually based in **Boston** who, ignoring colonial opposition, turned to making tax collecting a profitable exercise for themselves and the British government. The board members arrived on November 5, 1767, from Great Britain. They served as a target for dissatisfaction with British colonial policies and thereby helped to solidify opposition to the commissioners. Board members viewed themselves as political as well as economic reformers, which helped to also anger the colonists. The task of controlling **smuggling** and collecting import duties along the entire colonial coastline was simply too massive for the organization. *See also LIBERTY*.

AMERICAN COMMISSIONER. *See* COMMISSIONER.

AMERICAN MERCHANTS. *American merchants* is a term applied to English businessmen conducting a considerable portion of their **trade** with the American **colonies**. In 1765, the merchants formed a committee to gather political support for the American cause in matters of **taxation**. The merchants viewed colonial agitation over taxation as a threat to their business interests and generally supported the colonial position on trade.

AMERICAN PROHIBITORY ACT OF 1775. Following the **Battle of Lexington-Concord** and the **Olive Branch Petition**, **King George III** addressed Parliament on October 26, 1775. During his speech, the king warned of American colonial agitation and called for action. The American Prohibitory Act, passed by the British Parliament after lengthy debate on December 22, 1775, proved to be the government's response to King George's demands. The act replaced the civilian governments of the colonies with military rule, forbade **trade** with the rebellious American **colonies**, and announced that all American vessels and their cargoes belonged now to the British government. The act served to authorize the Royal Navy to seize American ships. The document included one clause that offered a type of amnesty for colonies or regions that proclaimed their loyalty to the Crown. The act had the opposite effect and tended to drive the colonies closer to independence despite several moves toward reconciliation by individual colonies. *See also* GREAT BRITAIN AND REVOLUTIONARY AMERICA.

AMERICAN REVENUE ACT OF 1764. *See* SUGAR ACT OF 1764.

AMERICAN REVOLUTION. *See* REVOLUTIONARY WAR.

AMERICAN RIFLE. The American rifle (also known as the Pennsylvania, Kentucky, or long rifle) was originally designed for hunting on the frontier. Unlike a musket, the barrel contained grooves known as rifling that increased the accuracy and distance of the weapon. Although more accurate than a musket, the rifle took longer to reload and could not hold a bayonet if utilized for military operations. Thus, the rifle did not replace the muskets carried by the majority of the **Continental Army**. *See also* FERGUSON RIFLE.

AMES, FISHER (1758–1808). Fisher Ames, a **Massachusetts** lawyer and noted **Federalist**, wrote the "Camillus" essays under the pen name Lucius Junius Brutus in March 1787. The essays supported the call for a new federal government during the period of **Shays's Rebellion**. The publications helped to herald the call for the **Constitutional Convention of 1787**. Fisher served later in the Massachusetts legislature and then the U.S. House of Representatives.

ANDREWS, JOHN (1746–1813). John Andrews, an Episcopal clergyman and educator, was a noted **loyalist** during the **Revolutionary War**. Despite Andrews's political leanings during the war, in 1782 he helped establish the Protestant Episcopal Church of Maryland as an independent entity from British jurisdiction. He is also known for an unsuccessful attempt to unify Episcopalians and Methodists in the United States. *See also* RELIGION.

ANNAPOLIS CONVENTION. At the conclusion of the **Alexandria Convention**, **Maryland** and **Virginia** agreed to call a second meeting to discuss economic differences between the states and common problems such as lawlessness among residents. All 13 states were invited to this gathering. In September 1786, five states (**Delaware**, **New Jersey**, **New York**, **Pennsylvania**, and **Virginia**) sent representatives to the meeting that became known as the Annapolis Convention or the Annapolis Trade Convention. With fewer than half of the states present, little could be accomplished in reference to developing means to solve economic differences between them. **James Madison** and **Alexander Hamilton** emerged as leaders during the meeting. Hamilton prepared a report that was unanimously adopted by the attendees. The document listed the weaknesses of the national government and the **Articles of Confederation** and suggested calling a convention of all 13 states to discuss strengthening the Articles. The **Congress of the Confederation** reluctantly agreed to endorse the report resulting from the Annapolis Convention and each state except **Rhode Island** appointed representatives to attend what would become the **Constitutional Convention of 1787**.

ANSON, LORD GEORGE (1697–1762). Lord George Anson, in his capacity as first lord of the admiralty, was instrumental in determining the policy of **Great Britain** to end the **smuggling** of the American colonists with French possessions. During the **French and Indian War**, the American colonists continued to **trade** with

French **colonies** in the West Indies despite the state of open conflict between **France** and Great Britain. The crackdown on illegal trade with the French islands became one of the many grievances that the American colonists would have with Great Britain, culminating in the **Revolutionary War**.

ANTI-FEDERALISTS. The anti-Federalists represented the individuals who opposed the ratification of the U.S. **Constitution**. Anti-Federalists tended to come from the less-populated and interior sections of the states and received the support of many farmers. The group feared that a strong federal government would impinge upon state power and individual freedoms. Prominent anti-Federalists included **Samuel Adams**, **Patrick Henry**, and **Richard Henry Lee**. Those who supported the ratification of the Constitution are often known as **Federalists**.

APPRENTICE. Apprentices were normally young men who signed a contract with a craftsman. Similar to an **indentured servant**, the apprentice provided a set length of service and was provided with clothing and money or tools upon completion. The craftsman was bound to teach the apprentice the skill of this trade.

ARANDA, COUNT DE (1718–1798). Count de Aranda served as the Spanish ambassador to **France** under Spanish Foreign Minister **Jerónimo Grimaldi**. Aranda, like Grimaldi, supported an early Spanish entry into the war against **Great Britain**. However, Aranda was wary of an independent United States and after the **Revolutionary War** correctly viewed the new country as an infant that would grow to demand more territory, including that held by Spain. *See also* SPAIN AND REVOLUTIONARY AMERICA.

ARANJUEZ, CONVENTION OF. *See* CONVENTION OF ARANJUEZ.

ARMSTRONG, FREEBORN. **James Otis** assumed the pen name Freeborn Armstrong during the **Stamp Act of 1765** crisis. Articles under this pen name were directed at **Thomas Hutchinson**. *See also* HAMPDEN, JOHN.

ARMSTRONG, JOHN (1717–1795). John Armstrong, a **Revolutionary War** officer, represented **Pennsylvania** in the **Second Continental Congress** from 1779–1780 and the **Congress of the Confederation** from 1787–1788.

ARNOLD, JONATHAN (1741–1793). Jonathan Arnold, a physician, represented **Rhode Island** in the **Congress of the Confederation** from 1782–1784. He actively supported the admission of **Vermont** as a state in the Union and later moved there.

ARTICLES OF CONFEDERATION. Officially known as the Articles of Confederation and Perpetual Union, this document established a confederation-based government in the United States. **Richard Henry Lee** introduced the idea of a governmental confederation for the 13 **colonies** as early as June 7, 1776. The **Second Continental Congress** established a committee and **John Dickinson** prepared the first draft of a constitutional document in July 1776. Delegates argued and debated the structure of a new national government for over a year and finally approved a draft document on November 15, 1777. Twelve states ratified the document but **Maryland** withheld its approval pending a feud with other states over claims to western lands. When these states surrendered their claims to the national government, Maryland ratified the Articles of Confederation on March 1, 1781. At this point, this book refers to Congress as the **Congress of the Confederation** rather than the Continental Congress.

Each state jealously guarded its sovereignty, thus ensuring the national government under the Articles of Confederation would be weak. The legislature remained unicameral in nature, meaning it consisted of only one House of Representatives. Each state had one vote in Congress regardless of size or population. Congress was politically weak and lacked the power to tax or regulate interstate commerce. Congress did have the power to conduct foreign relations, establish an army and navy, issue and borrow money, and oversee affairs with **Native Americans**. The federal government lacked a supreme court with national court system and an executive. The national legislature did elect a **president of Congress**, but he primarily presided over Congress and did not have the powers and duties of the president under the U.S. **Constitution**.

Numerous weaknesses emerged in the national government due to the Articles of Confederation. Many states began initiating their own **trade** agreements with other countries, undercutting the attempts by the national government to achieve national trade treaties. States established their own regulations for interstate commerce, taxed the goods of other states, and often printed their own **currency**. Citizens, protesting their personal **debt** and the poor economic conditions after the Revolution, took up arms against some states. The most famous of these incidents was **Shays's Rebellion** in 1786 **Massachusetts**. In 1786, delegates at the **Annapolis Convention** called for the formation of a national convention to revise the Articles. This second meeting, known as the **Constitutional Convention of 1787**, prepared a new Constitution that established a federal government at the national level. The Constitution officially replaced the Articles of Confederation when ratified by nine states on June 21, 1788. The signers of the Articles of Confederation are listed in appendix A and a biographical entry for each is included in the Dictionary section of this book.

ARTICLES OF WAR. *See* CONTINENTAL ARTICLES OF WAR.

ARTS. *See* CRAFTS; LITERATURE; MUSIC; PAINTING; THEATER.

ASSOCIATION. *See* CONTINENTAL ASSOCIATION.

ATHERTON, JOSHUA (1737–1809). Joshua Atherton, a **Massachusetts** lawyer, anti-**slavery** advocate, and **loyalist**, refused to join the **Sons of Liberty**. He was arrested and held from 1777–1778 for his political beliefs. After the surrender of British General John Burgoyne at the Battle of Saratoga, he agreed to take an oath of loyalty to **New Hampshire**. He served in the New Hampshire state convention that ratified the U.S. **Constitution**. However, he opposed the new document because it permitted slave **trade** in the United States until 1808.

ATTA-KULLA-KULLA. Atta-kulla-kulla, an elderly **Cherokee** war chief, signed a peace treaty following his defeat in the Cherokee

Campaign of 1776. During the process, he offered 500 Cherokee warriors to the patriot cause in **South Carolina**. The South Carolinians never accepted his offer. The treaty lasted until 1782. *See also* DRAGGING CANOE.

ATTUCKS, CRISPUS (c.1723–1770). Crispus Attucks is thought to have been a sailor. His origins are unknown although many believe he was an **African American** or a mulatto of mixed African American and **Native American** ancestry. It is also believed that he escaped **slavery** around 1760. Reports indicated that Attucks was a leader of the mob that precipitated the **Boston Massacre** in 1770. Some historians identify Attucks as the first African American to die for American independence. He fell when the British soldiers fired into the mass of people taunting them.

AUGUSTA, CONFERENCE OF, 1763. Following the conclusion of the **French and Indian War**, the governors of **Georgia**, **North Carolina**, **South Carolina**, and **Virginia** met with representatives of the Catawba, Chickasaw, Choctaw, and **Creek** in November 1763 to discuss commerce and establishing boundaries between the four colonies and **Native American** lands. The British **Proclamation of 1763** accomplished a similar task by establishing the border between American colonists and Native Americans along the entire length of territory between New York and Georgia. The British completed the development of the Proclamation of 1763 before information on the Augusta Conference arrived in London.

AUGUSTA, TREATY OF. **Georgia** concluded the Treaty of Augusta with the **Creeks** in November 1784. In the agreement, the Creeks surrendered enough land to allow the state borders to now reach the Oconee River. However, the Creeks, under the charismatic leadership of **Alexander McGillivray**, soon rejected the treaty. Georgia defeated the Creeks and their Florida-based allies in the spring of 1785 and forced them to sign the **Treaty of Galphinton** in November of that year.

AUSTIN, BENJAMIN (1752–1820). Benjamin Austin, the brother of **Jonathan Austin**, replaced **Samuel Adams** as the most important anti-British political agitator in **Boston**. Austin served in the **Massachusetts** state legislature in 1787 and then from 1789–1794.

AUSTIN, JONATHAN (1748–1826). Jonathan Austin, the brother of **Benjamin Austin**, worked for the American **commissioners** in Europe during the **Revolutionary War**. He carried the news of British General John Burgoyne's surrender at Saratoga to the American commissioners in **France**. **Benjamin Franklin** dispatched Austin on a secret mission to London in order to pass information to opposition leaders in government. In 1780, **Massachusetts** asked Austin to negotiate a European loan. While traveling to Europe, Austin fell into the hands of the British. However, British friends intervened on his behalf and he was released. Austin served later in the Massachusetts legislature.

AUSTRIA AND REVOLUTIONARY AMERICA. Austria, along with **Russia**, attempted to act as a mediator between **France** and **Great Britain** during the **Revolutionary War**. Austria was motivated by revenge against France rather than European peace. **John Adams** traveled to Vienna in 1781 to lobby for American independence. However, Austria's attempt at mediation was not successful and negotiations between the United States and Great Britain would commence the next year. *See also* LEAGUE OF ARMED NEUTRALITY.

– B –

BACHE, RICHARD (1737–1811). Richard Bache, a merchant and the son-in-law of **Benjamin Franklin**, served on the Committee of Nonimportation Agreements, the **Committee of Correspondence**, and the **Board of War**. He became postmaster general after Franklin and held the post until 1782.

BACON, JOHN (1738–1820). John Bacon, a judge, clergyman, and state legislator, stood firmly in favor of **African American** and **Native American** rights during the period of Revolutionary America. He opposed the ratification of the **Massachusetts** state constitution because the document did not grant suffrage for African Americans, Native Americans, and individuals of mixed blood. Although the legislature finally ratified a state constitution in 1780, these provisions that Bacon worked hard to include were not part of the document. Bacon served later in the U.S. House of Representatives.

BACON, THOMAS (1700–1760). Thomas Bacon, a clergyman and historian from **Maryland**, completed the book *The Laws of Maryland at Large* in 1765. The book was a great success and included colonial laws dating back to 1638. Today, the book offers researchers a view of early colonial laws in Maryland.

BAHAMAS AND REVOLUTIONARY AMERICA. The Bahamas, an English possession during the **Revolutionary War**, are located off the southern coast of Florida. The **Continental Navy** raided the islands twice during the war for powder, cannon, and other military supplies. The Spanish captured the islands on May 8, 1782.

BAILEY, ANN (1742–1825). Ann Bailey arrived in the American **colonies** in 1761. After the death of her husband, she began wearing men's clothing and served as a scout and messenger on the western frontier. She received the nickname "White Squaw of Kanawha."

BAILEY, FRANCIS (c.1735–1815). Francis Bailey, a **Revolutionary War** officer and printer, became the official printer of **Congress** after 1781. He printed official documents for the body.

BALDWIN, ABRAHAM (1754–1807). Abraham Baldwin, a chaplain in the American army of the **Revolutionary War** and later a lawyer, served in the **Georgia** legislature. He represented Georgia in the **Congress of the Confederation** in 1785 and the **Constitutional Convention of 1787**. In the latter, he proved to be an active member and played an important role in the discussions to determine the number of state representatives in Congress. Baldwin signed the **Constitution** for Georgia.

BALTIMORE. The port city of Baltimore, **Maryland**, served as the temporary location of the **Second Continental Congress** after its evacuation from **Philadelphia**. Congress convened its first session in Baltimore on December 20, 1776. It was from Baltimore on December 27, 1776, that Congress granted General **George Washington** nearly dictatorial powers in military matters for a six-month period. Congress reconvened in Philadelphia on March 12, 1777.

BANCROFT, EDWARD (1744–1821). Edward Bancroft, a sailor and writer, worked for **Benjamin Franklin** and **Silas Deane** as a spy. While assigned to London, Bancroft accepted a British offer to work as a double agent against the American cause. Bancroft remained in **Great Britain** after the **Revolutionary War** and became an inventor. He died in Great Britain.

BANISTER, JOHN (1734–1788). John Banister, a **Continental Army** officer and lawyer, served in the **Virginia** legislature. He represented Virginia in the **Second Continental Congress** from 1778–1779 and signed the **Articles of Confederation**. The British destroyed his property in retaliation for his political and military activity.

BANK OF NORTH AMERICA. The **Articles of Confederation** prohibited the national government from levying taxes. In response, the **Second Continental Congress** established the Bank of North America on December 31, 1781, in order to provide itself with **currency**. The bank opened with an initial $400,000 in assets. Disagreement over its role in the post-Revolution commerce and currency crisis led to the revocation of the bank's charter in 1785. In 1787, supporters of the bank managed to recharter it for a brief period. *See also* BINGHAM, WILLIAM; HILLEGAS, MICHAEL; TAXATION; WILLING, THOMAS.

BARBARY STATES AND REVOLUTIONARY AMERICA. The Barbary States included the North African governments of Algiers, Morocco, Tripoli, and Tunis. Collectively, the Barbary States preyed on shipping in the Mediterranean Sea unless paid hefty sums to allow vessels to sail unmolested. British ships protected American vessels until 1775 and the outbreak of the **Revolutionary War**. In February 1786, **John Adams** met with the Tripoli ambassador to **Great Britain** but withdrew from the negotiations when the latter demanded an outrageous sum of money to permit American vessels to sail freely in the Mediterranean Sea. **Thomas Jefferson**, in **France**, called for an international naval squadron to end the piracy of the Barbary States. However, **Congress** refused to participate in an international naval squadron. In June 1786, the United States obtained a free navigation treaty from Morocco for $10,000 worth of "gifts." Algiers, Tripoli, and Tunis refused to cooperate with the United States.

BARD, JOHN (1716–1799). John Bard, a physician, moved to **New York City** at the urging of **Benjamin Franklin**. Bard is known as the first American to conduct a human dissection for the purpose of medical instruction.

BARKER, JEREMIAH (1752–1835). Jeremiah Barker, a **Massachusetts** physician, served on a **privateer** and with the military during the **Revolutionary War**. Barker wrote texts on medicine during the Revolutionary period in American history and is noted for his belief that many diseases were caused by changes in the weather. He expended considerable effort in the attempt to prove this theory.

BARLOW, JOEL (1754–1812). Joel Barlow, a political philosopher and poet, moved from the United States to Europe in 1788. Barlow is known as a prominent liberal political philosopher of his period.

BARRÉ, ISAAC (1762–1802). Issac Barré, a member of the British Parliament, emerged as an early critic of **taxation** measures imposed on the American **colonies**. He is noted for utilizing the term "**sons of liberty**" during a speech in 1765 to describe those opposing British taxation. The American colonists soon adopted the term.

BARTLETT, JOSIAH (1729–1795). Josiah Bartlett, a physician, was selected to represent **New Hampshire** in the **First Continental Congress** but declined due to a fire at his home. Bartlett did travel to **Philadelphia** for the **Second Continental Congress** and represented New Hampshire in that body from 1775–1776 and then 1778–1779. He signed the **Declaration of Independence** and was the first to vote in favor of the **Articles of Confederation**. Later, Bartlett held the positions of chief justice and governor of New Hampshire.

BARTON, WILLIAM (1748–1831). William Barton, a **Revolutionary War** officer, actively supported the U.S. **Constitution** despite the opposition of his home state of **Rhode Island**. When Rhode Island refused to send delegates to the **Constitutional Convention of 1787**, Barton and others dispatched a letter to the convention attendees pledging their personal support for the process. Barton later served as an important figure in his state's 1790 convention to ratify the Constitution.

BARTRAM, JOHN (1695–1777). John Bartram, from **Pennsylvania**, and the cousin of **Humphrey Marshall**, the botanist, emerged as the first American-born naturalist in the American **colonies**. Bartram was possibly the first American to experiment with the hybridization of plants. In 1765, he received an appointment as a botanist to **King George III** of **Great Britain**. He conducted this royal service in the American colonies where he traveled extensively to study native plants. Bartram took an anti-**slavery** stand during his lifetime and freed his family's slaves. His son, **William Bartram**, became a botanist, too.

BARTRAM, WILLIAM (1739–1823). William Bartram, the son of famed botanist **John Bartram**, was also a noted American botanist during the Revolutionary period.

BASSETT, RICHARD (1745–1815). Richard Bassett emerged as an important political figure in **Delaware**, serving in that state's legislature from 1776–1786. He also commanded a troop of cavalry during the **Revolutionary War**. In 1787, Delaware selected Bassett as a delegate to the **Constitutional Convention of 1787**. He signed the document for the state and later served as a member of the U.S. Senate and as governor of Delaware.

BATTLE OF THE ALAMANCE. *See* ALAMANCE, BATTLE OF THE.

BATTLE OF BUSHY RUN. *See* BUSHY RUN, BATTLE OF.

BATTLE OF EDGEHILL. *See* EDGEHILL, BATTLE OF.

BATTLE OF LEXINGTON-CONCORD. *See* LEXINGTON-CONCORD, BATTLE OF.

BATTLE OF POINT PLEASANT. *See* POINT PLEASANT, BATTLE OF.

BAYARD, JOHN (1738–1807). John Bayard, a noted patriot from **Maryland**, joined the **Sons of Liberty** prior to the **Revolutionary War**. He was an avid supporter of **George Washington** as commander of the **Continental Army**, a **Revolutionary War** officer, and a staunch **Federalist** in his new home state of **Pennsylvania**.

BAYLEY, RICHARD (1745–1801). Richard Bayley, from **Connecticut**, served as a physician with the British army in the early years of the **Revolutionary War**. He departed British service in 1777 and moved to **New York**. His medical research included a keen interest in diseases. Many rumors emerged that he had performed inhumane experiments on soldiers who had contracted various diseases. In 1788, a crowd of agitated citizens broke into his office and ransacked it.

BEATTY, JOHN (1749–1826). John Beatty, a **Revolutionary War** officer from **New Jersey**, served in the **Congress of the Confederation** for his state from 1784–1785. He was also a member of the state convention during the ratification of the U.S. **Constitution** and later was elected to the U.S. House of Representatives.

BEAUMARCHAIS, PIERRE AUGUSTIN CARON DE (1732–1791). Pierre Beaumarchais, a French playwright and watchmaker, lived in London prior to the **Revolutionary War**. He served the French government as a secret agent during this period. In 1775, the **Continental Congress** formed a secret committee that requested **Arthur Lee**, an American commercial agent in London, to contact representatives of friendly European states. Lee met with Beaumarchais and the two discussed the possibility of secret French aid to the Americans. Beaumarchais is credited with establishing a dummy commercial company known as **Hortalez et Cie** as a means of transferring French and Spanish munitions to the Americans starting in June 1776. *See also* FRANCE AND REVOLUTIONARY AMERICA; SPAIN AND REVOLUTIONARY AMERICA.

BEDFORD, GUNNING (1742–1797). Gunning Bedford, sometimes known as Gunning Bedford Sr. to separate him from his cousin, known as **Gunning Bedford Jr**., served as an American officer in the **Revolutionary War** and sat in the **Delaware** legislature. He represented Delaware in the **Congress of the Confederation** from 1786–1787 and became a member of the state convention that ratified the U.S. **Constitution**. He later served as governor of Delaware. Bedford is frequently confused with his cousin.

BEDFORD, GUNNING, JR. (1747–1812). Gunning Bedford Jr., a lawyer and attorney general of **Delaware**, represented his state in the **Congress of the Confederation** from 1783–1785. He attended the **Constitutional Convention of 1787**. He signed the **Constitution** and later served as a U.S. district judge. Bedford should not be confused with his cousin, **Gunning Bedford Sr.**, a governor of Delaware.

BBEDFORD GANG. The Bedford Gang was the nickname for a group of British politicians loyal to the policies, including colonial, of **King George III** and **Lord North**.

EDINGER, GEORGE (1756–1783). George Bedinger, a **Revolutionary War** officer, was an early opponent of **slavery** in **Kentucky**. He later served in the U.S. House of Representatives from Kentucky.

BELKNAP, JEREMY (1744–1798). Jeremy Belknap, a clergyman and historian, is known for his research and publication of *The History of New Hampshire*. The three-volume collection took 20 years to complete and the first book of the collection was released in 1784.

BELL, ROBERT (c.1732–1784). Robert Bell, a publisher, stood adamantly for the free sale of books in the American **colonies**. In 1776, Bell published the first edition of **Thomas Paine's** classic work ***Common Sense***.

BELLY UP TO THE BAR. This expression emerged during Colonial America. To determine if an individual was old enough to consume an alcoholic beverage, tavern owners would ask the young man to stand up against the bar. His height then determined whether he received an alcoholic drink.

BENSON, EGBERT (1746–1833). Egbert Benson, a **Revolutionary War** officer and patriot, served in the **New York** legislature. He represented New York in the **Second Continental Congress** and **Congress of the Confederation** from 1781–1784. He also attended the **Annapolis Convention** in 1786. Benson later became a member of the U.S. House of Representatives and a justice of the New York Supreme Court.

BERMUDA AND REVOLUTIONARY AMERICA. The island of Bermuda is located off the eastern coast of the United States. During the Revolutionary period, Bermuda was a British **colony**. Although the island was British-held, locals tended to sell the Americans everything from military supplies to ships. American forces attacked Bermuda Island on August 14, 1775, captured the British fort, and removed all of the gunpowder stored in the facility. The British moved a permanent garrison onto the island on November 2, 1778, in order to maintain greater control of the area. *See also* BROWNE, WILLIAM.

BERNARD, SIR FRANCIS (1712–1777). Sir Francis Bernard served as the royal governor of **Massachusetts** from 1760–1767. Although he attempted to persuade the British government to drop or lower its various taxes, the citizens of the **colony** did not like him. Bernard found his position difficult—sitting between the British government and the hostile population of Massachusetts. Due to the rising popular opposition in Massachusetts to the Crown and his perceived ineffectiveness as governor, the British government removed him from the job in 1767.

BILLETING ACT OF 1765. *See* QUARTERING ACT OF 1765.

BILLETING ACT OF 1774. *See* QUARTERING ACT OF 1774.

BILLINGS, WILLIAM (1746–1800). William Billings was born in **Boston** in 1746. Billings is possibly the best known of the musicians from the Revolutionary America period and his works are frequently utilized in concerts today. He emerged as the first great American-born composer and his 1770 *New England Psalm-Singer* became the first published work of American **music**. His most famous songs were patriotic tunes composed just prior to and during the **Revolutionary War**. Billings excelled at music despite having a blind eye and being without the use of an arm and a leg.

BILL OF RIGHTS. The tradition of a bill of rights to protect citizens can be traced to the English Bill of Rights of 1689. **Virginia** incorporated the first state bill of rights into a state constitution in 1776 and other states followed. During the **Constitutional Convention of 1787**, many delegates, led by **James Madison**, demanded the adoption of a bill of rights into the proposed federal constitution in order to protect the personal freedoms of citizens from the national government. Originally, the Bill of Rights did not apply to state governments, which tended to have their own bills of rights. Over the years, this idea has been reversed and the U.S. Supreme Court has slowly applied the Bill of Rights to protect citizen freedoms from state governments.

Following the ratification of the U.S. **Constitution**, numerous proposed amendments were reviewed for incorporation into the document as a "bill of rights." Twelve amendments survived congressional vote and were sent to the states for ratification. Ten were then ratified, added to the Constitution, and became known as the Bill of Rights. The 10 became effective on December 15, 1791. One of the two amendments not ratified in 1791 became the 27th amendment in 1992. This particular amendment states that if Congress votes itself a pay raise, the increase does not take effect until after the next election. The Ten Bill of Rights amendments include:

1. Freedom of religion, speech, press; right to assemble peaceably, and the right to petition government.
2. Right to keep and bear arms.
3. Soldiers shall not, in peacetime, be quartered in homes without consent of the owner and only in wartime if in a manner prescribed by law.
4. Protection from unreasonable searches and seizures; warrants must be based on probable cause.
5. No person shall be held to answer for a capital crime unless a presentment or indictment of a grand jury exists; should face double jeopardy (tried twice) for a crime; be compelled in a criminal case to testify against himself; nor be deprived of life, liberty, or property without due process of the law.
6. Right to a speedy and public trial by an impartial jury; to be informed of the nature and cause of the accusation; to be confronted with the witnesses against him; to be able to obtain witnesses in his favor; and to have access to counsel for his defense.

7. Right to a trial by jury for specific cases and no facts tried by a jury shall be reexamined by another U.S. court except by the rules of common law.
8. Excessive bail shall not be required nor excessive fines imposed; cruel and unusual punishment shall not be inflicted.
9. Individuals have more personal rights than are codified in the Constitution.
10. Powers not delegated to the federal government by the Constitution nor prohibited to the states are reserved for the states or people.

See also FAYETTEVILLE STATE CONVENTION; HILLSBOROUGH STATE CONVENTION.

BINGHAM, WILLIAM (1752–1804). William Bingham served as the Continental agent in the West Indies from 1776–1780. After returning to the **Pennsylvania**, Bingham became a prominent banker and the director of the **Bank of North America**. He sat in the **Congress of the Confederation** from 1786–1789 and later in the U.S. Senate. He is also known for founding Binghamton, New York.

BLAIR, JOHN (1732–1800). John Blair, a jurist, represented **Virginia** at the **Constitutional Convention of 1787**. He signed the U.S. **Constitution** and later became an associate justice of the U.S. Supreme Court.

BLAND, RICHARD (1710–1776). Richard Bland served in the **Virginia** legislature. Although in favor of colonial rights, Bland believed that independence should be sought only as a last resort. He represented Virginia in the **First Continental Congress** in 1774 and was elected to the **Second Continental Congress** in 1776. However, he died after serving in this Congress for only a few days.

BLAND, THEODORICK (1742–1790). Theodorick Bland, a **Virginia Revolutionary War** officer and physician, represented his state in the **Second Continental Congress** and **Congress of the Confederation** from 1780–1783. After leaving Congress, Bland served in the Virginia legislature and was a member of the Virginia Convention for the ratification of the U.S. **Constitution**. He voted against the document.

BLEEKER, ANN (1752–1783). Ann Bleeker was a well-known poet from **New York** during the Revolutionary period. A collection of her poems was published in book form after her death in 1783.

BLODGET, SAMUEL (1724–1807). Samuel Blodget, a **Massachusetts** merchant, developed a device to raise sunken ships. He later constructed a canal.

BLOODWORTH, TIMOTHY (1736–1814). Timothy Bloodworth served in the **North Carolina** legislature and represented his state in the **Congress of the Confederation** from 1784–1787. He opposed ratification of the U.S. **Constitution**. Later Bloodworth served as a member of the U.S. Senate.

BLOODY BACKS. Bloody Backs was an American insult for British soldiers. The name derives from the severe treatment, including lashings, suffered by British soldiers. *See also* LOBSTER; LOBSTERBACK.

BLOODY RIDGE, BATTLE OF. *See* PONTIAC'S WAR.

BLOUNT, WILLIAM (1749–1800). William Blount of **North Carolina** fought for the American cause in the **Revolutionary War**. After the war he entered politics and was selected as a North Carolina delegate to the **Constitutional Convention of 1787**. After signing the U.S. **Constitution**, Blount went on to become U.S. territorial governor south of the Ohio River and later a U.S. senator from **Tennessee**. He was later expelled from the Senate

BOARD OF ADMIRALTY. *See* AMERICAN BOARD OF ADMIRALTY.

BOARD OF CUSTOMS COMMISSIONERS. *See* AMERICAN BOARD OF CUSTOMS COMMISSIONERS.

BOARD OF TRADE. *See* BOARD OF TRADE AND PLANTATIONS.

BOARD OF TRADE AND PLANTATIONS. The board, often simply referred to as the Board of Trade, was established in May 1696 along with the Navigation Act. The purpose of the board's establishment included meeting the growing demands of British merchants for a greater voice in colonial **trade** policy. The board consisted of the president of the Privy Council, seven individuals from the British executive department, and eight merchants or men with merchant interests. The board provided oversight and recommendations on all aspects of British colonial trade and **taxation**. Americans often complained that the board members lacked firsthand knowledge of the **colonies**. The prime minister stripped much of the board's authority in 1766 and passed it to government ministers after the repeal of the **Stamp Act of 1765**.

BOARD OF WAR. The **Second Continental Congress** established the Board of War on October 17, 1777, replacing the **Board of War and Ordnance**. The board originally consisted of three members of Congress and was increased to five on November 24, 1777. On October 29, 1778, Congress reorganized the board to include the provision that two members should be chosen from that particular body and three members be selected from outside the ranks of Congress. These were normally military officers. The board proved to be more efficient than its predecessor but still encountered numerous internal problems, including spats of jealousy between the military officers. The organization oversaw congressional actions necessary for conducting the war against **Great Britain**. It should be noted that the Congress was meeting in **York, Pennsylvania**, when it established the Board of War. The **Department of War** replaced the Board of War on February 7, 1781.

BOARD OF WAR AND ORDNANCE. The **Second Continental Congress** established the Board of War and Ordinance on June 13, 1776. The organization, consisting of five members of Congress, oversaw the actions necessary for conducting the war against **Great**

Britain. The organization suffered from inefficiency and was replaced with the **Board of War** in 1777. *See also* DEPARTMENT OF WAR.

BODY, THE. The Body was the name given to the individuals, including many merchants, who gathered to discuss the growing crisis in **Boston** in November and December 1773 following the passage of the **Tea Act of 1773**. The group served as the outlet for the people of Boston who opposed British tea policy; members of the organization conducted the **Boston Tea Party**.

BOLLAN, WILLIAM (c.1710–1776). William Bollan, a **Massachusetts** lawyer, served as an agent for his **colony** in London until 1762. He remained in London and wrote several pamphlets defending the colonial positions on political and economic issues prior to the **Revolutionary War**. **John Adams** and **John Hancock** spoke highly of Bollan and referred to him as a true friend of the **colonies**.

BOND, THOMAS (1712–1784). Thomas Bond, a physician, developed a splint for fractures and is credited with introducing mercury for medicinal use in **Philadelphia**. **Benjamin Franklin** wrote about Bond in his autobiography and noted that he was instrumental in the establishment of the Pennsylvania Hospital, the oldest hospital in the United States. Bond was also a patriot and served on the **Committee of Safety**.

BONVOULOIR, JULIEN ACHARD DE (1749–1783). Julien Bonvouloir secretly represented the French government in a fact-finding mission to the American **colonies** during 1775. His report helped to secure clandestine French military aid for the American cause. *See also* FRANCE AND REVOLUTIONARY AMERICA.

BOONE, DANIEL (1734–1820). Daniel Boone was a frontiersman known for encouraging settlement in **Kentucky**. Boone was hired by the **Transylvania Company**, a group of **land speculators**, to blaze the trail into Kentucky for settlers. He established the now famous Boonesborough as a base camp for arriving settlers. After the Revolutionary period, Boone pushed westward into Missouri.

BOONESBOROUGH. *See* BOONE, DANIEL; TRANSYLVANIA COMPANY.

BOSTON. The port city of Boston, **Massachusetts**, was the early seat of anti-British sentiment over the issue of **taxation**. The British garrisoned soldiers in the city starting in 1768. The city was the site of the **Boston Massacre** and **Boston Tea Party**, the latter resulting in the **Boston Port Act of 1774**. Following the **Battle of Lexington-Concord**, the Americans initiated the Siege of Boston, eventually forcing the British to withdraw from the city.

BOSTON MASSACRE. The British government dispatched two regiments of soldiers to **Boston** on October 1, 1768, in response to the refusal to negate the **Circular Letter**. In accordance with the **Quartering Act of 1765**, the British demanded that Bostonians provide housing for the soldiers. Despite this, Bostonians did not open their homes or inns to British soldiers, forcing General **Thomas Gage** to quarter them in expensive buildings. Tensions between the two groups continued to increase. Bostonians taunted British soldiers and the latter tended to conduct horse races and band music on the Sabbath. Off-duty soldiers competing with local residents for jobs added to the friction of having an occupation force within the city. A fight erupted between the two groups on March 5, 1770, setting the stage for mob action in the evening. One Bostonian mob taunted a lone British sentry on King Street in the early evening. The sentry responded by striking one of the youths with his musket and calling for help. The mob continued its taunting and began hurling chunks of ice at the sentry.

The British captain of the day ordered seven grenadiers to accompany him to rescue the sentry from the mob, which had grown to an estimated 300 people. Tensions increased as the mob turned on the newly arrived soldiers. Snowballs followed insults until someone threw a club, striking one of the British soldiers, who, in turn, fired his musket. Reports indicate that he fired into the air but his comrades fired their weapons upon hearing the first musket. Five Bostonians died of wounds they received from that volley. As a result of the shooting, the British troops departed the city and moved to Castle William. **John Adams** defended the soldiers involved in the incident.

Two soldiers were found guilty of manslaughter and the others were acquitted. Many of those killed or wounded in the incident were seamen and not native Bostonians. The most famous victim of the British volley was **Crispus Attucks**.

Paul Revere and other patriots capitalized on the "massacre" to solidify colonial opposition to the British. Some sources indicate that **Samuel Adams** orchestrated the incident. The Boston Massacre served to further degrade relations between Bostonians and the British army, five years before the start of the **Revolutionary War**. However, if the intent of the organizers was to begin the Revolutionary War in 1770, the event failed.

BOSTON PAMPHLET. The Boston **Committee of Correspondence** approved and presented two documents known as *The State of the Rights of the Colonists* and *The Enumeration of the Violations of Our Rights* at a **Boston** town meeting on November 20, 1772. The documents were well received and the committee wrote a report known informally as the Boston Pamphlet. The document outlined the various grievances of the populace, including **taxation** without representation and opposition to the **Declaratory Act**. The committee printed the document and had it distributed throughout **Massachusetts**. This action was the first attempt to go beyond the large cities and reach individuals in the small communities in an attempt to organize resistance to British policies. Many of these small towns established committees of correspondence to maintain communications with each other and Boston. The pamphlet helped to unite the communities of Massachusetts in their opposition to British policies.

BOSTON PORT ACT OF 1774. The Boston Port Act of 1774, also known as the Boston Port Bill, was one of the four **Intolerable Acts** passed by the British government in response to the **Boston Tea Party** of December 1773. It became effective on June 1, 1774. The act closed the port of **Boston** to all shipping until compensation was made for the dumping of tea into the harbor. The exceptions included the importation of military supplies and the intracolonial importation of fuel and food for the inhabitants. Many British supporters of the American **colonies** believed that the act was justified due to the actions of the Bostonians during the Tea Party. **Lord North** believed that the other colonial ports would be eager to replace Boston's commerce and would not lend support to the city. However, the act actually served to greatly solidify colonial resistance to British authorities. Communities throughout the colonies offered encouragement and supplies to Boston. The cooperation of the various colonies would continue into 1775 when a combined army would lay siege to the British garrison in Boston following the **Battle of Lexington-Concord**. *See also* LORD NORTH'S COASTERS; *SUMMARY VIEW OF THE RIGHTS OF BRITISH AMERICA*.

BOSTON PORT BILL OF 1774. *See* BOSTON PORT ACT OF 1774.

BOSTON TEA PARTY. The British government passed the **Tea Act** in 1773 in order to prevent the bankruptcy of the British East India Company. Under the Tea Act, the company could export its tea directly to agents in the American **colonies** without first going through British ports. By avoiding British middlemen and taxes, the tea could be sold much cheaper in the colonies than before the Tea Act. The low-priced tea threatened many prominent American merchants who made considerable sums of money smuggling the product. Following the passage of the Tea Act, three ships carrying British East India Company tea arrived in **Boston** in late 1773. Local opposition prevented the cargo from being transferred from the ships and the captains wanted to depart the port in order to avoid trouble. However, **Massachusetts** Governor **Thomas Hutchinson** refused to issue permits to allow the ships to leave the harbor. The opposition, led by **Samuel Adams**, formed an organization known as **The Body**, to coordinate their actions.

Merchants faced a 20-day period to pay duties on their cargo after arriving at the port. After this period, customs agents were permitted to seize the goods and auction them. The day before the deadline, members of The Body moved into action. During the evening of December 16, 1773, approximately 50 individuals partially dressed as Mohawks, watched by at least hundreds (some sources estimate thousands) of citizens, dumped 342 chests of tea from the ships. The rising tide carried the tea and chests out into the harbor. Despite modern renditions of the story, the event was quite organized and civil in its approach. The group avoided damaging property, with the exception of the tea, and everyone departed in an orderly manner.

The act proved to be very controversial among local residents and colonial leaders. While members of The Body tended to support the action, many merchants expressed concern over the attack on private property and offered compensation for the tea. **Benjamin Franklin** disapproved of the action while **John Adams** hailed the event. The British responded to the Boston Tea Party by passing the **Intolerable Acts** of 1774, which included the **Boston Port Act** of 1774. This in turn prompted the colonies to form the **First Continental Congress**. *See also* CHARLESTOWN; *ELEANOR*; *FORTUNE*; GREAT BRITAIN AND REVOLUTIONARY AMERICA.

BOTETOURT, NORBORNE BERKELEY, BARON DE (c.1718–1770). Baron Botetourt served as the governor of **Virginia** from 1768 to his death in 1770. He dissolved the Virginia legislature when its members complained about the British violations of colonial rights. Although he took a pro-British stand in colonial issues, many Virginians looked favorably upon Botetourt, knowing that his position placed him in a difficult position between the British government and the citizens of the **colony**.

BOUDINOT, ELIAS (1740–1821). Elias Boudinot, a lawyer, served in the **New Jersey** legislature. He represented New Jersey in the **Second Continental Congress**, from 1777–1784, and held the post of commissary-general of prisoners from 1777–1778. Boudinot became the **president of Congress** in 1782 and signed the **Treaty of Paris of 1783**. In 1783, Congress selected him as secretary of foreign affairs. Boudinot supported the U.S. **Constitution** and was a staunch **Federalist**.

BOUQUET, HENRY (1719–1765). Henry Bouquet, a British army officer, played a prominent role during **Pontiac's War**. Leading British regulars and American colonial troops, Bouquet defeated **Native American** forces at the **Battle of Edgehill** on August 5, 1763, and the **Battle of Bushy Run** the next day. In 1764, Bouquet led another successful column against the Native Americans, who respected him for his military leadership. In 1765, Bouquet received a promotion and other military honors but died the same year in Pensacola of a fever.

BOURNE, BENJAMIN (1755–1808). Benjamin Bourne, a **Revolutionary War** officer, served in the **Rhode Island** legislature. By January 1790, Rhode Island had not ratified the U.S. **Constitution** despite its acceptance by the other 12 states. Members of the U.S. **Congress** debated the issue and some called for economic measures against Rhode Island while others talked of dissolving the state and dividing its territory between **Connecticut** and **Massachusetts**. Some Rhode Island **Federalists** threatened to secede from Rhode Island and form their own state. Bourne, a Federalist, carried a petition to Congress and helped organize the pro-Constitution faction within his state. After considerable debate, Rhode Island finally ratified the Constitution. Bourne later served in the U.S. House of Representatives and became a U.S. District Court judge.

BOWDOIN, JAMES (1726–1790). James Bowdoin, a merchant in **Massachusetts**, showed himself to be a stout patriot in the years prior to the **Revolutionary War**. He served as a member of the governor's council between 1757 and 1774. Bowdoin became governor after the war and held that position during **Shays's Rebellion** before being voted out of office for his tough stance in putting down the uprising. Bowdoin proved to be influential in securing the ratification of the U.S. **Constitution** by Massachusetts. In 1785, Bowdoin spoke before the American Academy of Arts and Sciences and countered the racist attitudes of many Americans who claimed that **African Americans** were intellectually inferior. Bowdoin declared before the assembly that free African Americans lacked educational opportunities and were not intellectually inferior as a group.

BOYLSTON, ZABDIEL (1679–1766). In 1721, Zabdiel Boylston, a physician, was the first individual to introduce the controversial inoculation for **smallpox** in America. His tabulated results of the program became the first scientific clinical presentation by an American physician.

BRACKENRIDGE, HUGH (1748–1816). Hugh Brackenridge, a playwright, wrote plays during the **Revolutionary War**. He later emerged as one of the most noted **Federalists** in western **Pennsylvania**.

BRADFORD, WILLIAM (c.1721–1791). William Bradford, a printer and **newspaper** publisher in **Philadelphia**, was also a staunch patriot and member of the **Sons of Liberty**. His newspaper carried the famous political cartoon showing a dissected snake with each piece listed as one of the American **colonies**. The caption said, "Unite or Die." Bradford became the printer for the **First Continental Congress** and later served as an officer during the **Revolutionary War**. He was the father of **William Bradford** and they should not be confused.

BRADFORD, WILLIAM (1755–1795). William Bradford, the son of the printer **William Bradford**, served as an officer during the **Revolutionary War**. In 1780, he became the attorney general of **Pennsylvania**. Bradford should not be confused with his father.

BRANDT, JOSEPH (1742–1807). Brandt, known also by his **Native American** name Thayendanegea, was a Mohawk chief during the **Revolutionary War**. Brandt led Native American warriors fighting for the British throughout the war and is noted for leading a series of **loyalist** and Native American raids against patriot settlements. After the Revolution, Brandt continued his earlier work in life as a Christian missionary among the Mohawk.

BRAXTON, CARTER (1736–1797). Carter Braxton served in the **Virginia** legislature beginning in 1761. He represented Virginia in the **Second Continental Congress** from 1775–1776, from 1777–1783, and then again in 1785. During his first term, Braxton signed the **Declaration of Independence**.

BREARLEY, DAVID (1745–1790). David Brearley, a jurist, fought for the American cause in the **Revolutionary War** and became chief justice of the **New Jersey** Supreme Court in 1779. In 1787, New Jersey selected him as a delegate to the **Constitutional Convention of**

1787. Brearley signed the U.S. **Constitution**. He briefly served as a U.S. district judge before his death in 1790.

BRIG. A brig is a small, two-masted sailing vessel.

BRITISH EAST INDIA COMPANY. *See* BOSTON TEA PARTY; EAST INDIA COMPANY; TEA ACT OF 1773.

BRITISH MUTINY ACT OF 1765. Many British soldiers in the American **colonies** after the **French and Indian War** deserted with the encouragement and assistance of the local inhabitants. In response, the British government passed the British Mutiny Act in 1765. The act included provisions dealing with British military deserters and civilians assisting them. American colonists tended to ignore the act, claiming that its provisions did not apply to them. Ignoring the act helped to increase tensions between the colonies and the British government during the period leading to the opening of hostilities in 1775. This act is often associated with the **Quartering Act of 1765** and has also been referred to as the Mutiny and Quartering Act of 1765.

BROOM, JACOB (1752–1810). Jacob Broom, a surveyor, served as the postmaster of Wilmington, **Delaware**, and was a member of the state legislature. He represented Delaware in the **Constitutional Convention of 1787** and signed the U.S. **Constitution**. He later built the first cotton factory and mill in Delaware.

BROTHER JONATHAN. Brother Jonathan was British slang for American colonists. The term derives from Governor **Jonathan Trumbull's** name.

BROWN, JOHN (1736–1803). John Brown, the brother of **Joseph Brown**, led the group who burned the British vessel ***Gaspée*** in 1772. During the Revolution, he helped supply the **Continental Army**. **Rhode Island** elected him to serve in the **Congress of the Confederation** from 1784–1786. However, he never attended a meeting of Congress. He should not be confused with **John Brown** of **Kentucky**.

BROWN, JOHN (1757–1837). John Brown, a soldier in the **Revolutionary War**, moved to **Kentucky** in 1782. He emerged as a major leader in the statehood movement within Kentucky. In 1787, Brown met with Don Gardoqui, the **Spanish** minister, with regard to the possible secession of Kentucky from the United States in exchange for free navigation on the Mississippi River. The deal never materialized. Brown served in the **Virginia** legislature, as a representative from Kentucky, in 1787 and the **Congress of the Confederation** from 1787–1788. He voted against the ratification of the U.S. **Constitution** during the Virginia state convention. In 1792, Kentucky received statehood and Brown served in the U.S. Senate. He should not be confused with **John Brown** of **Rhode Island**.

BROWN, JOSEPH (1733–1785). Joseph Brown, the brother of **John Brown** of **Rhode Island**, emerged as a leading American scientific thinker during the Revolutionary period. He was an architect, amateur astronomer, and experimented with electricity.

BROWN, MATHER (1761–1831). Mather Brown, a well-known **Boston** portrait painter, began his work during the **Revolutionary War**. He moved to London and studied under **Benjamin West**. He painted members of the British royal family and later completed portraits of American presidents **John Adams** and **Thomas Jefferson**.

BROWN, THOMAS (?–1825). Thomas Brown refused to join the patriot cause and became an avid **loyalist** in the colonial politics of **Georgia**. After being **tarred and feathered**, he fled to Florida and formed a loyalist regiment that operated in Georgia throughout the duration of the Revolution.

BROWN, WILLIAM (1752–1792). William Brown, a physician, served with the colonial forces during the **Revolutionary War**. In 1778, he wrote the first pharmacopeia in the United States. He should not be confused with **William Browne**, the **loyalist** judge and governor of **Bermuda**.

BROWN BESS. The Brown Bess was the standard British musket during the **Revolutionary War**. Many American soldiers also carried

Brown Bess muskets until replaced by French muskets. The Brown Bess fired a .75 caliber round and had a maximum effective range of approximately 100 yards. The barrel of the weapon turned brown when oxidized, giving the musket its name.

BROWNE, WILLIAM (1737–1802). William Browne, a **loyalist**, served as a judge with the **Massachusetts** Supreme Court. He departed **Boston** with the British forces in 1776 and served as governor of **Bermuda** from 1782–1788. He should not be confused with **William Brown** the physician.

BULL, WILLIAM (1710–1791). William Bull, born in **South Carolina**, served as the acting royal governor of the **colony** for a total of eight years, including 1760–1761, 1764–1766, 1768, 1769–1771, and 1773–1775. He was the first person born in America to receive an actual degree in medicine but never practiced in the field. Bull was acting governor during the **Stamp Act of 1765** and **Tea Act of 1773** crises. He left South Carolina with the British troops in 1782. South Carolinians held an unusual respect for Bull despite his position.

BULLOCH, ARCHIBALD (c.1729–1777). Archibald Bulloch, a lawyer and planter, served in the **Georgia** legislature and briefly in the **Second Continental Congress** in 1775. When Sir James Wright, the royal governor of Georgia, departed, Bulloch became the president and commander in chief of the state.

BURKE, AEDANUS (1743–1802). Aedanus Burke, a **Revolutionary War** officer and judge, served in the **South Carolina** legislature. As a judge, he believed in extending leniency to **loyalists**. At the South Carolina convention on ratification of the U.S. **Constitution**, Burke voted against the document. He served later in the U.S. House of Representatives.

BURKE, EDMUND (1729–1797). Edmund Burke, a British statesman, held the position of secretary to **Marquis of Rockingham** from 1765–1782. Burke was a major influence in the opposition to the British government during the **Revolutionary War**. He believed that the British should offer conciliatory gestures to the American colonists and permit them all of the rights held by Englishmen.

BURKE, THOMAS (c.1747–1783). Thomas Burke, a physician and lawyer, represented **North Carolina** in the **Second Continental Congress** between 1777 and 1781. In 1781, Burke became governor of North Carolina and was captured during the raid on Hillsborough later that year. He escaped **parole** on James Island, **South Carolina**, and fled to the encampment of General Nathanael Greene.

BURNET, WILLIAM (1730–1796). William Burnet, a physician, served in the **Second Continental Congress** from 1776–1777 and then in 1780. Congress selected Burnet as the surgeon-general of the Eastern District. The British raided his property in retaliation for his service to the patriot cause. After the war, Burnet became a judge.

BUSHNELL, DAVID (c.1742–1824). David Bushnell, an accomplished inventor of the Revolutionary period, developed the submarine ***Turtle***.

BUSHY RUN, BATTLE OF. Henry Bouquet, a British officer, led a force of regular British soldiers and American colonial troops into what is now western **Pennsylvania** during **Pontiac's War**. He defeated a **Native American** force of Delaware and Shawnee warriors at the **Battle of Edgehill** on August 5, 1763 (at least one source claims the battle occurred on July 31, 1763). The next day, the Native Americans returned and attacked him at Bushy Run. Bouquet circled his troops around his baggage. He then made it look like a segment of the defensive perimeter was withdrawing. As the Native American warriors attacked into the supposed gap in the perimeter, Bouquet launched a bayonet attack. The Native American force collapsed, leaving Bouquet in control of the battlefield and earning him the respect of his opponents.

BUTLER, JOHN (1728–1796). John Butler, a **loyalist** and Indian agent, led **Native American** warriors against the patriots during the **Revolutionary War**.

BUTLER, PIERCE (1744–1822). Pierce Butler, a planter, was originally a British army officer born in Ireland. He resigned his commission in 1771 and served in the **South Carolina** legislature from 1778–1782 and then 1784–1789. In 1787, he represented South Carolina at the **Constitutional Convention of 1787** and signed the final draft of the U.S. **Constitution**. Butler authored the fugitive **slave** clause in the Constitution, mandating the return of fugitive slaves who escaped to free states. He served later in the U.S. Senate.

BUTLER, RICHARD (1743–1791). Richard Butler, a **Revolutionary War** officer, served as an Indian Commissioner at the request of **Congress** in 1784. He negotiated boundary treaties with the **Iroquois**, Wynadot, Delaware, Chippewa, Ottawa, and the Shawnee. He died in combat while fighting **Native American** warriors.

BUTLER, WILLIAM (1759–1821). William Butler, a **Revolutionary War** officer, served in the **South Carolina** legislature. At the South Carolina convention on the ratification of the U.S. **Constitution**, Butler voted against the document. Voters later elected him to the U.S. House of Representatives.

– C –

CABELL, SAMUEL (1756–1818). Samuel Cabell, a **Revolutionary War** officer and son of **William Cabell**, served in the **Virginia** legislature. At the Virginia convention for ratification of the U.S. **Constitution**, Cabell voted against the document. Voters elected him later to the U.S. House of Representatives.

CABELL, WILLIAM (c.1729–1798). William Cabell, the father of **Samuel Cabell**, served in the Virginia legislature. He voted against the U.S. **Constitution** at the **Virginia** convention to ratify the document.

CABOT, GEORGE (1752–1823). George Cabot, a merchant, was elected to represent **Massachusetts** at the **Annapolis Convention**. However, he did not attend the meeting. At the Massachusetts convention to ratify the U.S. **Constitution**, Cabot voted in favor of the document. He served later in the U.S. Senate.

CADWALDER, LAMBERT (1743–1823). Lambert Cadwalder, a **Revolutionary War** soldier and son of **Thomas Cadwalder**, served in the **Congress of the Confederation** from 1784–1787. He was elected later to the U.S. House of Representatives.

CADWALDER, THOMAS (c.1707–1799). Thomas Cadwalder, a physician and the father of **Lambert Cadwalder**, is known for his studies on the medical condition known as **dry gripes**.

CALDWELL, DAVID (1725–1824). David Caldwell, a Presbyterian clergyman, acted as a negotiator between **North Carolina** Governor **William Tryon** and the **regulators** and was active in pro-patriot state politics. During the **Revolutionary War**, the British plundered his home. Caldwell served in the North Carolina conventions to consider ratification of the U.S. **Constitution**. He voted against the Constitution due to the absence in the document of religious tests for government officials.

CALDWELL, JAMES (1734–1781). James Caldwell served as a chaplain with the American forces during the **Revolutionary War**. His wife was killed by a random shot fired by British forces. Within weeks of his wife's death, American forces fighting an engagement with British troops were running low on paper wadding for their musket rounds. Caldwell reportedly went into a local church and grabbed a handful of hymnals. He ripped out the pages for wadding and gave them to the American soldiers while declaring, "Give them Watts, boys." Isaac Watts was a noted writer of spiritual music during the period. An American sentry murdered Caldwell in an unusual episode in 1781.

CAMBRIDGE. Following the imposition of the **Intolerable Acts** after the **Boston Tea Party**, the **Massachusetts militia** began to remove weapons and ammunition from public arsenals and hide them in the event of a clash with British soldiers occupying **Boston**. On September 1, 1774, British General **Thomas Gage** sent a force to

Cambridge, located outside of Boston, to seize two brass cannons. At the same time, another British force moved to secure powder in **Charlestown**. The militia members were unprepared for the action and the British were successful. The operation, accompanied by false rumors of British atrocities, prompted the militia to disrupt the local courts in Cambridge and Worcester. The strain between the two groups would lead to the **Battle of Lexington-Concord** the following spring. *See also* NEWPORT; PORTSMOUTH; SALEM.

CAMM, JOHN (1718–1778). John Camm, a clergyman, challenged the Two Penny Act of 1755 and **Two Penny Act of 1758** in **Virginia**. His appeal to **Great Britain** won the king's approval and openly challenged the colonists' perceived right to make their own laws. Camm served as the president of William and Mary College from 1771–1777.

CAMMERHOFF, JOHN (1721–1751). John Cammerhoff, a Morovian missionary, arrived in America in 1746 and worked among the **Native Americans**. He was well received among many Native Americans, including the Oneida who adopted him into their tribe. However, Cammerhoff's journeys into the backcountry weakened his health and he died only five years after arriving in the American **colonies**.

CAMP FOLLOWERS. Camp followers were individuals who accompanied an army when it marched. Camp followers included sutlers, women, and children. Most of the women were the wives, legal and common law, of soldiers in the unit. They assisted their husbands with cooking, washing, and other domestic duties. The British army actually authorized a certain number of women to accompany their units and provided rations for them. Any women beyond the authorized limit had to provide their own food. At times, the numbers of the women swelled considerably and hampered the movement of the military units.

CAMPBELL, WILLIAM (?–1778). William Campbell, selected to serve as the royal governor of **South Carolina**, arrived in 1775 to find his power already usurped by patriots, including his own in-laws. He conducted secret negotiations with **loyalists** and **Native Americans** in the backcountry. However, he was not able to secure sufficient support to challenge the patriots in the coastal areas of the **colony**. He escaped to a British vessel and later commanded a gun deck on a warship during the 1776 Battle of Fort Sullivan. Campbell was wounded during the engagement and never fully recovered from his injuries.

CANADA ACT. *See* QUEBEC ACT of 1774.

CANADA AND REVOLUTIONARY AMERICA. On March 25, 1776, the **Second Continental Congress** dispatched **Benjamin Franklin**, **Charles Carroll**, and **Samuel Chase** to Canada for discussions with local leaders about joining the 13 American **colonies** in revolt against **Great Britain**. Canada, as a whole, chose to remain with Great Britain, although many individual Canadians fought with the American army. The Americans invaded Canada during 1775 and 1776 in an attempt to persuade the Canadians to join the revolt and expel the British from the area. However, the Americans were defeated in the campaign. A second invasion was planned but never carried out. During and after the war, many American **loyalists** moved to British areas of Canada such as Nova Scotia and New Brunswick rather than remain in the United States. The **Articles of Confederation** contained an article permitting the admission of Canada to the United States. However, Canadians remained loyal to the British Crown and never took advantage of the American offer. *See also* CANADIAN DEPARTMENT; QUEBEC ACT OF 1774.

CANADIAN DEPARTMENT. The **Second Continental Congress** established the Canadian Department as a **military department** in December 1775. The Canadian Department consisted of the British territory of Canada and represented the only military department not incorporated into the United States after the war. The Canadian Department ceased to exist when American forces withdrew from the area during the summer of 1776.

CANVAS TOWN. Canvas town was the nickname for an area of **New York City** after the **fire** following the American evacuation in 1776.

The area, gutted during the fire, consisted of shanties built from discarded lumber and sailcloth and was a haven for prostitutes, runaway **slaves**, and individuals living outside of the law.

CAPELLEN, JOHAN DERCK VAN DER, BARON (1741–1784). Baron Capellen, a member of the Dutch Parliament, served as the spokesman for the Liberals in the **Netherlands** on the issue of the **Revolutionary War**. Capellen opposed Dutch neutrality and returning the Scots Brigade to the British. He supported the American cause for freedom and felt that the Netherlands should also be active on behalf of the Americans. Capellen's remarks led to his dismissal from government.

CARLETON, GUY (1724–1808). Some historians credit British Major General Carleton as the author of the **Quebec Act of 1774**. Carleton was the governor of Quebec and commanded all British forces in **Canada** when the **Revolutionary War** erupted in 1775. He managed to defeat the American forces during the Battle of Quebec and pursued them as they retreated back into **New York** until being delayed at the Battle of Valcour Island. Dissatisfaction in **Great Britain** with his halted offensive led to Carleton's recall in 1778. In May 1782, Carleton replaced General Henry Clinton as commander in chief in America.

CARLISLE PEACE COMMISSION. By 1777, British opposition to Crown policies in the **Revolutionary War** was increasing. Higher **taxation** rates, the disruption of the profitable American **trade**, and the loss of an entire army at the Battle of Saratoga enflamed British merchants, parliamentarians, and other influential individuals. To continue the war in 1778 would demand more British troops and even higher taxes to fund them. **Lord North** proposed the **Conciliatory Propositions** and dispatched what has become known as the Carlisle Peace Commission to carry them to the American colonists. The commission consisted of Earl Carlisle, William Eden, and George Johnstone as well as the British army and navy commanders in the American **colonies**. The propositions offered an opportunity for reconciliation between the rebellious colonies and **Great Britain**. The commissioners were empowered to offer almost anything except independence to the Americans in order to secure the end of the rebellion. However, the American colonists, still beaming from their victory at Saratoga and hopeful of a French alliance, rejected the Conciliatory Propositions. In response, the commissioners announced the **Carlisle Proclamation**, calling for increased British military measures against the rebellious colonies.

CARLISLE PROCLAMATION. After the American rejection of the **Conciliatory Propositions** in 1778, the members of the **Carlisle Peace Commission** prepared what is known as the Carlisle Proclamation. The document called for settling the **Revolutionary War** through a policy of savage military reprisals against the American population. Under this policy, British forces carried out a series of brutal raids along the New England coast to burn vessels and destroy anything of economic value to the colonists.

CARPENTER'S HALL. The **First Continental Congress** met in Carpenter's Hall in **Philadelphia** in 1774.

CARROLL, CHARLES (1737–1832). Charles Carroll, the cousin of **Daniel Carroll** and **John Carroll**, served as an important statesman during the Revolutionary period. He joined his cousin John, **Benjamin Franklin**, and **Samuel Chase** on an unsuccessful expedition to persuade the Canadians to join the Americans in the **Revolutionary War**. He sat in **Maryland**'s legislature from 1777–1801. Carroll also represented Maryland in the **Second Continental Congress** from 1776–1778, during which time he signed the **Declaration of Independence**. Carroll later served as a U.S. senator. He was the last signer of the Declaration of Independence to die.

CARROLL, DANIEL (1730–1796). Daniel Carroll, the brother of **John Carroll** and the cousin of **Charles Carroll**, served in the **Maryland** legislature beginning in 1777. He represented Maryland in the **Second Continental Congress** and **Congress of the Confederation** from 1781–1783. Carroll signed the **Articles of Confederation**. Maryland selected Carroll as a delegate to the **Constitutional Convention of 1787**. He signed the final draft of the U.S. **Constitution** and later became a member of the U.S. House of Representatives.

CARROLL, JOHN (1735–1815). John Carroll, the brother of **Daniel Carroll** and the cousin of **Charles Carroll**, was a prominent religious leader during the Revolutionary period and in 1789 became the first Roman Catholic bishop in the United States.

CARTER, JOHN (1745–1814). John Carter, a **printer** and **newspaper** editor, was the editor of the *Providence Gazette* from 1768–1814. Under Carter's editorship, the newspaper proclaimed a pro-patriot and later an anti-**Constitution** stance in its stories and views.

CARVER, JOHN (1710–1780). In 1766, John Carver, from **Great Britain**, traveled west along the Great Lakes to what is now Minnesota. He returned to Great Britain and in 1778 published a very popular book detailing his adventure, titled *Travels in Interior Parts of America*. Other writers later accused Carver of plagiarizing his accounts of **Native American** culture.

CASWELL, RICHARD (1729–1789). Richard Caswell served in the **North Carolina** legislature and commanded the right wing of the state forces at the **Battle of the Alamance**. He sat in the **First Continental Congress** in 1774 and the **Second Continental Congress** from 1775–1776. Caswell was governor of North Carolina from 1776–1780 and 1785–1787. Although chosen as a delegate to the **Constitutional Convention of 1787**, he declined the offer. He did support the document during North Carolina's state conventions to consider its ratification.

CATHERINE THE GREAT. *See* RUSSIA AND REVOLUTIONARY AMERICA.

CATO. **George Clinton** wrote a series of anti–U.S. **Constitution** articles under the pen name Cato.

CAUCUS CLUB. The Caucus Club, formed as early as 1724, served as an unofficial governmental body for **Boston**. The members, local shopkeepers and artisans, organized Boston's opposition to British policies, including **taxation** schemes. **Samuel Adams** was a prominent member of the organization and used it to publicize his political views. *See also* LOYAL NINE.

CHARLESTON. Charleston, **South Carolina**, was the largest seaport in the south during the **Revolutionary War** and a prize for both sides. Patriot forces seized the powder supplies of this city on April 21, 1775. Charleston was seen by both sides as one of the primary keys for controlling the south during the war. A British attack on the city in 1776 failed. However, the city did fall to British forces in 1780 and the city remained under British occupation until 1782.

CHARLESTOWN. The American colonists living in **Massachusetts** opposed the imposition of the **Intolerable Acts** by the British in retaliation for the **Boston Tea Party**. Massachusetts **militia** members began taking powder and weapons from public arsenals and hiding them in case hostilities should erupt between the colonists and British forces. On September 1, 1774, British General **Thomas Gage** dispatched a force to seize powder stored at the arsenal in Charlestown and two brass cannons at **Cambridge**. Both towns were located just outside of **Boston**. The British forces caught the Massachusetts militia unprepared and successfully completed their missions. In response to these raids and false rumors of British atrocities, the Massachusetts militia disrupted the local courts in Cambridge and Worcester over the next three days. British troops made a second raid on Charlestown on September 8, 1774, to remove cannon from the harbor fortifications. However, this time the militia were one step ahead of the British and had already moved the cannon from the area. Tension between the two parties would lead to open conflict at the **Battle of Lexington-Concord** the following spring. *See also* NEWPORT; PORTSMOUTH; SALEM.

CHARTER COLONY. A charter **colony**, also known as a corporate colony, was actually chartered to an individual or company by the English Crown. The arrangement permitted the election of the governor, either directly or indirectly, by residents of the area holding the right to vote. After 1760, charter colonies included **Connecticut** and **Rhode Island**. See also PROPRIETARY COLONY; ROYAL COLONY.

CHASE, SAMUEL (1741–1811). Samuel Chase, a lawyer, represented **Maryland** in the **First Continental Congress** in 1774 and the **Second Continental Congress** from 1775–1778. He signed the **Declaration of Independence** for Maryland. He also accompanied **Benjamin Franklin** and **Charles Carroll** on the unsuccessful mission to persuade the Canadians to ally themselves with the Americans in the **Revolutionary War**. Chase later became a justice on the U.S. Supreme Court in 1796.

CHATEAU DE CHAUMONT. Chateau de Chaumont was **Benjamin Franklin's** residence in Paris.

CHECKS AND BALANCES. Checks and Balances, also known as the Madison Model, are the various methods within the U.S. **Constitution** that detail how the executive (president), legislative (Congress), and judicial (Supreme Court) branches of government oversee and prevent the unrestricted growth of power of one in relation to the other two. For example, the legislative branch can impeach members of the executive and judicial branches; must approve executive nominees for the Supreme Court, cabinet, and other high offices; and must ratify treaties negotiated by the executive branch. The executive branch nominates Supreme Court justices and can veto legislative bills. The judicial branch can declare acts of the executive and laws of the legislature unconstitutional and void. **James Madison** championed this system as a means to reassure opponents of the Constitution that the federal government would not grow too powerful.

CHEROKEE. The Cherokee **Native Americans** lived as farmers along the southern Appalachian Mountains during the Revolutionary period. Their lands lay in the modern states of **Georgia**, **North Carolina**, **South Carolina**, and **Tennessee** during this era. The Cherokee were in a continuous struggle to stem the westward movement of American colonists into their territory prior to the **Revolutionary War** despite the existence of various treaties. During the Revolution, the Cherokee sided with the British, who were seen as less inclined to take their lands than the American colonists. After the Revolution, the migration of settlers into Cherokee lands increased.

CHINA AND REVOLUTIONARY AMERICA. American relations with China during the Revolutionary period were based on **trade** and the need to counter the unfavorable balance of trade between the United States and Europe. In 1784, the *Empress of China* became the first U.S. vessel to visit China. The United States appointed Major Samuel Shaw as the first American consul to China in 1786. He established his post at the trading center of Canton.

CHITTENDEN, THOMAS (1730–1797). Thomas Chittenden was a leader in the movement to establish **Vermont** as a state within the United States. He served as the unofficial governor of Vermont from 1778–1797, with the exception of 1789–1790. Vermont became a state in 1791.

CHOISEUL, DUKE FRANÇOIS ETIENNE DE (1719–1785). The Duke of Choiseul served as the French chief minister during the **French and Indian War**. Choiseul realized after the war that the growing unrest between **Great Britain** and her American **colonies** could be of benefit to **France**. He maintained spies in the American colonies to observe this growing rift and offer discreet encouragement. In 1770, Choiseul left office and this policy was not continued by his successor. However, it was renewed in 1774 by **Count Charles Gravier de Vergennes**.

CHOVET, ABRAHAM (1704–1790). Abraham Chovet, a surgeon, arrived in **Philadelphia** in 1774. He delivered specialized classes in human dissection and human anatomy. Chovet is well known for his realistic wax models and paintings that he utilized to aid in his instruction due to the scarcity of human bodies for scientific research.

CHRISTIAN SERVANTS. *See* INDENTURED SERVANTS.

CIRCULAR LETTER OF MASSACHUSETTS. The **Massachusetts** legislature completed the Circular Letter, written primarily by **Samuel Adams**, on February 11, 1768. The document, sent to other colonial legislatures, requested their support in opposing the **Townshend Acts**. The British government ordered Governor **Francis Bernard** to order its withdrawal. However, the Massachusetts legislature voted overwhelmingly (a vote of 92-17) on June 30, 1768, to not rescind the Circular Letter. The number 92, like the number **45**, quickly became a symbol of colonial opposition to British **taxation**. As a result, Governor Bernard dissolved the legislature. The British Parliament extended the 16th-century **Treason Act** to Massachusetts and ordered two more regiments of soldiers to embark for **Boston**.

CLARK, ABRAHAM (1726–1794). Abraham Clark, a surveyor, represented **New Jersey** in the **Second Continental Congress** from 1776–1781 and the **Congress of the Confederation** from 1781–1783 and 1787–1788. He signed the **Declaration of Independence** for New Jersey. He was selected as a delegate in the **Constitutional Convention of 1787** but could not attend due to ill health. He later served in the U.S. House of Representatives.

CLAY, JOSEPH (1741–1804). Joseph Clay, a **Revolutionary War** officer and merchant, served in the **Second Continental Congress** from 1778–1780.

CLAYTON, JOHN (1685–1773). John Clayton was one of the earliest American-born botanists.

CLEAVELAND, MOSES (1754–1806). Moses Cleaveland, a **Revolutionary War** officer and lawyer, served in the **Connecticut** legislature. He attended the Connecticut convention to ratify the U.S. **Constitution**.

CLINGAN, WILLIAM (?–1790). William Clingan, a justice of the peace, represented **Pennsylvania** in the **Second Continental Congress** from 1777–1779. He signed the **Articles of Confederation** for Pennsylvania.

CLINTON, GEORGE (c.1686–1761). George Clinton, a British naval officer, served as the royal governor of **New York** from 1743–1753. His administration weakened the office due to quarrels with the New Yorkers. When he left the position, a significant amount of power had slipped to the populace of the **colony**. This helped to provoke future quarrels between the colony and British authorities. Clinton later became a member of the British Parliament. Clinton should not be confused with **George Clinton**, the American-born statesman who served as the governor of the state of New York.

CLINTON, GEORGE (1739–1812). George Clinton represented **New York** in the **Second Continental Congress** from 1775–1776. He missed signing the **Declaration of Independence** due to accepting a military assignment along the Hudson River and received a Continental commission as a brigadier general in 1777. Clinton was elected governor of New York and reelected for six consecutive terms. Clinton opposed the ratification of the U.S. **Constitution** and wrote anti-Constitutional letters in the press under the pen name **Cato**. His later election victories as governor resulted from questionable political tactics such as disqualifying the vote from entire counties that had leaned heavily toward his opponents. Clinton later became vice president of the United States. Clinton should not be confused with **George Clinton**, the British naval officer who served as royal governor of New York.

CLINTON, JAMES (1733–1812). James Clinton, a **Revolutionary War** officer, attended the **New York** convention to ratify the U.S. **Constitution**. Clinton voted against the document.

CLYMER, GEORGE (1739–1813). George Clymer, an early American patriot, represented **Pennsylvania** in the **Second Continental Congress** from 1776–1777 and 1780 and the **Congress of the Confederation** from 1781–1782. He signed the **Declaration of Independence**. He was selected to replace another delegate who refused to sign the Declaration. The British later sacked his home in retaliation for his signature. He attended the **Constitutional Convention of 1787** and signed the final draft of the U.S. **Constitution**. Clymer later served in the U.S. House of Representatives. He should not be confused with **George Clymer** the inventor.

CLYMER, GEORGE (1754–1834). George Clymer, an inventor, developed improved versions of the water pump and printing press. He should not be confused with **George Clymer** the statesman.

COCKE, WILLIAM (1748–1828). William Cocke was an important leader in the movements to establish Franklin, **Kentucky**, and **Tennessee** as states within the United States. The voters of Franklin elected him to the U.S. House of Representatives. However, **Congress** refused to seat him as a delegate since Franklin was not a state. Cocke moved numerous times during his lifetime and served in the state legislatures of Mississippi, **North Carolina**, Tennessee, and **Virginia**.

COERCIVE ACTS. *See* INTOLERABLE ACTS.

COKE, EDWARD (1552–1634). American colonists frequently quoted Edward Coke when protesting the various forms of British **taxation** after 1763. Coke, a prominent politician and parliamentarian, declared that Parliament should provide consent to all taxation. Coke implied that Parliament and not the king should have authority over taxation. However, the colonists borrowed the argument in defense of their declarations that colonial legislatures, chosen by the people, should have the power of taxation and not the British Parliament. Since the American colonists did not elect representatives to Parliament, the latter body should not impose taxes on them. *See also* GORDON, THOMAS; LOCKE, JOHN; TRENCHARD, JOHN.

COLDEN, CADWALLADER (1688–1776). Cadwallader Colden, a physician and the father of **Jane Colden**, served as the lieutenant governor of **New York**. In this position, he did not support the popular appeal to **Great Britain** for the removal of the **Stamp Act of 1765** and as a result was burned in effigy. Colden was an avid botanist and published works on medicine as well as botany.

COLDEN, JANE (1724–1766). Jane Colden, the daughter of **Cadwallader Colden**, was the first American **woman** to receive acclaim as a botanist.

COLLEGES. *See* EDUCATION.

COLLES, CHRISTOPHER (1738–1816). Christopher Colles, an inventor and engineer, proposed in 1774 the development of a water system to replace the private wells in **New York City**. However, this did not occur for many years. Colles was also one of the first Americans to design and build a steam engine.

COLLINS, JOHN (1717–1795). John Collins, a governor of **Rhode Island**, represented his state in the **Second Continental Congress** and the **Congress of the Confederation** from 1778–1781 and 1782–1783. He signed the **Articles of Confederation** for Rhode Island.

COLONIAL AGENT. A colonial agent was an individual hired to represent a specific **colony** or colonies as a lobbyist. Colonial agents presented colonial positions to the Privy Council, the **Board of Trade and Plantations**, or even Parliament. Their duties included seeking the passage of legislation or decrees that were favorable to the colonies. **Benjamin Franklin** was possibly the most famous colonial agent.

COLONY. A colony is a nonsovereign territory held by a country. Colonies were usually the source of raw materials, a location for migration of the home country's population, and a market for manufactured goods. There were three types of American colonies: **royal colonies**, **proprietary colonies**, and **charter colonies.**

COMMERCE. *See* TRADE.

COMMISSIONER. A commissioner, often referred to as an "American commissioner," was a representative, or ambassador, of the **Second Continental Congress** overseas. **Benjamin Franklin**, the commissioner in Paris, was the best-known individual holding the position. *See also* PLAN OF 1776.

COMMITTEE OF COMMERCE. The **Second Continental Congress** renamed the **Secret Committee** the Committee of Commerce in July 1777. The committee controlled all foreign **trade** between the United States and its allies and neutrals during the **Revolutionary War**.

COMMITTEE OF SECRET CORRESPONDENCE. The **Second Continental Congress** established the Committee of Secret Correspondence on November 29, 1775. The committee consisted of five members, namely **John Dickinson**, **Benjamin Franklin**, **Benjamin Harrison**, **John Jay**, and **Thomas Johnson**. Later members included **James Lovell** and **Robert Morris**. The organization conducted correspondence with individuals in **Great Britain** and the rest of Europe in order to learn which countries might offer support to the colonies in their struggle against the British. The body correctly assumed, based on correspondence, that **France** would offer the most sympathy and aid to the American cause. The members of the committee selected **Silas Deane** on March 3, 1776, to secretly approach France for assistance. Congress renamed the body the **Committee on Foreign Affairs** on April 17, 1777. This organization should not be confused with the **Secret Committee** of Congress chaired by Robert Morris or with **Committees of Correspondence**. *See also* PLAN OF 1776.

COMMITTEE ON FOREIGN AFFAIRS. The **Committee of Secret Correspondence** served as the confidential **foreign policy** arm of the **Second Continental Congress** between 1775 and 1777. On April 17, 1777, Congress reorganized the body and changed its name to Committee on Foreign Affairs. This committee conducted American diplomacy with other countries and served as the predecessor of the present-day Department of State. The organization suffered from various problems and was restructured into a position known as the **executive secretary of foreign affairs** on January 6, 1781, headed by **Robert Livingston**. *See also* PLAN OF 1776.

COMMITTEES OF CORRESPONDENCE. By 1771, radical American leaders had little to stir their fellow colonists. The **Stamp Act of 1765** and **Townshend Act of 1767** crises were over. In response to the need to keep the **colonies** united, Committees of Correspondence were developed to maintain contact between communities and coordinate actions in response to future British policies. Proposed by **Samuel Adams** in September 1771, **Boston** established the first committee in 1772 and urged the local communities to follow suit. By January 1773, approximately 80 **Massachusetts** communities boasted committees of correspondence. It was during January 1773 that the British announced the plan to arrest those responsible for the ***Gaspée*** affair and transport them to London for trial. This act helped spur the establishment of committees in other colonies.

The work of the Committees of Correspondence began to change during the time of the **First Continental Congress** and the **Continental Association**. The committees oversaw the enforcement of the Continental Association as well as establishing new organizations, including the **Committees of Observation** and **Committees of Inspection**. The Committees of Correspondence should not be confused with the **Committee of Secret Correspondence**. *See also* BOSTON PAMPHLET.

COMMITTEES OF INSPECTION. Local communities established Committees of Inspection generally to assist in the application of the **Continental Association**. However, enforcement of the boycott normally rested with **Committees of Correspondence**. *See also* COMMITTEES OF OBSERVATION.

COMMITTEES OF OBSERVATION. Local communities established Committees of Observation to assist in the application of the **Continental Association**. However, enforcement of the boycott normally rested with **Committees of Correspondence**. *See also* COMMITTEES OF INSPECTION.

COMMITTEES OF SAFETY. **Massachusetts** established the first Committee of Safety in February 1775. The committee held the authority to acquire military supplies and mobilize the **militia**. Other **colonies** followed the successful Massachusetts example. Some local committees formed to oversee merchant compliance with the **Continental Association** were referred to as Committees of Safety. *See also* COMMITTEES OF SAFETY MUSKETS.

COMMITTEES OF SAFETY MUSKETS. **Committees of Safety Muskets** were weapons manufactured locally under contracts with various **Committees of Safety**. Most of these muskets were based on the design of the British **Brown Bess**.

COMMON SENSE. **Thomas Paine** arrived in the American **colonies** from **Great Britain** in 1774. He found employment working with **Robert Aitken**, a **printer** and editor in **Philadelphia**. He wrote two articles that local patriots opted to publish under the title *Common*

Sense. They were published anonymously on January 10, 1776. The famous pamphlet offered a defense for American actions against Great Britain and was written in language easily understood by the average reader. Earlier documents were often very philosophical and difficult for the average reader of that period to fully understand. Some estimates indicate that approximately 500,000 copies of *Common Sense* were sold in the American colonies with 100,000 in the first three months after publication. *Common Sense* was one of the best-selling books of the Revolutionary period in American history. Many readers thought that **John Adams** had written the book. However, Adams actually criticized the work for the very reasons that the average reader enjoyed it—it was written in the language of the masses with the purpose of arousing the sentiment of the average person for independence. The document has been credited with persuading many Americans that independence was the only acceptable option. *See also CRISIS*; *PUBLIC GOOD*.

CONCILIATORY PROPOSITIONS. By the end of 1777, the British faced a lingering war in the American **colonies**, higher **taxes**, and the defeat of an entire army at the Battle of Saratoga. Before **France** could officially enter the war, **Lord North** offered peace terms to the American colonies in rebellion. Known as the Conciliatory Propositions, the British offer agreed to every American demand except independence. In the provisions, Parliament agreed to drop taxes on the colonies, repeal or amend the **American Prohibitory Act of 1775** and other legislation disliked by the colonists, and recognize **Congress** as a legitimate body for negotiations. The peace gesture floundered on the issue of American independence. Many Americans clung to the idea of independence, while others argued that they had pledged to France that they would not seek a separate peace with Great Britain. Some scholars have argued that Lord North did not really believe that the Americans would accept his proposals. Instead, the Conciliatory Propositions were an attempt to silence the opposition in Parliament favoring the American cause. The refusal of the Americans to accept the Conciliatory Propositions led to the enactment of the **Carlisle Proclamation**.

CONGRESS. Congress is the national legislature of the American **colonies** and then the United States of America beginning in 1774.

Congress can be classified by various names based on the foundation upon which it derived its authority. The following names are utilized in this text to describe Congress. The **First Continental Congress** is the body that met in 1774 to discuss united colonial action against British policies. The **Second Continental Congress** convened in 1775, issued the **Declaration of Independence**, and lasted until the ratification of the **Articles of Confederation** in 1781. At that point, the body became the **Congress of the Confederation**. This name and structure of the national legislature lasted until 1789 when a new body, **Congress of the United States of America**, was elected under the foundation of the **Constitution**. *See also* CONGRESS OF THE UNITED COLONIES; PRESIDENT OF CONGRESS.

CONGRESS MUSKET. The Congress Musket was an .80 caliber musket manufactured in small numbers in the United States for use by the **Continental Army** and **militia** units.

CONGRESS OF THE CONFEDERATION. The Congress of the Confederation (officially known as the **United States in Congress Assembled**) was the national legislature of the United States between 1781 and 1789. The body replaced the **Second Continental Congress** upon the ratification of the **Articles of Confederation** on March 1, 1781. The **Congress of the United States of America** replaced the Congress of the Confederation on March 4, 1789, following the elections resulting from the ratification of the **Constitution**. Each state could send multiple representatives to the Congress of the Confederation but had only one vote in the body regardless of physical size or population. Terms of office lasted one year. The organization was the only branch of the national government, since the Articles of Confederation did not provide for an executive or judicial branch of government. Members of Congress did select one representative to serve as the **president of Congress**. However, his duties were similar to those of the Speaker of the House in the Congress under the Constitution rather than a true national executive. The Congress of the Confederation was a very weak body lacking the authority to tax or pass national legislation that Americans would think common under the current Congress.

CONGRESS OF THE UNITED COLONIES. Congress of the United Colonies is the official name of the national legislature formed by the **colonies** prior to the **Declaration of Independence**. The first congressional gathering (1774) is more commonly known by its informal name as the **First Continental Congress**. The second (1775–1781) is more commonly known as the **Second Continental Congress**. The Congress of the United Colonies was actually the First Continental Congress and the Second Continental Congress until the signing of the Declaration of Independence. *See also* CONGRESS; CONGRESS OF THE CONFEDERATION; PRESIDENT OF CONGRESS.

CONGRESS OF THE UNITED STATES OF AMERICA. Congress of the United States of America is the official name of the national legislature established under the **Constitution**. The organization replaced the **Congress of the Confederation** on March 4, 1789, and consists of two houses. The first is the Senate with two representatives from each state. During the immediate post-Revolutionary historical period, the legislatures of each state selected the members of the Senate, who then served for six years. Membership in the second body, the House of Representatives, is based on state population and the representatives are elected by popular vote for two-year terms. Unlike the Congress of the Confederation, the Congress of the United States of America is one of three branches of government. Congress makes legislation but is balanced by (as it balances) executive and judicial branches of government. *See also* CONNECTICUT COMPROMISE; THREE-FIFTHS COMPROMISE.

CONNECTICUT. Connecticut, one of the **New England colonies**, was governed by **Great Britain** as a **charter colony** until the **Revolutionary War** and American independence. In 1766 the population stood at 130,612. By the end of America's Revolutionary period in 1790, the state boasted 237,946 people (1.9% slaves). The people of Connecticut generally supported **Massachusetts** and other **colonies** in their opposition to British **taxation** polices prior to the Revolution as seen in the **Farmington Resolves**. During the **Constitutional Convention of 1787**, representatives from the state were instrumental in developing what is known as the **Connecticut Compromise** to reconcile the differences between the large and small states during debates. The state ratified the U.S. **Constitution** on January 9, 1788. Connecticut was the largest producer and exporter of salted pork and the second-largest producer and exporter of salted beef in the United States during this period. However, most residents were small farmers who supplied food for nearby markets such as **New York City**. Notable individuals from Connecticut during this period include **Oliver Ellsworth**, **Samuel Huntington**, **William Johnson**, **Richard Law**, **William Williams**, and **Oliver Wolcott**.

CONNECTICUT COMPROMISE. The Connecticut Compromise, also known as the Great Compromise, served as a means to incorporate ideas of the rival **New Jersey Plan** and the **Virginia Plan** during the **Constitutional Convention of 1787**. The compromise included modified provisions found in both plans. The Connecticut Compromise included the following points:

1. A two-house national legislature. The upper house should be selected by state legislatures and the lower chamber elected by the residents of each state.
2. Representation in the upper house should be based on equality among the states while representation in the lower chamber should be based on state population.
3. The national legislature should have broad powers, including taxation and the regulation of commerce.
4. The national executive should consist of a single individual selected by an electoral college.
5. The national judiciary justices should be nominated by the president and confirmed by the upper chamber of the national legislature.

The acceptance of these provisions after considerable debate and threats of secession may have saved the union. Other compromises between the delegates can be found in the entry on the Constitutional Convention of 1787. *See also* THREE-FIFTHS COMPROMISE.

CONSTITUTION. The document known as the Constitution (with a capital "C") is actually the second constitution (with a small "c") of the United States. The first document, the **Articles of Confederation**, proved to be too weak and after the **Revolutionary War** the national government was on the verge of collapse as each state tended to exert its interpretation of sovereignty at the expense of the other states. A poor **economy**, unfavorable **trade** conditions with most foreign countries, interstate rivalry, and a restless population represented just four of the many problems faced by the new country. After two preliminary discussions (the **Alexandria Convention** and the **Annapolis Convention**), the states gathered for the **Constitutional Convention of 1787**. Considerable heated debate and tense compromises led to the drafting of the Constitution before the end of 1787. Ratification of the Constitution occurred on June 21, 1788, when **New Hampshire** became the ninth state to grant final approval to the document. More than one state convention refused to ratify the document until assured that a **Bill of Rights** to protect individual freedoms would follow. The U.S. Constitution is the oldest written constitution currently in use by any country today. The government system outlined by the Constitution is reviewed under the entry **Connecticut Compromise**. A list of everyone who attended at least part of the Constitutional Convention of 1787 is included as appendix B of this book. *See also* CHECKS AND BALANCES; FAYETTEVILLE STATE CONVENTION; HAMILTON PLAN; HILLSBOROUGH STATE CONVENTION; NEW JERSEY PLAN; THREE-FIFTHS COMPROMISE; SEPARATION OF POWERS; VIRGINIA PLAN.

CONSTITUTIONAL CONVENTION OF 1787. The national government under the **Articles of Confederation** faced many challenges after the **Revolutionary War**, including the inability to tax and regulate commerce. Restless Americans were demanding social and economic justice during a period when the **economy** was poor and many farmers were in **debt**. **Shays's Rebellion** stood out as an example of what could happen in any state as farmers opposed local and state government. Concerned states met at the **Alexandria Convention** and then the **Annapolis Convention** to discuss how to strengthen the Articles of Confederation and hold the country together. Attendees at the Annapolis Convention proposed the convening of a national convention to discuss amending the Articles of Confederation. The **Congress of the Confederation** gave its consent for that specific purpose.

Twelve states sent a total of 55 delegates to the convention that opened on May 25, 1787, in Independence Hall, **Philadelphia**. **Rhode Island** was wary of national government interference in state affairs and did not send a delegation. The attendees quietly changed the purpose of their gathering from amending the Articles of Confederation to drafting a new federal constitution to replace the articles. The delegates met behind closed doors with the windows closed in order to maintain the confidentiality of the discussions. Guards blocked the doors and dirt was thrown on the cobblestone street in front of Independence Hall so that the noise of passing horses and carts would not disturb the delegates.

The attendees were a "who's who" of the United States. **George Washington** represented **Virginia** and sat as the president of the convention. **James Madison**, often referred to now as the "father of the Constitution," proved to be one of the main driving forces behind the new document. The journal kept by Madison is one of the few primary-source materials that relate the proceedings of the convention. **Benjamin Franklin**, **Robert Morris**, and **Alexander Hamilton** represent just three of the many great personalities present at the convention. **John Adams** and **Thomas Jefferson** were prevented by other governmental responsibilities from being able to attend. **John Jay** and **Samuel Adams** did not receive appointments to represent their states. **Patrick Henry** opposed a stronger national government and declined to attend. Other prominent founding fathers who did not attend included **John Hancock** and **Richard Henry Lee**.

Compromises among the delegates were often reached after considerable debate and threats of secession by those representatives who believed their states would suffer under the provisions suggested by other individuals. The **Connecticut Compromise**, also known as the Great Compromise, settled the divisions between the **New Jersey Plan** and **Virginia Plan.** The Connecticut Compromise established the structure of the new U.S. government and representation within the national legislature. The **Three-Fifths Compromise** ended a stalemate over the issue of counting slaves toward representation in Congress and direct taxation. Other compromises during the convention included:

1. **Slavery**:
   a. States could determine whether slavery would be accepted within their borders.

   b. States could not harbor escaped slaves from other states.
   c. The importation of slaves in the country was permitted until 1808.
   d. Slavery was prohibited in the **Northwest Territory**.

2. Voting qualifications to be set by individual states.
3. Economic issues:

   a. Congress has the power to levy taxes and spend money.
   b. Congress could regulate interstate and foreign commerce.
   c. States are prohibited from establishing tariffs for interstate or foreign commerce.
   d. Only Congress can print or coin money and regulate its value.

Of the 55 delegates, 39 signed the Constitution. Not all of those who did not sign the document opposed it. See appendix B for a list of the 55 delegates who attended at least part of the convention. Each signer and nonsigner listed in the appendix has a separate biographical entry in this book. *See also* CHECKS AND BALANCES; SEPARATION OF POWERS.

CONTINENTAL. The term *continental* refers to almost anything associated with the Continental Congress (national government) rather than an individual state. Soldiers serving with the **Continental Army** were called Continentals. They enlisted for set periods of time and represented the United States rather than the individual states, in contrast to the **militia**. The term has also been applied to the paper **currency** issued by the **Second Continental Congress**. As the war progressed, the paper money steadily lost its value when compared to European currencies, leading to the phrase "**not worth a continental**."

CONTINENTAL ARMY. The Continental Army was the military ground force authorized by the **First Continental Congress** and the **Second Continental Congress**. The Continental Army consisted of soldiers pledged to the Continental Congress and not individual states. Enlistments in the Continental Army were generally for the duration of the conflict, in contrast to those of the state **militia** members. The original two Marine battalions raised by Congress were also part of the Continental Army. Congress authorized the raising of 88 battalions on September 16, 1776, to replace the troops who had enlisted until the end of 1776. Members of the new units would be required to serve for the duration of the **Revolutionary War**. Although commonly portrayed in blue uniforms, Congress did not officially authorize the color for all soldiers in the Continental Army until 1782. *See also* CONTINENTAL; CONTINENTAL LINE; CONTINENTAL NAVY.

CONTINENTAL ARTICLES OF WAR. The **Second Continental Congress** adopted the Continental Articles of War on June 30, 1775, and amended them on November 7, 1775. In general terms, articles of war provide for the administrative and disciplinary needs of an army. The Continental Articles of War were based on a set of articles of war written by **Massachusetts** on April 5, 1775, which had been derived from the British Articles of War of 1765. The Massachusetts Articles provided for the order of military units and outlined crimes, punishments, and legal procedures. The Continental Articles added provisions covering administrative forms, pardons, sutters, and other items from the original British articles. The revision of November 7, 1775, increased the range of capital crimes including treason.

CONTINENTAL ASSOCIATION. The delegates to the **First Continental Congress** approved the Continental Association, often referred to as "the Association," on October 20, 1774. This hotly debated agreement proved to be the most important act during the short duration of the First Continental Congress. The document, based on the **Virginia Association**, called for unified colonial agreement to halt economic relations with **Great Britain**. The American **colonies** would cease importing British goods on December 1, 1774. This **trade** embargo included the importation of slaves and demonstrates the influence of the anti-**slavery** movement at this point of time. The colonies would also cease exporting material to Great Britain on September 10, 1775. **Georgia**, lacking delegates at the First Continental Congress, agreed to modified provisions of the document on January 23, 1775. Congress relied more on recommendations for adherence by the colonies since the body was not authorized to produce legislation in the form of mandatory laws. Various committees (of various names including the **Committees of Safety**, **Committees of Inspection**, and **Committees of Observation**) and the **Sons of Liberty** served to enforce the provisions of the Continental Association. Punishment for merchants violating the Association included **tarring and feathering**. The boycott of trade with Great Britain was very successful and led many British merchants to demand that Parliament repair relations with the colonies. The Continental Association can be seen as one of the first unified efforts of all the American colonies against Great Britain and the predecessor of a government representing all of the colonies.

CONTINENTAL CONGRESS, FIRST. Representatives of 12 **colonies** met at **Carpenter's Hall** in **Philadelphia** on September 5, 1774, in response to the British **Intolerable Acts** of 1774. The Congress was envisioned as a means to demonstrate unified protest to British policies. The delegates selected **Peyton Randolph** as **president of Congress**. It is interesting to note that of the 56 delegates to the First Continental Congress (all but seven between the ages of 30 and 60) only one was not born in the American colonies. **Georgia** was the only colony without representation at the gathering. That colony's royal governor prevented a delegation from attending the Congress. The delegates met as representatives of individual colonies and not citizens of a single country. Thus, each colony, regardless of population, wielded a single vote throughout the proceedings.

Delegates were divided into three groups: the radicals who demanded immediate action against **Great Britain**, the conservatives who called for reconciliation with the mother country, and the moderates who hovered somewhere between the two extremes. Congress was thus divided on the issue of how to respond to the Intolerable Acts. The body did denounce the Intolerable Acts, as well as the **Quebec Act of 1774** in a **Statement of Rights and Grievances** and it endorsed the **Suffolk Resolves**. However, the group disagreed on exactly how to respond to the British government. A call for the establishment of a Grand Council and a new relationship with the British, known as the **Galloway Plan of Union**, was defeated after receiving an initial warm reception by many delegates.

Delegates agreed that Parliament had the right to regulate **trade** but that the British body should not pass any colonial laws without consent. Toward the end of the gathering, Congress drafted a petition to **King George III** presenting its grievances with colonial policy. The body endorsed an economic boycott of British goods known as the **Continental Association**. This could be seen as the most important act of the Congress. The First Continental Congress adjourned on October 26, 1774, after agreeing to meet again on May 10, 1775. *See also* CONTINENTAL CONGRESS, SECOND; GRAND COMMITTEE.

CONTINENTAL CONGRESS, SECOND. The Second Continental Congress convened on May 10, 1775, in **Philadelphia** as requested by members of the **First Continental Congress**. The **Battle of Lexington-Concord**, recognized by most historians as the first military engagement of the **Revolutionary War**, occurred just prior to the convening of Congress. Thus, Congress had to immediately deal with the escalation of the confrontation between the **colonies** and **Great Britain**. Delegates tended to lean more toward the radical opinion than those of the First Continental Congress. Congress established the **Continental Army**, named **George Washington** as the commander in chief, and began requesting the colonies to furnish new units. The members also asked **Canada** to join the revolt. Congress originally attempted reconciliation with Great Britain via the **Olive Branch Petition**. However, this attempt failed and **King George III** declared the colonies to be in a state of rebellion. By early 1776, the members began discussing the merits of declaring independence from Great Britain. These debates led to the signing of the **Declaration of Independence** on July 4, 1776.

Congress continued to administer the national **economy** and war effort in the absence of a true central government. The body passed the **Articles of Confederation** in November 1777 to establish a central government but they were not ratified until 1781. The Second Continental Congress transformed itself into the **United States in Congress Assembled** (more commonly known as the **Congress of the Confederation**) on March 3, 1781, with the ratification of the articles. Overall, the Second Continental Congress was seen as a fairly weak organization with the colonies adhering to its requests, such as for logistical support or money, when it was in their interests. *See also* COMMISSIONER; COMMITTEE OF COMMERCE;

COMMITTEE OF SECRET CORRESPONDENCE; COMMITTEE ON FOREIGN AFFAIRS;

CONTINENTAL LINE. The Continental Line is another name for the **Continental Army**. The term "line" refers to the linear battle formations of the time period.

CONTINENTAL NAVY. The **Second Continental Congress** established a navy on October 13, 1775. On this day, Congress authorized the fitting of two ships to intercept British vessels carrying supplies to the garrison besieged at **Boston**. On December 13, 1775, Congress authorized the construction of 13 **frigates**, to include five 32-gun, five 28-gun, and three 24-gun ships. The Continental Navy, like its **Continental Army** counterpart, was pledged to serve the Continental Congress and not the individual states. Eventually, 57 ships would serve under the banner of the Continental Navy at some point between 1775 and 1783. *See also* NAVAL CONSTRUCTION ACT OF 1775; NAVAL CONSTRUCTION ACT OF 1776; NAVAL CONSTRUCTION ACT OF 1777.

CONVENTION OF ARANJUEZ. **Spain** entered the war against **Great Britain** by signing the Convention of Aranjuez, a secret treaty with **France,** on April 12, 1779. The document was followed by a formal declaration of war against Great Britain on June 21, 1779. Under the terms of the convention, Spain entered the war on the side of the French and France promised to back the transfer of Gibraltar to Spain in any treaty with Great Britain. Spain did not extend recognition to the United States and did not pledge soldiers to assist the American war effort as France had promised.

CONWAY CABAL. Several American military officers and political leaders, including General **Thomas Mifflin**, General Thomas Conway, **Samuel Adams**, and **Benjamin Rush** questioned the ability of General **George Washington** to lead the Continental Army following the string of military defeats in 1776–1777. Many called for the replacement of Washington with General Horatio Gates, the victor at the Battle of Saratoga. Word of a possible cabal leaked to Washington who confronted Conway and others on the matter. The **Second**

Continental Congress did not attempt to replace Washington and both Mifflin and Conway resigned from the army. Historians still disagree as to whether a cabal actually existed.

COOPER, EZEKIEL (1763–1847). Ezekiel Cooper, a clergyman, was a pioneer in the development of the Methodist church in the United States. *See also* RELIGION.

COOPER, MYLES (1737–1785). Myles Cooper, a **loyalist** clergyman, departed **New York** to **Great Britain** in 1775. Local patriots considered him one of the most despised loyalists in New York.

COOPER, SAMUEL (1725–1783). Samuel Cooper, a patriot clergyman, fled **Boston** in 1775 ahead of British troops sent to arrest him for his staunch anti-British stance.

COPLEY, JOHN (1738–1815). John Copley, born in **Boston**, emerged as the first American painter to receive international recognition for his work. A portrait painter, Copley traveled to London in 1774 at the urging of **Benjamin West**, another famous American painter of the Revolutionary period. He remained in **Great Britain** for the rest of his life.

COPPER INDUSTRY. A small copper industry existed in Revolutionary America with the largest deposits in **Connecticut**, **New Jersey**, and **New York**. Copper is the main ingredient in the production of bronze and is an important additive to tin for the production of some types of pewter.

CORNPLANTER (1740–1836). Cornplanter, a Seneca chief, fought for the British during the **Revolutionary War**. After the war, Cornplanter played a significant role in negotiating treaties to ensure peaceful relations between his people and American settlers. *See also* IROQUOIS; NATIVE AMERICANS.

CORNSTALK (c.1720–1777). Cornstalk, a Shawnee chief, led the uprising against encroaching American colonial settlers that became known as **Lord Dunmore's War**. During the **Revolutionary War**, the British encouraged **Native Americans** to assist them in defeating the American colonial bid for independence. In 1777, some of the Shawnee planned to launch a series of raids in support of the British. However, Cornstalk opted to honor his treaty and preserve the peace. As a result, he went to warn the settlers. The Americans held Cornstalk and his son out of mistrust and murdered them after a soldier was killed by a Native American. This murder proved to be the pivotal point in persuading the Shawnee to ally themselves with the British during the Revolution. *See also* POINT PLEASANT, BATTLE OF.

CORPORATE COLONY. *See* CHARTER COLONY.

COURT OF QUARTER SESSIONS. A Court of Quarter Sessions is another name for a county-level **court**. *See also* CRIMINAL JUSTICE SYSTEM.

COURTS. The court system was fairly similar within all 13 **colonies** and then states of Revolutionary America. The courts were based on the English system and normally included a justice of the peace at the lowest level. The latter individual, appointed to the position, handled most simple civil court cases. Above this level, one could find the county courts, which were often the most important governmental agencies in rural areas. The general circuit courts were at the next level in the court system. Judges at this level sometimes rode a "circuit" to hear cases in various areas within their territory. A colonial court with judges appointed by the governor could be found at the highest level. *See also* COURT OF QUARTER SESSIONS; CRIMINAL JUSTICE SYSTEM; LEGAL PROFESSION.

COX, LEMEUL (1736–1806). Lemeul Cox, a loyalist during the **Revolutionary War**, was one of the most successful American bridge builders during the Revolutionary period. From 1785–1786, Cox supervised the construction of the first bridge built on the Charles River between **Boston** and **Charlestown**. The bridge was considered remarkable for its time. He built other bridges in the United States before traveling to Ireland where he constructed several major bridges.

CRAFTS. Many Americans rose to national and international prominence for their craft working during the period of Revolutionary America. Notable craftsmen included **John Goddard**, **Jonathan Gostelowe**, **Thomas Harland**, **Nathaniel Hurd**, **Paul Revere**, **Joseph Richardson**, and **David Tannenberger**. *See also* PAINTING.

CRAIGIE, ANDREW (1743–1819). Andrew Craigie, an apothecary and surgeon, became the first **Continental** apothecary in 1775.

CRAIK, JAMES (1730–1814). James Craik, a physician and surgeon, served with the **Continental Army**. He became the director general of Hospital Development for the United States. Craik treated **George Washington** and was in attendance when the former president and Continental Army commander in chief died.

CREEK. The Creek were **Native Americans** who lived as farmers in a political confederation within the modern states of Alabama and **Georgia**. The Creek struggled during the Revolutionary period to stem the westward migration of American colonists into their lands despite the existence of various treaties. *See also* AUGUSTA, CONFERENCE OF, 1763; AUGUSTA, TREATY OF; GALPHINTON, TREATY OF.

CREVECOEUR, MICHEL-GUILLAUME JEAN DE (1735–1813). In 1759, Crevecoeur, a Frenchman, traveled to the American **colonies** and became a naturalized citizen in 1765. He married an American in 1769 and established a farm along the frontier. In 1780, he returned to **France** and wrote a successful book about his life in America. In 1783, he returned to find his wife dead and farm destroyed by a **Native American** raid. He served as the French consul in **New York City**, sailed for France in 1790, and never returned to the United States.

CRIMINAL JUSTICE SYSTEM. Most towns and cities hired individuals to serve as a public police force, and at night citizens frequently were assigned to perform a night watch in their communities. The latter were assigned to watch for **fires** as well as criminal activity. While there were many **courts** established in cities, towns, and rural areas, they were frequently packed with lawsuits and lawyers were eager to make money from the judicial process. Most hearings in courts utilized the jury system. If convicted, individuals found that the conditions in most jails during this period were miserable. Jails constructed to house prisoners were rare and most were incarcerated in any building designated for that purpose. **Connecticut** housed many of its prisoners in an abandoned **copper** mine. Men and women were housed together in the same prisons, leading to even more problems such as rape. Every state except **New Jersey** forced prisoners to pay for their own room and board. As a result, those unable to meet the costs might be sold into **indentured servitude** when released. Many individuals formed societies to argue for reform of the prison systems in various states.

Punishment for crimes in Revolutionary America included incarceration with hard labor, branding, mutilation, placement in **stocks** or a **pillory**, public whipping, and the death penalty. The death penalty normally involved hanging the offender. Debate over the death penalty existed as early as the period of Revolutionary America. After the Revolution, **Thomas Jefferson** and **James Madison** argued in favor of eliminating the death penalty for all crimes in **Virginia** except murder and treason. In 1786, **Pennsylvania** dropped the death penalty for robbery. Most states maintained strict guidelines on the death penalty and permitted it as a form of punishment for a large variety of crimes. Many groups were active during this period, protesting the harshness of the laws on debtors who could be thrown into prison for lengthy terms for trivial **debts**. *See also* COURTS; LEGAL PROFESSION.

***CRISIS*.** **Thomas Paine** published the first edition of his political pamphlet *Crisis* on December 19, 1776, in **Philadelphia**. The document began with the famous line, "These are the times that try men's souls." Paine served as an enlisted soldier on General Nathanael Greene's staff at this period. He wrote the document during a period of dark despair among Americans. The British had captured **New York City** and had chased General **George Washington**'s army across **New Jersey**. American officers read *Crisis* to the meager American army facing the British across the Delaware River and the document is credited with bolstering the resolve of the **Continental**

Army prior to the First Battle of Trenton six days later. *See also COMMON SENSE.*

CROGHAN, GEORGE (?–1782). George Croghan was a very prominent **Native American** agent. His personal journals and letters present some of the best historical sources on the areas west of the Appalachians from 1745–1775. He was involved in the attempt to form **Vandalia**.

CRUGER, JOHN (1710–1791). John Cruger, a staunch patriot, served as the mayor of **New York City** from 1756–1765. He was also a member of the **New York** colonial legislature.

CUFFEE, PAUL (1759–1817). Paul Cuffee, a freeborn **African American** from **Massachusetts**, was a sailor and successful owner of many sailing vessels. In 1780, Cuffee filed a case in the Massachusetts **court** system challenging the state's denial of suffrage to those who pay taxes. Although he lost the case, his efforts were significant in the 1783 state act that granted African Americans legal rights in the state. He supported returning freed slaves to Africa and traveled to Sierra Leone to establish the program.

CUMBERLAND AGREEMENT. Richard Henderson, after failing to settle land he claimed that he acquired for his **Transylvania Company** at the **Treaty of Sycamore Shoals**, moved inland along the Cumberland River. At least 250 settlers purchased land from Henderson in the area of modern Nashville, **Tennessee**. Since it was over 200 miles from the nearest large settlement, the individuals opted to establish their own system of government and signed the Cumberland Agreement on May 13, 1780. The agreement lasted until the area was officially absorbed by **North Carolina** in 1783.

CURRENCY. Currency in the form of precious metals was scarce in Revolutionary America. First, gold and silver mines did not exist in the 13 **colonies**. This eliminated a source of precious metals for the local minting of coins. Second, the colonies maintained an unfavorable balance of **trade** with **Great Britain**. Thus, gold and silver were not flowing to the American colonies in exchange for commodities. Third, the

British forbade the export of coins to the American colonies. The majority of coins held by Americans were of French, Portuguese, or Spanish origins and obtained via the favorable balance of trade with the colonies of these countries in the West Indies. Americans turned to alternatives, including the barter of goods, establishing new mediums of exchange such as **tobacco**, **rice** and other products, and the printing of paper money. Paper money was unpopular and usually depreciated very quickly. However, debtors liked the idea of being able to pay off their bills in paper money that was actually worth less than the amount they borrowed. Some colonies established controversial land banks to issue paper money backed by land.

Currency problems increased during the **Revolutionary War** as American trade with the West Indies decreased and the **Second Continental Congress** and the states issued more paper money backed by only a promise to redeem the bills later for specie. Toward the end of the war, paper money was essentially worthless and valued at approximately two or three cents on the dollar, leading to the popular cultural phrase "**not worth a continental**." Congress did borrow money from **France**, **Netherlands**, and **Spain** during the war but the currency it obtained did not come close to meeting the needs of the new country. In 1780, Congress issued new treasury notes to replace the nearly worthless continentals in circulation at an exchange rate of 40 to 1. However, even the new notes depreciated to a value of approximately 20 cents on the dollar.

Currency problems continued immediately after the Revolution. Trade restrictions imposed on the United States by the European states after the war quickly drained the little specie still in the country, adding to the currency woes. In 1785, Congress established a coinage system but lacked the bullion required to meet the needs of the country. Seven states issued paper money with laws making its acceptance mandatory. As before, paper money simply depreciated in value. Many individuals clipped or sheared the edges of the coins to remove the precious metals. As a result, most coins were not accepted in exchange for their original face value. The currency issue was one of the causes of the **economic** crisis that led to **Shays's Rebellion** in 1786. *See also* BANK OF NORTH AMERICA; CURRENCY ACT OF 1751; CURRENCY ACT OF 1764; DEBT, PERSONAL; DEBT, PUBLIC; MORRIS, ROBERT.

CURRENCY ACT OF 1751. While the passage of this act is actually prior to the Revolutionary America period, it is important for understanding **currency** issues in the American colonies and the **Currency Act of 1764**. The British government passed the Currency Act of 1751 in an attempt to regulate the paper money being issued in the **New England colonies**. New England colonial governments could issue paper money to cover expenses if they levied taxes to cover the bill within two years. However, paper money could not be used to pay private debts. The British did not enforce the act during the **French and Indian War** due to the need for paper money to cover the mounting debt of the colonies. The British government passed the Currency Act of 1764 after the war.

CURRENCY ACT OF 1764. British Prime Minister **George Grenville** persuaded Parliament to pass the Currency Act of 1764, the same year as the **Sugar Act of 1764**. While the Sugar Act had its greatest impact on the northern **colonies**, the Currency Act of 1764 added a new burden on the **southern colonies**. Parliament had passed the **Currency Act of 1751** to control the issuing of paper money in the **New England colonies**. During and after the **French and Indian War**, the American colonies faced a scarcity of precious metals. Merchants throughout the American colonies experienced difficulties paying their British counterparts and turned to paper **currency** as a solution. As the value of the colonial paper money decreased, British merchants petitioned the government for assistance. The Currency Act of 1764 resulted from this action and extended the provisions of the Currency Act of 1751 from New England to all 13 American colonies. Royal governors could not authorize the issuance of bills of credit as legal tender (paper currency). Any governor who refused to abide by the act could be fined 1,000 pounds, lose his position, and be disbarred from public office.

The American colonists viewed the Currency Act with disdain, especially since it was passed around the same time as the Sugar Act of 1764 and the Navigation Acts. The Currency Act is significant in that it reduced the monetary supply within the colonies during the period of crisis initiated by the Sugar Act of 1764. The latter act reduced the influx of hard currency into the colonies as merchants faced obstruction in acquiring inexpensive non-British sugar. The Currency Act served to increase the currency shortage and helped raise the ire of the colonists against the government in London. *See also* TAXATION.

CUSHING, THOMAS (1725–1788). Thomas Cushing served in the **Massachusetts** legislature and as a delegate to the **First Continental Congress** and **Second Continental Congress** from 1774–1776. He did not support independence from **Great Britain** and was replaced by **Elbridge Gerry**, who signed the **Declaration of Independence** for Massachusetts. Despite his opposition to independence, Cushing still considered himself a patriot and was elected as the lieutenant governor of Massachusetts.

CUSHING, WILLIAM (1732–1810). William Cushing, a lawyer, served as the chief justice of **Massachusetts**. He was the vice president of the state convention for ratification of the U.S. **Constitution**. Later he became the first associate justice of the U.S. Supreme Court.

CUTLER, MANASSEH (1742–1823). Manasseh Cutler can be described as a clergyman, physician, botanist, and amateur astronomer. He was one of the original cofounders of the **Ohio Company**. Due to his many experiences, Cutler's suggestions were incorporated into the **Northwest Ordinance**.

CUTTER. A cutter was a small naval vessel with a single mast.

– D –

DAME SCHOOLS. *See* EDUCATION.

DANA, FRANCIS (1743–1811). Francis Dana, a diplomat, jurist, and the son of **Richard Dana**, was a member of the **Sons of Liberty** but urged reconciliation between the American **colonies** and **Great Britain**. After returning from a trip to Great Britain in 1776, Dana realized that his hopes for reconciliation were out of the question. He represented **Massachusetts** in the **Second Continental Congress** and the **Congress of the Confederation** from 1777–1778 and then in

1784. He signed the **Articles of Confederation**. Congress dispatched Dana to serve as the secretary to **John Adams** in **France**. From France, he was then sent on to **Russia** in 1781 to secure that country's recognition and assistance for the United States. During his two years in Russia, Dana failed to gain American membership in the **League of Armed Neutrality** or Russian support for the American cause. Catherine the Great of Russia never received Dana in his official capacity as a representative of the United States. Dana was selected to attend the **Constitutional Convention of 1787**. However, he did not attend due to ill health. Dana did serve as a delegate in the Massachusetts state convention to ratify the U.S. **Constitution**. He later held the position of chief justice of the Supreme Court of Massachusetts.

DANA, RICHARD (1700–1772). Richard Dana, a lawyer and father of **Francis Dana**, was an original member of the **Sons of Liberty**. He was the force behind the **Massachusetts** opposition to the **Stamp Act of 1765** and served as a member of the committee that investigated the **Boston Massacre**.

DANE, NATHAN (1752–1835). Nathan Dane, a lawyer, represented **Massachusetts** in the **Congress of the Confederation** from 1785–1788. He helped draft the **Northwest Ordinance** and wrote the article within the document that prohibited **slavery** in the **Northwest Territory**. He opposed the U.S. **Constitution** and was not elected to serve on the state convention that ratified the document. He served later in the Massachusetts legislature.

DARKE, WILLIAM (1736–1801). William Darke, a **Revolutionary War** officer, served in the **Virginia** convention to ratify the U.S. **Constitution**. He was in favor of ratification. Darke sat later in the Virginia legislature and returned to the Army.

DAVIE, WILLIAM (1756–1820). William Davie, a former American officer in the **Revolutionary War**, represented **North Carolina** in the **Constitutional Convention of 1787**. He favored approval of the resulting **Constitution** but was absent from the convention and not able to add his signature. Davie was later governor of North Carolina and proved to be significant in the establishment of the University of North Carolina.

DAWES, WILLIAM (1745–1799). William Dawes, a tanner and grocer, carried news of the British troop movements from **Boston** prior to the **Battle of Lexington-Concord** along with **Paul Revere**.

DAWSON, JOHN (1762–1814). John Dawson served in the **Virginia** legislature. He attended the state convention for ratification of the U.S. **Constitution**. **James Madison** wrote that Dawson was a leading opponent of the ratification of the document.

DAYTON, JONATHAN (1760–1824). Jonathan Dayton served as an American officer in the **Revolutionary War**. He represented **New Jersey** in the **Congress of the Confederation** from 1787–1788. Dayton attended the **Constitutional Convention of 1787** and signed the U.S. **Constitution**. He later sat in the New Jersey legislature.

DE BERDT, DENNYS (c.1694–1770). Dennys De Berdt served as a **colonial agent** for **Delaware** and **Massachusetts** in London. He is noted for his help in securing the British repeal of the **Stamp Act of 1765**.

DE BRAHM, WILLIAM (1717–c.1799). William De Brahm, a surveyor and engineer, constructed several forts along the coasts of **Georgia** and **South Carolina**.

DEANE, SILAS (1737–1789). Silas Deane sat as a delegate from Connecticut in the **First Continental Congress** and the **Second Continental Congress** from 1774–1776. In 1776, Congress selected him to represent the American **colonies** in **France**. Congress ordered him to procure military supplies for secret shipment back to America and discuss the possibility of French diplomatic recognition. Deane helped to establish **Hortalez et Cie** to handle supplies destined for America. **Benjamin Franklin** and **Arthur Lee** joined him after the American colonies declared independence. Deane was accused of using his position for personal gain and Congress recalled him after France entered the war in 1778. However, the charges against Deane were never proven. In 1781, he returned to Europe as a private citizen and began to question the wisdom of American independence. Labeled a traitor by the United States, the bankrupt Deane remained in Europe after the war and died in 1789 before he was due to sail to **Canada**.

DEATH PENALTY. *See* CRIMINAL JUSTICE SYSTEM.

DEBT, PERSONAL. Debt was treated very harshly in the **criminal justice system** of Revolutionary America. After the **Revolutionary War**, many farmers found themselves deeply in debt. With a shortage of **currency**, the debtors pushed the states to issue paper money and legal tender laws to back it. With the inflation of the period, debtors could pay their bills with paper money that was actually worth less than its face value in specie. Despite legal tender laws, many individuals refused to accept paper money for the payment of debt. Such debt by farmers led to **Shays's Rebellion**, one of the sparks leading to the **Constitutional Convention of 1787**. Many prominent Americans fell into debt after the Revolution, including **Robert Morris** who played a significant role in shoring up the finances of the United States during the war. Morris spent time in a debtor's prison at the end of his life. **William Duer** also spent time imprisoned for debt. **Daniel Boone**, **Carter Braxton**, **Silas Deane**, **Nathaniel Gorham**, and **Thomas Nelson Jr.** were other Americans who fell into debt late in life, although Boone did manage to settle his financial obligations. *See also* DEBT, PUBLIC.

DEBT, PUBLIC. Public, or governmental debt, plagued Revolutionary America. During the **Revolutionary War**, **Congress** and the states accumulated large sums of debt due to many reasons, including **trade** restrictions imposed on the new country during the war, the lack of sufficient **currency**, and the costs associated with fighting **Great Britain**. After the Revolution, public debt increased as new trade restrictions were applied against the United States. Even former European allies imposed trade restrictions on the new country. States and the national government found it difficult to meet their financial obligations. A post-Revolution **economic** recession simply made the debt situation worse and Congress found itself nearly bankrupt. In 1783, the national government owed over $43,000,000 and borrowed $2,000,000 from the **Netherlands** just to pay interest on the debt. The states, in debt themselves, either refused to pay their assessments to the national government or offered a fraction of their assessments. The situation became so bad that **Robert Morris** resigned from his position as superintendent of finance. Congress opted to sell land in the newly organized **Northwest Territory** as one means of collecting money to pay its debts. The inability of Congress to force the states to deal with the national debt is cited as one of the weaknesses of the **Articles of Confederation**. *See also* DEBT, PERSONAL.

DECLARATION OF INDEPENDENCE. **Richard Henry Lee** of Virginia submitted the **Lee Resolution** to the **Second Continental Congress** and called for the complete independence of the 13 American **colonies**. Supporters of Lee included **John Adams** and **George Wythe**, while the opponents included **James Dickinson**, **Robert Livingston**, **Edward Rutledge**, and **James Wilson**. After introducing the resolution for debate on June 7, 1776, Congress voted to postpone debate on the Lee Resolution for three weeks in order to allow delegates to review the proposal and consult their colonial governments. Initially, only nine colonies favored the resolution. Further debate persuaded the other colonies to move in favor of the resolution. It should be noted that only 12 colonies were in attendance at this time. **Pennsylvania** finally swung in favor of the resolution after **Robert Morris** and Dickinson opted to not attend Congress during the vote. **South Carolina**'s delegates altered their anti-independence stance when it was known that the other 11 colonies demonstrated their intent to approve the resolution. These delegates had been instructed by South Carolina to join the others in any measures deemed best to support all of the colonies. **New York**'s delegates did not cast their votes until after the new elections for the colonial assembly. New York joined the other colonies in favor of the resolution when its delegates arrived in **Philadelphia**. **Delaware**'s delegates had been split on the decision so the colony dispatched **Caesar Rodney** to Philadelphia to cast the deciding colonial vote in favor of the Lee Resolution.

The actual Declaration of Independence was written primarily by **Thomas Jefferson** based on the proposal within the Lee Resolution. The Second Continental Congress approved the Declaration of Independence, on July 4, 1776. As noted, the New York delegates did not sign the document until later. The declaration announced that the colonies had severed their ties with **Great Britain** and were now independent under a still-to-be-determined central government of their own. The document borrowed many of the concepts of the Enlightenment philosophers, including **John Locke**. Appendix C of this book contains a list of the signers of the Declaration of Independence. A biographical entry for each signer is also included within the Dictionary section of this book.

DECLARATION OF RIGHTS AND GRIEVANCES (1765). Nine **colonies** formed the **Stamp Act Congress** in October 1765 to formulate a common response to the **Sugar Act of 1764** and **Stamp Act of 1765**. Delegates approved the Declaration of Rights and Grievances on October 14, 1765. The document acknowledged colonial "subordination" to the British Crown and Parliament but objected to the authority of Parliament to tax them. The colonists believed that only their elected officials in the colonial assemblies held the authority for **taxation**. The document also noted the colonial concerns over the expansion of the **Admiralty Courts** to handle tax cases. Although the declaration itself had little impact on the repeal of the Stamp Act, the document is important as a precedent for future colonial agreements opposing **Great Britain**, including the **Declaration of Independence** 11 years later. The Declaration of Rights and Grievances (1765) should not be confused with the **Declaration of Rights and Grievances (1774)**.

DECLARATION OF RIGHTS AND GRIEVANCES (1774). On October 14, 1774, members of the **First Continental Congress** approved the Declaration of Rights and Grievances. The declaration noted the loyalty of the **colonies** to **King George III** but stated that Parliament did not have the right to **tax** them. The document continued with the colonial opposition to the **Admiralty Courts**, payment of colonial officials by the British crown, permanent stationing of soldiers in America, the passage of the **Intolerable Acts**, and power of Parliament to dissolve colonial assemblies. The declaration also highlighted the demand for the protection of Enlightenment principles such as life, liberty, and property. The Declaration of 1774 should not be confused with the **Declaration of Rights and Grievances (1765)**.

DECLARATION OF THE CAUSES AND NECESSITIES OF TAKING UP ARMS. After adopting the **Olive Branch Petition**, the **Second Continental Congress** passed the Declaration of the Causes and Necessities of Taking Up Arms on July 6, 1775. **Thomas Jefferson** and **John Dickinson** were the primary authors of the declaration. The document was written as an address to General **George Washington** and the **Continental Army**. The declaration discussed the rationale for fighting and traced British actions back to 1763. The declaration did not propose independence but noted that the **colonies** should maintain their armed resistance until the British had ceased hostilities.

DECLARATORY ACT. The British Parliament and Prime Minister **Lord Rockingham** decided to repeal the **Stamp Act of 1765** on March 17, 1766, after an intense opposition campaign by the colonists and their British supporters. On the same day as the repeal of the Stamp Act, the British passed the Declaratory Act. The document was similar to the Navigation Act of 1651 and the Irish Declaratory Act of 1719. The act officially noted the government's refusal to acknowledge the colonial opposition to British laws. It stated that Parliament had the legal right to make laws that applied to the **colonies**. The document did not directly mention the right of **taxation** but left the subject vague in order to reduce friction.

DELANCEY, JAMES (1746–1804). James DeLancey, a prominent **New York loyalist** and owner of racehorses, was the main political rival of **Lewis Morris**. DeLancey moved to **Great Britain** at the start of the **Revolutionary War** and suffered the confiscation of his personal property left in New York. After the war, he emerged as a major leader in the fight to receive compensation for seized property.

DELAWARE. Delaware was officially part of **Pennsylvania** until the outbreak of the **Revolutionary War**. Delaware selected its own legislature since 1704 but Pennsylvania governors sat as the chief executives of both areas. Delaware sent its own delegates to the **First Continental Congress** and the **Second Continental Congress** and voted for independence from **Great Britain**. On June 15, 1776, Delaware declared itself a sovereign entity separate from Pennsylvania and officially became one of the 13 states of the United States upon passage of the **Declaration of Independence**. The two members in attendance at the Second Continental Congress were split on their decisions whether to sign the declaration. **Caesar Rodney**, later the first governor of the state, hurriedly rode 80 miles to **Philadelphia** to cast the deciding vote in favor of American independence. By the end of America's Revolutionary period in 1790, the state boasted 50,094 people (15% slaves). Delaware ratified the U.S. **Constitution** on December 7, 1787, becoming the first state to sign the document. Most residents of Delaware were small farmers who produced food for the major towns of the area, including Philadelphia. Notable individuals from Delaware include **Gunning Bedford**, **Gunning Bedford Jr**., **Thomas McKean**, **George Read**, Caesar Rodney, and **Nicholas Van Dyke**.

DENMARK AND REVOLUTIONARY AMERICA. The Danish island of **Saint Croix** (now part of the American Virgin Islands) served as a haven for American ships operating in the eastern Caribbean.

DENTISTS. *See* HEALTH.

DEPARTMENT, MILITARY. The Military Departments were geographical divisions for organizing the **Continental Army** and delineating military responsibilities. Each department had its own troop authorization based on **Continental** soldiers and/or **militia**. In addition, each department was authorized a major general and two brigadier generals. However, the authorization of general officers and numbers of soldiers changed according to the military situation facing a department. The divisions included the **Canadian**, **Eastern**, **Highlands**, **Middle**, **Northern**, **Southern**, and **Western Departments**.

DEPARTMENT OF WAR. The **Second Continental Congress** replaced the **Board of War** with the Department of War on February 7, 1781. The department oversaw the conduct of the war and was led by the secretary of war.

DERBY, RICHARD (1712–1785). Richard Derby, a merchant ship owner in **Massachusetts**, is known for his February 1775 stand with the **militia** of Salem when British forces arrived to seize cannon and powder stored in the town. Derby reportedly stated to the British commander that he and the militia would not surrender the weapons. Rather than risk starting the **Revolutionary War** in **Salem**, the British forces withdrew. After the **Battle of Lexington-Concord**, Derby offered his schooner, *Quero*, to patriot leaders so they could dispatch their version of the armed engagement to the British government ahead of the British army report. The *Quero* arrived two weeks before the British vessel.

DICKINSON, JOHN (1732–1808). Dickinson was an early vocal advocate of the patriot cause prior to the **Revolutionary War** and sat as a delegate in the legislatures of **Pennsylvania** and **Delaware**. He is known for writing the series of articles known as the ***Letters from a Farmer in Pennsylvania*** *to the Inhabitants of the British Colonies*. The series is often simply referred to as the *Farmer's Letters* or *Letters from a Farmer*. Dickinson did not agree with the calls for the use of force against the British. He represented Pennsylvania in the **First Continental Congress** and the **Second Continental Congress** from 1774–1776 and then sat in the latter body for Delaware in 1779. Dickinson authored the **Olive Branch Petition**. He opposed the **Lee Resolution** and voted against the **Declaration of Independence**. However, Dickinson did leave Congress to serve in the military. Dickinson fought at the Battle of Brandywine as a private but later received a commission as a **militia** brigadier general. Dickinson served as the president (governor) of Delaware in 1781 and Pennsylvania from 1782–1785. He signed the **Articles of Confederation** and represented Delaware in the **Constitutional Convention of 1787**, playing a significant role in the drafting of the U.S. **Constitution**. Although not present at the signing of the Constitution, he asked a fellow delegate to affix his name to the document. *See also* DICKINSON REPORT; LIBERTY SONG.

DICKINSON REPORT. In 1776, **John Dickinson** chaired a committee of the **Second Continental Congress** to prepare an outline for a new governmental structure for the United States. The committee completed the report on July 12, 1776, and delegates hotly debated the document. In November 1777, the delegates to Congress finally agreed on a compromise governmental structure known as the **Articles of Confederation**.

DOCTORS' MOB. The acquisition of bodies for dissection by **health** care specialists proved to be challenging during the period of Revolutionary America. Human bodies were required for medical experimentation and education and most of the available bodies were executed criminals or "unknowns" relegated to potter's fields. In some cases, illegal means were utilized to acquire the bodies of recently deceased individuals not fitting either of these two categories. On April 12, 1788, a mob attacked the **New York** Hospital claiming that their loved ones were being illegally exhumed and sold to the hospital for dissection. The riot lasted for two days and the medical students had to be evacuated for their protection. The incident is known as the Doctors' Mob.

DOCK YARDS ACT OF 1772. The Dock Yards Act of 1772 permitted trials of colonists to be conducted in other areas of the British Empire for certain offenses. The American colonists disagreed with the provisions of this act and declared that they had the right to face trial at home. *See also* ADMIRALTY COURT.

DRAFT. Service in the **Continental Army** was voluntary throughout most of the **Revolutionary War**. However, on February 26, 1778, the **Second Continental Congress** requested the states to begin drafting men from their **militias** for nine months of service in the Continental Army. This is the first American national draft.

DRAGGING CANOE (1732?–1792). Chief Dragging Canoe persuaded several hundred **Cherokee** warriors and family members to join Alexander Cameron and continue resistance against the patriot cause in **South Carolina** despite a peace treaty at the conclusion of the Cherokee Campaign of 1776.

DRAYTON, WILLIAM (1742–1779). William Drayton, a planter, served in the **South Carolina** legislature and as chief justice for the state. Initially, Drayton called for restraint and reconciliation with **Great Britain** but slowly developed into an avid patriot. He represented South Carolina in the **Second Continental Congress** from 1778 until his death of typhus in 1779. During this period, Drayton signed the **Articles of Confederation**.

DRY GRIPES. Dry gripes was a medical problem during the Revolutionary period. It occurred from drinking too much **punch** made with Jamaican rum that was often distilled using lead pipes. The condition was a type of lead poisoning. *See also* CADWALDER, THOMAS.

DUANE, JAMES (1733–1797). James Duane, a jurist, represented **New York** in the **First Continental Congress** in 1774, the **Second Continental Congress** from 1775–1779, and the **Congress of the Confederation** from 1781–1783 but opposed the calls for independence from **Great Britain**. He believed that the **colonies** were acting too hastily in breaking the bonds with Great Britain. Duane played a significant role in drafting the **Articles of Confederation** and signed that document. After the **Revolutionary War**, Duane was mayor of **New York City** from 1784–1789 and later a federal judge.

DUER, WILLIAM (1749–1799). William Duer, a former military officer and businessman, moved to **New York** from **Great Britain** in 1773. He quickly immersed himself in politics and represented New York in the **Second Continental Congress** between 1777 and 1778 and signed the **Articles of Confederation**. After the **Revolutionary War**, Duer served on the Board of Treasury and became a **land speculator**. After the ratification of the U.S. **Constitution**, Duer worked with **Alexander Hamilton** in the Department of the Treasury. In his later years, Duer's personal fortune collapsed and he spent time imprisoned for **debt**.

DUMPLIN CREEK, TREATY OF. In May 1785, residents of the self-proclaimed state of Franklin, in what is now **Tennessee,** signed the Treaty of Dumplin Creek with a group of minor **Cherokee** chiefs. The treaty ceded land between the Holston and Little Rivers to Franklin. The United States refused to recognize the treaty or even admit Franklin as a state within the union. Many Cherokee chiefs were upset with the Treaty of Dumplin Creek. As a result, the United States signed the Treaty of Hopewell with them in November 1785 in order to validate the 1777 land claims of the Cherokee.

DUNMORE, LORD JOHN (1732–1809). Lord John Dunmore served as the royal governor of **Virginia** when the Revolution erupted in 1775. Dunmore actively opposed the growing patriot sentiment in Virginia. Unlike many governors who fled their **colonies**, Dunmore offered armed resistance. He freed the **slaves** of patriots if they would agree to fight for him and gathered **loyalist** forces to his side. After losing the Battle of Great Bridge, Dunmore launched the Battle of Norfolk and later departed the area. **Smallpox** and the Battle of Gwynn Island decimated the loyalist forces with Dunmore. *See also* LORD DUNMORE'S WAR.

DUTCH TREATY OF AMITY AND COMMERCE. **John Adams**, who replaced the captured **Henry Laurens** as American commissioner to the **Netherlands**, arrived in that country in June 1780. **France** wanted the Netherlands to remain neutral in the war so the latter could continue carrying commercial goods from French colonies safely past British warships. **Great Britain** wanted the Netherlands to enter the war on the side of France so she could reduce the Dutch commercial fleet and halt the country's **trade** with the rebellious American **colonies**. The Dutch, wanting to ensure a bountiful share of American trade after the **Revolutionary War**, secretly and unofficially negotiated a Treaty of Amity and Commerce with the United States in 1780. The treaty would commence upon the recognition of independence by Britain. Henry Laurens was transporting the document to the Netherlands when his vessel was halted by a British warship. Laurens threw the treaty into the ocean to avoid capture. The British spotted the package, which did not sink, and discovered the treaty inside. They attempted to use the documents to pressure the Dutch not to join the **League of Armed Neutrality**. The British eventually declared war on the Netherlands on December 20, 1780. *See also* FRENCH TREATY OF AMITY AND COMMERCE.

DUTIES. *See* TAXATION.

DUTY ACT. *See* TOWNSHEND REVENUE ACT OF 1767.

– E –

EARLE, RALPH (1751–1801). Ralph Earle was the best-known portrait painter in **Connecticut** during the Revolutionary period. He traveled to **Great Britain** in 1779 and remained there until the 1780s. During his visit to Europe, Earle studied under **Benjamin West**.

EAST INDIA COMPANY. In 1772, the East India Company faced severe economic difficulties due to mismanagement, corruption, British wars in the Far East, and a decline in American purchases of tea due to the **nonimportation agreements**. The British government needed to prevent an impending bankruptcy of the company, which would have had national ramifications on the **economy** if panic spread to other businesses. Parliament passed the **Tea Act of 1773** to save the company. The East India Company held a surplus of tea so the British government permitted it to export the product directly to the American **colonies** under the Tea Act. Normally, the tea had to be transshipped through **Great Britain**. The East India Company now held a tea monopoly in the American colonies and could sell it cheaply without the cost of English middlemen and taxes during transshipment. However, the **Townshend Revenue Act of 1764** tax on tea still applied to the imports. Americans reacted negatively to the Tea Act and Bostonians conducted what is known as the **Boston Tea Party** to prevent the product from being brought into their city.

EASTERN DEPARTMENT. The **Second Continental Congress** established the Eastern Department in April 1776 when General **George Washington** placed his army in **New York City**. The Eastern Department was one of the **Continental Army**'s military departments and covered the geographical area of **Connecticut**, **Massachusetts**, **New Hampshire**, and **Rhode Island**.

EASTON, TREATY OF. **Pennsylvania** signed the Treaty of Easton with several **Native American** groups in October 1758. The treaty acknowledged that Pennsylvania would not establish settlements in the western areas of the **colony**. Individuals broke the treaty the following year despite an attempt by the British to enforce the agreement. Following a British inquiry, London issued the Mohawk Valley

Report. British opposition to Americans moving into western lands reserved for Native Americans would be one of the grievances that eventually led to the **Revolutionary War**.

ECONOMY. Economic relations between **Great Britain** and the American **colonies** proved to be a major wedge between the two entities and a major cause of the deteriorating relations that led to the **Revolutionary War**. American production related to **agriculture**, **fishing**, **fur**, **industry**, **iron**, **lumber**, **manufacturing**, **naval stores**, **potash**, and **whaling** was heavily export-oriented to either Great Britain or British and French colonies in the Caribbean. British **trade** restrictions limited American economic growth and encouraged **smuggling**. At the same time, London imposed tight **currency** restrictions, including the **Currency Act of 1751** and the **Currency Act of 1764**, on the American colonies. After the Revolutionary War, the United States suffered a harsh postwar economic depression and had to negotiate with European states reluctant to freely trade with the new country. European trade attitudes were a reflection of the general policies of **mercantilism**. Debt (**public debt** and **personal debt**) was a major problem across the United States. Frustration over debt and postwar economic issues in **Massachusetts** helped initiate **Shays's Rebellion** and eventually prompt the **Constitutional Convention of 1787** when states realized the central government was too weak to deal with economic and other problems. *See also* BANK OF NORTH AMERICA; COPPER INDUSTRY; CRAFTS; PRINTING; SLAVERY.

EDEN, ROBERT (1741–1784). Robert Eden served as royal governor of **Maryland** from 1769–1776. Eden attempted to take a political middle ground between the British government and the colonists during the years leading up to the **Revolutionary War**. He left Maryland in June 1776, just prior to American independence. He returned to Maryland after the war to retrieve some personal property and died prior to his departure.

EDES, BENJAMIN (1732–1803). Benjamin Edes, an early patriot, edited an influential **Boston newspaper** during the Revolutionary period. His newspaper carried pro-patriot stories and emerged as an important voice for many of the Bostonians espousing anti-British sentiments. During the siege of **Boston** by American forces early in the war, Edes dismantled his printing press, smuggled it out of the city in pieces, and continued his operations from outside the town.

EDGEHILL, BATTLE OF. **Henry Bouquet**, a British officer, led a mixed force of British regulars and American colonial troops to relieve Fort Pitt during **Pontiac's War**. On August 5, 1763, a **Native American** force of Delaware and Shawnee warriors struck Bouquet's column. Bouquet repulsed the attack and then delivered a sound defeat of the Native Americans the next day at the **Battle of Bushy Run**.

EDUCATION. American colonists pioneered the move toward public education as early as the 17th century. By the Revolutionary period in all 13 **colonies**, one could find public and private schools, as well as private tutors for those wealthy enough to afford them. Most towns in the **New England** and the **middle colonies** had public schools that imparted educational basics. The **southern colonies**, having fewer towns and a more scattered population, tended to have fewer public schools. Areas without formal public schools normally had "dame" schools where a woman would bring children into her home and teach them to read and write. Students learned to read from *The New England Primer*, written in 1690, and still in use in many areas throughout the Revolutionary period.

Americans established colleges unusually early for a colonial area. Harvard, the first college in what is now the United States, was founded as early as 1636. By 1763 and the beginning of the Revolutionary period, there were six colleges in the colonies and this number grew to nine within six years with the founding of what are now Brown University (1764), Rutgers (1766), and Dartmouth (1769). The Revolutionary period also witnessed an important change in college curricula, led by **Benjamin Franklin** among others. Beginning around 1765, colleges began to move away from curricula that emphasized ancient languages, logic, ethics, and rhetoric for future theologians and began to teach more English grammar, modern European languages, and history.

The **Revolutionary War** helped lead to a greater emphasis in education in the United States. States talked of more funds for public education and the building of schools, although the money often did not materialize due to the economic difficulties of the period. Eight new colleges were established between 1783 and 1789. On January 27, 1785, the University of Georgia became the first public, nondenominational state university in the United States. Education for **women** lagged behind that of men in Revolutionary America. However, changes could be seen after the Revolution. In 1787, the publication of *Thoughts on Female Education* challenged many notions on the education of women. The book noted the importance of educated mothers in the education of their children. Education for **slaves** essentially did not exist although there are accounts of some individuals teaching slaves working within their households the skill of reading. Prominent educators of Revolutionary America included **John Bard**, **Abraham Chovet**, **William Davie**, **James Hutchinson**, **Ebenezer Kinnersley**, **Adam Kuhn**, **John Kunze**, **Samuel Langdon**, **James Madison** (not the future president of the United States), **James Manning**, **Robert Molyneux**, **Benjamin Moore**, **John Morgan**, **Robert Proud**, **John Redman**, **Nicholas Romayne**, **Benjamin Rush**, **William Shippen**, **Noah Webster**, **Eleazar Wheelock**, **Edward Wigglesworth**, and **Joseph Willard**.

EIGHT MONTHS ARMY. The American forces besieging **Boston** in early 1775 consisted of **militia** units from the **New England colonies**. The various units mistrusted each other and individual militia members tended to come and go as they pleased. To alleviate the situation, the men were enlisted in April 1775 until the end of the year. In other words, the men were enlisted for eight months and, thus, the term "Eight Months Army" developed to describe the collection of units outside of Boston.

ELBERT, SAMUEL (1740–1788). Samuel Elbert emerged as an early patriot and **Son of Liberty** in **Georgia**. During the Revolution, he served as a **Continental** officer. In 1783, Elbert was chosen to negotiate a treaty with the **Creeks** and **Cherokee**. He declined an opportunity to serve in the **Congress of the Confederation** in 1784 but did become governor of Georgia in 1785.

ELEANOR. The British vessel *Eleanor* carried tea into **Boston** Harbor on December 2, 1773, under the provisions of the **Tea Act of 1773**.

Locals dumped the tea overboard, along with the cargo of the *Dartmouth*, during the **Boston Tea Party**.

ELLERY, WILLIAM (1727–1820). William Ellery, a lawyer and businessman, represented **Rhode Island** in the **Second Continental Congress** from 1776–1781 and the **Congress of the Confederation** from 1783–1786. He signed the **Declaration of Independence** as well as the **Articles of Confederation**. The British burned his home in retaliation for his signature on the former document. He served later as the chief justice of the Rhode Island Supreme Court.

ELLSWORTH, OLIVER (1745–1807). Oliver Ellsworth, a lawyer, represented **Connecticut** in the **Second Continental Congress** from 1778–1781 and the **Congress of the Confederation** from 1781–1783. He also represented Connecticut in the **Constitutional Convention of 1787**. Although absent during the signing, he did approve the new U.S. **Constitution**. Later, Ellsworth served as a U.S. senator, chief justice of the U.S. Supreme Court, and played a significant role in writing the Judiciary Act of 1789.

ELMER, JONATHAN (1745–1817). Jonathan Elmer, a physician, represented **New Jersey** in the **Second Continental Congress** from 1776–1778 and the **Congress of the Confederation** from 1781–1784 and 1787–1788. He later served in the U.S. Senate.

EMPRESS OF CHINA. *See* CHINA AND REVOLUTIONARY AMERICA; TRADE.

ENUMERATED ARTICLES. The enumerated articles were goods produced in British **colonies** that could be transported and sold only to **Great Britain**, Ireland, or other British colonies. The practice of placing colonial products on the enumerated list began in the early 17th century and continued up to the **Revolutionary War**. Early products on the list included **tobacco**, sugar, **indigo**, cotton, wool, certain woods, and various spices. Later, the British added **rice**, **furs**, **naval stores**, **copper**, and **iron** to the enumerated list. As late as 1764, the British declared **potash** as an enumerated article. Although the enumerated list guaranteed colonial producers a market within the British

Empire, it also prevented them from seeking higher prices in other locations. The enumerated articles helped encourage American **smuggling** to the Caribbean colonies of other European countries.

ERSKINE, ROBERT (1735–1780). Robert Erskine, a Scot, traveled to America in 1771 in order to represent a group of British investors. By 1774, Erskine displayed pro-American sentiments in the various disagreements with **Great Britain**. In 1777, he became the geographer and surveyor-general to the **Continental Army**. In 1780, he died following an illness that he contracted while working in the wilderness.

EVANS, NATHANIEL (1742–1767). Nathaniel Evans, a Church of England clergyman, was known for his contributions to the embryonic field of lyric **poetry** in America.

EVE, JOSEPH (1729–1799). Joseph Eve, an inventor, built an early cotton gin in the **Bahamas** in 1787—six years before Eli Whitney built his device in **Georgia**. He later moved to Georgia and **South Carolina** and built cotton gins in those states.

EXECUTIVE SECRETARY OF FOREIGN AFFAIRS. The **Committee on Foreign Affairs** transformed itself into the executive secretary of foreign affairs under **Robert Livingston** on January 6, 1781. The office conducted the foreign relations of the United States before the ratification of the **Constitution**.

– F –

FACING THE MUSIC. "Facing the music" became a popular American phrase in 1785. The term has origins in the **theater** where actors used it to refer to the challenges of going out and facing floodlights, the orchestra, and audience.

FAESCH, JOHN (1729–1799). John Faesch, an **iron** master, is known as one of the major manufacturers of musket and cannon balls for the **Continental Army** during the **Revolutionary War**. He utilized the labor of 300 **Hessian** prisoners of war in his business.

FANEUIL HALL FRIENDS. **Boston** merchants who supported the continuation of **nonimportation** in mid-1770 were often referred to as the Faneuil Hall Friends. The name derives from Faneuil Hall, where the group met for discussions. *See also* REAL MERCHANTS.

FARMING. *See* AGRICULTURE.

FARMINGTON RESOLVES. Locals wrote and passed the Farmington Resolves in Farmington, **Connecticut**, on May 19, 1774. The document expressed the community's opposition to British policies. The citizens erected a liberty pole and burned a copy of the **Boston Port Act of 1774**. The document referred to those behind the latter act as "pimps and parasites."

FATHER OF THE REVOLUTION. "Father of the Revolution" is a nickname often given to **Samuel Adams** due to his efforts to ignite a war between the American **colonies** and **Great Britain**.

FAUQUIER, FRANCIS (c.1704–1768). Officially, Francis Fauquier served as the lieutenant governor of **Virginia** from 1758–1768. For all practical purposes, Fauquier functioned as the governor since each governor-in-chief appointed by the British actually lived in **Great Britain**. He understood the people of his **colony** and warned the British government not to **tax** the Americans.

FAY, JONAS (1737–1818). Jonas Fay, a physician and politician, represented the residents of **Vermont** in the attempts to persuade **Congress** to recognize the area as a new state.

FAYETTEVILLE STATE CONVENTION. **North Carolina** failed to ratify the U.S. **Constitution** at the **Hillsborough state convention** of July 21 to August 2, 1788. In response to the concerns of North Carolina and other states, **Congress** forwarded 12 proposed amendments to the new Constitution (10 of these would eventually become the **Bill of Rights** and an eleventh would be ratified over 200 years later). North Carolina called for a new convention to be held in Fayetteville. On November 21, 1789, the Fayetteville state convention ratified the U.S. Constitution.

FAYSSOUX, PETER (1745–1795). Peter Fayssoux, a physician from **South Carolina**, served with the **Continental Army** of the south. He is known for utilizing the yellow fever treatments developed by **Benjamin Rush**.

***FEDERALIST PAPERS*.** The *Federalist Papers* is a collection of 85 **newspaper** letters written by **Alexander Hamilton**, **James Madison**, and **John Jay**. These three men, members of the group of **Constitution** supporters known as the **Federalists**, wrote the letters in 1787 and 1788 in the attempt to persuade the **New York** ratification convention to vote in favor of the document. Most of the articles carried the pen name Publius. Hamilton prepared 51 letters; Madison wrote 29, and Jay penned 5 of the manuscripts. The letters reminded readers of the weaknesses within the **Articles of Confederation** and highlighted the need for a strong central government. Many of the letters emphasized the inclusion of the **checks and balances** system to protect against one element of the federal government from growing too powerful. The letters were very persuasive among many Americans and even today are utilized as a means to help understand the original intent of the **Founding Fathers** when writing the Constitution.

The best known of the 85 essays are "Federalist Number 10" and "Federalist Number 51." James Madison wrote both of these documents. "Federalist Number 10" examines "factions," which are described as a cause of political conflict. "Federalist Number 51" discusses the **separation of powers** and checks and balances. In 1788, the essays were published as a single volume titled ***The Federalist***. The Federalists who wrote the *Federalist Papers* should not be confused with the post-1789 Federalists who would become the Federalist Party.

FEDERALIST, THE*.** In 1788, the ***Federalist Papers were published in a single volume known as *The Federalist*. The book utilized the essays written by **Alexander Hamilton**, **James Madison**, and **John Jay** as a means to highlight the weaknesses of the **Articles of Confederation** and the need for ratification of the new U.S. **Constitution**. The book proved so influential and persuasive that even opponents of the Constitution such as **Thomas Jefferson** often praised it as an important piece of political discourse.

FEDERALISTS. The Federalists, also known as the Constitutionalists, were a group of influential Americans who supported the ratification of the U.S. **Constitution**. Federalists tended to come from the more populated areas of the eastern United States and were supported by businessmen, merchants, southern planters, and lawyers. Prominent Federalists included **Alexander Hamilton**, **John Jay**, **James Madison**, and **George Washington**. The first three men were responsible for writing the **newspaper** letters collectively known as the ***Federalist Papers*** in support of the Constitution during the ratification process of 1787 and 1789. The Federalists were opposed by individuals known as the **anti-Federalists**. The 1787–1789 Federalists should not be confused with the group known as the Federalists who emerged after 1789 and later formed the Federalist Party.

FELL, JOHN (1721–1798). John Fell, a patriot, judge, and legislator, served in the **New Jersey** legislature. He also represented New Jersey in the **Second Continental Congress** from 1778–1780.

FERGUSON, ELIZABETH (1737–1801). Elizabeth Ferguson was a noted poet of Revolutionary America. At one point she was engaged to **William Franklin**, the son of **Benjamin Franklin**.

FERGUSON RIFLE. British Major Patrick Ferguson developed the weapon known as the Ferguson rifle. This breech-loading rifle offered rapid fire and long range to the soldier wielding it in combat. Approximately 200 were manufactured, although the British never adopted the weapon on a widespread scale during the **Revolutionary War**. *See also* AMERICAN RIFLE.

FEW, WILLIAM (1748–1828). William Few, a pro-**regulator** in **North Carolina**, fought for the American cause in the **Revolutionary War** and served in the **Georgia** legislature. He represented Georgia in the **Second Continental Congress** from 1780–1781 and the **Congress of the Confederation** from 1781–1782 and 1785–1788. Georgia sent Few as a delegate to the **Constitutional Convention** of 1787. He signed the final draft of the **Constitution** and later became a federal circuit judge and a U.S. senator from **New York**.

FILSON, JOHN (c.1747–1788). John Filson, an explorer and historian, produced the first map and wrote the first history of **Kentucky**. Filson is also the first individual to publish a biography of **Daniel Boone**. The piece appeared as an appendix within the Kentucky history book.

FINDLEY, WILLIAM (1741–1821). William Findley, a member of the **Pennsylvania** state legislature, opposed the ratification of the U.S. **Constitution**. He served as a delegate to the state constitutional convention and later as a member of the U.S. House of Representatives.

FIRE PROTECTION. Fire proved to be an ever-present reality due to the construction of buildings with wood, the use of candles and fireplaces, and the close proximity of buildings in towns and cities. It was not uncommon for fires to obliterate entire city blocks or multiple blocks. Some municipalities established public fire companies while most organized volunteers to be ready to fight fires in their neighborhoods. Private fire companies also existed during the period and citizens could acquire individual fire protection policies from these groups who would roll out to protect their subscribers when the peril struck. *See also* NEW YORK CITY.

FIRST CONTINENTAL CONGRESS. *See* CONTINENTAL CONGRESS, FIRST.

FIRST RESTRAINING ACT. On March 30, 1775, the British government enacted the First Restraining Act, sometimes known as the Fisheries Act, in response to growing American agitation against British policies. The act, following the **Intolerable Acts**, limited New England commerce and permitted **trade** with only **Great Britain**, Ireland, and British West Indies. The **New England colonies** were not allowed to even conduct trade among themselves. At the same time, the act forbade New England fishermen and **whalers** from working in the waters off Newfoundland and Nova Scotia. The provisions of the act were difficult to enforce and widely ignored. *See also* SECOND RESTRAINING ACT.

FISHERIES ACT. *See* FIRST RESTRAINING ACT.

FISHING INDUSTRY. Commercial fishing proved to be one of the most profitable industries in Revolutionary America. Not only did the industry serve as a source of food and **trade** but also stimulated a **shipbuilding industry** among the American colonists. The Grand Bank and St. Pierre Bank off Newfoundland and the Sable Island Bank off Nova Scotia attracted European fisherman since the early 16th century and some writers claim even prior to 1492. New England fishermen were also attracted to these rich waters and entire communities developed around the industry. Notable fishing towns include Marblehead, New Bedford, Mystic, Gloucester, and Sag Harbor. Fishing and **whaling** emerged as the primary economic wealth of the **New England colonies**. Some estimates place the number of commercial fishermen in 1765 at 10,000 with 665 vessels. Fishermen preferred cod but also caught bluefish, herring, mackerel, salmon, and shad. Large fish were sold locally in the colonies while smaller fish were cured and exported to Europe. Damaged or poor quality varieties were traded with the West Indies as **slave** food in exchange for rum.

New England political agitation against the British government resulted in the passage of the **First Restraining Act** in 1775 in an attempt to prevent fishermen from working the banks off Newfoundland and Nova Scotia. During the **Revolutionary War**, many fishermen became **privateers** in the hope of becoming wealthy from captured British shipping. At the same time, American colonial fishermen were subject to capture by British vessels during the war. American negotiators demanded that fishermen of the new United States have access to the banks off Newfoundland and Nova Scotia after the Revolution and the right to dry fish on land. While the British resisted this demand, their negotiators finally backed down and this provision was added to the final peace treaty.

After the Revolution, American fishermen attempted to revive their industry. Fishermen require markets and Americans encountered stiff European opposition and tariffs to their products. The fishermen found that the British prohibited them from trading with Newfoundland and the other areas of **Canada**. At the same time **Great Britain** and **France** offered substantial subsidies to develop their own domestic fishing fleets. The American fishing industry grew slowly and in 1784 France eliminated the restrictions on American trade with its possessions in the West Indies. This move permitted fishermen to trade their catch with the islands. **Spain** finally allowed Americans access to the ports of Havana and Trinidad. American trade with the West Indies recovered its pre-Revolution strength by 1788.

FITCH, JOHN (1743–1798). John Fitch, an inventor and craftsman, produced the first working **steamboat** in the United States. The craft steamed on the Delaware River in 1787.

FITZSIMONS, THOMAS (1741–1811). Thomas FitzSimons, a businessman, represented **Pennsylvania** in the **Congress of the Confederation** from 1782–1783. He also served as a delegate at the **Constitutional Convention** of 1787 and signed the U.S. **Constitution**. Later, FitzSimons was a member of the U.S. House of Representatives and became director of the **Bank of North America**.

FIVE NATIONS. *See* IROQUOIS.

FLAGG, JOSIAH (1737–1795). Josiah Flagg emerged as one of the greatest American musicians and band directors during the Revolutionary period. *See also* MUSIC.

FLINTLOCK. The flintlock is another name for a musket. The name comes from the flints that were used to ignite the powder inside the musket.

FLORIDABLANCA, COUNT JOSE DE (1728–1808). Count Jose de Floridablanca replaced **Jerónimo Grimaldi** as Spanish foreign minister in 1777. Unlike Grimaldi, Floridablanca did not want to enter the conflict against **Great Britain**. He believed that Great Britain could seize Spanish territory during a war and an independent United States would be just as dangerous as the British. Floridablanca attempted to use Spanish neutrality as a means for negotiating concessions, especially the recovery of Gibraltar, from the British. However, **Spain** finally entered the war by signing the **Convention of Aranjuez** with

France on April 12, 1779, and officially declared war on Great Britain on June 21, 1779.

FLOYD, WILLIAM (1734–1821). William Floyd, a farmer, served in the **New York militia** and represented New York in the **First Continental Congress** in 1774, the **Second Continental Congress** from 1775–1777 and 1778–1781, and **Congress of the Confederation** from 1781–1783. He signed the **Declaration of Independence** and the British destroyed his home in retaliation. Later, he served in the U.S. House of Representatives.

FOLSOM, NATHANIEL (1726–1790). New Hampshire selected Nathaniel Folsom as a delegate to the **First Continental Congress** in 1774 and the **Second Continental Congress** from 1777–1778 and 1779–1780.

FOREIGN POLICY. American foreign policy can trace its origins to the **Secret Committee** and the **Committee of Secret Correspondence** in 1775. The **Second Continental Congress** tasked the Secret Committee with establishing **trade** and clandestinely importing arms. The five-man Committee of Secret Correspondence carried out the responsibility for initiating and conducting correspondence with individuals in Europe who might be willing to offer support to the American **colonies**. Although the 13 colonies had not declared their independence, the Committee of Secret Correspondence acted on behalf of them through Congress. The body made the initial contact with citizens of **France**, which eventually would lead to a political and military alliance with Paris. In 1777, the body evolved into the **Committee of Foreign Affairs** and then the **executive secretary of foreign affairs** in 1781. The latter office oversaw U.S. foreign policy under the **Articles of Confederation** and was replaced by the **State Department** in 1789 under the U.S. **Constitution**.

Between 1775 and 1781, American foreign policy centered on the securing of economic aid and military assistance from any country opposed to **Great Britain**. After the **Revolutionary War**, trade and **economic** relations became the focal point of American foreign policy. Until 1789, American foreign policy suffered due to the weak central governments of the Second Continental Congress and the **Congress of the Confederation**. European states frequently worked to negotiate directly with the states and to avoid the central government. This allowed countries to force states to compete for trade. Despite this problem, the central government did secure a number of post-Revolutionary War trade and aid deals with European states. Important American diplomats during the period of Revolutionary America included **Benjamin Franklin**, **Silas Deane**, **Thomas Jefferson**, **Robert Livingston**, **John Adams**, **Robert Morris**, and **John Jay**. *See also* AUSTRIA AND REVOLUTIONARY AMERICA; BARBARY STATES AND REVOLUTIONARY AMERICA; CHINA AND REVOLUTIONARY AMERICA; DENMARK AND REVOLUTIONARY AMERICA; NETHERLANDS AND REVOLUTIONARY AMERICA; PORTUGAL AND REVOLUTIONARY AMERICA; PRUSSIA AND REVOLUTIONARY AMERICA; RUSSIA AND REVOLUTIONARY AMERICA; SPAIN AND REVOLUTIONARY AMERICA; SWEDEN AND REVOLUTIONARY AMERICA; TUSCANY AND REVOLUTIONARY AMERICA.

FORESTRY PRODUCTS. *See* LUMBER INDUSTRY; NAVAL STORES INDUSTRY; SHIPBUILDING INDUSTRY.

FORGE. *See* IRON INDUSTRY.

FORT FINNEY, TREATY OF. The United States negotiated a series of treaties with **Native American** groups in 1784 and 1785 to secure the **Northwest Territory** for settlers. The Shawnees refused to agree to the **Second Treaty of Fort Stanwix** or the **Treaty of Fort McIntosh**. Continued negotiation and threats resulted in the Treaty of Fort Finney between the United States and Shawnees in January 1786. In this treaty, the Shawnees agreed to abide by the Treaty of Fort McIntosh. However, the Shawnees backed out of the agreement, encouraging other Native Americans to join them in a series of raids against the settlers throughout the summer of 1786. The United States, unable to solve the crisis by military means, established the **Ordinance of 1786** in an attempt to end the warfare through diplomacy. This measure failed and violence between both parties continued until 1795.

FORT GEORGE. *See* NEWPORT.

FORT MCINTOSH, TREATY OF. In order to secure the **Northwest Territory**, the United States sought to secure the withdrawal of **Native American** land claims to much of the area. The **Iroquois** surrendered their claims to lands west of the Niagara River with the **Second Treaty of Fort Stanwix** in October 1784. However, the Delaware, Ottawa, and Wyandot refused to recognize the agreement. American commissioners, backed by the military, forced the latter three groups to withdraw their claims to the area now known as Ohio via the Treaty of Fort McIntosh in January 1785. The treaty did permit a Native American reservation between the Cuyahoga and Maumee Rivers. The Shawnees refused to become a party to either agreement until forced to sign the **Treaty of Fort Finney**.

FORT STANWIX, SECOND TREATY OF. In order to secure the **Northwest Territory**, the United States negotiated the Second Treaty of Fort Stanwix with the **Iroquois** in October 1784. In the treaty, the Iroquois surrendered their claims to land west of the Niagara River. Other tribes refused to recognize this agreement until forced to do so by the **Treaty of Fort McIntosh**. *See also* FORT FINNEY, TREATY OF; FORT STANWIX, TREATY OF.

FORT STANWIX, TREATY OF. The British concluded the Treaty of Fort Stanwix with the **Iroquois** in November 1768. In return for many gifts, the Iroquois relinquished claim over the territory east of Fort Stanwix and extending as far as the mouth of the Tennessee River. This treaty represents one of the moves by the British to extend the territorial boundary of the **Proclamation of 1763** westward to provide more territory for settlement by Americans. *See also* FORT STANWIX, SECOND TREATY OF; HARD LABOR, TREATY OF; LOCHABER, TREATY OF.

FORT WILLIAM AND MARY. *See* PORTSMOUTH.

FORTUNE. The *Fortune* arrived in **Boston** Harbor in March 1774 carrying a small quantity of tea. Reportedly, the owners of the ship did not know that the tea was on board and agreed to return the cargo to

England. However, customs officials refused to allow the ship to depart without paying a duty on the tea. In response, local patriots boarded the ship and dumped the cargo into the harbor in an action similar to the **Boston Tea Party** three months earlier.

45. American colonists adopted the number 45 as an important symbol of resistance to British **taxation** policies. The number comes from *The North Briton No. 45*, a pamphlet written by **John Wilkes** to protest the **Treaty of Paris of 1763**. The colonists approved of the way Wilkes criticized **King George III** and the British government in the document. Wilkes was briefly held in the Tower of London for his work. *See also* LIBERTY BOWL.

FOSTER, ABIEL (1735–1806). Abiel Foster, a clergyman, represented **New Hampshire** in the **Congress of the Confederation** from 1783–1785. He later served as a member of the U.S. House of Representatives following the ratification of the U.S. **Constitution**.

FOUNDING FATHERS. "Founding Fathers" is a nickname for the men who led the pre-Revolution anti-British protests, the American government during and after the Revolution, and participated in the **Constitutional Convention** of 1787 and the post-Convention ratification process. While there is not a set list of the Founding Fathers, men such as **John Adams**, **Benjamin Franklin**, **Alexander Hamilton**, **John Jay**, **James Madison**, and many others would easily be included in any collection under this name.

FRANCE AND REVOLUTIONARY AMERICA. France authorized the secret shipment of munitions to the Americans on May 2, 1776. The French continued to secretly support the American war effort as a means of achieving revenge for their losses in the **French and Indian War** with **Great Britain**. France finally recognized the United States and agreed to an alliance in 1778 after receiving news of the American victory at the Battle of Saratoga. France would eventually dispatch soldiers and naval vessels to assist the Americans in the military struggle. However, the number of troops and the amount of naval support varied since France placed an emphasis on battling the British in the Caribbean. French military equipment, loans, and soldiers were instrumental in securing the American military victory, as evidenced by the cooperation of the two countries in the Battle of Yorktown.

During the **Revolutionary War**, American aristocracy admired anything "French." French fashion, language, and literature became the "rage" of society thanks to excitement over the alliance with France. Across the Atlantic, French society was infatuated with **Benjamin Franklin** as a representative of the American people. After the Revolution and the defeat of Great Britain, French attitudes began to change toward the inferior, backwoods Americans. Not wanting to rely on the American **criminal justice system**, France demanded that she be allowed to establish tribunals to try her own citizens accused of crimes and other offenses. The United States refused to grant France this extraterritorial right. At the same time, France demanded that the United States begin repaying her debts from the Revolution. However, the poor American **economy** in the post-Revolution years, combined with various European **trade** restrictions, prevented the new country from meeting its **debt** obligations in a timely manner.

In 1784, France imposed trade restrictions upon her former ally and did not withdraw them until requested by her West Indies colonies. France finally opened six ports to limited American trade. The Americans could export anything except pork, and exchange it for rum or molasses. Once trade was renewed with France, the United States found itself with a favorable balance. This is mainly because Americans preferred to import goods from Great Britain. By 1786, the United States maintained a 400 percent favorable trade balance with France. **Tobacco** proved to be the major product purchased by France from the United States thanks to a deal arranged by **Robert Morris**. However, this deal was associated with a program to lower the price of tobacco in the United States, leading to considerable controversy over the price of the product and the business arrangement with France. **Thomas Jefferson**, as U.S. ambassador to France, played a major role in ending this price system in 1787. *See also* FRENCH TREATY OF AMITY AND COMMERCE.

FRANCHISE. Prior to the **Revolutionary War**, most free males in America were eligible to vote. Originally in America, church membership was an important factor in determining the right to vote. By the 18th century, ownership of property became the most important factor in determining the eligibility of free males to vote. Each **colony** established its own property criteria for voting. Some colonies set the requirement based on land while others demanded only the ownership of "personal property" or either of the two criteria. Those colonies basing voting criteria on land could set either a minimal acreage or monetary value to the property. Free **African Americans** were often prohibited from voting even if they owned property.

FRANKLIN. *See* DUMPLIN CREEK, TREATY OF; TENNESSEE.

FRANKLIN, BENJAMIN (1706–1790). Benjamin Franklin's only challenger to the title of "best-known individual from the period of Revolutionary America" is **George Washington**. Franklin was an internationally known writer, **printer**, **scientist**, inventor, diplomat, negotiator, and philosopher. He was born in **Boston** and attended only two years of formal school. He taught himself mathematics, grammar, physical science principles, and five languages. During the colonial period of American history, Franklin worked as a printer, conducted scientific experiments with electricity (he proved that lightning is electricity and invented the lightning rod), served as a **colonial agent** in **Great Britain** for **Pennsylvania**, established the first subscription library, organized the first hospital in America, and greatly improved postal services in the American colonies. In 1754, he wrote the **Albany Plan of Union**, a document that would serve as a predecessor to the **Articles of Confederation** and the U.S. **Constitution**.

The period of Revolutionary America witnessed even more accomplishments. As a colonial agent, Franklin convincingly argued the colonial case against the **Stamp Act of 1765** before the British Parliament. His persuasive presentations have been credited for helping ensure that the British government repealed the act. Franklin returned to Pennsylvania in 1775 after nearly 18 continuous years in Great Britain. He was elected to the **Second Continental Congress** in 1775 and served on the unsuccessful commission to persuade the Canadians to join the American **colonies** in their revolt. Selected in 1775 as postmaster general, Franklin soon reorganized the postal service and ensured it operated efficiently. He helped draft the **Declaration of Independence** and signed the document.

In 1776, Congress selected Franklin as one of its three commissioners to France where he enjoyed overnight popularity. He worked diligently to secure French money, military aid, military specialists, and later diplomatic recognition for the American cause. In 1781, Congress named Franklin to be one of the three American negotiators of the **Treaty of Paris of 1783**. After two years of holding a position that is equivalent to being governor of Pennsylvania, the state sent Franklin as a delegate to the **Constitutional Convention of 1787**. He was the oldest delegate at the convention and his health prevented him from taking a direct, active part in the proceedings. However, his influence and advice were an important part of the meeting and he was one of the authors of the **Connecticut Compromise**. He signed the U.S. **Constitution**. In 1788, Franklin became president of the first anti-**slavery** society in America and later petitioned Congress to abolish slavery.

FRANKLIN, WILLIAM (1731–1813). William Franklin, the son of **Benjamin Franklin**, traveled to **Great Britain** with his father. He received an appointment as the royal governor of **New Jersey** in 1763. Franklin, a **loyalist**, often clashed with the patriots of New Jersey. He refused to depart the colony and was arrested in 1776. After being exchanged in 1778, Franklin left America for Great Britain.

FRAUNCES' TAVERN. General **George Washington** delivered his farewell address to his officers at Fraunces' Tavern in **New York City** on December 4, 1783.

FREE AFRICAN SOCIETY. *See* AFRICAN AMERICANS AND REVOLUTIONARY AMERICA; ALLEN, RICHARD.

FREE PORT ACT OF 1766. *See* WEST INDIES FREE PORT ACT OF 1766.

FREE-WILLERS. *See* INDENTURED SERVANTS.

FRELINGHUYSEN, FREDERICK (1753–1804). Frederick Frelinghuysen, a lawyer and **New Jersey** patriot, served in the provincial assembly as well as the **militia**. He represented New Jersey in the

Second Continental Congress from 1778–1779 and the **Congress of the Confederation** from 1782–1783. He returned to the state legislature and also attended the state convention to ratify the U.S. **Constitution**. Following ratification of the Constitution, Frelinghuysen represented his state in the U.S. Senate.

FRENCH AND INDIAN WAR. It is common for historians to mark 1763 and the end of the French and Indian War as the transitional point from Colonial America to Revolutionary America. The conflict, known in Europe as the Seven Years' War, began in 1754 but can be seen as the flare-up of ongoing hostilities between **France** and **Great Britain** on the North American and European continents. The French and Indian War, concluded with the **Treaty of Paris of 1763**, had several important implications for Revolutionary America. First, the peace treaty officially marked the transfer of **Canada** from France to Great Britain. Second, **Spain**, a French ally, surrendered West and East Florida to Great Britain. France would later transfer its Louisiana territories to Spain by a separate treaty. Third, Great Britain opted to permanently garrison soldiers on the American frontier and tax the American **colonies** in order to pay the costs of the stationing. Although 1763 is often considered the commencement of the political crisis that led to open warfare in 1775, tensions between the American colonies and Great Britain can be traced back many years prior to the end of the French and Indian War.

FRENCH TREATY OF AMITY AND COMMERCE. The United States signed the Treaty of Amity and Commerce with **France** in 1778. The treaty became effective when **Great Britain** recognized the independence of the United States. *See also* DUTCH TREATY OF AMITY AND COMMERCE.

FRENEAU, PHILIP (1752–1832). Philip Freneau was born in 1752 and entered Princeton in 1768 where he roomed with **James Madison**. His interests included literature and poetry, and today he is often referred to as the "Father of American Literature" and "Poet of the Revolution." He is known for a series of 1775 satires about the British. Most of his poetry emerged in the early 1780s following his service in the **Revolutionary War**. A collection of his poems, titled *The Miscellaneous Works of Freneau*, was published in 1788.

FRIENDS OF LIBERTY AND TRADE. New Yorkers formed the Friends of Liberty and Trade in early 1770. The body opposed continuing the colonial strategy of **nonimportation** as a counter to the **Townshend Acts of 1767** but believed in the basic principles of those individuals supporting nonimportation. The Friends believed that nonimportation damaged the American colonial economy, as much as it impacted British merchants.

FRIGATE. A frigate was a naval vessel with three masts specially designed to carry cannon on two decks and the forecastle.

FUR INDUSTRY. The once-profitable fur industry, centered in the Great Lakes region, had been declining toward the mid-18th century. With the British acquisition of **Canada** in 1763, the American fur industry declined even faster. Acquiring and trading furs would remain an important source of income for many individual Americans before, during, and after the **Revolutionary War**. However, the industry should be seen as a minor one when compared to the economic impact of **shipbuilding** and other **industries** in Revolutionary America.

FURMAN, RICHARD (1755–1825). Richard Furman, a Baptist clergyman, patriot, and **Federalist**, proved to be influential in the uniting of Baptist churches in **South Carolina** after the **Revolutionary War**. Furman also argued for the establishment of a Baptist college for residents of South Carolina and **Georgia**. The college, founded later, carries his name—Furman University.

FURNACE. *See* IRON INDUSTRY.

– G –

GADSDEN, CHRISTOPHER (1724–1805). Christopher Gadsden, a merchant, served as a brigadier general in the **Continental Army** and represented **South Carolina** in the **First Continental Congress** in 1774 and the **Second Continental Congress** from 1775–1776. The British captured Gadsden after the fall of **Charleston** in 1780 and held him in Florida. After his release, Gadsden worked diligently within the state government and championed the protection of **loyalist** property.

GAGE, THOMAS (1719–1787). Thomas Gage served as the British commander in chief in America between 1763 and 1775. Gage faced the difficult task of being the military commander in America during the crises leading to the **Revolutionary War**. In 1774, the British government appointed him as the governor of **Massachusetts**. After the **Battle of Lexington-Concord** and the Battle of Bunker Hill, the British government opted to recall him from America, citing his lack of clear, decisive action.

GAINE, HUGH (1726/1727–1807). Hugh Gaine, a patriot, **printer**, and bookseller, lived in **New York City**. He moved his printing press to **New Jersey** and continued printing his **newspaper** during the British occupation of the city. Gaine later became a public printer and reproduced laws, journals, and **currency** for the state government.

GALE, BENJAMIN (1715–1790). Benjamin Gale, a physician, introduced mercury in the process to inoculate individuals against **smallpox**. He claimed that the use of mercury on a patient prior to receiving a smallpox inoculation cut the death rate from 1:100 to 1:800. Gale also assisted David Bucknell in developing the ***Turtle***, an early type of submarine.

GALLOWAY, JOSEPH (1731–1803). Joseph Galloway, a lawyer, was a prominent **Pennsylvania loyalist** prior to and during the **Revolutionary War**. He sat in the Pennsylvania legislature and was a delegate to the **First Continental Congress**, during which he wrote the **Galloway Plan of Union**. Galloway administered the government of **Philadelphia** during the British occupation and departed with the British army. He sailed to **Great Britain** and fought for a reconciliation between London and the American **colonies**. Pennsylvania declared him a traitor and the state government authorized the sale of his possessions. After the Revolution, Galloway's request to return to Pennsylvania in 1793 was disapproved.

GALLOWAY PLAN OF UNION. On September 28, 1774, **Joseph Galloway** proposed his Plan of Union to the members of the **First Continental Congress**. The plan, developed as a compromise between factions within the Congress, envisioned a reorganization of the British system for governing the American **colonies**. Galloway's plan called for the British to appoint a president-general to oversee royal affairs within the colonies. Every three years, the colonial assemblies would elect members to a Grand Council, which would serve as a national legislative body. All British colonial legislation involving issues between **Great Britain** and the American colonies as a whole or between two or more colonies would have to be approved by both the Grand Council and Parliament. The plan did acknowledge Parliament as holding superior power over the Grand Council. **John Jay** and **Edward Rutledge** supported the plan. The Continental Congress voted 6 to 5 to table the Plan of Union until a future date and later rejected the proposal. The significance of the plan is that it demonstrated the desire of many colonists to reduce the influence of the British government in colonial affairs while rejecting independence from the mother country.

GALPHINTON, TREATY OF. Following the defeat of the **Creeks** in the spring of 1785, **Georgia** forced them to conclude the Treaty of Galphinton in November 1785. The terms of this treaty included those of the **Treaty of Augusta** (surrender of territory up to the Oconee River) and forced the Creeks to also withdraw from their land south of the Altamaha River. Fighting between Georgia residents and the Creeks did not end after the conclusion of the treaty.

GAMBIER, JAMES (1723–1789). James Gambier, a British admiral, served as commander in chief of the American Station naval squadron between 1770 and 1773. Following his promotion to the rank of rear admiral in 1778, Gambier served as the deputy to Admirals Richard Howe and John Byron until departing **New York City** in 1779.

GANSEVOORT, LEONARD (1751–1810). Leonard Gansevoort, a lawyer, represented **New York** in the **Congress of the Confederation** in 1788. He later served as a county judge.

GARDEN, ALEXANDER (c.1730–1791). Alexander Garden, a physician and naturalist, was the first person of European descent to discover numerous plants and animals in America. After patriots seized his property, Garden left America for **Great Britain**.

GARDOQUI AND SONS. The firm of Gardoqui and Sons served as a front for the distribution of aid from **Spain** to the United States in 1777 and 1778.

GARRETTSON, FREEBORN (1752–1827). Freeborn Garrettson proved instrumental in the establishment of the Methodist Church in America.

***GASPÉE*.** **Smuggling** proved to be a very profitable enterprise for many American merchants prior to the **Revolutionary War**. The British revenue ship *Gaspée* patrolled Narragansett Bay in search of colonial smugglers. The captain of the vessel angered many locals by sending shore parties to chop wood and steal pigs and chickens from the local inhabitants of the many islands in the bay. During the night of June 9, 1772, the British vessel ran aground while chasing a possible smuggler near Providence, **Rhode Island**. Local patriots (the numbers vary depending upon the source) attacked and burned the stranded British vessel. British authorities offered a reward for information about the attack, but they were never able to bring those responsible to trial. The "*Gaspée* Incident" is one of the sparks that resulted in the establishment of the **Committees of Correspondence** by the colonial assemblies as they offered their moral support to Rhode Island.

GEORGE III (1738–1820). King George III of **Great Britain** adamantly supported the right of the British government to **tax** the American **colonies** and pursued the war against his rebellious colonies despite the shock of the Battle of Saratoga and the introduction of the French military to the conflict. King George III assumed a more direct role in British politics than his two German-speaking predecessors, King George I and King George II. For example, he selected **Lord North** as prime minister because of the latter's tendency to agree with the king's views on politics. The Battle of Yorktown signaled to King George III that the end had finally come. At this point, he allowed Lord North to resign as prime minister and permitted the negotiations that would lead to the **Treaty of Paris of 1783**.

GEORGIA. Georgia, one of the **southern colonies**, was governed by **Great Britain** as a **royal colony** until the **Revolutionary War** and American independence. Georgia was the youngest of the 13 British colonies that formed the United States and its population included a high percentage of those who remained loyal to the British Crown during the Revolutionary War. By the end of America's revolutionary period in 1790, the state boasted 85,548 people (35.5% slaves). The state ratified the U.S. **Constitution** on January 2, 1788. After the Revolutionary War, **Spain** disputed the border between Florida and Georgia but the United States was too weak to effectively deal with the issue. Georgia was the second-largest producer and exporter of **rice** and the third-largest producer and exporter of **tobacco** and pine boards in the United States during this period. Notable individuals from Georgia include **William Few**, **Button Gwinnett**, **Lyman Hall**, **Edward Telfair**, and **George Walton**.

GÉRARD, CONRAD (1729–1790). Conrad Gérard served as the French ambassador to the United States between 1778 and 1779.

GERMAIN, GEORGE SACKVILLE (1716–1785). Lord George Germain, who went by the title Viscount Sackville after 1782, served as the British secretary of state for the American **colonies** between 1775 and 1782. Germain is often cited as being a major factor in the British loss of the American colonies. Germain feuded with Generals Henry Clinton, **Guy Carleton**, and William Howe and tended to try to control the war from London.

GERRY, ELBRIDGE (1744–1814). Elbridge Gerry, a businessman, served in the **Massachusetts** legislature. He represented Massachusetts in the **Second Continental Congress** from 1776–1780. He signed the **Declaration of Independence** and the **Articles of Confederation**. In 1787, Massachusetts selected Gerry as a delegate to the **Constitutional Convention**. However, he refused to sign the document. Later, Gerry served as governor of Massachusetts, minister to **France**, member of the U.S. House of Representatives, and vice president of the United States.

GIBAULT, PIERRE (1737–1804). Pierre Gibault served as a Roman Catholic priest and vicar-general at Kaskaskia in what is now Illinois. When George Rogers Clark arrived at Kaskaskia in 1778 with his military force, he allowed the Roman Catholic Church to continue unmolested. This action won Gibault's favor as well as that of the French people living in the area. Gibault declared his allegiance to the American cause in the Revolution and helped persuade others to do the same. Gibault also assisted Clark to secure French volunteers for his force. After the Revolution, Gibault moved into Spanish territory.

GIBBONS, WILLIAM (1726–1800). William Gibbons, a patriot and lawyer, sat in the **Georgia** provincial assembly. He represented Georgia in the **Congress of the Confederation** from 1784–1786. Gibbons later served in the state legislature and as the president of the Georgia state convention to ratify the U.S. **Constitution**.

GILL, JOHN (1732–1785). John Gill, a journalist from **Massachusetts**, published the *Boston Gazette* with **Benjamin Edes**. The **newspaper** took a pro-patriot editorial slant and became an important voice of the patriot cause. The office of the paper served as the gathering point for those individuals participating in the **Boston Tea Party**. After the Americans established a siege of **Boston**, Edes escaped with the press and Gill was arrested. Gill later established his own newspaper.

GILLAN, ALEXANDER (1741–1794). Alexander Gillan, a merchant and naval officer, served in the **South Carolina** provincial assembly. He represented the state in the **Congress of the Confederation** in 1784 and then returned to the state legislature. Voters later elected Gillan to the U.S. House of Representatives and he also served as a financial agent for Congress.

GILMAN, NICHOLAS (1755–1814). Nicholas Gilman fought for the American cause in the **Revolutionary War** and represented **New Hampshire** in the **Congress of the Confederation** from 1786–1788. New Hampshire selected him as a delegate to the **Constitutional Convention** in 1787 and he signed the U.S. **Constitution**. Gilman later served in the U.S. House of Representatives and the U.S. Senate.

GIST, CHRISTOPHER (c.1706–1759). Christopher Gist was the first European explorer in southern Ohio and northeast **Kentucky**, even before **Daniel Boone**. Gist carefully recorded his observations of these areas.

GLOVER, JOHN (1732–1797). John Glover, an early patriot and military officer, served in the **Massachusetts** state convention to ratify the U.S. **Constitution**.

GODDARD, JOHN (1723/1724–1785). John Goddard of **Massachusetts** was a well-known furniture **craftsman** of the Revolutionary period.

GODDARD, WILLIAM (1740–1817). William Goddard, a **printer**, established his own independent postal system. The United States later absorbed Goddard's system into the new national postal service.

GODFREY, THOMAS (1736–1763). Godfrey was one of the greatest playwrights of Revolutionary America. In 1767, four years after his death, Godfrey's *The Prince of Parthia* became the first American tragedy to be staged. *See also* THEATER.

GOLDEN HILL. Tensions between the colonists and British soldiers deteriorated in **New York City** after the imposition of the **Quartering Act of 1765** and later the **New York Restraining Act of 1767**. The **Sons of Liberty** opposed the Quartering Act as well as the New York Assembly's move to comply with the British legislation. On January 19, 1770, several British soldiers were apprehended while distributing leaflets questioning the legitimacy of the Sons of Liberty. Additional armed soldiers arrived at the mayor's office to rescue their comrades. By this time, a mob armed with clubs contested the soldiers, who withdrew to Golden Hill. The two groups fought at Golden Hill, leaving one person dead and many seriously injured. The next day, the groups renewed the conflict. The confrontation at Golden Hill increased the tensions between the colonists and British soldiers stationed on their soil and served as a forerunner to the more famous clash known as the **Boston Massacre**.

GOLDSBOROUGH, ROBERT (1733–1788). Robert Goldsborough, a lawyer, represented **Maryland** in the **First Continental Congress** of 1774. He was later chosen to serve on the state convention to ratify the U.S. **Constitution** but did not attend.

GOODHUE, BENJAMIN (1748–1814). Benjamin Goodhue, a merchant, served as a member of the **Maryland** convention to ratify the U.S. **Constitution**. Later voters elected Goodhue to the U.S. House of Representatives.

GORDON, THOMAS (?–1750). Thomas Gordon, an English politician and philosopher, was quoted by the American colonists during the various crises over **taxation** after the conclusion of the **French and Indian War**. Gordon, borrowing from **John Locke**, wrote that liberty was a "fragile good" that could be threatened by abusive rulers. The role of government is to protect the liberties of the people. Therefore, it should be the will of the people to check these abusive rulers. Gordon collaborated with **John Trenchard** until the death of the latter in 1723.

GORHAM, NATHANIEL (1738–1796). Nathaniel Gorham, a businessman, served in the **Massachusetts** legislature. He represented Massachusetts in the **Congress of the Confederation** from 1782–1783 and 1785–1787 and was **president of Congress** in 1786. He presided briefly over the **Constitutional Convention** of 1787 and signed the U.S. **Constitution**. Later Gorham lost his fortune in a failed **land speculator** scheme. *See also* DEBT, PERSONAL.

GOSTELOWE, JONATHAN (1744–1795). Jonathan Gostelowe of **Pennsylvania** was known for his furniture **craftsmanship** during the Revolutionary period in American history.

GRAHAM, ISABELLA (1742–1814). Isabella Graham, a philanthropist, moved to **New York** in 1789. She opened a school for young **women** that was known for its academic excellence.

GRAHAM, JOSEPH (1759–1836). Joseph Graham, a **Revolutionary War** officer, sat in the **North Carolina** state conventions to ratify the U.S. **Constitution**.

GRAND COMMITTEE. The **First Continental Congress** established the Grand Committee to draft what became known as the **Statement of Rights and Grievances**. The committee consisted of 24 members and dealt with issues that included developing the statement of American rights and grievances and the method for securing British compliance with American demands.

GRAND UNION FLAG. The Grand Union Flag, adopted on September 3, 1775, served as the flag for the 13 American **colonies** until 1777. The flag consisted of 13 horizontal alternating red and white stripes representing each colony. The upper corner contained the **Union Jack** of **Great Britain**. The **Stars and Stripes** replaced the Grand Union in June 1777.

GRAPESHOT. Grapeshot were iron balls, normally nine in number. They were tied into tiers of three balls that resembled a grape cluster. When fired, the balls separated into multiple projectiles. Grapeshot was effective against massed soldiers and naval vessels.

GRASSHOPPER. "Grasshopper" was the nickname for a small field cannon. The name comes from the fact that the gun jumps into the air when fired, much like the movement of a grasshopper.

GRATIOT, CHARLES (1757–1817). Charles Gratiot worked as a trader in what are now Illinois and Missouri. He helped provide supplies for George Rogers Clark during the latter's **Revolutionary War** expedition.

GRATZ, BARNARD (1738–1805). Barnard Gratz, a Jewish patriot, merchant, and the brother of **Michael Gratz**, challenged the **Penn-**

sylvania and **Maryland** state constitutions on the requirement to swear religious oaths in order to hold political office. For example, the Maryland constitution required an official to profess allegiance based on true faith as a Christian. Gratz noted that an individual of the Jewish faith could obviously not hold office based on the oath requirement.

GRATZ, MICHAEL (1740–1811). Michael Gratz, a merchant and the brother of **Barnard Gratz**, served the patriot cause by running the British blockade in order to bring supplies into the United States during the **Revolutionary War**.

GRAY, ROBERT (1755–1806). Robert Gray served as the captain of the **sloop** *Columbia*, the first American vessel to sail up the Columbia River. Gray acquired sea otter pelts and carried them for the first American **trade** with **China**.

GRAY, WILLIAM (1750–1825). William Gray, a **Massachusetts** merchant, owned numerous **privateers** during the **Revolutionary War**. He served as delegate to the state convention to ratify the U.S. **Constitution**. After ratification, voters elected Gray as lieutenant governor under Governor **Elbridge Gerry**.

GRAYSON, WILLIAM (c.1736–1790). William Grayson, a **Virginia** lawyer and **Revolutionary War** officer, served as a commissioner on the **Board of War** in 1779. He held a seat in the Virginia legislature and represented the state in the **Congress of the Confederation** from 1785–1787. Grayson sat on the state convention to ratify the U.S. **Constitution**. He opposed the document but did serve in the U.S. Senate following ratification.

GREAT AWAKENING. The Great Awakening was a significant religious revival movement within the American **colonies**. The leaders of the movement frequently espoused the need for individuals to seek the truth within the Bible rather than rely strictly on the creeds and sermons of men. The Great Awakening began in the early 18th century and increased the size of church memberships while weakening the influence of conservative religious leaders who had controlled many societies, especially in **New England**. A renewed interest in sending missionaries among the **Native Americans** emerged from the movement, and many who were influenced by the Great Awakening formed groups opposed to **slavery** in the colonies. One long-range major impact of the Great Awakening proved to be the influence of "individualism" among Americans. Such thoughts would help stir Americans to questions British colonial policies prior to the Revolution. *See also* RELIGION.

GREAT BRITAIN AND REVOLUTIONARY AMERICA. Before the **French and Indian War**, Great Britain controlled most of North America situated east of the Appalachian Mountains, south of the Great Lakes, and north of present-day Florida. London applied the economic policy of **mercantilism** to this vast territory, eventually divided into 13 **colonies**. Examples of British economic policies toward its American colonies can be seen in the **Currency Act of 1751**, **Hat Act of 1732**, **Iron Act of 1750**, **Molasses Act of 1733**, **Plantation Duty Act of 1673**, and **Woolens Act of 1699**. The purpose of these various acts was to promote the British **economy**. However, the British applied **salutary neglect** in its economic policies. Colonists tended to ignore or evade duties while the British government did little to actively enforce them. Each territorial area was governed as a **charter colony**, **proprietary colony**, or **royal colony**.

The end of the French and Indian War in 1763 altered the relationship of Great Britain with its American colonies. London acquired what is now **Canada** as well as the most of the vast lands between the Appalachian Mountains and Mississippi River. It also gained Florida from **Spain**. With the **Proclamation of 1763**, the British imposed migration restrictions on the American colonists in an attempt to establish a broad zone of **Native American** lands between the Appalachian Mountains and the Mississippi River. The colonists resented this attempt to restrict their free movement in search of land. London also felt the American colonists should help pay some of the costs associated with the French and Indian War as well as the need to permanently station British troops on American soil. One of the easiest ways involved enforcing the various duties associated with mercantilism. The British chose this route as well as developed plans to impose new types of **taxation** on the American colonists. Examples of these programs included the **Currency Act of 1764**, **First Re-**

straining Act, **Intolerable Acts**, **Revenue Act of 1766**, **Second Restraining Act**, **Stamp Act of 1765**, **Sugar Act of 1764**, **Tea Act of 1763**, and **Townshend Acts of 1767**. The colonists complained, although in many cases they actually lowered duties but increased enforcement.

The American colonists, spurred on by agitators such as **Samuel Adams**, as well as great statesmen like **Thomas Jefferson**, **John Adams**, and **Benjamin Franklin**, began to actively oppose British policies. Relations between the colonies and the mother country became increasingly tense and bitter. However, not everyone in Great Britain supported the government's policies toward the American colonies. Many businessmen, political philosophers, and statesmen viewed the British enforcement of mercantilistic policies as harmful to trade and transatlantic relations. By 1775, the situation reached a critical point and open warfare broke out between Great Britain and her colonies. The Americans declared independence in 1776 and in 1783 achieved recognition of this move at the conclusion of the **Revolutionary War**.

British economic attitudes toward the United States changed little after 1783. While the British did recognize American independence, they now treated the United States as the foreign state that it was and imposed trade restrictions such as large duties on American goods. Political disagreements also existed between the two countries and included the exact demarcation of the border between Canada and the United States, the removal of British troops from forts in what would become the **Northwest Territory**, and the impressments of American sailors. The conflicts between Great Britain and the United States would eventually culminate in the War of 1812 early in the next century.

GREAT COMPROMISE. *See* CONNECTICUT COMPROMISE.

GREAT PHILADELPHIA WAGON ROAD. The Great Philadelphia Wagon Road ran from the **Philadelphia** area to the backcountry of the Carolinas. Emigrants utilizing the road greatly increased the non-**Native American** population of backcountry **North Carolina**, **South Carolina**, and **Virginia**.

GREEN, FRANCIS (1742–1809). Francis Green, a prominent **Massachusetts loyalist**, commanded a volunteer pro-British military unit during the American siege of **Boston**. He departed America with the British forces.

GREEN, JACOB (1722–1790). Jacob Green, a **New Jersey** Presbyterian clergyman and patriot, served as a member of the provincial assembly. Green and other clergymen split from the Presbyterian Church. Green also took a firm stand against **slavery** in America.

GREEN, JONAS (1712–1767). Jonas Green, a noted printer, worked briefly for **Benjamin Franklin**.

GREEN, JOSEPH (1706–1780). Joseph Green, a prominent **loyalist** merchant and writer, escaped to **Great Britain** after patriots defaced his home.

GREEN, THOMAS (1735–1812). Thomas Green worked as a printer in **Connecticut**. Although a well-known printer, Green's **newspaper** carried little political news and editorials during the **Revolutionary War**. This was unusual since most newspapers of the period maintained a lively debate on political issues.

GREEN DRAGON TAVERN. Patriot leaders, including those of the **Caucus Club** and **Sons of Liberty**, frequently conducted their business in **Boston**'s Green Dragon Tavern.

GREENE, WILLIAM (1731–1809). William Greene served in the **Rhode Island** colonial assembly. He became chief justice of Rhode Island in 1777 and governor of the state in 1778. Green held the latter position until 1786.

GREENWOOD, JOHN (1760–1819). John Greenwood, a revolutionary officer and dentist, developed a foot-powered drill and spiral springs to hold artificial teeth plates together. He also pioneered the use of porcelain for artificial teeth. Greenwood served as dentist for **George Washington**.

GRENVILLE, GEORGE (1712–1770). George Grenville served as prime minister of **Great Britain** between 1763 and 1765. Grenville planned to lower land taxes in Great Britain and increase various taxes in the American **colonies** to ensure the latter paid for a greater percentage of the burden of maintaining British troops in North America. During his administration, he persuaded the government to pass the **Currency Act of 1764**, the **Sugar Act of 1764**, and the **Stamp Act of 1765**. The three **taxation** bills angered the American colonists and helped to pave the way to the **Revolutionary War**.

GRIDLEY, JEREMIAH (1701/1702–1767). Jeremiah Gridley, a lawyer from **Massachusetts**, argued the government's case over the **Writs of Assistance** in 1761. The opposing lawyer was **James Otis**. During his arguments, Gridley acknowledged that some individual rights would be denied by the government under the Writs. Despite defending the British governmental position in the case, Gridley maintained a solid reputation among the populace.

GRIFFIN, CYRUS (1748–1810). Cyrus Griffin, a lawyer, arrived in **Virginia** from **Great Britain** in 1774. He sat in the Virginia legislature and argued for reconciliation between the American colonies and Great Britain. He represented Virginia in the **Second Continental Congress** from 1778–1780 and the **Congress of the Confederation** from 1786–1789. Griffin was elected as the last **president of Congress** in 1788. Later, Griffin held a seat as a federal district judge and served as a member of the commission to secure a treaty between **Georgia** and the **Creeks**.

GRIFFITH, BENJAMIN (1688–1768). Benjamin Griffith, a Baptist clergyman, is often referred to as the first official historian of the American Baptists.

GRIM, DAVID (1737–1826). David Grim is known for his series of sketches of Revolutionary period **New York City**. All of the sketches were made from memory later in Grim's life.

GRIMALDI, JERÓNIMO (1720–1786). Jerónimo Grimaldi was the Spanish foreign minister during the early years of the **Revolutionary War**. He was an enthusiastic supporter of joining **France** in a war against **Great Britain**. Grimaldi saw a conflict with Great Britain as an opportunity to defeat **Portugal** and demand territorial concessions in the New World. He also considered a proposal to use New Orleans as a means of supplying the American cause. Grimaldi was replaced by the **Count Jose de Floridablanca**. *See also* SPAIN AND REVOLUTIONARY AMERICA.

GRIMKE, JOHN (1752–1819). John Grimke, a jurist, served as a member of the **South Carolina** state convention to ratify the U.S. **Constitution**. Grimke voted in favor of the new constitution and later served as a presidential elector for South Carolina.

GRISWOLD, MATTHEW (1714–1719). Matthew Griswold, an early patriot, served in the **Connecticut** assembly. He held the governorship of his state from 1784–1786. Griswold presided over the convention held in Connecticut to debate and vote on the new U.S. **Constitution**.

GRUBE, BERNHARD (1715–1808). Bernhard Grube, a Morovian missionary, is known for his work among **Native Americans**. He was often in trouble with both Native Americans and white settlers because of his missionary work. The **Paxton Boys** once threatened to attack a town in which he was living. Grube was a personal friend of **Benjamin Franklin**.

GWINNETT, BUTTON (1735–1777). Button Gwinnett, a planter and merchant, served in the **Georgia** legislature prior to the Revolution. He represented Georgia in the **Second Continental Congress** from 1776–1777 and signed the **Declaration of Independence**. The British destroyed his home for the latter action. He also briefly held the governorship of Georgia. In 1777, Gwinnett died in a duel with General Lachlan McIntosh over who was to blame for a failed military expedition into Florida.

– H –

HABERSHAM, JAMES (1712–1775). James Habersham, a merchant and the father of **Joseph Habersham**, unsuccessfully attempted the production of silk and grapes in **Georgia**. When these commodities did not succeed, he turned to the cultivation of **rice**. Habersham was an early advocate behind the introduction of **slavery** to Georgia, in particular for work in the rice fields. He served as a member of the Georgia colonial assembly and held the position of acting governor from 1771–1773.

HABERSHAM, JOSEPH (1751–1815). Joseph Habersham, an early patriot and the son of **James Habersham**, served as a **Continental Army** officer during the **Revolutionary War**. After the war, Habersham sat in the **Georgia** state legislature and represented his state in the **Congress of the Confederation** from 1785–1786. In 1788, he served as a delegate to Georgia's convention to ratify the **Constitution** of the United States. He later held the position of postmaster general of the United States.

HALBERD. A halberd is a blade with a metal point resembling a large spear attached with an ax head on a long pole. Noncommissioned officers used the halberd as a symbol of rank during the period of Revolutionary America. *See also* SPONTOON.

HALBERT. A halbert was the staff used by artillery personnel to sponge out the barrel of a cannon after it had been fired. The purpose of the wet sponge on the end of the halbert was to extinguish any sparks that could ignite the new powder being placed inside the barrel. The device was also known as a "sponge."

HALE, NATHAN (1755–1776). Nathan Hale, a **Continental Army** officer, volunteered to gather intelligence on the British positions located on Long Island. The British captured Hale on his return journey and hanged him for espionage. Hale is often credited with declaring, "I only regret that I have but one life to lose for my country."

HALIFAX. Halifax is a port in what is now Nova Scotia, **Canada**. The British established one of four North American **Admiralty Courts** in Halifax. Thus, Americans could face trial outside of the 13 American **colonies**.

HALL, DAVID (1714–1772). David Hall, a **printer**, served as an apprentice to **Benjamin Franklin**. He later became Franklin's business partner and then the official printer for the government of **Pennsylvania**.

HALL, LYMAN (1724–1790). Lyman Hall, a doctor and planter, was an early advocate of the patriot cause prior to the **Revolutionary War**. He represented **Georgia** in the **Second Continental Congress** from 1775–1777 and signed the **Declaration of Independence**. Hall represented his parish in the Second Continental Congress before being officially selected as a Georgia delegate. In 1778, the British burned his home in retaliation for the act. In 1783, he became governor of Georgia and later returned to his role as a planter.

HALL, PRINCE (1735–1807). Prince Hall, a mulatto slave from Barbados, secured his freedom and arrived in **Boston** in approximately 1752. He emerged as an active abolitionist in **Massachusetts**. In 1777, Hall and seven other **African Americans** petitioned the state court system to end **slavery** within Massachusetts. However, the state did not abolish slavery until 1783. In 1786, Hall offered to form a 700-man African American **militia** unit to help Massachusetts end **Shays's Rebellion**. Hall continued to fight for African American political and social equality throughout his life. Working to secure **educational** opportunities for African Americans became one of his greatest achievements.

HALL, SAMUEL (1740–1807). Samuel Hall, a **printer**, emerged as an early patriot. He utilized his profession to support the cause of patriots in **New England**.

HALLMAN, LEWIS (c.1740–1803). Lewis Hallman was a prominent actor and **theater** manager in Revolutionary America.

HAMDEN. **Benjamin Rush** utilized the pen name Hamden in 1773 while attacking the plan to import tea into **Philadelphia**. Hamden should not be confused with the pen names **Hampden** and **John Hampden**.

HAMILTON, ALEXANDER (c.1757–1804). Alexander Hamilton arrived in the American **colonies** from the West Indies in 1772 in order to complete his education. When the **Revolutionary War** began, he fought for the American cause in the battles around **New York City**. In 1777, he became secretary to General **George Washington**. After the war, Hamilton represented **New York** in the **Congress of the Confederation** from 1782–1783. He perceived the weaknesses in the **Articles of Confederation** and played a key role in the **Annapolis Convention** of 1786. Hamilton played a significant part in calling for a second convention of all the states to discuss revising the articles. He attended the resulting **Constitutional Convention of 1787** and fought vigorously for the new U.S. **Constitution**. He was the only delegate from New York to sign the Constitution. During the ratification process, Hamilton wrote some of the documents known collectively as ***The Federalist***. He later served as secretary of the treasury and died in a duel with Vice President Aaron Burr. *See also* HAMILTON PLAN.

HAMILTON, JAMES (c.1710–1783). James Hamilton, a lawyer and member of the **Pennsylvania** assembly, served as the colonial lieutenant governor from 1749–1754 and then from 1759–1763. He assumed the duties as the acting governor from 1771–1773. As a **loyalist**, Hamilton faced tense relations with the many patriots in the colonial assembly. Patriots arrested Hamilton in 1777 but later released him.

HAMILTON, PAUL (1762–1816). Paul Hamilton, a member of the **South Carolina militia** during the **Revolutionary War**, served in the state legislature after the war. Hamilton sat as a delegate to the South Carolina convention called to ratify the **Constitution** of the United States. He later became governor of South Carolina.

HAMILTON PLAN. During the **Constitutional Convention of 1787**, **Alexander Hamilton** presented the Hamilton Plan as an alterative to the **Virginia Plan** and **New Jersey Plan**. The Hamilton Plan of government proposed a strong central government. The legislature would include a bicameral congress. An individual known as the governor and chosen by an electoral college would serve as the executive. There would also be a 12-justice Supreme Court. Details of the plan offered considerable power to the central government and it was not seriously considered by the delegates at the convention. Even advocates of the new **Constitution** shunned the Hamilton Plan as being too conservative.

HAMMON, JUPITER (c.1720-c.1806). Jupiter Hammon, a slave, emerged as a prominent poet before **Phillis Wheatley**, who is perhaps better known as a poet of Revolutionary America. Hammon wrote about the abolition of **slavery**.

HAMPDEN. Hampden was the pen name assigned to the ***Alarm*** **newspaper** articles that appeared in **New York** protesting British tea policy in 1773. This pen name should not be confused with **Hamden** used by **Benjamin Rush**. *See also* HAMPDEN, JOHN.

HAMPDEN, JOHN. **James Otis** assumed the pen name of John Hampden during the **Stamp Act of 1765** crisis. *See also* ARMSTRONG, FREEBORN.

HAMPTON, WADE (1751 or 1752–1835). Wade Hampton, a **South Carolina** planter, fought with the **militia** of Thomas Sumter during the **Revolutionary War**. Hampton served in the state legislature and sat as a delegate to the state convention to ratify the **Constitution** of the United States. He opposed ratification of the document but later served his state in the U.S. House of Representatives.

HANCOCK, JOHN (1737–1793). John Hancock, a wealthy businessman and **smuggler**, owned the ***Liberty***, which was seized by British customs officials. The incident brought Hancock to the forefront of American opposition to British **taxation** policies. Hancock emerged as a popular figure among the residents of **Boston** and he entered the **Massachusetts** legislature. The British considered him a dangerous revolutionary and he was one of the men they planned to capture in the raid that resulted in the **Battle of Lexington-Concord**. Hancock represented Massachusetts in the **First Continental Congress** and the **Second Continental Congress** from 1774–1780. He served as **president of Congress** from 1775–1777. As president, he was the first to sign the **Declaration of Independence**. He also signed the **Articles of Confederation**.

Holding a commission as a **militia** major general, Hancock participated in the Battle of **Newport** in 1778. In September 1780, he became the first governor of Massachusetts. He resigned in 1785, prior to **Shays's Rebellion** and returned to the post in 1787. In 1785, delegates to Congress elected him as the president of Congress. However, he was not a delegate to the body at the time but did accept the honor. **David Ramsay** of **South Carolina** chaired Congress for him. Hancock continued to serve as governor of Massachusetts until his death in 1793.

HANCOCK, THOMAS (1703–1764). Thomas Hancock, the uncle of **John Hancock**, was a prominent and successful merchant during the early years of the Revolutionary period of American history.

HAND, EDWARD (1744–1802). Edward Hand, a physician, served as an American officer during the **Revolutionary War**. After the war, Hand represented **Pennsylvania** in the **Congress of the Confederation** from 1784–1785. He sat in the Pennsylvania legislature from 1785–1786 and was a **Federalist** delegate to his state's convention to ratify the **Constitution** of the United States.

HANNOVER AND REVOLUTIONARY AMERICA. **King George III** of **Great Britain**, an elector of Hannover, requested the assistance of this small state early in the **Revolutionary War**. Hannover formed five battalions of infantry and sent them to Gibraltar and Minorca, where they replaced British soldiers who were then transferred to North America. *See also* HESSIANS.

HANSON, JOHN (1721–1783). John Hanson was an early advocate of the patriot cause prior to the **Revolutionary War** and served in the **Maryland** legislature. He advocated military confrontation with British soldiers as early as 1769. He represented Maryland in the **Second Continental Congress** from 1780–1782 and was selected as **president of Congress** in 1781 for his work in securing Maryland's ratification of the **Articles of Confederation**. Hanson signed the document for Maryland after the other states surrendered their claims to land west of the Appalachian Mountains to the national government. Hanson died one year after leaving Congress.

HARD LABOR, TREATY OF. In October 1770, the British concluded the Treaty of Hard Labor with the **Cherokee**. The treaty moved the boundary between Cherokee and colonial land westward from the point originally designated in the **Proclamation of 1763**. *See also* LOCHABER, TREATY OF; FORT STANWIX, TREATY OF.

HARDENBERGH, JACOB (1736–1790). Jacob Hardenbergh, an avid patriot, was a Dutch Reformed Church clergyman. He served in the **New Jersey** Provincial Congress and General Assembly. Hardenbergh became the first president of Rutgers University in 1786.

HARDY, SAMUEL (c.1758–1785). Samuel Hardy served in the **Virginia** legislature and became that state's lieutenant governor in 1782. He represented Virginia in the **Congress of the Confederation** from 1783–1785 and is noted for having been a very active member of that body. During the 1784 recess of Congress, Hardy chaired the Committee of States.

HARLAND, THOMAS (1735–1807). Thomas Harland was a noted **Connecticut** watch and clock maker as well as silversmith during the period of Revolutionary America.

HARMAR, FORT. The United States established Fort Harmar in 1785 following the conclusion of a treaty with the Chippewas, Delawares, Ottawas, and Wyandots living in the area known as the **Northwest Territory**. Soldiers assigned to the fort provided security for the surveyors working under the provisions of the **Land Ordinance of 1785**.

HARNETT, CORNELIUS (1723–1781). Cornelius Harnett, known as the "**Samuel Adams** of **North Carolina**," was a member of the **Sons of Liberty** and the North Carolina legislature. He represented North Carolina in the **Second Continental Congress** from 1777–1780 and he signed the **Articles of Confederation**. The British captured Harnett in 1781 and he died while on **parole** the same year.

HARRISON, BENJAMIN (1726–1791). Benjamin Harrison served in the **Virginia** legislature and was active in the opposition to British policies prior to the **Revolutionary War**. He represented Virginia in the **First Continental Congress** in 1774 and the **Second Continental Congress** from 1775–1778. He chaired the Committee of the Whole that debated the **Declaration of Independence** and signed the document. Harrison was governor of Virginia and later served in the state legislature until his death in 1791. His son, William Henry Harrison, and great-grandson, Benjamin Harrison, were elected presidents of the United States.

HARRISON, PETER (1716–1775). Peter Harrison is often acclaimed as the most notable architect of Colonial America.

HARROD, JAMES. *See* KENTUCKY.

HARRODSBURG. *See* KENTUCKY.

HART, JOHN (1711–1779). John Hart, a farmer, served in the **New Jersey** legislature beginning in 1761. He was an avid and early backer of the patriot cause prior to the **Revolutionary War**. Hart represented New Jersey in the **Second Continental Congress** for three months in 1776 and signed the **Declaration of Independence**. The British burned his home in retaliation for his signature on the document. Hart and his wife narrowly escaped capture and hid in the woods for months. This proved to be hard on his wife and she died as result. Hart was able to resurface after **George Washington**'s victories at Trenton and Princeton. However, the long months of hiding had also taken a toll on his health. He retired in 1778 and died the next year.

HART, NANCY. Legend states that six **loyalists** arrived at Hart's **Georgia** home in search of a patriot. She killed one man, wounded a second, and kept the remaining four at musket point until the return of her husband, who with the assistance of other patriots, hanged them. While the story has been considered a myth, curious investigation in later years revealed that railroad crews laying track over the Hart homesite uncovered the skeletons of six men.

HARTFORD CONFERENCE. Baron Rochambeau of **France** met with General **George Washington** at Hartford, **Connecticut**, on September 20–22, 1780. The conference is significant since it represents the first meeting between the French and American commanders to plan a combined strategy for defeating the British. Although Washington wanted to attack **New York City**, both men agreed that a larger French fleet was required for such an action. Rochambeau favored military action in the Chesapeake Bay region. The latter's ideas would prevail when British General Charles Cornwallis moved into Yorktown and the combined American and French military forces laid siege to the British force, forcing its surrender in the last major action of the **Revolutionary War**.

HARTLEY, THOMAS (1748–1800). Thomas Hartley, a **Revolutionary War** officer and lawyer, served in the **Pennsylvania** legislature. He sat as a delegate in the Pennsylvania convention to ratify the U.S. **Constitution**, where he supported the document. Hartley later served as a member of the U.S. House of Representatives.

HARVIE, JOHN (1742–1807). John Harvie, a lawyer, represented **Virginia** in the **Second Continental Congress** from 1776–1778, during which time he signed the **Articles of Confederation**. Harvie became the mayor of Richmond later in life.

HAT ACT OF 1732. The British government imposed the Hat Act on American hat manufacturers in 1732 in order to protect the domestic English hat industry. Americans were producing hats from beaver and exporting them outside of the **colonies**. The Hat Act forbade the export of hats between colonies and from the colonies to other areas, including England itself. Other restrictions included a control on the number of apprentices who could train to become hatters. The Hat Act, along with the earlier **Woolens Act** and later **Iron Act**, tended to anger Americans, who complained that these **economic** restrictions were an imposition on their individual rights. The acts helped fuel the growing fires of American resistance to colonial commercial restrictions.

HAWKINS, BENJAMIN (1754–1818). Benjamin Hawkins, a French-language interpreter for General **George Washington**, represented **North Carolina** in the **Second Continental Congress** in 1781 and the **Congress of the Confederation** from 1781–1784 and 1786–1787. He later served as a U.S. senator for North Carolina.

HAWLEY, GIDEON (1727–1807). Gideon Hawley was a prominent Christian missionary among the **Native Americans**.

HAWLEY, JOSEPH (1723–1788). Joseph Hawley, a **Massachusetts** lawyer and member of the **Sons of Liberty**, was elected to represent his colony in the **First Continental Congress** in 1774. However, he declined to serve due to his health and was replaced by **John Adams**. Hawley favored the adoption of the **Declaration of Independence** and suffered insanity problems after 1776.

HAYS, MARY LUDWIG (1754–1832). The exploits of Mary Ludwig Hays, also known as "Molly Pitcher," represent one of the great legends of Revolutionary America. Hays was the wife of an artilleryman in the **Continental Army**. During the Battle of Monmouth Courthouse on June 28, 1778, she carried water to wounded American soldiers. Legend stemming from the journals and letters of battle participants claim that Hays assumed the duties of her husband, John, at his cannon after he fainted from the extreme heat of the day. Although documentary evidence of this feat does not exist, the **Pennsylvania** legislature voted to award her a pension in 1822. The legend of Molly's exploits may have been derived from the actions of another **woman**, Margaret Cochran Corbin, known also as Captain Molly.

HAZARD, EBENEZER (1744–1817). Ebenezer Hazard served as postmaster general of the United States from 1782–1789. He later published extensive volumes of historical document collections from the Revolutionary period and afterward.

HAZARD, JONATHAN (1744–?). Jonathan Hazard served in the **Rhode Island** assembly and represented his state in the **Congress of the Confederation** from 1787–1789. He opposed the ratification of the U.S. **Constitution** in the state convention of 1790.

HAZARD, THOMAS (1720–1798). Thomas Hazard, a notable abolitionist, advocated for an act in 1787 to abolish all **slavery**.

HEALTH. Many individuals exhibited poor overall health during Revolutionary America and life expectancy was half of what it is today due to disease, poor nutrition, lack of medical knowledge, and the lack of trained physicians in many areas. Frequent diseases included **smallpox**, yellow fever, measles, diphtheria, influenza, scarlet fever, and malaria. Families maintained personal medicine chests and often applied home cures to those who were ill. Apothecary shops were located in larger cities. Physicians exhibited various degrees of medical knowledge and many applied home cures in their work. Some doctors did receive medical training in Europe before coming to the **colonies**. During the Revolutionary period, medical departments were established at the University of **Pennsylvania** (1765) and Columbia University (1768). Harvard medical school opened in 1782. Surgery, mostly amputations, was crude by modern standards, with liquor or "biting the bullet" offered as an anesthetic. Some of the most common cures involved bleeding the patient or making the patient sweat in order to purge impurities within the body. The pulling of teeth, without anesthetic, was the main duty of those practicing dentistry. Prominent physicians and dentists of Revolutionary America included **John Bard**, **Jeremiah Barker**, **Richard Bayley**, **Thomas Bond**, **Zabdiel Boylston**, **William Brown**, **Thomas Cadwalder**, **Abraham Chovet**, **Andrew Craigie**, **James Craik**, **Peter Fayssoux**, **Benjamin Gale**, **Alexander Garden**, **John Greenwood**, **Edward Holyoke**, **James Hutchinson**, **David Jackson**, **John Jeffries**, **John Jones**, **Adam Kuhn**, **John Morgan**, **Bodo Otto**, **Jonathan Potts**, **John Redman**, **Nicholas Romayne**, **Benjamin Rush**, **William Shippen**, **Cotton Tufts**, and **Benjamin Waterhouse**. *See also* DOCTORS' MOB; DRY GRIPES.

HEATH, WILLIAM (1737–1814). William Heath, a **Revolutionary War** officer, served as a delegate to the 1788 **Massachusetts** convention to ratify the U.S. **Constitution**. He later served in the U.S. Senate for Massachusetts.

HECK, BARBARA (1734–1804). Barbara Heck, known as the "mother of Methodism in America," initiated the Wesleyan movement in America. She was a **loyalist** during the **Revolutionary War** and moved to **Canada**.

HECKEWELDER, JOHN (1743–1823). John Heckewelder was a prominent Christian missionary among the **Native Americans** for the Moravian Church.

HELFFENSTEIN, JOHN (1748–1790). John Helffenstein, a German Reformed clergyman, arrived in America in 1772. He is known for his services among **Hessian** prisoners of war held in Lancaster, **Pennsylvania**.

HELL AFLOAT. *Hell Afloat* was the American nickname for the British prison ship *Jersey*.

HENDEL, JOHN (1740–1798). John Hendel, a German Reformed clergyman, is remembered for his work among Americans living in remote areas. He was also the eventual leader of the movement that formed the Synod of the United States in 1793.

HENDERSON, RICHARD (1735–1785). Richard Henderson, a lawyer and judge in **Virginia**, established the **Transylvania Company** with a group of **land speculators**. *See also* CUMBERLAND AGREEMENT.

HENRY, JOHN (1750–1798). John Henry, a lawyer, represented **Maryland** in the **Second Continental Congress** from 1778–1780 and the **Congress of the Confederation** from 1785–1787. He is remembered for his active participation in committee work within Congress and later served in the U.S. Senate for Maryland.

HENRY, PATRICK (1736–1799). Patrick Henry, a lawyer, displayed avid support for the patriot cause prior to the **Revolutionary War**. In 1764, Henry entered the **Virginia** legislature and quickly became a leading delegate thanks to his oratory skills. He represented Virginia as a delegate in the **First Continental Congress** in 1774 and the **Second Continental Congress** in 1775. Henry is credited in 1775 with giving a speech before the Virginia Provincial Convention where he declared, "Give me liberty or give me death." He departed Congress to assume command of Virginia's military forces and, in 1776, worked on the committee to draft the new Virginia constitution.

Henry became the first governor of the state of Virginia and held that post several times up to 1786. Although initially opposed to the U.S. **Constitution**, he accepted the document after its ratification by Virginia and later proved to be instrumental in the adoption of the **Bill of Rights**. He returned to his law practice. In 1799, Henry won election to the state legislature but died before assuming the office.

HENRY, WILLIAM (1729–1786). In 1763, William Henry attempted the first **steamboat** experiment in America. The experiment failed. Henry served in the **Pennsylvania** legislature and represented his state in the **Congress of the Confederation** from 1784–1786.

HERON, WILLIAM (1742–1819). William Heron served the British as a spy during the **Revolutionary War**. Heron held a seat in the **Connecticut** legislature.

HESSELIUS, JOHN (1728–1778). John Hesselius was a well-known portrait painter, especially in **Maryland**, during the Revolutionary America period.

HESSIANS. The states of Brunswick, Hesse-Cassel, Hesse-Hanau, Waldeck, Anspach-Bayreuth, and Anhalt-Zerbst supplied an estimated 30,000 soldiers to the British during the **Revolutionary War**. Known collectively as Hessians, these soldiers were mercenaries from the German states fighting for the British. **King George III** turned to the German states after **Russia** refused to provide troops for the conflict in America. Approximately 12,000 Hessians never returned home, including 5,000 soldiers who deserted and remained in North America and 7,000 who died during the conflict. Most of the men were from Hesse-Cassel, from which the name "Hessian" is derived. The British provided the German rulers with cash for each soldier sent to North America and an additional sum for each death. Often, three wounded soldiers earned the ruler the same amount of money as a single death. Most Hessian soldiers wore blue uniforms. However, special units of **Jaegers** wore green uniforms. The Hessians earned a mixed record of service during the war. Some Hessian soldiers and units provided distinguished service to the British while others quickly deserted. In addition, the Hessians achieved an early reputation for cruelty and were often criticized in the British Parliament.

HEWAT, ALEXANDER (c.1745–c.1829). Alexander Hewat, a **loyalist**, was a Presbyterian clergyman and historian. He moved to England in 1775 as the **Revolutionary War** erupted and later wrote historical volumes on **South Carolina**.

HEWES, JOSEPH (1730–1779). Joseph Hewes served in the **North Carolina** legislature from 1766–1773. He represented North Carolina in the **First Continental Congress** in 1774 and the **Second Continental Congress** from 1775–1777 and again in 1779. He signed the **Declaration of Independence**. Other than being a signer of the Declaration, Hewes is best known for his appointment of John Paul Jones to a U.S. naval commission and providing him with a ship. He died in 1779 while serving in Congress.

HEYWARD, THOMAS, JR. (1746–1809). Thomas Heyward Jr., after studying law in **Great Britain**, served in the **South Carolina** legislature from 1774–1775. He then represented South Carolina in the **Second Continental Congress** from 1776–1778 and signed the **Declaration of Independence** and the **Articles of Confederation**. He fought with the South Carolina **militia** and was captured after the fall of **Charleston** to the British in 1780. After his exchange in 1781, Heyward returned and reentered the South Carolina legislature, where he served until 1784 and became a circuit judge until 1789.

HIESTER, DANIEL (1747–1804). Daniel Hiester, the cousin of **Joseph Hiester**, was a farmer and **Revolutionary War** officer. He served in the **Pennsylvania** Assembly and represented his state in the **Congress of the Confederation** in 1788. Hiester was an **anti-Federalist**.

HIESTER, JOSEPH (1752–1832). Joseph Hiester, the cousin of **Daniel Hiester**, was a merchant and **Revolutionary War** officer. He served in the **Pennsylvania** Assembly and opposed ratification of the U.S. **Constitution** in the Pennsylvania convention. He later represented his state in the U.S. Senate and served as a presidential elector.

HIGHLANDS DEPARTMENT. **Congress** established the Highlands Department as a **military department** in November 1776. The department consisted of the area that included the lower Hudson River Valley north of **New York City**.

HILLEGAS, MICHAEL (1729–1804). Michael Hillegas, a **Pennsylvania** merchant, served as the first treasurer of the United States beginning in 1777. He was an avid supporter of the **Bank of North America**.

HILLHOUSE, JAMES (1754–1832). James Hillhouse served in the **Connecticut** legislature. He was selected to represent his state in the **Congress of the Confederation** from 1786–1788 but did not attend any sessions. He later served in the U.S. House of Representatives.

HILLSBOROUGH STATE CONVENTION. Representatives from across **North Carolina** gathered in Hillsborough between July 21 and August 2, 1788, to debate the ratification of the U.S. **Constitution**. **Anti-Federalists** dominated the convention and following days of intense debate, the body voted 184 to 83 against ratifying the Constitution until the document included a bill of rights. Eleven other states had previously ratified the Constitution; therefore, the document had already officially replaced the **Articles of Confederation**. After the 10 amendments of the **Bill of Rights** were passed by **Congress**, North Carolina agreed to hold a second gathering, the **Fayetteville state convention**.

HINDMAN, WILLIAM (1743–1822). William Hindman sat in the **Maryland** legislature and represented his state in the **Congress of the Confederation** from 1785–1788. He later served in the U.S. House of Representatives.

HOBART, JOHN (1738–1805). John Hobart sat in the **New York** legislature and became a justice of the New York Supreme Court. He attended the state convention to ratify the U.S. **Constitution** in 1788 and later served in the U.S. Senate.

HODENOSAUNEE LEAGUE. *See* IROQUOIS.

HOLKER, JEAN (1745–1822). Jean Holker served as the French consul to the United States between 1777 and 1781. *See also* FRANCE AND REVOLUTIONARY AMERICA.

HOLLAND AND REVOLUTIONARY AMERICA. *See* NETHERLANDS AND REVOLUTIONARY AMERICA.

HOLTEN, SAMUEL (1738–1816). Samuel Holten, a physician, was a member of the **Sons of Liberty** and served in the **Massachusetts** legislature. He represented Massachusetts in the **Second Continental Congress** from 1778–1780 and signed the **Articles of Confederation**. He opposed ratification of the U.S. **Constitution** in the 1788 state convention but left early due to an illness. He later served in the U.S. House of Representatives.

HOLYOKE, EDWARD (1728–1829). Edward Holyoke, a **Massachusetts** physician, was an early advocate of **smallpox** vaccination. He became one of the most important doctors and medical **educators** of the northeast during the Revolutionary America period.

HOMESPUN. Homespun was cloth made within a family household and sold across all of the American **colonies**. The manufacture of this cloth was part of the austerity measures introduced in the colonies to reduce British imports in protest of **taxation** measures. After the outbreak of the **Revolutionary War** and the introduction of a British embargo, the manufacture of homespun became essential in the new United States.

HOOPER, WILLIAM (1742–1790). William Hooper, a lawyer trained by **James Otis**, served in the **North Carolina** legislature. He represented North Carolina in the **First Continental Congress** in 1774 and the **Second Continental Congress** from 1775–1777 and signed the **Declaration of Independence**. The British burned his home in retaliation for his signature. Hooper is best remembered as a political moderate and advocated lenient polices toward **loyalists**. After the Revolution, he returned to his law practice and again served in the North Carolina legislature.

HOPEWELL, TREATY OF. *See* DUMPLIN CREEK, TREATY OF.

HOPKINS, STEPHEN (1707–1785). Stephen Hopkins sat in the **Rhode Island** assembly and attended the **Albany Congress**. He served as colonial governor numerous times between 1755 and 1767. Hopkins represented his colony and then state in the **First Continental Congress** in 1774 and the **Second Continental Congress** from 1775–1776 and signed the **Declaration of Independence**. Hopkins served again later in the Rhode Island legislature.

HOPKINSON, FRANCIS (1737–1791). Francis Hopkinson, a lawyer, represented **New Jersey** in the **Second Continental Congress** for five months in 1776 and signed the **Declaration of Independence**. The British looted his home in retaliation for his patriotic stance. He is credited with designing the American flag in 1777. Hopkinson was also one of the greatest musicians of the Revolutionary period and is often credited with being the first native-born American to compose a major song (1759). After the **Revolutionary War**, Hopkinson served as a judge for the state of **Pennsylvania** and the United States. *See also* MUSIC.

HORNBLOWER, JOSIAH (1729–1809). Josiah Hornblower, a farmer and engineer, served in the **New Jersey** legislature. He represented his state in the **Congress of the Confederation** from 1785–1786 and later became a judge.

HORTALEZ ET CIE. The firm of Hortalez et Cie was a fictitious company established by **Pierre Augustin Caron de Beaumarchais** in June 1776 as a means of transferring French and Spanish weapons and munitions to the Americans. **France** and **Spain** each loaned one million livres to the firm for the purchasing of weapons and munitions. The Americans, in turn, paid for the material with rice, tobacco, and other products. However, these items were frequently not available for transfer to the company in payment. Ships carrying the military aid sailed to the West Indies and then to the United States. The organization of this system was plagued with controversy and scandal, as seen in the case of **Silas Deane**. Hortalez et Cie continued to operate after the signing of the official Franco-American alliance permitted open shipments of military aid between the two countries. The company was officially terminated in 1783.

HOSMER, TITUS (1737–1780). Titus Hosmer, a lawyer, served in the **Connecticut** legislature and represented his state in the **Second Continental Congress** from 1778–1780. He signed the **Articles of Confederation**. Hosmer died after being appointed a judge on the national **court** for maritime affairs.

HOUSTON, WILLIAM (1746–1788). William Houston, an educator, represented **New Jersey** in the **Second Continental Congress** from 1775–1776 and 1779–1781 and the **Congress of the Confederation** from 1784–1786. He attended the **Annapolis Convention** and was selected as a delegate to the **Constitutional Convention of 1787**. Houston, although favoring the document, departed early due to illness. He died the next year of tuberculosis. Houston should not be confused with **William Houstoun** (note spelling of name) of **Georgia** who also attended the Constitutional Convention of 1787.

HOUSTOUN, JOHN (1744–1796). John Houstoun, a lawyer, served in the **Georgia** legislature and represented his state in the **Second Continental Congress** from 1775–1776. Elected governor of Georgia in 1778, Houstoun accompanied the failed American expedition into British-held Florida. He served a second term as governor in 1784.

HOUSTOUN, WILLIAM (1755–1813). William Houstoun, a lawyer, represented **Georgia** in the **Congress of the Confederation** from 1784–1786. He served as a delegate to the **Constitutional Convention of 1787**. Houston departed the Convention prior to the signing of the U.S. **Constitution** but did favor the document. He should not be confused with **William Houston** (note spelling of name) of **New Jersey** who also attended the Constitutional Convention of 1787.

HOVERING ACT. The Hovering Act, dating from the reign of King George I, was applied to the American **colonies** after the **French and Indian War**. The act required all ships traveling more than two leagues from the coast to maintain a list of all contents that it carried. The purpose of the act was to permit easier inspection and collection of duties. Many Americans chose to falsify the list in order to avoid **taxation** on the goods carried in the vessels.

HOWE COMMISSION. The British dispatched Lord Richard Howe to the American **colonies** with a proposal for peaceful restoration of relations. Howe arrived off the American coast in late June 1776, just prior to the signing of the **Declaration of Independence**. The new British proposal called for the colonists to end all committees and congresses formed outside of the structure of the royal governments; disband all military units raised to oppose the British; and declare their intention to remain loyal to **King George III**. In return for these actions, the British would not **tax** the American **colonies** and would lift the various **trade** restrictions placed on them. **Congress** learned of the Howe Commission's offer after signing the Declaration of Independence. Continued British attempts to persuade the Americans to accept the terms failed.

HOWELL, DAVID (1747–1824). David Howell, a jurist, represented **Rhode Island** in the **Congress of the Confederation** from 1782–1785. He later served as a federal judge and the Rhode Island state attorney general.

HOWITZER. A howitzer was a short-barreled weapon on a wheeled carriage used to fire projectiles in a high arc onto enemy defensive positions during a siege operation.

HOWLEY, RICHARD (1740–1784). Richard Howley served in the **Georgia** legislature and represented his state in the **Second Continental Congress** from 1780–1782. From 1782–1784, Howley sat as the chief justice of Georgia.

HUCK, CHRISTIAN (?–1780). Christian Huck commanded a troop of Banastre Tarleton's British Legion in **South Carolina** during the **Revolutionary War**. A lawyer from **Philadelphia**, he exhibited a violent temper and was a firm **loyalist**. His reprisal raids against patriots in the South Carolina backcountry illustrate the vicious civil war nature of the conflict in that state. His campaign ended with his death at daybreak on June 12, 1780, in a battle known today as Huck's Defeat.

HUNTINGTON, JEDEDIAH (1743–1818). Jedediah Huntington, a **Revolutionary War** officer from **Connecticut**, sat as a delegate at his state's convention to ratify the U.S. **Constitution**. He later served as a federal customs collector at the port of New London.

HUNTINGTON, SAMUEL (1731–1796). Samuel Huntington represented **Connecticut** in the **Second Continental Congress** and **Congress of the Confederation** from 1775–1784. He signed the **Declaration of Independence**. Huntington served as the **president of Congress** from 1779–1781. He later became governor of Connecticut.

HURD, NATHANIEL (1730–1777). Nathaniel Hurd was a noted **Massachusetts** silversmith during the Revolutionary America period.

HUTCHINS, THOMAS (1730–1789). Thomas Hutchins, an engineer and geographer from **New Jersey**, held a commission in the British military. He refused to serve against his fellow Americans and was jailed from 1779–1780. In 1781, he became a geographer to the United States and surveyed the **Land Ordinance of 1785**.

HUTCHINSON, JAMES (1752–1793). James Hutchinson, a physician, was the surgeon general of **Pennsylvania** and a noted medical **educator**.

HUTCHINSON, THOMAS (1711–1780). Thomas Hutchinson, a Bostonian by birth, served as the royal governor of **Massachusetts** between 1771 and 1774. It was Hutchinson who had to deal with the Massachusetts patriots in the matters of the **Boston Tea Party** and other acts of defiance against British **taxation**. Hutchinson sailed for **Great Britain** after 1774.

HUTSON, RICHARD (1748–1795). Richard Hutson served in the **South Carolina** legislature and represented his state in the **Second Continental Congress** from 1778–1779 and signed the **Articles of Confederation**. The British imprisoned Hutson in Florida after the fall of **Charleston** until 1781. Hutson was later a member of the U.S. House of Representatives and a judge.

– I –

IMPARTIAL ADMINISTRATION OF JUSTICE ACT. *See* ADMINISTRATION OF JUSTICE ACT OF 1774.

IMPRESSMENT. The practice of seizing men against their will for service in the navy was known as impressment. Despite the British prohibition of impressment under the **Sixth of Anne**, it still occurred in North America. The American colonists deeply resented the British practice of impressing the inhabitants of coastal towns for service in the British navy. Such actions helped to stir Americans to oppose British policies and demand independence.

INDENTURED SERVANTS. Indentured servants, sometimes known as Christian servants or free-willers, were individuals who offered their labor for set periods in exchange for transportation and basic necessities in the Americas. The contracts were often seven years in length but the duration did fluctuate based on negotiations. At the end of the contracted service, the former servant was free to leave the service of the individual to whom he was indentured. Indentured servants received clothing and basic farming instruments upon completing the contract. Some negotiated for the receipt of land upon finishing the contracted service.

INDIGO. Indigo, along with **rice**, **tobacco**, and **wheat**, proved to be an important export crop during the period of Revolutionary America. Indigo was second only to rice in the economy of **South Carolina**. By 1775 and the opening of the Revolution, South Carolina exported 1,250,000 pounds of indigo residue while **Georgia** exported approximately 16,000 pounds of the product. Indigo exports suffered during the Revolution due to hostilities and immediately after the war due to European **trade** restrictions. However, the indigo trade recovered within a few years of the war's conclusion due to the inability of **Great Britain** to acquire adequate supplies of similar quality from other sources. *See also* AGRICULTURE; PINCKNEY, ELIZABETH.

INDUSTRY. Manufacturing in Revolutionary America tended to be at three levels: items produced by individual families for their personal consumption, products intended for colonial consumption, and goods intended for export to Europe or other **colonies**. Most families produced their own basic necessities such as food, cloth, soap, basic furniture, and candles. At the second level, artisans made manufactured goods that were sold to neighbors and others within the colony, or possibly in other colonies. These items included furniture, farm implements, wagons, and most things made from metal. The third level involved manufacturing goods intended for export as well as local consumption. However, London placed many restrictions on manufactured exports from the American colonies. Under **mercantilism**, colonies were expected to export raw materials to the home country and in return import manufactured goods. Hats made from beaver pelts proved to be one of the early exceptions and were exported to southern Europe and Ireland. However, these American-manufactured hats competed with British goods, leading to trade restrictions imposed by London. As a result of British **trade** restrictions, many Americans turned to **smuggling** as a method of exporting manufactured goods to other colonies as well as importing items without paying duties. After the Revolution, American goods continued to be restricted in Europe by the implementation of stiff tariffs. *See* COPPER INDUSTRY; FUR INDUSTRY; IRON INDUSTRY; LUMBER INDUSTRY; NAVAL STORES INDUSTRY; POTASH PRODUCTION; PRINTING; SHIPBUILDING INDUSTRY; WHALING.

INGERSOLL, JARED (1749–1822). Jared Ingersoll, a lawyer, represented **Pennsylvania** in the **Second Continental Congress** in 1780. He served as a delegate to the **Constitutional Convention** of 1787 and signed the U.S. **Constitution**. He later became attorney general of Pennsylvania.

INTOLERABLE ACTS. The Intolerable Acts is a name applied by the American **colonies** to a collection of bills passed by Parliament under **Lord North** in response to colonial opposition to the **Tea Act of 1773**. The Intolerable Acts, also known as the Coercive Acts, were actually four separate pieces of legislation: the **Massachusetts Government Act of 1774**, the **Quartering Act of 1774**, the **Administration of Justice Act of 1774**, and the **Boston Port Act of 1774**. The Intolerable Acts served to solidify colonial opposition to **Great Britain** and led to the formation of the **First Continental Congress**. *See also* QUEBEC ACT OF 1774.

IRON ACT OF 1750. Parliament passed the Iron Act of 1750 as a means of restricting the growth of manufacturing and industry in the

American **colonies**. Under **mercantilism**, colonies should buy manufactured goods from the mother country and supply her with raw materials. The act permitted the duty-free importation of American pig and bar iron needed by British industry. However, the construction of new iron mills, furnaces, or forges was forbidden. The act was difficult to enforce in the American colonies but it helped to fuel the colonial displeasure that would erupt into the **Revolutionary War** a quarter-century later. *See also* HAT ACT OF 1732; IRON INDUSTRY; WOOLENS ACT OF 1699.

IRON INDUSTRY. Iron ore proved to be abundant in the American **colonies**. The first working iron furnace was established at Lynn, **Massachusetts**, in 1643. The iron industry grew quickly and the total number of American furnaces and forges outnumbered those in England and Wales by 1775 while the American colonial output of bar and pig iron exceeded the production totals of **Great Britain** at the opening of the Revolution. The British attempted to slow this growth as early as 1750 with the passage of the **Iron Act of 1750**. However, enforcement of the act proved to be nearly impossible. American exports of iron to Great Britain totaled 8,000 tons in 1770. In 1775, the first year of the **Revolutionary War**, the colonies produced one-seventh of the world's supply of iron. Many American communities, such as Valley Forge, **Pennsylvania**, were named after the iron forge located in their vicinity.

IROQUOIS. The Iroquois were actually a **Native American** confederation, known as the Hodenosaunee League, that included the Cayuga, Mohawk, Oneida, Onondaga, Seneca, and Tuscarora during the Revolutionary period. They are sometimes known as the Six Nations. The Iroquois were farmers living along the southern edge of the Great Lakes in what is now **New York** and **Pennsylvania**. It is believed that their unity under a single government was a model for the **Albany Plan of Union** and the 13 **colonies** as they formed a new government under the **Articles of Confederation**. During the **Revolutionary War**, the Oneida and Tuscarora sided with the American colonists and the other four groups allied with the British. After the Revolution, the Iroquois steadily declined as a political confederation. *See also* ALBANY CONGRESS.

IRVINE, WILLIAM (1741–1804). William Irvine, a **Revolutionary War** officer, represented **Pennsylvania** in the **Congress of the Confederation** from 1786–1788. Irvine also sat in the state convention to ratify the U.S. **Constitution**.

IZARD, RALPH (1742–1804). The **Second Continental Congress** selected Ralph Izard as the American commissioner to **Tuscany**. However, Tuscany refused to receive the new commissioner and he remained in **France**. Izard and **Benjamin Franklin** developed a dislike for each other while both were in Paris. Congress recalled Izard in 1779. He represented **South Carolina** in the Second Continental Congress from 1782–1783 and later served in the U.S. Senate.

– J –

JACKSON, DAVID (1747–1801). David Jackson, a physician and **Continental Army** surgeon, represented **Pennsylvania** in the **Congress of the Confederation** in 1785.

JACKSON, HALL (1739–1797). Hall Jackson, a physician and **Continental Army** surgeon, was one of the first to introduce foxglove (digitalis) as a heart stimulant.

JACKSON, WILLIAM (1759–1820). William Jackson, a **Revolutionary War** officer, served as the secretary during the **Constitutional Convention of 1787**. He burned his records after the conclusion of the convention, as ordered, destroying what could have become one of the most important records in American history.

JACKSONBORO. Jacksonboro, located west of **Charleston**, **South Carolina**, served as the seat of government of South Carolina from the winter of 1781–1782 until the British departed Charleston in 1783.

JAEGER. Jaegers were former hunters and gamekeepers of the German states fighting for the British in the American **colonies** under the general title of **Hessian**. The green-uniformed Jaegers carried rifles and were expert marksmen. British commanders used the Jaegers as special troops due to their marksmanship skills.

JAILS. *See* CRIMINAL JUSTICE SYSTEM.

JAPAN AND REVOLUTIONARY AMERICA. *See* KENDRICK, JOHN.

JAY, JOHN (1745–1829). John Jay, a lawyer, represented **New York** in the **First Continental Congress** and the **Second Continental Congress** and served as president of the latter body between December 1778 and September 1779. At this point, Congress selected Jay to represent the United States in **Spain**. Jay managed to obtain a loan for the United States but failed to persuade Spain to recognize the new country. He also served on the committee that completed the **Treaty of Paris of 1783**. Jay held the post of secretary of foreign affairs from 1784–1790 for the United States.

JEFFERSON, THOMAS (1743–1826). Thomas Jefferson, originally a lawyer, is one of the best-known **Founding Fathers** of America's Revolutionary period. An early patriot, Jefferson served in the **Virginia** legislature from 1769–1775. Jefferson wrote ***A Summary View of the Rights of British America*** in 1774. He represented Virginia in the **Second Continental Congress** from 1775–1776. Jefferson chaired the congressional committee that drafted the **Declaration of Independence** and he is credited with personally writing much of the document. He signed the Declaration of Independence. Jefferson left Congress and became governor of Virginia from 1779–1781. After a brief term in the legislature, he sat in the **Congress of the Confederation** from 1783–1784, where he emerged as an important voice behind the adoption of a decimal-based American coin system. Congress selected him as **trade** minister to **France** in 1784. He then succeeded **Benjamin Franklin** as minister to France and remained in Europe until 1789.

Jefferson was not able to directly participate in the debates on the U.S. **Constitution** since he was in France. However, he actively expressed his opinion on the document to friends via letters. Initially, Jefferson opposed the Constitution because it lacked a bill of rights to protect individual liberties. His opinion changed when learning of the preparation of the amendments that would become the **Bill of Rights**. Jefferson returned to the United States in 1789 and served as the federal secretary of state under President **George Washington**, vice president under President **John Adams**, and then as president from 1801–1809.

JEFFRIES, JOHN (1744 or 1745–1819). John Jeffries, a **Massachusetts loyalist** physician, conducted experiments on air. He gathered air samples via balloon flights between 1784 and 1785 in Europe. In 1790, he returned to **Boston** and opened a medical practice.

JENIFER, DANIEL OF ST. THOMAS (1723–1790). Daniel of St. Thomas Jenifer (the origins of the "of St. Thomas" are lost to history but most likely were added to his name to differentiate him from other individuals of the same name), a planter, served in the **Maryland** legislature. He represented Maryland in the **Second Continental Congress** and the **Congress of the Confederation** from 1778–1782. Jenifer attended as a delegate for his state during the **Alexandria Convention**. He signed the U.S. **Constitution** at the **Constitutional Convention** of 1787.

JOHNSON, GUY (c.1740–1788). Guy Johnson, a **loyalist**, served as the British superintendent of Indian affairs from 1774–1782. In this capacity, Johnson organized **Native Americans** in upper **New York** and southern **Canada** against patriot interests during the **Revolutionary War**. He was replaced by **John Johnson**.

JOHNSON, JOHN (1742–1830). John Johnson, a **loyalist**, replaced **Guy Johnson** as the British superintendent of Indian affairs in 1782 and held the position until 1790.

JOHNSON, THOMAS (1732–1819). Thomas Johnson represented **Maryland** in the **First Continental Congress** in 1774 and the **Second Continental Congress** from 1775–1776. He nominated **George Washington** as commander in chief of the newly organized **Continental Army**. He was not in attendance to sign the **Declaration of**

Independence. Johnson sat in the Maryland state convention to ratify the U.S. **Constitution** and later served as a justice on the U.S. Supreme Court.

JOHNSON, WILLIAM (1727–1819). William Johnson, a lawyer, served in the **Connecticut** legislature and represented his state in the **Congress of the Confederation** from 1785–1787. He attended the **Constitutional Convention** of 1787 and proved to be active in the debates over the new document. Johnson signed the **Constitution** and later became a U.S. senator and president of Columbia College.

JOHNSTON, SAMUEL (1733–1816). Samuel Johnston sat in the **North Carolina** legislature and represented his state in the **Second Continental Congress** in 1780. He declined the presidency of Congress in 1781. He served as the governor of North Carolina from 1787–1789 and the president of the state convention to ratify the U.S. **Constitution** in 1788. He was later a member of the U.S. Senate.

JOHNSTON, ZACHARIAH (1742–1800). Zachariah Johnston, a **Revolutionary War** officer, sat in the **Virginia** legislature. He also attended the state convention to ratify the U.S. **Constitution** in 1788. He later served as presidential elector.

JOHNSTON ACT. The Johnston Act, also known as the Riot Act, consisted of measures to control the **regulators** in **North Carolina** in late 1770. Following a series of riots in the western areas of the **colony**, the colonial legislature passed the Johnston Act. The document authorized the governor to use force in order to end riot conditions, declared anyone resisting arrest as an outlaw, and permitted any county to place those accused of rioting on trial. The act tended to have the opposite of its intended effect and actually helped increase the number of regulators.

JOIN OR DIE. The motto "Join or die" was written on a famous drawing first published by **Benjamin Franklin**. The banner, reproduced in many forms and in various media, included a snake cut into pieces representing the American **colonies**. The motto "Join or die" meant that the American colonies had to unite in their opposition to British **taxation** or fall individually.

JONES, ALLEN (1739–1807). Allen Jones, the brother of **Willie Jones**, served as a **Revolutionary War** officer and a member of the **North Carolina** legislature. Jones represented North Carolina in the **Second Continental Congress** from 1779–1780.

JONES, GABRIEL (1724–1806). Gabriel Jones, a lawyer, served in the **Virginia** legislature. Although elected to the **Second Continental Congress** in 1779, he did not attend any sessions of that body. Jones, a **Federalist**, did sit in the state convention to ratify the U.S. **Constitution** in 1788.

JONES, JOHN (1729–1791). In 1775, John Jones, a physician, authored the first surgical textbook written in America. He helped organize the medical department of the **Continental Army**.

JONES, JOSEPH (1727–1805). Joseph Jones, a jurist, sat in the **Virginia** legislature. Although selected to the **Second Continental Congress** in 1778, Jones declined in order to serve as a Virginia judge. He did represent his state in the Second Continental Congress from 1780–1781 and the **Congress of the Confederation** from 1781–1783 but later declined to serve another term in 1786.

JONES, NOBLE (c.1724–1805). Noble Jones, a prominent **Georgia** patriot and physician, was captured by the British after the fall of **Charleston, South Carolina**. After being exchanged, Georgia selected him to represent the state in the **Second Continental Congress** from 1781–1782. He returned to Georgia in 1782 and sat in the state legislature.

JONES, WILLIE (c.1741–1801). Willie Jones, a prominent **North Carolina** patriot and the brother of **Allen Jones**, sat in the state legislature and represented his state in the **Second Continental Congress** in 1780. Jones declined an opportunity to attend the **Constitutional Convention of 1787**. He opposed the U.S. **Constitution** at the **Hillsborough**

state convention and did not attend the **Fayetteville state convention** that ratified the document.

JOUETT, JOHN (1754–1822). British General Charles Cornwallis dispatched Banastre Tarleton to make a raid deep into **Virginia** to capture **Thomas Jefferson** and the members of the state legislature. John Jouett, a Virginia patriot, rode ahead of Tarleton's men to Charlottesville and warned Jefferson, who managed to escape. Jouett later served in the Virginia legislature and became very active in **Kentucky** politics and the movement to gain statehood for the area.

***JOURNAL OF THE TIMES*.** **Samuel Adams** published the *Journal of the Times* as a means of publicizing incidents between British soldiers and citizens of **Boston** following the arrival of the former in late 1768. Such incidents, as reported by Adams, stirred he local population and would eventually lead to the **Boston Massacre**.

JUDICIARY. *See* COURTS; CRIMINAL JUSTICE SYSTEM.

JUNGMAN, JOHN (1720–1808). John Jungman was a noted Moravian missionary among the **Native Americans** during the Revolutionary America period.

– K –

KENDRICK, JOHN (c.1740–1794). John Kendrick commanded the expedition of the *Columbia* and *Washington* to the Pacific Northwest in 1787. He sailed onward to **China** in the *Washington* (some sources indicate the name of the vessel was actually the *Lady Washington*) in 1789. He also visited Japan, becoming the first captain of a U.S. vessel to visit that country. *See also* TRADE.

KENTUCKY. **North Carolina** and **Virginia** claimed areas that today form the single state of Kentucky. During the Revolutionary period, the British attempted to reserve the area for **Native Americans** by issuing the **Proclamation of 1763** to prevent the westward migration of settlers. American colonists tended to ignore the proclamation and in 1774 James Harrod brought a group of individuals from **Pennsylvania** to central Kentucky. The settlers founded the town of Harrodsburg, which was soon destroyed by the Shawnee in **Lord Dunmore's War**. In 1775, Harrodsburg was rebuilt and the **Transylvania Company** arrived in Kentucky in an attempt to attract settlers through land sales. **Daniel Boone** founded Boonesborough on April 1, 1775, as a base for the Transylvania Company. North Carolina and Virginia refused to recognize or back the Transylvania Company, which was forced to move to the Cumberland River area. Migration into Kentucky continued and a number of skirmishes, including the Battle of Blue Licks, were fought in the area during the **Revolutionary War**.

Many in Kentucky wanted to form their own state but met with resistance from North Carolina and Virginia. The latter states withdrew their claims on the territory by 1784 but this did not lead to immediate statehood for Kentucky. In 1787, a prominent Kentuckian, **John Brown**, met with a Spanish official and reportedly discussed the secession of Kentucky from the United States in exchange for a Spanish guarantee of free navigation on the Mississippi River. The deal never materialized and some believe it was just a ploy to prod **Congress** into admitting Kentucky as a state. In 1792, Kentucky became a state within the Union. *See also* JOUETT, JOHN; LOGAN, BENJAMIN.

KENTUCKY RIFLE. The Kentucky rifle was another name for the **American rifle**.

KING, RUFUS (1755–1827). Rufus King, a lawyer from **Massachusetts**, emerged as a leading American politician after the Revolution. He served as a delegate to the **Congress of the Confederation** from 1784–1786 and was selected to represent his state in the **Constitutional Convention of 1787**. King was known for his many speeches during the convention. He sat on the committee that arranged the **Constitution**'s final draft and signed the document. He also helped draft the **Northwest Ordinance of 1787** and was instrumental in the successful debate to exclude **slavery** from the **Northwest Territory**. He served later as a U.S. senator from **New York** and as the U.S. minister to **Great Britain**.

KING, SAMUEL (1748–1819). Samuel King was a noted portrait painter from **Rhode Island**.

KINNERSLEY, EBENEZER (1711–1778). Ebenezer Kinnersley was a prominent teacher and scientist from **Pennsylvania**. He experimented with electricity and was better known for his work in this field at that time than **Benjamin Franklin**.

KIRKLAND, SAMUEL (1741–1808). Samuel Kirkland spent many years as a Christian missionary among the Oneida. He had considerable influence among the Oneida and other **Native American** groups and persuaded many to remain neutral during **Lord Dunmore's War**. He is also credited with helping to persuade the Oneida to maintain their neutrality during the **Revolutionary War**.

KLINE, GEORGE (c.1757–1820). George Kline was a frontier publisher and **newspaper** editor in Carlisle, **Pennsylvania**.

KNOX, HENRY (1750–1806). Henry Knox served as the American commander of artillery throughout the **Revolutionary War**. He rose to become one of General **George Washington**'s most trusted officers and attained the rank of major general. When Washington resigned in 1783, Knox assumed the position of commander in chief of the army until 1784. He conceived and formed the **Society of the Cincinnati** to preserve the ties forged between the American officers during the Revolution. In 1785, Knox accepted an appointment as secretary of war and became the first secretary of war after the ratification of the **Constitution**.

KNOW YE ALL MEN. The phrase "Know ye all men" emerged as a slogan to identify those who supported the **printing** and distribution of paper money as **currency** in **Rhode Island** after the Revolution

KUHN, ADAM (1741–1817). Adam Kuhn, a physician, emerged as one of the more prominent **educators** in **Pennsylvania** during the Revolutionary America period.

KUNZE, JOHN (1744–1807). John Kunze was a noted Lutheran clergyman and **educator** in Revolutionary America.

– L –

LABOR STRIKES. *See* STRIKES.

LADD, JOSEPH (1764–1786). Joseph Ladd, a **poet** from **Rhode Island**, moved to **Charleston**, **South Carolina**, where he died in a 1786 duel.

LANCASTER. The **Second Continental Congress** met in Lancaster, **Pennsylvania**, on September 27, 1777, after departing **Philadelphia** due to the approach of the British army. The members would proceed from Lancaster to **York**, Pennsylvania.

LAND ORDINANCE OF 1785. The newly independent United States developed plans to organize and settle the **Northwest Territory** after the **Revolutionary War**. **Thomas Jefferson** played a significant role in preparing what would become the Land Ordinance of 1785. The ordinance was a compromise between two groups divided over how to settle the Northwest Territory. The document called for surveying the area into six-square-mile townships. Every other township would be further divided into 36 sections, each comprising 640 acres (one square mile). The sale of one section of each township was reserved to support a school and four sections were reserved by the national government for sale or use at a later date. The land was sold at auction for a minimum of $1 per acre. The average American could not afford the minimum $640 required to purchase a tract and this opened the door for **land speculators**. The land sold more slowly than predicted, prompting Congress to cut deals with companies and dispose of tracts at more favorable terms than those listed in the Land Ordinance of 1785. *See also* HUTCHINS, THOMAS; NORTHWEST ORDINANCE OF 1787; OHIO COMPANY; ORDINANCE OF 1784.

LAND SPECULATORS. Land speculators normally operated in organized companies in order to pool their monetary resources. The groups, or companies, purchased large tracts of land to the west of the original 13 **colonies** with the purpose of reselling them to individuals or families in smaller parcels for a profit. Land speculators were active immediately following the conclusion of the **French and Indian War** as

Americans sought to move into the former French territories. The companies tended to violate the British **Proclamation of 1763**, established to reserve western lands for **Native Americans**.

Land speculators remained active throughout the Revolutionary period, including after the **Revolutionary War** itself. These groups had the resources to purchase the minimum tracts of land of the **Land Ordinance of 1785** that were too costly and too large for small farmers to acquire. They could then subdivide the large tracts and offer them at more affordable rates. However, the land speculators often caused more harm than good during the Revolutionary period. Many land speculators did not operate in the **Northwest Territory** under the Land Ordinance of 1785 but moved into **Kentucky**, **Tennessee**, or areas claimed by **Spain**. They frequently agitated the Native American groups and even the Spanish during a critical period as the United States was trying to establish itself after the Revolution. *See also* LOYAL LAND COMPANY; MISSISSIPPI LAND COMPANY; OHIO COMPANY; TRANSYLVANIA COMPANY.

LANGDON, JOHN (1741–1819). John Langdon, a businessman and the brother of **Woodbury Langdon**, represented **New Hampshire** in the **Second Continental Congress** and **Congress of the Confederation** in 1775, 1783, and 1787. He served also as a **militia** commander during the Revolution and fought at the Battle of Saratoga. New Hampshire selected him to represent the state in the **Constitutional Convention of 1787**. He arrived late to the convention due to his other duties. After considerable debate over the draft document by the delegates, Langdon signed the U.S. **Constitution** on behalf of New Hampshire. Langdon later represented New Hampshire in the U.S. Senate, where he rose to the become president pro tempore.

LANGDON, SAMUEL (1723–1797). Samuel Langdon, a clergyman from **Massachusetts**, served as a delegate to his state's 1788 convention to ratify the U.S. **Constitution**. He also held the presidency of Harvard from 1774–1780.

LANGDON, WOODBURY (1738 or 1739–1805). Woodbury Langdon, the brother of **John Langdon**, was selected to represent **New**

Hampshire in the **Second Continental Congress** and **Congress of the Confederation** from 1779–1781 and again in 1785. Although chosen as a delegate, he declined to attend sessions of Congress from 1780–1781 and then 1785. Later, Langdon served as a controversial judge.

LANGWORTHY, EDWARD (c.1738–1802). Edward Langworthy represented **Georgia** in the **Second Continental Congress** from 1777–1779, during which time he signed the **Articles of Confederation**. He later opposed demanding the American right to **fish** off Newfoundland as an ultimatum in the peace negotiations leading to the **Treaty of Paris of 1783**.

LANSING, JOHN (1754–1829). John Lansing, a lawyer, served as a soldier in the Revolution, a member of the **New York** legislature, and represented his state in the **Congress of the Confederation** from 1784–1785. He became mayor of Albany in 1786. New York selected Lansing as one of the state's delegates to the **Constitutional Convention of 1787**. He disagreed with the direction of the convention and charged that its members were going beyond their instructions to amend the **Articles of Confederation**. In protest, Lansing departed the convention. In 1829, Lansing disappeared and is believed to have been murdered.

LAURENCE, JOHN (1750–1810). John Lawrence, a **Revolutionary War** officer, represented **New York** in the **Congress of the Confederation** from 1785–1787. He later served in the state legislature, the U.S. House of Representatives, and U.S. Senate.

LAURENS, HENRY (1724–1792). Henry Laurens, a planter of **rice** and **indigo** and the father of **John Laurens**, represented **South Carolina** in the **Second Continental Congress** from 1777–1780 and signed the **Articles of Confederation**. He became **president of Congress** in November 1777 but resigned in 1778. In 1779, Congress selected Laurens to negotiate with the **Netherlands** and secure a treaty that was being discussed between **William Lee** and a minor Dutch official. A British warship captured Laurens off Newfoundland and discovered his secret instructions, which had been thrown overboard.

Held in the Tower of London, Laurens was finally granted bail in December 1781 and exchanged for British General Charles Cornwallis who had surrendered at the Battle of Yorktown. After his release, Laurens participated in the negotiations leading to the **Treaty of Paris of 1783**. He played a major role in securing a British pledge to grant **fishing** rights off Newfoundland to American seamen and a promise to not remove **slaves** or American property when the British army evacuated the cities it held in the United States. The British did not carry through with their pledge on the fishing rights. South Carolina selected Laurens as a delegate to the **Constitutional Convention of 1787** but he was too ill to attend.

LAURENS, JOHN (1754–1782). John Laurens, the son of **Henry Laurens**, served as a **Revolutionary War** officer. In 1780, **Congress** selected Laurens to represent the United States in **France**. Laurens later sat in the **South Carolina** legislature.

LAW, ANDREW (1748–1821). Andrew Law was born in **Connecticut** and became a popular musician, **music** teacher, and author of music books during the Revolutionary period. He is known for his patriotic tunes, including one entitled *Bunker Hill*.

LAW, RICHARD (1733–1806). Richard Law, a **Connecticut** patriot, was selected to represent his colony and then state in the **First Continental Congress** in 1774, the **Second Continental Congress** from 1776–1777 and 1780–1781, and the **Congress of the Confederation** from 1781–1783. He did not attend the sessions in 1774 and 1776 due to ill health. Law sat as a delegate in the 1788 state convention to ratify the U.S. **Constitution**.

LAWYERS. *See* CRIMINAL JUSTICE SYSTEM; LEGAL PROFESSION.

LEAGUE OF ARMED NEUTRALITY. The League of Armed Neutrality, formed in 1780, included **Austria**, **Denmark**, the Kingdom of the Two Sicilies, **Portugal**, **Russia**, and **Sweden**. Russia's Catherine the Great initiated the development of the league in response to British threats against her shipping. Russia did not have the naval resources to stand alone against British threats. However, a league or alliance with other states would permit the development of a neutral shipping policy. The league's provisions included the exclusion of naval stores, the nonrecognition of blockaded ports without sufficient naval vessels to enforce the declaration, and the right of neutral vessels to sail between the ports of a belligerent. The United States sought but failed to secure membership in the league due to its participation in the war against **Great Britain**, the primary target of the agreement. Some sources declare that the league was a success and note that Great Britain eased her blockade policies against **France** and **Spain** in response to the league. Others state that the league was a failure and cite Catherine's description of the alliance as the "League of Armed Nullity" and the refusal to admit the **Netherlands** to the organization as examples. A more accurate evaluation lies between these two extremes. While the league never accomplished all that the members intended, it did persuade the British to be less restrictive in the enforcement of its blockade of France and Spain.

LEAMING, JEREMIAH (1717–1804). Jeremiah Leaming, a **Connecticut loyalist**, emerged as a prominent Episcopal clergyman in Revolutionary America.

LEE, ANN (1736–1784). Ann Lee, often called Mother Ann, arrived from **Great Britain** in 1774. She founded the Shaker movement, a conservative religious group, in America.

LEE, ARTHUR (1740–1792). Arthur Lee, a medical doctor and later lawyer, was the brother of **Francis Lee**, **Richard Henry Lee**, and **William Lee**. In the late 1760s, Lee wrote many pro-American letters opposing British **taxation** in the **colonies**. In 1774, he became a commercial agent for **Massachusetts** and traveled to London. The next year, the **Second Continental Congress** requested Lee to contact friendly European representatives in order to discuss secret aid to the American colonies. Lee met with French playwright and agent **Pierre Augustin Caron de Beaumarchais**. The latter helped arrange secret French military aid. Congress selected Lee to serve as one of three **commissioners** to **France** in October 1776. Lee replaced **Thomas Jefferson**, who declined a nomination to fill the post. He traveled to **Spain** in 1777 to negotiate a commercial treaty and obtain military and monetary aid from that country. He then returned to France and it was Lee who exposed the financial dealings of **Silas Deane**, leading to the recall of the latter. Lee is also known for his controversial relations with **Benjamin Franklin**, which led to his own recall to America in 1779. He served in the **Congress of the Confederation** from 1782–1784 and helped negotiate the **Second Treaty of Fort Stanwix**. *See also LIBERTY SONG.*

LEE, EZRA. *See TURTLE.*

LEE, FRANCIS (1734–1797). Francis Lee, a brother of **Arthur Lee**, **Richard Henry Lee**, and **William Lee**, was active in **Virginia** politics and opposed the various British **taxation** schemes in the 1760s and 1770s. He served in the Virginia legislature and represented his state in the **Second Continental Congress** from 1775–1779. Lee signed the **Declaration of Independence** and the **Articles of Confederation** while a member of Congress.

LEE, HENRY (1756–1818). Henry Lee, known as Light Horse Harry, served as an American cavalry commander during the **Revolutionary War**. He was a relative of **Arthur Lee**, **Francis Lee**, and **William Lee**. After the Revolution, Lee served in the **Virginia** legislature and the state selected him as a delegate to **Congress of the Confederation** from 1785–1788. Later, he became governor of Virginia, commanded the soldiers who ended the Whiskey Rebellion, served in the U.S. House of Representatives, spent time in jail for **debt**, and fathered Robert E. Lee—the future commander of the Army of Virginia during the American Civil War.

LEE, RICHARD HENRY (1732–1794). Richard Henry Lee, an early **Virginia** patriot and the brother of **Arthur Lee**, **Francis Lee**, and **William Lee**, served in the colonial legislature from 1758–1775. He was very active in Virginia's resistance to the various British **taxation** schemes for the **colonies**. Lee represented Virginia in the **First Continental Congress** in 1774, the **Second Continental Congress** from 1775–1779, and the **Congress of the Confederation** from 1784–1785 and then in 1787. He initially favored the implementation of an **economic** boycott against the British government. However, during the Second Continental Congress, he slowly turned toward a more radical approach to the political confrontation and introduced the resolution that eventually became the **Declaration of Independence**. He signed the **Articles of Confederation**, became **president of Congress** in 1784, and later opposed his state's ratification of the **Constitution**. As an **anti-Federalist**, Lee wrote the ***Letters from the Federalist Farmer to the Republican***. He served later as a U.S. senator from Virginia. *See also* ADAMS, JOHN.

LEE, THOMAS (1745–1819). Thomas Lee served as the governor of **Maryland** from 1779–1783. During his administration, Lee proved to be an active supporter of the **Continental Army** during periods when others hesitated or refused to provide for the needs of the American troops during the Revolution. He represented his state in the **Congress of the Confederation** from 1783–1784 and later became a national presidential elector and, again, governor of Maryland.

LEE, WILLIAM (1739–1795). William Lee, a brother of **Arthur Lee**, **Francis Lee**, and **Richard Henry Lee**, served as an American commercial agent in **France**. In May 1777, **Congress** selected Lee as the American commissioner to **Prussia** and **Austria**. However, neither country would officially receive him. He did negotiate a draft commercial treaty with a minor Dutch official and dispatched it to Congress for review. **Henry Laurens** was carrying a copy of this draft treaty when apprehended by the British. Congress recalled Lee in 1779 and he returned to his native **Virginia** in 1783. *See also* NETHERLANDS AND REVOLUTIONARY AMERICA.

LEE RESOLUTION. **Richard Henry Lee** submitted a resolution to the **Second Continental Congress** in the summer of 1776. **Virginia** instructed Lee to prepare the resolution and call for the complete independence of the 13 American **colonies**. **John Adams** offered his second to the resolution when it was introduced for debate on June 7, 1776. Prominent supporters included Lee, Adams, and **George Wythe**. Opponents included **John Dickinson**, **Robert Livingston**, **Edward Rutledge**, and **James Wilson**. The main argument against the resolution involved its timing. Many who might have initially favored the proposal noted that it was too early to be calling for independence. Congress voted to postpone debate for three weeks while delegates reviewed the proposal and consulted their colonial governments. Debate renewed on July 1, 1776, and eventually led to the passage of the **Declaration of Independence** on July 4, 1776.

LEEDS, JOHN (1705–1790). John Leeds, a **loyalist**, was a noted mathematician and astronomer in Revolutionary America.

LEGAL PROFESSION. Young men wanting to be lawyers either attended the Inns of Court in London or served as apprentices under practicing lawyers. Bar associations did exist to control who was allowed to practice law in the court system. Half of the signers of the **Declaration of Independence** were lawyers. The English legal system was prevalent in Revolutionary America. The legal profession in Revolutionary America was similar in many ways to the profession today. Reviews of legal cases from this period show that lawyers argued the law in front of juries consisting of laymen, confusing them in the process with technicalities and trivial interpretations. Immediately after the Revolution, students wanting to study law could do so in only selective locations. William and Mary offered the only formal law program and the only school devoted exclusively to law was a private college in **Connecticut**. A large percentage of America's founding fathers were lawyers by training or profession. Some of the individuals who stood out in the legal profession (as lawyers and/or judges) rather than just politics during the Revolutionary America period included **Andrew Adams**, **John Adams**, **Gunning Bedford Jr**., **Egbert Benson**, **John Blair**, **Benjamin Bourne**, **David Brearley**, **William Cushing**, **Francis Dana**, **William Ellery**, **Oliver Ellsworth**, **William Few**, **Leonard Gansevoort**, **Cyrus Griffin**, **Patrick Henry**, **Thomas Heyward Jr**., **John Hobart**, **David Howell**, **Richard Hutson**, **Thomas Johnson**, **Joseph Jones**, **Woodbury Langdon**, **Richard Law**, **Daniel Leonard**, **Levi Lincoln**, **Luther Martin**, **Thomas McKean**, **Stephen Mitchell**, **James Otis**, **William Paca**, **Robert Paine**, **Theophilus Parsons**, **William Paterson**, **John Pickering**, **Richard Potts**, **Jesse Root**, **Increase Sumner**, **George Thatcher**, **William Tilghman**, **George Tucker**, **John Williams**,

William Williams, and **James Wilson**. *See also* CRIMINAL JUSTICE SYSTEM.

LEIPER, THOMAS (1745–1823). Thomas Leiper, a **Pennsylvania** merchant and military officer, contributed considerable personal sums of money to help finance the patriot struggle during the **Revolutionary War**. Although an **anti-Federalist**, Leiper later served as a presidential elector.

LELAND, JOHN (1754–1841). John Leland, a Baptist clergyman from **Massachusetts**, proved to be an avid supporter of the U.S. **Constitution** and active in the anti-**slavery** movement.

LENNOX, CHARLOTTE (1720–1804). Charlotte Lennox, a novelist born in **New York**, moved to England at an early age.

LEONARD, DANIEL (1740–1829). Daniel Leonard, a **loyalist** born in **Massachusetts**, became the chief justice for Bermuda.

LETTER OF MARQUE. A letter of marque is a document authorizing a ship's crew to act as **privateers** and seize enemy vessels and cargoes. The letter established the fine line between a crew being privateers or pirates. The availability of such letters prompted many sailors to sign on with privateering vessels in the hopes of securing personal wealth from their share of the profits from seized ships.

***LETTERS FROM A FARMER IN PENNSYLVANIA*.** The 12 letters known as the *Letters from a Farmer in Pennsylvania* were actually a series of **newspaper** articles authored by **John Dickinson** and printed from 1767–1768. The letters denounced the **Townshend Revenue Act of 1767** and the **New York Restraining Act of 1767**. The collected letters were published in pamphlet form in the American **colonies** as well as England, Ireland, and the **Netherlands** in 1769. They were highly effective in solidifying resistance to the renewed British attempts at colonial **taxation**.

***LETTERS FROM THE FEDERALIST FARMER TO THE REPUBLICAN*.** **Richard Henry Lee**, an **anti-Federalist**, wrote the *Letters* *from the Federalist Farmer to the Republican* in 1787 as a means to derail ratification of the U.S. **Constitution**. Lee's essays are often considered the most persuasive articles authored by anti-Federalist writers.

LEWIS, FRANCIS (1713–1802). Francis Lewis arrived in North America in 1738. He became a merchant and represented **New York** in the **Second Continental Congress** from 1775–1779. He signed the **Declaration of Independence** as well as the **Articles of Confederation**. His signature was appended to the former document in August 1776 because the New York delegation did not have voting instructions upon the completion of the document in July. In retaliation for his signature, the British burned his home and imprisoned his wife. She died soon after being exchanged. Lee served as a commissioner on the **Board of Admiralty** from 1779–1781.

LEWIS, WILLIAM (1751–1819). William Lewis, a lawyer, served in the **Pennsylvania** legislature after the **Revolutionary War**. In 1789, he sat as a delegate in the state convention to ratify the U.S. **Constitution**. Lewis later held positions as a federal attorney and judge.

LEXINGTON-CONCORD, BATTLE OF. A review of the military engagements at Lexington and Concord, **Massachusetts**, is important for understanding the pivotal point where the political and **economic** frustrations of the American colonists turned to open warfare with **Great Britain**. By 1775, Massachusetts grew weary of the **Intolerable Acts**, imposed on them following the **Boston Tea Party** in 1774. Relations between the colonists, especially those in **Boston**, and the British were strained to the maximum and by 1775 Massachusetts **militia** units were stockpiling ammunition and other military stores in the towns outside of Boston. In March 1775, British General **Thomas Gage** learned through his intelligence sources that the nearby town of Concord housed military supplies for the Massachusetts militia. Although Gage planned a secret military expedition to secure or destroy the supplies, locals quickly recognized the signs of an impending military operation as light infantry and grenadiers were removed from normal duties on April 15, 1775, in preparation for the expedition.

Patriot legislators meeting in Concord in defiance of the British adjourned and two of the more famous and radical members, **John Hancock** and **Samuel Adams**, traveled to nearby Lexington to stay with a friend. Military supplies, including light cannon, were moved to another town. In Boston, **Paul Revere** arranged for a signal to be broadcast from the North Church steeple. If the British departed by land across the narrow neck that joined Boston to the rest of Massachusetts, a single lantern would be displayed in the steeple. However, if the British crossed by boat to the **Charlestown** peninsula in the attempt to keep their expedition a secret, two lanterns would be displayed in the church. In the early evening hours of April 18, 1775, 700 British soldiers, commanded by Lieutenant Colonel Francis Smith, quietly prepared to depart Boston and crossed by small boats to the Charlestown peninsula. Ahead of the British rode several patriots, including Revere and **William Dawes**, who warned the local militia of the march of the British regulars. The two **alarm riders** met **Samuel Prescott** along the road and he joined them in their ride. Revere was captured by a British patrol just west of Lexington on the road to Concord. Dawes and Prescott managed to escape and continue the alert. The British soldiers released Revere around 2:30 the next morning, 30 minutes after the British departed Charlestown on their way to Concord.

The **Minutemen** of Lexington, numbering 77 men, assembled on Lexington Green around 4:00 a.m. on April 19. British marines were acting as an advance guard for the main body of soldiers and entered Lexington at approximately 5:00 a.m. Captain John Parker, commanding the militia at Lexington that morning, realized that he was outnumbered and ordered his men to withdraw. A single shot erupted and was followed by two British volleys and a bayonet charge. Eight militia members died and 10 were wounded in the exchange. Despite speculation about who fired first at Lexington, the origin of that single shot has never been positively identified. The British forces resumed their march toward Concord.

Approximately 150 militia members spotted the British column just east of Concord and withdrew into the village. British soldiers chased a group of militia from the village and onto a ridge known as Ripley Hill half a mile north of Concord without exchanging a shot. Colonel James Barrett, commanding the militiamen assembled at

Concord, shifted the force from Ripley Hill to Punkatasset Hill. When they numbered approximately 400 men, the militia moved from the hill toward the North Bridge. The British had been searching for ammunition and in the process set fire to two buildings. The smoke from these buildings helped to provoke the militia to action. Thinking that the British intended to burn the village, Barrett ordered his men to march into the center of Concord but to only fire their weapons if fired upon by the British. The militia quickly approached a small group of British soldiers working to remove the planks of the North Bridge. The British regulars fired three individual shots followed by a complete volley. Two militia members fell dead following the volley. Major John Buttrick ordered the men of the militia to return fire and the British received a volley from their opponents. The British soldiers retreated from the bridge, leaving two dead comrades. Lieutenant Colonel Smith ordered his men to gather and withdraw from the town but not before the British force lost another man killed and nine wounded.

The first mile of the withdrawal passed without any trouble, but as the British approached Meriam's Corner, they encountered opposition from the militia. The British soldiers would face a running gauntlet of fire from the patriot militia for the next 16 miles. The militia frequently fought as individuals or small groups behind trees, rocks, and fences rather than organized in large European-style ranks. British flank guards attempted to force the Americans to withdraw or at least remain beyond effective range of their muskets. The British continued their bloody retreat until reaching a 1,400-man force led by Lord Hugh Percy that had been dispatched by General Gage earlier in the day. Percy's command provided Smith's men a chance to catch their breath and then both units continued the retreat to Boston where they arrived back in the early evening. The militia units settled outside of the town and would eventually form the nucleus of the Grand American Army laying siege to Boston.

It has been estimated that approximately 3,700 militiamen engaged the British force along their retreat. Units would arrive, fire upon the British, and then depart to be replaced by other militiamen. Some militia units continued the pursuit the entire length of the retreat. The Americans lost 39 men killed, 41 wounded, and 5 missing. The British suffered 269 total casualties, including 73 deaths. Most of the casual-

ties on both sides occurred in the town of Menotomy (now Arlington). The battle is significant in that it marked the beginning of the armed hostilities known as the **Revolutionary War**. The British realized that the American militia members were better organized and more willing to engage regular forces than expected. The American opposition set the stage that would lead to the siege of Boston and then the **Declaration of Independence** the following summer. *See also* CAMBRIDGE; CHARLESTOWN; NEWPORT; PORTSMOUTH.

L'HOMMEDIEU, EZRA (1734–1811). Ezra L'Hommedieu, a lawyer, represented **New York** in the **Second Continental Congress** and **Congress of the Confederation** from 1779–1783.

***LIBERTY*.** The *Liberty* was a merchant **sloop** owned by **John Hancock**. Hancock tended to defy British attempts at **taxation** and **trade** restrictions imposed on the American **colonies**. Officials with the **American Board of Customs Commissioners** were looking for reasons to counter Hancock. Customs personnel seized Hancock's sloop on June 10, 1768. However, accounts differ as to the actual rationale for the act. Most sources state that Hancock was offloading wine for which he had not paid duties. Other sources claim that the customs officers were enforcing a little-used law that demanded bonding prior to loading a vessel with export goods. Regardless of the reason, the British officials seized the sloop and towed it alongside the warship *Romney*. Bostonians protested the action, forcing the responsible officials to flee. These actions were instrumental in prompting the British to send two regiments of soldiers to **Boston**. The British troops arrived on October 1, 1768, and set the stage for even greater confrontations between the Bostonians and British officials. The continued clashes between the two groups would eventually lead to the **Boston Massacre** and later the siege of the city by colonial forces who would form the nucleus of the **Continental Army**. The British utilized the *Liberty* as a customs vessel along the **Rhode Island** coast. During the summer of 1769, a group of **Newport** residents seized the armaments and rigging of the vessel and scuttled her. *See also LYDIA*.

LIBERTY BOWL. **Paul Revere** crafted the Liberty Bowl as a means of commemorating the numbers 92 and **45**. Each of these numbers held a special significance to patriots. The bowl weighed 45 ounces, held 45 gills of liquid, and was inscribed to the "Ninety-Two" of the **Massachusetts** Assembly. *See also* CIRCULAR LETTER OF MASSACHUSETTS.

LIBERTY BOYS. The Liberty Boys was another name for the **Sons of Liberty**.

LIBERTY POLE. *See* LIBERTY TREE.

LIBERTY SONG. **John Dickinson**, with the assistance of **Arthur Lee**, wrote the *Liberty Song*. Groups throughout the American **colonies** adopted the song as their anthem. *See also* MUSIC.

LIBERTY TREE. **Boston** emerged as the home of the first "liberty tree." On August 14, 1765, patriots placed the effigies of British officials **Andrew Oliver** and Lord Bute on an elm tree to protest British colonial **taxation**. The idea quickly spread to the other **colonies**. Patriots also erected "liberty poles" to celebrate events such as the repeal of the **Stamp Act of 1765** and to provide a center for opposition to British taxation. The **Sons of Liberty** frequently rallied their supporters at the base of the liberty trees and poles. In **New York City**, British troops frequently cut down liberty poles erected by the locals. By the next day, these symbols of opposition were normally replaced. At other times, colonists confronted British soldiers exhibiting the intention of destroying a liberty pole. In January 1770, colonists and British forces tangled in the area known as **Golden Hill**. During this confrontation, many individuals on both sides were injured.

LIBRARIES. Revolutionary America boasted a considerable number of college, parish, public, and subscription libraries. **Benjamin Franklin** founded the first subscription library in the American **colonies** in 1731. The existence of libraries helped encourage many educated individuals to read and write on numerous topics. The events of the **Revolutionary War** prompted many participants to write about their experiences, making this conflict well documented by late 18th-century standards.

LINCOLN, BENJAMIN (1733–1810). Benjamin Lincoln, a major general during the **Revolutionary War**, led the **Massachusetts militia** in the suppression of **Shays's Rebellion**. In 1788, he sat as a delegate in the state convention to ratify the U.S. **Constitution** and later served as the state lieutenant governor.

LINCOLN, LEVI (1749–1820). Levi Lincoln, a lawyer, sat in the **Massachusetts** legislature. In 1781, he was a member of a team that won a significant state court case against the institution of **slavery** within Massachusetts. He later served in the U.S. House of Representatives and became governor of Massachusetts.

LIQUOR. *See* ALCOHOL.

LITERATURE. There was a large number of writers during the Revolutionary period, even though few became famous for their work. Some of the best-known examples of American literature from this period are political in nature and include ***Letters from a Farmer in Pennsylvania*** by **John Dickinson** and ***Common Sense*** by **Thomas Paine**. **Philip Freneau** is often referred to as the "Father of American Literature" and concentrated also on political themes before and after the Revolution. One of the more famous authors of the era was **Noah Webster**, who developed a series of spellers and later his famous dictionary. Along with writing, Americans, including **Benjamin Franklin**, carried on a long tradition of **printing**. In 1782, **Robert Aitken** printed the first Bible in the United States. **Great Britain** had prevented the printing of Bibles in the American **colonies** by citing copyright laws and forcing Americans to purchase British-printed Bibles. Other prominent writers of the Revolutionary period include **Peter Markoe** and **Susanna Rowson**. *See also* POETRY.

LIVINGSTON, PHILIP (1716–1778). Philip Livingston, the cousin of **Robert Livingston** and brother of **William Livingston**, was a merchant and served in the **New York** colonial legislature. Livingston represented New York in the **First Continental Congress** in 1774 and the **Second Continental Congress** from 1775–1778 while simultaneously holding his seat in the New York legislature. He signed the **Declaration of Independence** in August 1776 due to the lack of instructions from New York when the document was completed in July. Livingston has been credited as a very active member of Congress before his death in 1778.

LIVINGSTON, ROBERT (1746–1813). Robert Livingston, a cousin of **Philip Livingston** and **William Livingston**, was a farmer and lawyer from **New York**. He represented New York in the **Second Continental Congress** and the **Congress of the Confederation** from 1775–1776, 1779–1781, and 1784–1785 while simultaneously holding his seat in the New York legislature. Livingston did not sign the **Declaration of Independence**. Although he sat on the committee to draft the document, the New York delegation did not have instructions regarding signing it in July 1776. While the other New York delegates signed the Declaration in August 1776, Livingston was back at the state legislature and never penned his name to the document after retuning to **Philadelphia**. He was a very active member of Congress and served there 1775–1776, 1779–1781, and 1784–1785. Congress named him the **executive secretary of foreign affairs** from 1781–1782, during which time he was upset that **France** was not a party to the **Treaty of Paris of 1783**. He later administered the presidential oath of office to **George Washington**, served as minister to France, and negotiated the Louisiana Purchase.

LIVINGSTON, WILLIAM (1723–1790). William Livingston, the brother of **Philip Livingston** and a cousin of **Robert Livingston**, practiced law and became the first governor of **New Jersey** in 1776. He held this position until his death in 1790. Livingston represented New Jersey in the **First Continental Congress** in 1774 and **Second Continental Congress** from 1775–1776. He accepted a commission in the New Jersey **militia** one month prior to the signing of the **Declaration of Independence**. He attended the **Constitutional Convention of 1787** and signed the U.S. **Constitution** for New Jersey and was instrumental in ensuring his state's ratification of the document. Livingston was the father-in-law of **John Jay**.

LLOYD, JAMES (1728–1810). James Lloyd, from **Massachusetts**, was the first physician to practice midwifery in America. Normally,

women with little, if any, training acted as midwives for other women delivering children during Revolutionary America.

LOBSTER. Lobster was an American colonial insult for British soldiers, who wore red jackets with their uniforms. Some sources credit the name from the red backs of the frequently flogged British soldiers. *See also* LOBSTER BACK.

LOBSTER BACK. Lobster back was an American colonial insult for British soldiers, who wore red jackets with their uniforms. Some sources credit the name from the red backs of the frequently flogged British soldiers. *See also* LOBSTER.

LOCHABER, TREATY OF. The British concluded the Treaty of Lochaber with the **Cherokee** in October 1770. This treaty modified the **Treaty of Hard Labor** and increased the size of the Cherokee-claimed lands turned over to **Virginia** for settlement. *See also* AUGUSTA, TREATY OF; FORT STANWIX, TREATY OF; PROCLAMATION OF 1763.

LOCKE, JOHN (1632–1704). John Locke, an English philosopher, exhibited considerable philosophical influence on American intellectuals before, during, and after the **Revolutionary War**. Locke's ideas, as discussed in his 1689 book *Two Treatises of Government*, made a considerable impact on **Thomas Jefferson** as he wrote the **Declaration of Independence**. Locke believed that all individuals have "natural rights"—life, liberty, and property—given to them by God. Individuals do not surrender their natural rights when they join an organized society. According to Locke, these individuals make contracts with the rulers of the organized societies. The rulers provide protection in return for the obedience of the individuals in society. However, if the rulers violate the natural rights of their subjects, the latter are no longer under any obligation to obey and have the right to replace these leaders.

This philosophical relationship between rulers and the ruled is evident in Thomas Jefferson's drafting of the Declaration of Independence. Jefferson wrote that individuals have "unalienable rights," including "life, liberty, and the pursuit of happiness." He also added that "whenever any Form of Government becomes destructive of these ends, it is the Right of the People to alter or to abolish it." *See also* COKE, EDWARD; GORDON, THOMAS; TRENCHARD, JOHN.

LOCKE, MATTHEW (1730–1801). Matthew Locke, a **North Carolina** patriot, served in the state legislature. Locke opposed the ratification of the U.S. **Constitution** and attended the **Hillsborough state convention** in 1788 and the **Fayetteville state convention** in 1789. He later sat as a member of the U.S. House of Representatives.

LOGAN, BENJAMIN (c.1743–1802). Benjamin Logan, an early pioneer and settler in **Kentucky**, sat in the **Virginia** legislature. He proved to be an avid advocate for Kentucky statehood and later served on the U.S. **Board of War** under President **George Washington**.

LOGAN, JAMES (c.1725–1780). James Logan, a **Native American** Mingo leader with the birth name of Tahgahjute, was an early friend of the American colonists. However, his friendship soured as the colonists continued to stream into Native American lands and ignore treaties. After the **Battle of Point Pleasant**, Logan refused to join the other Native Americans who sought peace. He sided with **Great Britain** in the **Revolutionary War** and died under unknown circumstances.

LONDON. The *London* carried tea into **Charleston** harbor in December 1773 under the provisions of the **Tea Act of 1773**. When unpaid duties on the tea reached the 20-day period due to local opposition to the cargo, customs officials seized the entire shipment and it remained in storage until the outbreak of open warfare in the **colonies**. At that point, the tea was confiscated and sold to benefit the patriot cause.

LONG RIFLE. The long rifle was another name for the **American rifle**.

LONGSTREET, WILLIAM (1759–1814). William Longstreet moved to **Georgia** and experimented with steam engines and a cotton gin. He later patented a horse-powered breast roller gin.

LOPEZ, AARON (1731–1782). Aaron Lopez, a merchant, emerged as a prominent individual in the shipping industry during Revolutionary America.

LORD DUNMORE'S ETHIOPIAN REGIMENT. **Lord John Dunmore**, the royal governor of **Virginia**, formed this military unit from freed **slaves** in November 1775 in response to the patriot attempt to seize control of the government. Dunmore offered freedom to any slave willing to join the British forces against the American patriots who now controlled the colony. The unit numbered 300 men and wore uniforms upon which "Liberty to Slaves" was printed. Dunmore's action in forming this unit tended to help unite Virginia landowners against the British government and aided the patriot cause.

LORD DUNMORE'S WAR. Movement by settlers into **Native American** territory despite the **Proclamation of 1763** prompted renewed violence between the two groups. In 1774, the Shawnee, led by **Cornstalk**, initiated open warfare along the western borders of **Pennsylvania** and **Virginia**. Their initial successes persuaded other Native Americans to join the Shawnee. The governor of Virginia, **Lord John Dunmore**, organized two military parties against the Shawnee. Together, these expeditions are known as Lord Dunmore's War. The first military unit dispatched to the west was ambushed by the Shawnee along the Kentucky River in July 1774. In response, Lord Dunmore mobilized 1,500 **militia** members from western Virginia. This second expedition defeated Cornstalk at the **Battle of Point Pleasant** on October 10, 1774. Diplomatic negotiations successfully placed a wedge between the Shawnee and their allies. As a result, the Shawnee were forced to surrender their claims to all territory in what is now **Kentucky**. Many historians credit Lord Dunmore's War with discouraging the Shawnee from doing more to aid the British during the **Revolutionary War**. *See also* KIRKLAND, SAMUEL.

LORD NORTH'S COASTERS. The term "Lord North's Coasters" was applied to the wagons utilized to transfer cargo from ships to **Boston** during the period of the **Boston Port Act of 1774**. The act closed the port, forcing coastal vessels carrying essentials for the town of Boston to transfer their cargo to wagons outside of the district.

LOTTERY. On November 18, 1776, the **Second Continental Congress** established a national lottery to help fund the national government and the American war effort in the **Revolutionary War**. Congress offered up to 100,000 tickets for sale in four price categories. Ticket sales were slow and when combined with the inflation of continental **currency**, the lottery can be considered a failure.

LOUDON, SAMUEL (c.1727–1813). Samuel Loudon, a patriot, became an important **printer** and publisher in **New York City**. He later served as a state printer and reproduced state **currency** and copies of the **New York** constitution.

LOUISA COMPANY. *See* TRANSYLVANIA COMPANY.

LOVELL, JAMES (1737–1814). James Lovell, a schoolmaster from **Massachusetts** and the son of **John Lovell**, was arrested by the British in 1775 as an American spy. He represented Massachusetts in the **Second Continental Congress** from 1777–1782. In Congress, Lovell was not a supporter of either **Silas Deane** or **George Washington** and participated in the **Conway Cabal**. He did sign the **Articles of Confederation** for his state.

LOVELL, JOHN (1710–1778). John Lovell, a prominent **Massachusetts** schoolmaster, a **loyalist**, and the father of **James Lovell**, arranged for his son's exchange after capture as an American spy.

LOW, ISAAC (1735–1791). Isaac Low, a merchant, and the brother of **Nicholas Low**, represented **New York** in the **First Continental Congress**. Although an early patriot, he did not favor complete independence and became a **loyalist** in his beliefs.

LOW, NICHOLAS (1739–1826). Nicholas Low, a **New York** patriot, merchant, and brother of **Isaac Low**, sat as a delegate in the state legislature and the 1789 state convention to ratify the U.S. **Constitution**.

LOWELL, JOHN (1743–1802). John Lowell, a politician and jurist, served as a member of the **Massachusetts** legislature and represented his state in the **Congress of the Confederation** from 1782–1783.

LOWNDES, RAWLINS (1721–1800). Rawlins Lowndes sat in the **South Carolina** legislature. Although a patriot, he opposed complete American independence. In 1779, he departed office as the last president of South Carolina. After the **Revolutionary War**, he returned to the legislature and opposed the ratification of the U.S. **Constitution**.

LOYAL LAND COMPANY. The Loyal Land Company represented a group of **land speculators** who were active after the **French and Indian War**. The company actively lobbied to move the **Proclamation of 1763** boundary along **Virginia** westward to permit more territorial expansion for Americans. A leader of the company proved to be instrumental in assisting with the negotiations for the **Treaty of Fort Stanwix** and the **Treaty of Lochaber**. *See also* OHIO COMPANY; MISSISSIPPI LAND COMPANY.

LOYAL NINE. The Loyal Nine were a group of **Boston** artisans and shopkeepers who met during 1765. The group worked with other organizations to promote opposition to the British **Stamp Act of 1765**. For example, the members of the Loyal Nine persuaded the **South-End Mob** of Boston to rise in protest against the stamp distributor in the city. *See also* CAUCUS CLUB.

LOYALISTS. Loyalists were those who remained "loyal" to the British Crown before, during, and after the Revolution. It has often been estimated that the American population during the Revolution can be equally divided into thirds: those supportive of the American cause, the loyalists, and those who supported neither cause and just wanted to be left alone. **Committees of Safety** sought to identify those within the population who harbored loyalist sympathies. Loyalists tended to be in greater numbers in the **southern colonies**. For example, the Revolution in rural **South Carolina** is often seen in terms of a civil war between patriot farmers and their loyalist neighbors. Savage brutality often accompanied the political divisions between the two groups. Loyalists lost their property and some states passed laws to exile them.

Many loyalists joined the British military and fought as regular **provincial** forces against patriot **militia** and the **Continental Army**. Others formed loyalist militia bands that fought against patriot militia. During the Battle of King's Mountain, Major Ferguson, the British commander, was the only regular army officer on both sides in the engagement. At the end of the **Revolutionary War**, an estimated 60,000 loyalists departed with the British troops. Many traveled to what is now **Canada**. The inability of the U.S. government to enforce compensation of the loyalists by state governments for their loss of land and businesses was presented as the reason for **Great Britain**'s refusal to negotiate a **trade** treaty with the newly independent country. By the end of the Revolutionary period in 1787, most states had repealed their anti-loyalist laws and many former loyalists became productive citizens of the new country. *See also* HUCK, CHRISTIAN.

LUMBER INDUSTRY. Forestry products, especially lumber, were an important **industry** in Revolutionary America. Forests covered nearly the entire eastern coast of North America and provided an abundance of trees for the needs of Europe as well as the American colonists. Wood from maple, sweet gum, walnut, cedar, and cypress trees provided the material for specialty wood products such as furniture, while oak and pine were utilized for barrels, boards, and shingles. The forests were also important for the **shipbuilding industry** and **naval stores industry**. Lumbering in the **New England colonies** was often a winter industry conducted by farmers waiting for their fields to thaw from the harsh cold. In 1770, the American colonies exported over 42,000,000 board feet of lumber; 15,000 tons of uncut timber; 20,000,000 barrel staves; and 3,000,000 wooden hoops. British industry demanded all the lumber that the American **colonies** could provide and London attempted to prevent the product from being exported to other countries. Despite British efforts, Americans did manage to export considerable amounts of lumber to **Spain**, **Portugal**, and the West Indies.

LUZERNE, ANNE-CESAR DE LA, CHEVALIER (1741–1791) Anne-Cesar de la Luzerne replaced **Conrad Gérard** as the French minister to the United States in 1777. He displayed considerable power in his position and is reported to have persuaded **Maryland** to sign the **Articles of Confederation** by threatening to deny the state French naval support.

LYDIA. **John Hancock**, a wealthy merchant and patriot, owned the sailing vessel *Lydia*. Hancock, like most American merchants, tended to avoid paying British-imposed **taxes** on his goods and ignored British restrictions on trading. During April 1768, *Lydia* arrived home to **Boston** at the same time that British custom authorities were increasing their enforcement of duties on Madeira wine. Customs officials boarded the *Lydia* for a routine inspection to ensure that nothing would be offloaded until the proper paperwork had been completed. One of the customs officers went below decks without authorization and was caught by the crew. Hancock promptly threw the man out of the hold, angering the British customs officials, who would soon take their revenge on the Bostonian merchant by seizing the vessel ***Liberty***.

LYNCH, THOMAS, JR. (1749–1779). Lynch, a planter, represented **South Carolina** in the **Second Continental Congress** from 1776–1777. He attended as an extra delegate in order to care for his ill father, **Thomas Lynch Sr.** Thomas Lynch Jr. signed the **Declaration of Independence** but then returned home due to his own ill health. He was lost at sea in 1779.

LYNCH, THOMAS, SR. (1727–1776). Thomas Lynch, a **rice** planter, represented **South Carolina** in the **First Continental Congress** and the **Second Continental Congress** from 1774–1776. Following a stroke, Lynch was joined in Congress by his son, **Thomas Lynch Jr**. The senior Lynch died in 1776 while journeying with his son back to South Carolina.

– M –

MACINTOSH, EBENEZER. Mackintosh, the captain of Boston's **South-End Mob** and one of the **Sons of Liberty**, led the attacks upon the houses of Oliver and **Thomas Hutchinson** during the **Stamp Act**

of 1765 crisis. After the union with the **North-End Mob**, Mackintosh led the combined group of Bostonian Sons of Liberty in actions protesting British **taxation**.

MACON, NATHANIEL (1758–1837). Nathaniel Macon, a **Revolutionary War** officer, sat in the **North Carolina** legislature. Although selected to represent the state in the **Congress of the Confederation** in 1786, he declined to attend. Macon opposed ratification of the U.S. **Constitution** but later served in the U.S. House of Representatives.

MACWHORTER, ALEXANDER (1734–1807). Alexander MacWhorter, a Presbyterian clergyman and patriot, served as a chaplain in the **Continental Army**. The British ransacked his home in retaliation for his political stance.

MADISON, JAMES (1749–1812). James Madison, a bishop of the Episcopal Church, is known for his work as a professor and the president of William and Mary College from 1777–1812. He should not be confused with **James Madison**, the politician and future president of the United States.

MADISON, JAMES (1751–1836). James Madison served in the **Virginia** legislature in 1776 and represented his state in the **Second Continental Congress** from 1780–1781 and **Congress of the Confederation** from 1781–1783. As a delegate, Madison noted the problems associated with a weak national government such as that of the United States under the **Articles of Confederation**. He played a significant role in the **Annapolis Convention** and represented his state in the **Constitutional Convention of 1787**. He quickly emerged as probably the most important individual associated with the debate over the new document. Madison, although favoring a strong central government, was known as a compromiser and frequently brought opposing groups together under alternative solutions. Madison signed the U.S. **Constitution** and played a significant role in the ratification of the document. He was one of the authors of the ***Federalist Papers*** calling for the ratification of the Constitution. He later served Virginia in the House of Representatives of Congress, emerged as a leader in the drafting of the **Bill of Rights**, became secretary of state, and was president of the United States from 1809–1817. He should not be confused with **James Madison**, the Episcopal bishop and president of William and Mary College. *See also* CHECKS AND BALANCES.

MADISON MODEL. *See* CHECKS AND BALANCES.

MAGAZINES. *See* PUBLICATIONS.

MALCOLM, JAMES (1767–1815). James Malcolm, a **Pennsylvania loyalist**, is known as one of America's best line engravers during the Revolutionary period.

MANIGAULT, PETER (1731–1773). Peter Manigault, a planter, served as the speaker of the **South Carolina** assembly from 1765–1772. He was a patriot and actively opposed the **Stamp Act of 1765**.

MANNING, JAMES (1738–1791). In 1765, James Manning, a Baptist clergyman, became a founder and the first president of **Rhode Island** College (now Brown University).

MANUFACTURING. *See* INDUSTRY.

MARCHANT, HENRY (1741–1796). Henry Marchant, a jurist, represented **Rhode Island** in the **Second Continental Congress** from 1777–1779 and signed the **Articles of Confederation**. He was also selected as a delegate to the **Congress of the Confederation** in 1780 and 1783 but did not attend any of the sessions. In 1784, Marchant was again selected as a congressional delegate but resigned before attending any sessions. He sat as a delegate in Rhode Island's state constitutional convention and led the struggle in his state for the ratification of the U.S. **Constitution**. He later served as a federal judge.

MARIETTA. *See* OHIO COMPANY.

MARINE COMMITTEE. The **Second Continental Congress** renamed its **Naval Committee** as the Marine Committee on December

14, 1775, to reflect that body's new mission of constructing and maintaining ships for the **Continental Navy**. The 13-member committee later became the **American Board of Admiralty** in October 1779 in an attempt to control internal controversy within the Marine Committee and the inability of the latter to properly oversee American vessels at sea. *See also* AGENT OF THE MARINE; NAVAL BOARD; NAVAL CONSTRUCTION ACT OF 1775; NAVAL CONSTRUCTION ACT OF 1776; NAVAL CONSTRUCTION ACT OF 1777.

MARINES. The **Second Continental Congress** established the U.S. Marines on November 10, 1775.

MARKOE, PETER (c.1752–1792). Peter Markoe was a noted **poet** and dramatist of Revolutionary America.

MARLBOROUGH. The *Marlborough* was the most successful of the larger-size American **privateers**. She captured 28 British vessels during her career.

MARRIAGE. *See* WOMEN AND REVOLUTIONARY AMERICA.

MARSHALL, DANIEL (1706–1784). Daniel Marshall, a clergyman and missionary among the **Native Americans**, emerged as one of the most important figures behind the growth of the Baptist church in the southern states. In particular, Marshall was a leader of what is known as the "separate Baptists." The mainstream Baptist church of the northern states disagreed with the energetic methods and practices of this new branch of the church.

MARSHALL, HUMPHREY (1760–1841). Humphrey Marshall, a **Revolutionary War** officer, settled in **Kentucky**. However, unlike many of his contemporaries there, he opposed the separation of Kentucky from **Virginia**. As a delegate to the Virginia convention, he supported the ratification of the U.S. **Constitution**. Marshall later served in the Kentucky legislature and the U.S. Senate.

MARSHALL, HUMPHREY (1722–1801). Humphrey Marshall, the cousin of **John Bartram**, was a noted American botanist of the Revolutionary period.

MARSHALL, JOHN (1755–1835). John Marshall served in the **Virginia** legislature. One of his greatest accomplishments during the America's Revolutionary period involved the ratification of the U.S. **Constitution**. Marshall proved to be instrumental in ensuring the U.S. Constitution was submitted to the Virginia convention without the inclusion of instructions for amendments that could have hampered its passage by the body. He then attended the state convention, although many sources indicate that his role at this point was more subdued. Marshall's greatest achievement in American history would emerge later when he held the post of chief justice of the U.S. Supreme Court.

MARSHALL, THOMAS (1730–1802). Thomas Marshall, a **Revolutionary War** officer and surveyor, served in the **Virginia** legislature. After the **Revolutionary War**, he became very important in the affairs of **Kentucky** and represented the area in the Virginia legislature.

MARTIN, ALEXANDER (1740–1807). Alexander Martin fought in the **Revolutionary War** and served as a delegate in **Congress of the Confederation** in 1782 and from 1786–1787. He was also one of **North Carolina**'s delegates to the **Constitutional Convention of 1787**. Martin is known as the North Carolina delegate least inclined toward strong federalism. He departed **Philadelphia** in August 1787, prior to the completion of the draft, and did not sign the U.S. **Constitution**. He also served as governor of North Carolina in 1782 and later as a U.S. senator.

MARTIN, JOSIAH (1737–1786). Josiah Martin was the governor of **North Carolina** from 1771–1775. He frequently clashed with the colonial legislature over funding and judicial issues. Martin fled his capital in 1775 after the **Battle of Lexington-Concord** in **Massachusetts**. He actively aided various British military campaigns in the south during the **Revolutionary War** but never regained his post.

MARTIN, LUTHER (1748–1826). Luther Martin, a lawyer, was selected by **Maryland** as an honorary delegate to the **Congress of the Confederation** in 1785. He was also the first attorney general for the state of Maryland. He attended the **Constitutional Convention of 1787**.

Martin opposed the proceedings to write a new U.S. **Constitution** and walked out of the meeting with **John Mercer**.

MARTINIQUE AND REVOLUTIONARY AMERICA. The French port of Martinique in the Caribbean served as a haven for American vessels and a location for selling prize ships captured from the British by American **privateers**. *See also* FRANCE AND REVOLUTIONARY AMERICA.

MARYLAND. Maryland, one of the **southern colonies**, was governed by **Great Britain** as a **proprietary colony** until the **Revolutionary War** and American independence. By the end of America's Revolutionary period in 1790, the state boasted 319,728 people (32% slaves). In 1763, a border quarrel with **Pennsylvania** resulted in a settlement based on the **Mason-Dixon Line**. Maryland refused to sign the **Articles of Confederation** until the other states agreed to surrender their claims to western lands to the United States. On March 7, 1781, it became the last state to ratify the articles and officially make this document the first constitution of the United States. Maryland proved to be a leader in the discussions to strengthen the articles and helped organize the **Alexandria Convention** and the **Annapolis Convention** with other states. The state ratified the U.S. **Constitution** on April 28, 1788. Maryland was the second-largest producer and exporter of **tobacco** and flour and the third-largest producer and exporter of **wheat** and corn in the United States during this period. Notable individuals from Maryland include **Charles Carroll**, **Daniel Carroll**, **Samuel Chase**, **Daniel of St. Thomas Jenifer**, **Thomas Johnson**, **James McHenry**, and **William Paca**.

MASON, GEORGE (1725–1792). Mason, a planter, early patriot, and uncle of **Stevens Mason**, wrote the **Virginia Resolves** and was prominent in **Virginia** politics throughout the period before and during the **Revolutionary War**. He also wrote the Virginia Declaration of Rights, a bill of rights for Virginians. **Thomas Jefferson** borrowed ideas from this document when drafting the **Declaration of Independence**. The same document served later as a model for the U.S. **Bill of Rights**. Mason attended the **Constitutional Convention of 1787** as a delegate from Virginia. He supported the new U.S. **Con-**

Patrick Henry, after a portrait by J. B. Longacre. The Virginia-born orator led that colony's opposition to the Stamp Act and subsequent measures from the time he delivered his "If this be treason" speech in that cause to the Virginia House of Burgesses.

Samuel Adams, from a portrait by John Singleton Copley. Adams was no doubt the most influential spokesman among the people of Boston in the years before the Revolution and the first in the colonies to commit himself to independence. John Adams was his second cousin.

John Hancock, from a Copley portrait. Hancock, the richest man in Boston before the Revolution, was President of the Second Continental Congress and the first to sign the Declaration of Independence.

Thomas Jefferson, after a print by Desnoyers. Largely at the suggestion of John Adams, Jefferson was the member of the committee of Congress asked to write the Declaration of Independence. He was charged with the task of preparing the Declaration and was selected to do the actual writing.

John Adams, from a portrait by Gilbert Stuart. Adams was the most effective debater in the Congress as he urged adoption of Jefferson's Declaration.

Benjamin Franklin, engraving of a portrait of Franklin from a painting by Duplessis.

Alexander Hamilton, from a minature by Archibald Robertson.

James Madison, from a portrait by Gilbert Stuart.

John Jay, in an engraving by Asher B. Durand from a portrait by Stuart and Trumbull.

George Washington, after a Gilbert Stuart portrait.

stitution but disagreed with many of the compromises between northern and southern states. He insisted on the inclusion of a bill of rights and disagreed with permitting **slavery** within the United States. He suggested educating slaves and then gradually freeing them. He also did not like the compromise on tariffs. Although he worked feverishly on the document, he refused to sign the Constitution due to the above issues. Later, the inclusion of the 11th Amendment to the Constitution, defining the boundaries of the federal judiciary, resulted from Mason's ideas.

MASON, STEVENS (1760–1803). Stevens Mason, an aide to General **George Washington** during the **Revolutionary War** and the nephew of **George Mason**, served in the **Virginia** legislature. In 1788, he sat as a delegate in the Virginia convention to ratify the U.S. **Constitution** and opposed the document. Mason also opposed the amendments forwarded to the states by **Congress**. He declared that these proposed amendments, 10 of which became the **Bill of Rights**, were inadequate for the protection of liberties. He later served as a member of the U.S. Senate.

MASON-DIXON LINE. While the Mason-Dixon Line is often associated with the Missouri Compromise and the division of the United States in terms of **slavery** vs. nonslavery states, the demarcation actually was completed during the period of Revolutionary America for different reasons. **Pennsylvania** and **Maryland** maintained a long-lasting disagreement over the exact border between the two colonies. Charles Mason and Jeremiah Dixon were appointed to survey and mark the exact border. They completed their work in 1768, although others later continued the survey and extended the line beyond their original 244-mile demarcation.

MASSACHUSETTS. Massachusetts, one of the **New England colonies**, was governed by **Great Britain** as a **royal colony** until the **Revolutionary War** and American independence. By the end of America's revolutionary period in 1790, the state boasted 378,787 people (0% slaves). Massachusetts was the only state without slaves in 1790. Considerable opposition to British **taxation** policies could be found in the colony due to the importance of **trade** to the local **economy**.

Famous pre-Revolutionary War events include the **Boston Massacre** and then the **Boston Tea Party** with the resulting **Intolerable Acts**. The Revolutionary War began in Massachusetts with the **Battle of Lexington-Concord**. Massachusetts was the largest producer and exporter of **fish**, **whale** oil, pine boards, and oak boards in the United States during this period. It also had the largest merchant marine fleet. The post-Revolutionary War depression, **personal debt**, and scarcity of **currency** were particularly hard on the state's small farmers, leading to the incident known as **Shays's Rebellion**. The shock of this event and similar incidents helped lead to the **Massachusetts Resolves** and spurred others in calling for a revision of the **Articles of Confederation** and the eventual ratification of the U.S. **Constitution**. The state ratified the U.S. Constitution on February 6, 1788. Notable individuals from Massachusetts include **John Adams**, **Samuel Adams**, **Francis Dana**, **Elbridge Gerry**, **John Hamilton**, **Rufus King**, **John Hancock**, **James Otis**, **Robert Paine**, and **Roger Sherman**.

MASSACHUSETTS ACTS. The **Massachusetts** Provincial Congress adopted the Massachusetts Acts on October 26, 1774, following the British imposition of the **Intolerable Acts** on the **colony**. The Massachusetts Acts established the **Committees of Safety** and reorganized the **militia** of the colony. Militia units were to drill according to the latest British manual on the subject and conduct new elections for officers in order to remove loyalists. Despite the purge, **loyalists**, including Major General William Brattle, did remain within the ranks of the militia officers. The Massachusetts Acts reorganized the colonial militia by forming companies of **Minutemen** who would be able to respond quicker to a crisis than regular units. Eventually, one-quarter of all militia members in the colony became Minutemen.

MASSACHUSETTS ARTICLES OF WAR. *See* CONTINENTAL ARTICLES OF WAR.

MASSACHUSETTS CIRCULAR LETTER. *See* CIRCULAR LETTER OF MASSACHUSETTS.

MASSACHUSETTS GOVERNMENT ACT OF 1774. In retaliation for the **Boston Tea Party** and other acts of colonial opposition to

British policies, the British Parliament passed the Massachusetts Government Act on May 20, 1774. This act was one of the four **Intolerable Acts** placed on the colony. The Massachusetts Government Act essentially removed all governmental functions from the inhabitants of the colony and placed them in the hands of the royal governor. All members of the **Massachusetts** Council would now be selected by the British and the governor could select and remove judges within the **colony**. The governor also exercised considerable authority over the business conducted by town meetings. The people of **Salem** met in a council in defiance of the act, prompting General **Thomas Gage**, the royal governor, to dispatch troops to disperse the gathering. The soldiers arrived after the conclusion of the meeting, averting what could have been the first battle of the **Revolutionary War**. The Massachusetts Government Act, along with the other Intolerable Acts, helped to solidify colonial resistance to the British and led to the formation of the **First Continental Congress**.

MASSACHUSETTS RESOLVES. **Rufus King** and **Elbridge Gerry** presented the Massachusetts Resolves to the **Congress of the Confederation** in 1785. The resolves called for a convention to change the **Articles of Confederation**, which were proving to be inefficient at framing an effective national government.

MATHEWS, GEORGE (1739–1812). George Mathews, a **Revolutionary War** officer, became governor of **Georgia** in 1787. He later served in the U.S. House of Representatives and then completed another three years as governor.

MATHEWS, JOHN (1744–1802). John Mathews, a lawyer, represented **South Carolina** in the **Second Continental Congress** from 1778–1782. He signed the **Articles of Confederation** and later fought the proposal for a separate peace between the northern **colonies** and **Great Britain** without the participation of **Georgia**, **North Carolina**, and South Carolina. After leaving Congress in 1782, Mathews became the governor of South Carolina.

MCCAULEY, MARY LUDWIG HAYS. *See* HAYS, MARY LUDWIG.

MCCLURG, JAMES (1746–1823). James McClurg, a physician and medical professor, represented **Virginia** in the **Constitutional Convention of 1787**. He argued for presidential life tenure among other issues. McClurg departed from the convention prior to the signing of the **Constitution** but he did favor the document.

MCDOUGALL, ALEXANDER (1732–1786). Alexander McDougall, a **New York** merchant, received a commission as a brigadier general in August 1776 and fought for American independence in the **Revolutionary War**. **Congress** promoted McDougall to the rank of major general in October 1777. McDougall also represented New York in the **Second Continental Congress** in 1781 and the **Congress of the Confederation** between 1781 and 1782. He also served as a state senator from 1783–1786.

MCDOWELL, JOSEPH (1756–1801). Joseph McDowell, a Revolutionary officer from **North Carolina**, sat in the state legislature after the war. He served as a delegate to the **Hillsborough state convention** and the **Fayetteville state convention** to consider the ratification of the U.S. **Constitution**. He initially opposed ratification because the document did not contain a bill of rights. He later sat as a member of the U.S. House of Representatives.

MCGILLIVRAY, ALEXANDER (c.1759–1793). Alexander McGillivray, a **Creek** chief, envisioned a confederation that would encompass all **Native Americans** in the southern United States. In 1786, he engaged in a war with the United States, utilizing Spanish-supplied weapons. The United States under the **Articles of Confederation** was too weak to aid the individual southern states and effectively counter the Creeks.

MCHENRY, JAMES (1735–1816). James McHenry moved to America in 1771 from Ireland. McHenry, a businessman and doctor, represented **Maryland** in the **Congress of the Confederation** from 1783–1786. He attended the **Constitutional Convention of 1787** as a delegate and kept a private diary of its events, which is today one of the few firsthand records of the proceedings. McHenry signed the **Constitution** and later served as secretary of war. Fort McHenry, associated with the United States national anthem, is named after him.

MCINTOSH, LACHLAN (1725–1806). **Georgia** selected Lachlan McIntosh, a **Revolutionary War** officer, to represent the state in the **Congress of the Confederation** in 1784. However, McIntosh did not attend any sessions.

MCKEAN, THOMAS (1734–1817). Thomas McKean, a lawyer and politician from **Delaware**, represented his state in the **First Continental Congress** in 1774, the **Second Continental Congress** from 1775–1776 and 1778–1781, and the **Congress of the Confederation** from 1781–1783. He signed the **Declaration of Independence** and the **Articles of Confederation**. His vote in favor of the Declaration tied the second Delaware delegate who opposed the document. In response to McKean's appeal, Delaware's third delegate, **Caesar Rodney**, quickly rode to **Philadelphia** and cast his vote in favor of independence. McKean was a very active member of Congress and served as the **president of Congress** in 1781. McKean attended the **Pennsylvania** state convention to ratify the U.S. **Constitution** and later became chief justice of the Pennsylvania Supreme Court and governor of Pennsylvania.

MCKINLEY, JOHN (1721–1796). John McKinley, a physician, sat in the **Delaware** legislature and became the first president (governor) of the state in 1777. The British captured McKinley and exchanged him. Upon his release, he returned to medicine.

MEASON, ISAAC (1742–1818). Isaac Meason was a pioneer in the development of the **iron industry** west of the Allegheny Mountains. Meason also served in the **Pennsylvania** legislature.

MECKLENBURG RESOLVES. On May 31, 1775, a committee formed in Mecklenburg County, **North Carolina**, passed a series of 20 resolutions known collectively today as the Mecklenburg Resolves. The collection included resolutions that declared all British laws as "null and void" within the county; ordered the establishment and equipping of nine **militia** companies; and set up a local governmental body. The county forwarded the resolves to the North Carolina delegates to the **Second Continental Congress**. However, the resolves were never reviewed and discussed by Congress.

MEDICINE. *See* HEALTH; SMALLPOX.

MERCANTILISM. Mercantilism is an **economic** philosophy that advocates the maintenance of a favorable **trade** balance with **colonies** and other countries. Colonies are acquired in order to provide the home country with raw materials that are, in turn, manufactured into finished goods and then sold back to the colonies or other areas. On the one hand, the colonies have a guaranteed market but, on the other, they are restricted to trading exclusively or almost exclusively with the home country despite opportunities for more favorable trade with other countries or colonies. The home country utilizes its military force, especially naval power, to maintain the lines of communication with the colonies and to ensure the availability of raw materials. The mercantilistic practices of **Great Britain** were among the major causes of the **Revolutionary War** and American independence. They limited American trading partners, attempted to control prices via duties, and ensured a shortage of hard **currency** in the colonies. After the Revolutionary War, Great Britain attempted to maintain a mercantilistic relationship with the United States by controlling the prices of the goods it purchased as well as sold to the new country. The principle of mercantilism also impacted American trade with **France**, **Spain**, the **Netherlands**, and their West Indies colonies after the Revolutionary War.

MERCER, JAMES (1736–1793). James Mercer, an active patriot, represented **Virginia** in the **Second Continental Congress** in 1779. He served later as a state judge.

MERCER, JOHN (1759–1821). John Mercer, a lawyer and soldier in the **Revolutionary War**, served in the **Virginia** legislature. He represented Virginia in the **Congress of the Confederation** from 1782–1783. He attended the **Constitutional Convention of 1787** for **Maryland** (not Virginia). However, Mercer opposed the proceedings to write a new U.S. **Constitution** and walked out of the meeting with **Luther Martin** and did not sign the document. He also sat in the Maryland convention to ratify the Constitution and again opposed the document. He later served in the U.S. House of Representatives and as governor of Maryland.

MEREDETH, SAMUEL (1741–1817). Samuel Meredeth, a financier and **Revolutionary War** officer, served in the **Pennsylvania** legislature. He represented his state in the **Congress of the Confederation** from 1786–1788 and later became the first treasurer of the United States under the **Constitution**.

MIDDLE COLONIES. The middle colonies included **Delaware**, **New Jersey**, **New York**, and **Pennsylvania**. *See also* AGRICULTURE.

MIDDLE DEPARTMENT. The **Second Continental Congress** established the Middle Department as a **military department** on February 27, 1776. Congress originally authorized the assignment of a major general and two brigadier generals to each department. However, the Middle Department was the exception and included four brigadier generals due to the size of the area, which consisted of **Delaware**, **Maryland**, **New York**, and **Pennsylvania**. New York was originally considered its own department prior to the establishment of the Middle Department. When the **Continental Army** moved its operations to the **New York City** vicinity, the areas of New York north of the Pennsylvania and **Connecticut** borders became the **Northern Department** and New York City joined the Middle Department.

MIDDLETON, ARTHUR (1742–1787). Arthur Middleton, a planter and the son of **Henry Middleton**, represented **South Carolina** in the **Second Continental Congress** from 1776–1777 and 1781–1782. He signed the **Declaration of Independence**. Although reelected to Congress in 1778, 1779, and 1780, he failed to attend. The British captured Middleton when he was helping to defend **Charleston** in 1780. He was held at Saint Augustine and exchanged in 1781.

MIDDLETON, HENRY (1717–1784). Henry Middleton, a planter and the father of **Arthur Middleton**, represented **South Carolina** in the

First Continental Congress and the **Second Continental Congress** from 1774–1775. He served as the second **president of Congress** of the First Continental Congress. Middleton took the oath of loyalty offered by the British after the fall of **Charleston,** although this apparently did little damage to his reputation in South Carolina.

MIFFLIN, THOMAS (1744–1800). Thomas Mifflin, an active patriot, wrote under the pen name of **Scaevola** during the tea crisis of 1773. He represented **Pennsylvania** in the **First Continental Congress** and entered military service in 1775, rising as high as major general in February 1777. Mifflin served twice as the quartermaster general for the **Continental Army**. His increasing incompetence is often blamed for the shortages during the winter encampment at Valley Forge. Mifflin was also a supporter of the **Conway Cabal**. He resigned in 1779 but later became a delegate to the **Second Continental Congress** where he served from 1782–1784. He held the position of **president of Congress** from 1783–1784. As a delegate to the **Constitutional Convention of 1787**, Mifflin signed the new document for Pennsylvania.

MILITIA. Militia members were part-time state soldiers, like today's National Guard, who could be called to service for short periods of time, generally up to three months. Militia units normally received minimal training and equipment and their performance varied greatly. They tended to form when there was a threat to their general area and disband as the threat moved on to another area. For example, as British General Charles Cornwallis moved from **South Carolina** into **North Carolina**, the militia of the former state tended to return to their homes while those of the latter state gathered to assist American General Nathanael Greene to counter him. In a battle, the militia could be an asset to assist the regular forces or a considerable liability. In some engagements, such as the Battles of Long Island and Camden, the militia melted away at the sight of British bayonets or after offering token resistance. At other engagements, such as the Battles of Bunker Hill, Bennington, Saratoga, Cowpens, King's Mountain, and Eutaw Springs, the militia stood firmly in the face of the British. In the South, many of the battles fought during the **Revolutionary War** were between militia units with few, if any, regular army soldiers in the engagement. This is particularly true of the many small engagements in South Carolina where the Revolutionary War degenerated into a sort of civil war between neighbors as patriot and **loyalist** militia units roamed the state depending upon which regular forces were present. For example, only one regular soldier (the British commander) fought at the Battle of King's Mountain but the combatants included militia members from what are now **Georgia**, North Carolina, South Carolina, **Virginia**, and **Tennessee**. After the Revolutionary War, local communities continued to maintain a militia military system. Many **Massachusetts** militia members faced each other during **Shays's Rebellion**. *See also* ALAMANCE, BATTLE OF THE; CAMBRIDGE; CHARLESTOWN; LEXINGTON-CONCORD, BATTLE OF; MASSACHUSETTS ACTS; MINUTEMEN; NEWPORT; PORTSMOUTH; SALEM; STATE TROOPS.

MIND YOUR 'Ps' AND 'Qs'. This expression emerged during Colonial America. Today, it means for an individual to behave and pay attention to his or her surroundings. In Colonial America, the expression was common in taverns where owners wanted to make sure that their pints (Ps) and quarts (Qs) of **alcoholic** beverages were accounted for and not missing.

MINUTEMEN. Minutemen were members of special **militia** units, known as Minute Companies, in **Massachusetts**. They were formed by direction of the **Massachusetts Acts**, which were in response to the British-imposed **Intolerable Acts of 1774**. The militia members assigned to be Minutemen underwent additional training and were supposed to be ready to form "at a minute's notice" to counter any British military foray from their garrison in **Boston**. Minutemen challenged the British at the **Battle of Lexington-Concord**. **Connecticut**, **Maryland**, **New Hampshire**, and **North Carolina** later formed Minuteman-based units following a request by the **Second Continental Congress** on July 18, 1775. The formation of the **Continental Army** in 1775 outside of Boston led to the elimination of the Minutemen in Massachusetts. Today, the term *Minuteman* has evolved to symbolize all militia units in the early stages of the **Revolutionary War**.

MISSISSIPPI LAND COMPANY. The Mississippi Land Company was a group of **land speculators** who were active after the **French and Indian War**. The company was founded by individuals originally associated with the **Ohio Company**. *See also* LOYAL LAND COMPANY.

MITCHELL, JOHN (?–1768). John Mitchell, a botanist and author from **Virginia**, is perhaps best known for a map of North America that he drew in 1755. His map was reprinted numerous times in various countries and became a standard for use by the British and American governments. American and British negotiators utilized Mitchell's map during the peace talks that led to the **Treaty of Paris of 1783**.

MITCHELL, NATHANIEL (1753–1814). Nathaniel Mitchell, a **Revolutionary War** officer, represented **Delaware** in the **Congress of the Confederation** from 1787–1788. He later served as governor of Delaware.

MITCHELL, STEPHEN (1743–1835). Stephen Mitchell, a **Connecticut** jurist, represented his state in the **Congress of the Confederation** from 1783–1788. Mitchell held numerous judicial positions within Connecticut and later in life sat in the U.S. Senate to fill the unexpired term of **Roger Sherman**.

MOHAWK VALLEY REPORT. The British government prepared the Mohawk Valley Report following the breaking of the **Treaty of Easton** by Americans seeking land in western **Pennsylvania**. The report, completed in November 1761, faulted colonial governors for granting land in areas that the British wanted left as preserves for **Native Americans**. One result of the Mohawk Valley Report and similar documents was the British attempt to demarcate the boundary between colonists and Native Americans. *See also* AUGUSTA, CONFERENCE OF, 1763; AUGUSTA, TREATY OF.

MOHAWKS. American colonists sometimes utilized the names of **Native American** groups as symbols of defiance to the British. In November 1773, announcements signed by "The Mohawks" warned the inhabitants of **New York City** that anyone assisting in the transfer or storage of British tea would face the consequences of their actions. In December 1773, **Boston** locals dressed as Mohawks carried out the **Boston Tea Party**.

MOLASSES ACT OF 1733. The British imposed the Molasses Act on the American **colonies** in 1733. The act placed a six-pence-per-gallon tax on imported molasses. **New England** merchants were importing large quantities of inexpensive molasses from French islands in the Caribbean. French sugar growers, thanks to better management and lower taxes, could offer their product at considerable savings over British-grown sugar. More importantly, the French were often willing to **trade** their sugar for American products such as food and **lumber**. Deals with the French also netted the Americans hard **currency**, which they required in their trade for items directly from **Great Britain**. Naturally, the trade with the French islands economically hurt British sugar growers in the Caribbean. The Molasses Act attempted to provide these British sugar growers with a monopoly in the American market. New Englanders viewed the tax as a danger to their trade and tended to avoid the tax through bribery and **smuggling**. The British actually spent more money on the customs bureaucracy than it received in molasses tax. In response, the British passed the **Sugar Act of 1764** as a measure to correct the flaws in enforcing the Molasses Act. However, this revised tax and its associated increased enforcement procedures further angered the colonists, who saw it as a violation of their rights. The Molasses Act was a precedent for the various taxes imposed on the colonists after the **French and Indian War** and helped generate the conditions that would lead to the **Revolutionary War**. *See also* TAXATION.

MOLLY PITCHER. *See* HAYS, MARY LUDWIG.

MOLYNEUX, ROBERT (1738–1808). Robert Molyneux was a well-known Roman Catholic priest of **Philadelphia** during the period of Revolutionary America. A Jesuit, Molyneux supported **education** and later became the president of Georgetown College.

MONEY. *See* CURRENCY.

MONROE, JAMES (1758–1831). James Monroe, a **Revolutionary War** officer, sat in the **Virginia** legislature and represented his state in the **Congress of the Confederation** from 1783–1786, where he actively supported amendments to strengthen the power of the national government under the **Articles of Confederation**. He attended the **Annapolis Convention** in 1786 but was not a member of the **Constitutional Convention of 1787**. Monroe did sit as a delegate in the Virginia state convention to ratify the U.S. **Constitution**. He later sat in the U.S. Senate and served as the president of the United States from 1817–1825.

MOODY, JAMES (1744–1809). James Moody, a **New Jersey loyalist**, worked as one of the most noted spies for the British military during the **Revolutionary War**. His exploits included escaping from an American jail and the unsuccessful attempt to steal the papers and journals of the **Second Continental Congress** in **Philadelphia**.

MOORE, ANDREW (1752–1821). Andrew Moore, a **Revolutionary War** officer, supported the ratification of the U.S. **Constitution** as a delegate in the **Virginia** state convention of 1788. Moore later served in the U.S. House of Representatives and the U.S. Senate.

MOORE, BENJAMIN (1748–1816). Benjamin Moore, a prominent Episcopal bishop and educator, became president of Columbia College in 1784.

MOREY, SAMUEL (1762–1843). Samuel Morey, an inventor and scientist, is best known for his work on steam engines after 1789. However, he began his initial research and experiments with light and heat around 1780 during the period of Revolutionary America.

MORGAN, GEORGE (1743–1810). George Morgan, a **land speculator**, served as a **Native American** agent for the United States during the **Revolutionary War**.

MORGAN, JOHN (1735–1789). John Morgan, a prominent physician and medical director for the **Continental Army**, founded the University of **Pennsylvania** medical school in 1787.

MOROCCO AND REVOLUTIONARY AMERICA. *See* BARBARY STATES AND REVOLUTIONARY AMERICA.

MORRIS, CADWALDER (1741–1795). Cadwalder Morris, a merchant, was a founder and director of the **Bank of North America**. Cadwalder represented **Pennsylvania** in the **Congress of the Confederation** from 1783–1784.

MORRIS, ELIZABETH (c.1753–1826). Elizabeth Morris was possibly the best-known actress in America immediately after the **Revolutionary War**. She was especially known for her roles in comedies and is said to have attracted considerable attention in public. *See also* THEATER.

MORRIS, GOUVERNEUR (1752–1816). Gouverneur Morris, a half-brother of **Lewis Morris** and **Richard Morris**, represented **New York** in the **Second Continental Congress** from 1778–1779 and signed the **Articles of Confederation**. Morris represented **Pennsylvania** in the **Constitutional Convention** of 1787, where he is reported to have been very active in debate over the new document. He favored a strong central government and a president for life. Morris headed the committee tasked to draft the U.S. **Constitution** and he is credited with much of the specific wording within the document. He signed the Constitution for New York when it was completed. Later, Morris was named minister to **France** and represented New York in the U.S. Senate.

MORRIS, LEWIS (1726–1798). Lewis Morris, the brother of **Richard Morris** and the half-brother of **Gouverneur Morris**, served as a general of the **New York militia** during the **Revolutionary War** and as a member of the New York legislature. From 1775–1776, he represented New York in the **Second Continental Congress** where he signed the **Declaration of Independence**. Lewis supported the ratification of the U.S. **Constitution** at the New York convention of 1788.

MORRIS, RICHARD (1730–1810). Richard Morris, the brother of **Lewis Morris** and half-brother of **Gouverneur Morris**, sat in the

New York legislature. In favor of the U.S. **Constitution**, Morris attended the 1788 New York convention to ratify the document. However, he was absent on the day the delegates signed the ratification resolution.

MORRIS, ROBERT (1734–1806). Robert Morris arrived in America from **Great Britain** in 1747. He became a successful merchant and represented **Pennsylvania** in the **First Continental Congress** in 1774 and the **Second Continental Congress** from 1775–1778 where he signed the **Declaration of Independence**, served on the **Secret Committee**, and became active in the acquisition of munitions and naval vessels for the **Continental** military. Morris became a member of the executive committee of the Second Continental Congress in 1776 and signed the **Articles of Confederation** in 1778.

In 1778, Morris departed Congress and returned home where he served in the Pennsylvania Assembly. He faced accusations of being involved in the controversy that erupted around **Hortalez et Cie** company. An investigation cleared Morris in the matter. He assumed the duties of the superintendent of finances on February 20, 1781, in an attempt to stabilize the American **economy**. Morris has been called the "Financier of the **Revolutionary War**." He established the **Bank of North America**, primarily backed by French money and his own personal credit. Morris resigned in January 1783 due to mounting **debts** and out of frustration with the failure of the states to support the new national government. He changed his mind and remained in office until September 1784 and oversaw the final payments to the demobilizing American army. Morris attended the **Annapolis Convention** of 1786 and represented Pennsylvania at the **Constitutional Convention of 1787**. He signed the U.S. **Constitution** and later served in the U.S. Senate. Toward the end of his life, Morris lost his fortune in **land speculating** and was imprisoned for his debts.

MORTON, JOHN (1724–1777). John Morton served in the **Pennsylvania** legislature early in his life. He represented Pennsylvania in the **First Continental Congress** in 1774 and the **Second Continental Congress** from 1775–1777. Morton signed the **Declaration of Independence**.

MOULTRIE, WILLIAM (1730–1805). William Moultrie, a **Revolutionary War** officer from **South Carolina**, sat in the state legislature after the war and became governor in 1785. Moultrie attended the state convention that ratified the U.S. **Constitution** and later served as governor again.

MUHLENBERG, FREDERICK (1750–1801). Frederick Muhlenberg, a Lutheran clergyman, represented **Pennsylvania** in the **Second Continental Congress** from 1779–1780. In 1787, he presided over the state convention to ratify the U.S. **Constitution**. Muhlenberg later served in the U.S. House of Representatives.

MUHLENBERG, HENRY (1711–1787). Henry Muhlenberg was a noted Lutheran clergyman during the period of Revolutionary America.

MURRAY, JOHN (1741–1815). John Murray, a controversial clergyman, founded the Universalism movement in America.

MURRAY, JUDITH (1751–1820). Judith Murray was a well-known **poet** and author of dramas and comedies during the period of Revolutionary America, although the majority of her work was published after 1789.

MUSIC. Independent nonreligious music developed slowly in Colonial America due to Church opposition to secular tunes, the lack of affordable musical instruments, and a general cultural belief that the profession was beneath a gentleman. Other than religious themes, music during the period of Revolutionary America tended to revolve around political issues. Numerous musical societies did develop prior to the Revolution in many cities throughout the **colonies**. Some of the best-known American musicians emerged at the end of the colonial period and include **William Billings**, **Josiah Flagg**, **Francis Hopkinson**, **Andrew Law**, James Lyon, **Daniel Read**, and **William Tuckey**. Perhaps the most famous song from the **Revolutionary War** period is *Yankee Doodle*, penned in 1767, and adopted by the **Continental Army** soldiers as a marching song. The latter was actually a British-written song intended to make fun of the colonists and their unique culture. Orchestras did exist in Revolutionary America. In

1771, the orchestra of Bethlehem, **Pennsylvania**, boasted 20 musicians playing 11 different instruments. In 1784, the German Reformed Church of **Philadelphia** sold an impressive 2,000 tickets to a concert it organized featuring 250 singers and 50 instruments performing many American-composed works.

MUTINY AND QUARTERING ACT OF 1765. *See* BRITISH MUTINY ACT OF 1765; QUARTERING ACT OF 1765.

MUTINY OF 1780. Some units of the **Continental Army** mutinied late in the **Revolutionary War**. In May 1780, two **Connecticut** regiments mutinied due to cuts in rations during the previous winter and the failure of **Congress** to pay them. **Pennsylvania** troops remained loyal to Congress and prevented the Connecticut troops from deserting as a unit. *See also* MUTINY OF 1781; MUTINY OF 1783.

MUTINY OF 1781. Some units of the **Continental Army** mutinied on three separate occasions in 1781. In January 1781, troops from **Pennsylvania** mutinied against perceived pay problems. They seized weapons, injured several officers who attempted to stop them, and marched on **Congress** in **Philadelphia**. Concessions prompted many to end their mutiny while others left the service. **New Jersey** soldiers mutinied prior to the end of January, prompting General **George Washington** to dispatch a separate force to halt them. The New Jersey men returned to their quarters and two of their leaders were executed in response to the uprising. A third event occurred in May when Pennsylvania troops mutinied. Other continental soldiers persuaded the Pennsylvania men to end their revolt; the leaders of this mutiny were also executed. *See also* MUTINY OF 1780; MUTINY OF 1783.

MUTINY OF 1783. Although **Continental Army** officers did not take up arms against the government in 1783, they did threaten to defy **Congress** if their grievances were not met. In January 1783, numerous officers expressed their concerns about the failure of Congress to pay them. One officer circulated what is known as the Newburgh Address, declaring the right of the men to oppose Congress if that body did not pay them properly. General **George Washington** ended the affair by a personal appeal to the officers. The respect they held for

Washington carried the day and the declaration was withdrawn. *See also* MUTINY OF 1780; MUTINY OF 1781.

– N –

NASH, ABNER (c.1740–1786). Abner Nash sat in the **North Carolina** legislature and became governor of the state between 1780 and 1782. He represented North Carolina in the **Congress of the Confederation** from 1782–1783 and 1785–1786. Although elected as a delegate to the **Annapolis Convention** of 1786, he did not attend and died while a member of Congress that same year.

NATIVE AMERICANS AND REVOLUTIONARY AMERICA. Most Native American groups had been pushed westward past the Appalachian Mountains or into western **New York** and **Pennsylvania** and beyond by the middle of the 18th century. The Revolutionary period opened with the defeat of the French and their Native American allies in the **French and Indian War**. After the war, the British realized they needed to pacify the Native Americans and the most important method involved stemming the eager American colonists who wanted to push westward into Native American lands. As a result, the British announced the **Proclamation of 1763** in a belated attempt to halt the westward migration of colonists. However, the proclamation did little to stop the colonists and prevent warfare with the Native Americans. The largest conflicts between Native Americans and the colonists between the French and Indian War and the **Revolutionary War** were **Pontiac's War** from 1763–1766 and **Lord Dunmore's War** in 1774. During the Revolution, most Native American groups sided with the British. While they did not trust either the British or the Americans, the Native Americans viewed the American colonists as being more dangerous due to the aggressive manner in which they violated the Proclamation of 1763 and other land treaties.

During and after the Revolutionary War, American colonists continued to stream westward. The United States established the first reservation for Native Americans in 1786. Notable Native Americans during the Revolutionary America period included **Atta-Kulla-Kulla**, **Cornplanter**, **Cornstalk**, **Dragging Canoe**, **James Logan**,

Alexander McGillivray, **Oconostota**, **Outacity**, **Pontiac**, **Red Jacket**, **Skenandoa**, **Nancy Ward**, and **White Eyes**. Some of the more prominent Christian missionaries among the Native Americans during this period included **Joseph Brandt** (a Native American), **Gideon Hawley**, **John Heckewelder**, **John Jungman**, **Samuel Kirkland**, **Daniel Marshall**, **Christian Post**, **William Savery**. Traders and merchants among the Native Americans included **James Adair**, **George Croghan**, **George Morgan**, **William Panton**, and **James Robertson**. *See also* ALBANY CONGRESS; ALBANY PLAN OF UNION; AUGUSTA, CONFERENCE OF, 1763; AUGUSTA, TREATY OF; BACON, JOHN; CHEROKEE; CREEK; EASTON, TREATY OF; IROQUOIS; MOHAWK VALLEY REPORT; FORT STANWIX, SECOND TREATY OF; FORT STANWIX, TREATY OF.

NAVAL BOARD. The **Second Continental Congress** established the Naval Board on November 6, 1776, to oversee the operations of the **Continental Navy**. The Naval Board served under the **Marine Committee**.

NAVAL COMMITTEE. The **Second Continental Congress** established the Naval Committee on October 30, 1775, to replace a three-man congressional committee tasked to review naval policy. The newly established Naval Committee consisted of seven members who were responsible for the purchase and arming of vessels for the **Continental Navy**, officially established on November 25, 1775. On December 14, 1775, Congress changed the name of the body to the **Marine Committee** and altered its size to reflect its new mission of actually constructing and maintaining a navy rather than purchasing secondhand ships. *See also* NAVAL CONSTRUCTION ACT OF 1775.

NAVAL CONSTRUCTION ACT OF 1775. The **Naval Committee** of the **Second Continental Congress**, with a congressional budget of $100,000, approved the construction of the first new vessels for the **Continental Navy** on December 13, 1775. Up to this point, ships for the navy had been purchased from private sources. The new ships were to be **frigates** and included the *Raleigh*, *Hancock*, *Warren*, *Washington*, *Randolph*, *Providence*, *Trumbull*, *Congress*, *Virginia*, *Effingham*, *Boston*, and *Montgomery*. Additional ships were acquired for the Continental Navy either individually or under the **Naval Construction Act of 1776** or the **Naval Construction Act of 1777**.

NAVAL CONSTRUCTION ACT OF 1776. The **Marine Committee** of the **Second Continental Congress** approved the construction of 10 new vessels for the **Continental Navy** in November 1776. The planned vessels included three 74-gun **ships of the line**, five 36-gun **frigates**, one 18-gun **brig**, and one packet ship. The *Alliance* was the only frigate completed based on appropriations from this act, and the *America* was the only ship of the line completed out of the three planned. Congress presented the *America* to **France** as a gift. Additional ships were acquired for the Continental Navy either individually or under the **Naval Construction Act of 1775** or the **Naval Construction Act of 1777**.

NAVAL CONSTRUCTION ACT OF 1777. The **Marine Committee** of the **Second Continental Congress** approved the construction of two new vessels for the **Continental Navy** on January 23, 1777. These vessels were the **frigates** *Bourbon* and *Confederacy*. The Act of 1777 followed the **Naval Construction Act of 1776** by only two months. The Act of 1777 in many ways an amendment to the Act of 1776, involved state politics. **Connecticut** had not been included as a building site for any of the vessels appropriated under the Act of 1776. The Act of 1777 named Connecticut as the construction site of the two new frigates. Additional ships were acquired for the Continental Navy under the **Naval Construction Act of 1775** or individually.

NAVAL STORES INDUSTRY. Naval stores included the production of rope, pitch, tar, and turpentine for the **shipbuilding industry** as well as general maintenance of naval vessels. Most of these products were derived from the **lumber industry**. The British encouraged this industry within the American **colonies**. In 1768, 140,000 barrels of pitch, tar, and turpentine were exported to **Great Britain**. This amount does not take into account the many thousands of barrels produced for the domestic American shipbuilding industry. The **economic** fate of this industry hinged on the domestic shipbuilding industry and the lack of commercial treaties with Great Britain and other countries after the **Revolutionary War**. The naval stores industry required several years to recover after the Revolution.

NAVY BOARD OF THE EASTERN DEPARTMENT. A Navy Board established in **Boston**, on April 17, 1777, assumed naval jurisdiction for the **Eastern Department**. The three members of the board have been praised for their diligence and knowledge of naval affairs and the board continued in existence until 1781. *See also* BOARD OF ADMIRALTY; NAVAL BOARD; NAVY BOARD OF THE MIDDLE DEPARTMENT.

NAVY BOARD OF THE MIDDLE DEPARTMENT. A Navy Board established in **Philadelphia** in October 1776 assumed naval jurisdiction for the **Middle Department**. The three commissioners appointed to the board conducted little business, since most ships of the **Continental Navy** chose to avoid Philadelphia due to the dangers of encountering the British. In addition, individuals tended to avoid the board and conduct business directly with the **Marine Committee** or the **Board of Admiralty**. *See also* NAVAL BOARD; NAVY BOARD OF THE EASTERN DEPARTMENT.

NELSON, THOMAS, JR. (1738–1789). Thomas Nelson, a merchant, sat in the **Virginia** legislature and represented the **colony** and then the state in the **Second Continental Congress** from 1775–1777 and then again in 1779. He signed the **Declaration of Independence** in 1776. Nelson held a state commission as a brigadier general in the **militia** and helped to organize the resistance to the British raids in Virginia during 1779. As governor of Virginia in 1781, Nelson personally led the state militia to join the army of General **George Washington** at the Battle of Yorktown. He resigned before the end of 1781 due to ill health.

NETHERLANDS AND REVOLUTIONARY AMERICA. **King George III** of **Great Britain**, in need of soldiers to suppress the **Revolutionary War**, requested that a Scots mercenary unit, known as the Scots Brigade, serving with the Dutch army be released to the British. The Dutch leaders declined the request, forcing King George to turn to recruiting **Hessians**.

Officially neutral for most of the Revolutionary War, the Dutch provided and transshipped military supplies to the Americans. The Dutch West Indies port of **Saint Eustatius** served as an early haven for American vessels operating in the Caribbean. In addition, Dutch ports serviced American vessels including the *Serapis*, captured and commanded by John Paul Jones after losing the *Bonhomme Richard*. Some historians believe that Jones held secret orders to utilize a Dutch rather than French port, if possible, to help fan the discord between the Netherlands and Great Britain.

The **Second Continental Congress** dispatched **Henry Laurens** to negotiate an alliance; however, he was captured by the British while at sea. Congress then sent **John Adams** to replace Laurens and he arrived in the Dutch capital in June 1780. **France** worked behind the scenes to keep the Netherlands as a neutral state. At this time neutral countries were permitted, with many exceptions, to ship goods in and out of the ports of belligerents. Great Britain wanted to see the Netherlands enter the conflict in order to curtail the growing Dutch commercial fleet and its operations with London's enemies. Great Britain, citing the papers it had captured from Henry Laurens, declared war on the Netherlands in December 1780.

The Dutch finally officially recognized the United States of America as an independent country on April 19, 1782. The United States then negotiated a loan and treaty of commerce with the new ally. American exports to the Dutch included **naval stores**, **rice**, and **tobacco** while the United States imported very little from the Netherlands. As a result, American ships brought much needed specie for use as **currency** back home. Trade with the Netherlands proved to be favorable in economic terms and beneficial to the United States as a path to good relations with the European country. The positive state of relations between the two can be seen in the Dutch offer to assume the entire American debt through a buy-out process. *See also* CAPELLEN, JOHAN DERCK VAN DER, BARON.

NEVILLE, JOHN (1731–1803). John Neville, a **Revolutionary War** officer, sat as a delegate in the **Pennsylvania** state convention to ratify the U.S. **Constitution**.

NEW ENGLAND ARMY. Discussions about coordinating the **militia** units of New England to counter possible British military operations led to the **Massachusetts** Provincial Congress adopting a proposal to establish a New England Army on April 8, 1775. Little work on this proposal was accomplished until after the **Battle of Lexington-Concord** later that same month. General Artemas Ward, the commander of the troops besieging **Boston**, offered a series of unit organizational proposals on April 23, 1775, which the Provincial Congress accepted. Under this plan, the New England Army would consist of 30,000 men, with Massachusetts providing 13,600 troops. The other colonies included in the New England Army were **Connecticut**, **New Hampshire**, and **Rhode Island**. Despite the participation of all four colonies, the New England Army never achieved a strength above 20,000 men during its short life.

The New England Army fought its first battle at Bunker Hill on June 17, 1775. Despite inflicting a massive 42% casualty rate on the attacking force of General William Howe, it was forced to withdraw from the hills on **Charlestown** Peninsula. The New England Army suffered from a lack of coordination and a strong centralized authority, which would help lead to the establishment of a **Continental Army** under the control of the **Second Continental Congress** on June 14, 1775, three days prior to the Battle of Bunker Hill. With the establishment of the Continental Army, Congress agreed to accept responsibility for the New England Army and to incorporate it into the Continental Army.

NEW ENGLAND COLONIES. The New England colonies included **Connecticut**, **Massachusetts**, **New Hampshire**, and **Rhode Island**. *See also* AGRICULTURE; FISHING INDUSTRY; POTASH PRODUCTION; SHIPBUILDING INDUSTRY.

NEW ENGLAND CURRENCY ACT OF 1751. *See* CURRENCY ACT OF 1751.

NEW HAMPSHIRE. New Hampshire, one of the **New England colonies**, was governed by **Great Britain** as a **royal colony** until the **Revolutionary War** and American independence. By the end of America's revolutionary period in 1790, the state boasted 141,885 (0.1% slaves). New Hampshire supported the pre-Revolutionary War opposition to British **taxation** policies. In 1774, **militia** members from the **colony** seized British cannons in **Portsmouth** and in 1775 rushed to neighboring **Massachusetts** to help engage the

British in **Boston** after the **Battle of Lexington-Concord**. New Hampshire is the only one of the 13 original states in which a battle with the British did not occur during the Revolutionary War. New Hampshire adopted its own constitution in January 1776, essentially declaring itself independent of Great Britain and then signed the Declaration of Independence with the other 12 states in July. The state ratified the U.S. **Constitution** on June 21, 1788. New Hampshire produced few exports and most residents were small farmers who might also work in the **lumber industry**. Notable individuals from New Hampshire during this period include **Josiah Bartlett**, **Nicholas Gilman**, John Longdon, **John Sullivan**, **Matthew Thornton**, and **William Whipple**.

NEW JERSEY. New Jersey, one of the **middle colonies**, was governed by **Great Britain** as a **royal colony** until the **Revolutionary War** and American independence. By the end of America's revolutionary period in 1790, the state boasted 180,139 people (6.2% slaves). Located between **New York City** and **Philadelphia**, New Jersey became a major battleground during the Revolutionary War with the British occupying the former and the American capital in the latter for most of the conflict. New Jersey delegates to the **Constitutional Convention of 1787** were instrumental in helping develop what became known as the **New Jersey Plan**, a proposal for a governmental structure intended to limit the power of larger states under a new U.S. **Constitution**. The **Connecticut Compromise** merged this plan with the competing **Virginia Plan**. The state ratified the U.S. Constitution on December 18, 1787. New Jersey was the largest producer and exporter of **copper** and the second-largest producer and exporter of **iron** in the United States during this period. Notable individuals from New Jersey during this period include **Abraham Clark**, **Frederick Frelinghuysen**, **John Hart**, **William Livingston**, **William Paterson**, **Jonathan Sergeant**, and **John Witherspoon**.

NEW JERSEY PLAN. **William Paterson** of **New Jersey** proposed the New Jersey Plan at the **Constitutional Convention of 1787** as a means to enhance the power of the states with smaller populations and ensure that the states with larger populations did not completely control the new government. The New Jersey Plan included the following provisions:

1. A single-house national legislature with each state having equal representation.
2. The national legislature would have the existing legislative powers of the **Articles of Confederation** with the addition of the ability to levy limited taxes and regulate commerce.
3. A national executive consisting of multiple members elected by the national legislature. State governors would have the power to remove members of the national executive.
4. A national judiciary appointed by the national executive.

After considerable debate, delegates at the Constitutional Convention reached an agreement, known as the **Connecticut Compromise**, that incorporated ideas from both the New Jersey Plan and the rival **Virginia Plan** with the large population states.

NEW YORK. New York, one of the **middle colonies**, was governed by **Great Britain** as a **royal colony** until the **Revolutionary War** and American independence. By the end of America's revolutionary period in 1790, the state boasted 340,170 people (6.2% slaves). A large percentage of New York's population remained loyal to the British Crown during the Revolutionary War and the state produced an equal number of **Continental** and **loyalist** regiments. The greatest occurrences of anti-British political resistance prior to the Revolution occurred in **New York City** as demonstrated by the **New York Restraining Act of 1767** and the incident at **Golden Hill** in 1770. At least 30,000 residents departed with the British at the end of the war. The state ratified the U.S. **Constitution** on October 26, 1788, due in part to the influence of the ***Federalist Papers***. New York was the largest producer and exporter of flax seed, the second-largest producer and exporter of **wheat**, and the fourth-largest producer and exporter of flour and corn in the United States during this period. Notable individuals from New York during this period include **George Clinton**, **James Duane**, **William Floyd**, **Alexander Hamilton**, **John Jay**, **Francis Lewis**, **Philip Livingston**, **Gouverneur Morris**, and **Lewis Morris**.

NEW YORK CITY. Like today, New York City was an important American port city during Revolutionary America. The **Continental Army** under General **George Washington** shifted operations to New York City in April 1776 after the British evacuated **Boston**. The British military began arriving off New York City on June 25, 1776. Following a series of defeats during the summer and fall of 1776, Washington withdrew his reduced force and moved into **New Jersey** to protect the **Second Continental Congress** gathered in **Philadelphia**. A fire erupted in New York City during the early morning hours of September 21, 1776, during the British occupation. Nearly 500 buildings were consumed before British soldiers and locals extinguished the flames. Although patriots were blamed as the arsonists, proof of this accusation has never materialized. The destruction caused by the fire made quartering British soldiers in the city difficult. The British occupied New York City until the end of the **Revolutionary War**.

NEW YORK DEPARTMENT. *See* NORTHERN DEPARTMENT.

NEW YORK RESTRAINING ACT OF 1767. After the **French and Indian War**, the British government wanted to force the American **colonies** to pay more of the burden for their own defense. The **Townshend Acts of 1767** included the New York Restraining Act of 1767, sometimes known as the New York Suspending Act of 1767. The New York Assembly had refused to comply with the **Quartering Act of 1765** and a large percentage of British troops were based in **New York City**. The assembly declared that the colony of New York should not have to bear such a large share of the cost for the maintenance of British soldiers in the American colonies. The New York Restraining Act of 1767 went into effect on October 1, 1767, and suspended the legislative authority of the New York Assembly until it complied with the Quartering Act of 1765.

The New York Assembly opted to provide limited funding for the British soldiers. However, the British still dissolved the assembly under the provisions of the New York Restraining Act of 1767 for failing to fully comply. A new assembly, elected in January 1769, agreed to fulfill the requirements of the Quartering Act of 1765. At this point, the British government lifted the New York Restraining Act of 1767. These actions further strained relations between the colonial government of New York and the British government in London. Relations between the citizens of New York and the British soldiers stationed in the colony also deteriorated, leading to the clash at **Golden Hill** in 1770.

NEW YORK SUSPENDING ACT OF 1767. *See* NEW YORK RESTRAINING ACT OF 1767.

NEW YORK VOLUNTEERS. Oliver DeLancey organized three battalions of **provincials** under the title "New York Volunteers." One battalion fought in the northern theater of operations while the other two fought for the British in the south. The New York Volunteers represent one example of the many regular military units formed of **loyalist** Americans to fight for the British against those Americans desiring independence.

NEWCOMER, CHRISTIAN (1749–1830). Christian Newcomer, a clergyman, was one of the founders of the Church of the United Brethren in Christ.

NEWPORT. The **New England colonies** grew weary of the British **Intolerable Acts** imposed after the **Boston Tea Party** in 1774. In December of that year, Rhode Island **militia** seized 44 cannon at Fort George in **Newport**. Militia units throughout New England conducted similar raids in order to secure weapons and ammunition for storage in case hostilities erupted with the British garrison in **Boston**. Tense relations between the colonists and British would eventually lead to open conflict at the **Battle of Lexington-Concord** the following spring. *See also* CAMBRIDGE; CHARLESTOWN; PORTSMOUTH.

NEWSPAPERS. Newspapers flourished in Revolutionary America and most were vehicles of debate for issues such as **taxation** of the **colonies**. Most newspapers were published three or fewer times a week, consisted of up to four pages, and were not widely circulated outside of the cities in which they were printed. Newspapers frequently received their stories from distant areas by acquiring copies of newspapers from other colonies and repeating their material. At the opening of the Revolution there were 37 newspapers in the 13 colonies (one-third of the newspapers were published in the **New England colonies**). Of these, 23 newspapers displayed a pro-patriot leaning in their stories and editorials while 7 can be considered loyalist and an additional 7 seen as neutral in the political struggle leading to the **Revolutionary War**. The number of newspapers grew to 43 by 1783 and continued to increase throughout the rest of the century. On May 30, 1783, the *Pennsylvania Evening Post* of **Philadelphia** became the first daily newspaper in the United States. Prominent newspaper editors and publishers included **William Bradford**, **John Carter**, **Benjamin Edes**, **Thomas Green**, **George Kline**, and **Samuel Loudon**. *See also JOURNAL OF THE TIMES*; PUBLICATIONS.

NICHOLAS, GEORGE (c.1754–1799). George Nicholas, the brother of **Wilson Nicholas**, sat as a delegate in the 1788 **Virginia** state convention to ratify the U.S. **Constitution**. He later emerged as an important figure in the movement to establish **Kentucky** as a separate state.

NICHOLAS, WILSON (1761–1820). Wilson Nicholas, a member of the **Virginia** legislature and the brother of **George Nicholas**, attended the 1788 state convention to ratify the U.S. **Constitution**. Nicholas later held seats in the U.S. Senate and U.S. House of Representatives.

NONIMPORTATION AGREEMENTS. On August 1, 1768, merchants in **Boston** established the first nonimportation agreements to counter the **Townshend Acts of 1767**. The merchants agreed to not import or purchase most British goods through 1769. They also called for locals to produce their own substitutes for the imports. Merchants in other **colonies** slowly adopted their own nonimportation agreements. The **Sons of Liberty** frequently oversaw the enforcement of nonimportation agreements. *See also* TRADE.

NORMAN, JOHN (c.1748–1817). John Norman was a prominent engraver and publisher during the period of Revolutionary America.

NORTH, LORD FREDERICK (1732–1792). Lord North served as the British prime minister between 1770 and 1782. He assumed the office following a very controversial parliamentary election in 1769. Throughout his administration, Lord North supported **King George III**, who helped put him into power. He entered office and removed the **Townshend Acts of 1767**, which were so dreaded by the American colonists. However, this action represented Lord North's conciliatory gesture to British merchants rather than the American colonists. He did leave the duty on tea in place since this commodity did not originate in **Great Britain**. Following the **Boston Tea Party** in 1774, North took a hard stance against the American colonists and the **Intolerable Acts** were a result of his call for action against the **colonies**. After the prolongation of the **Revolutionary War** and a growing political opposition in Parliament, Lord North agreed to introduce two conciliatory bills in 1777, known as the **Conciliatory Propositions**, and terms for a peaceful solution. The **Carlisle Peace Commission**, an unsuccessful offer of peace, was followed by the retaliatory **Carlisle Proclamation**. Lord North resigned in 1782 after learning of General Charles Cornwallis's surrender at the Battle of Yorktown.

NORTH AMERICAN SQUADRON. The North American Squadron was the British naval unit assigned to the waters of North America. In January 1775, it consisted of 24 vessels. Although the squadron contained a mix of vessels, only four ships (all assigned to **Boston** at this time) mounted 50 or more guns. The majority of the squadron's ships were smaller and faster vessels that served as customs enforcers. By the end of the war, the North American squadron had greatly increased in size in order to protect merchant vessels from American **privateers**.

NORTH BRIDGE. The North Bridge, located in the town of Concord, **Massachusetts**, is the location where patriot **militia** engaged British forces in the opening of the fighting that would become known as the **Battle of Lexington-Concord**.

NORTH BRITON NO. 45. *See* 45.

NORTH CAROLINA. North Carolina, one of the **southern colonies**, was governed by Great Britain as a **royal colony** until the **Revolutionary War** and American independence. By the end of America's Revolutionary period in 1790, the state boasted 393,751 people (25.5% slaves). Farmers, now known as **regulators**, in western North Carolina rebelled against the colonial government in the east in 1771. They complained about **taxation**, corrupt officials, and general neglect by the government in the eastern part of the **colony**. The regulators were dispersed after the **Battle of the Alamance**. Many North Carolinians supported the anti-British measures of the **New England colonies** on the issues of taxation and liberties as seen in the development of the **Mecklenburg Resolves** in 1775. The initial attempt to ratify the U.S. **Constitution** failed at the state's **Hillsborough convention** due to concerns about the protection of individual liberties. The state ratified the Constitution on November 21, 1789, at its **Fayetteville convention** after **Congress** proposed the **Bill of Rights**. North Carolina was the largest producer and exporter of pitch and tar, the second-largest producer and exporter of turpentine, and the fifth-largest producer and exporter of **tobacco** in the United States during this period. Notable individuals from North Carolina during this period include **Cornelius Harnett**, **Benjamin Hawkins**, Joseph Hewes, **John Penn**, and **Richard Spaight**.

NORTH CHURCH. The North Church in **Boston** was the location where patriots agreed to hang lanterns to signal that British troops were departing the city for raids into local towns.

NORTH-END MOB. The North-End Mob was a loose organization of individuals living in the northern sections of **Boston**. The mob was well known for its rowdy confrontations with a similar group known as the **South-End Mob** every November 5th (the anniversary of Guy Fawkes's gunpowder plot). The two groups became organizers for action against British **taxation** plans in Boston. *See also* LOYAL NINE.

NORTHERN DEPARTMENT. **Congress** established what is known as the Northern Department as a **military department** on June 25, 1775. Originally, it was known as the New York Department and consisted of

New York and the future **Vermont**. When the **Continental Army** moved its operations to the **New York City** vicinity, the areas of New York north of the **Pennsylvania** and **Connecticut** borders were renamed the Northern Department. The southern areas of New York and New York City joined the **Middle Department**. In November 1776, the lower Hudson Valley became a separate department known as the **Highlands Department**.

NORTHWEST ORDINANCE OF 1787. Following the passage of the **Land Ordinance of 1785**, **Congress** turned to discussing a governmental system for the **Northwest Territory**. **Thomas Jefferson** played a major role in developing the **Ordinance of 1784**, the Land Ordinance of 1785, and the Northwest Ordinance of 1787. The Ordinance of 1784 proved inoperable so Congress decided to revise the document. Under the Northwest Ordinance of 1787, the Northwest Territory would be divided into between three and five territorial units that could eventually apply for statehood. Each territory was governed by a congressionally appointed governor and three judges. When the male population reached 5,000 eligible voters, the territory could elect a legislature and send a nonvoting member to Congress. The area could request statehood when the population reached 60,000. **Slavery** was prohibited in any new state carved out of the Northwest Territory. The Northwest Ordinance of 1787 set the precedent of offering American territories the opportunity for statehood and equality with other states rather than remaining as forms of "colonial" holdings of the United States.

NORTHWEST TERRITORY. The Northwest Territory was the first public domain of the United States. The territory, consisting of nearly 200,000,000 acres, lay north and west of the Ohio River and east of the Mississippi River. The original territory had been claimed by various **colonies**/states before, during, and after the Revolution. **Virginia** dropped its claim to the majority of the area in 1784. **Massachusetts** followed Virginia's lead in 1785 and **Connecticut** withdrew its claim in 1786. These acts officially transferred the territory to national authority. **Congress** viewed the area as a means to eliminate the **public debt** and repay **Continental** soldiers who were promised land in exchange for military service during the Revolution. After

Virginia withdrew its claim, Congress passed the **Ordinance of 1784**, the **Land Ordinance of 1785**, and the **Northwest Ordinance of 1787** as means to organize the territory. Congress signed treaties with several **Native American** groups in order to eliminate their claims to land in the eastern and southern part of the territory. On October 22, 1784, the Six Nations withdrew their claims to **Pennsylvania** or territory north of the Ohio River. On January 21, 1785, the Delawares, Chippewas, Ottawas, and the Wyandots withdrew their claims over southern Ohio. Eventually, the states of Illinois, Indiana, Michigan, Ohio, and Wisconsin emerged from the Northwest Territory. The northeastern third of Minnesota was also once part of the Northwest Territory.

NOT WORTH A CONTINENTAL. This expression emerged as a result of the drastic devaluation of American continental **currency** during the **Revolutionary War**. The original issue of continental paper money eventually lost nearly all of its value. Thus, anything with little value would often be referred to as "not worth a continental."

NOVANGLUS LETTERS. In 1774, **John Adams** wrote a series of letters justifying colonial opposition to British policies. These documents were published in the *Boston Gazette* and known as the Novanglus Letters.

– O –

OCCOM, SAMSON (1723–1792). Samson Occom was a noted Christian missionary among the **Native American** Montauk and Oneida tribes.

OCONOSTOTA (?–1785). Oconostota was a **Cherokee** chief prior to and throughout most of Revolutionary America. He fought for **Great Britain** during the **Revolutionary War**.

ODELL, JONATHAN (1737–1818). Jonathan Odell, a **loyalist**, served as an agent for the British military. Odell assisted in passing communications between American turncoat Benedict Arnold and his British contact, Major John André.

OGILVIE, JOHN (1724–1774). John Olgilvie was a noted Church of England clergyman in **New York** during the period of Revolutionary America.

OHIO COMPANY. The Ohio Company, officially known as the Ohio Company of Associates, was organized on March 1, 1786. The company petitioned **Congress** for land in the **Northwest Territory**. Congress granted 750,000 acres in what is now southeast Ohio to the company for settlement under the provisions of the **Northwest Land Ordinance of 1787**. The company set aside two townships to support an institution of higher learning (this school later emerged as Ohio University). The Ohio Company established the first settlement under the Northwest Ordinance of 1787 on April 7, 1788, and named it Marietta. The national government placed the first capital of the Northwest Territory in Marietta on July 15, 1788.

OLD IMPORTERS. "Old Importers" was a nickname given to the **Boston** merchants who refused to comply with the strategy of **nonimportation agreements**. *See also* REAL MERCHANTS.

OLIVE BRANCH PETITION. After the opening shots of the **Revolutionary War**, many members of the **Second Continental Congress** still preferred a political settlement to the crisis between the American **colonies** and **Great Britain**. **John Dickinson** headed a committee that prepared what is known as the Olive Branch Petition and the other members of Congress signed it on July 8, 1775. The document listed the grievances of the colonies and pledged their desire for reconciliation. The petition reminded readers of the beneficial relations between the colonies and their mother country before 1763 and stressed a desire to return to those conditions. **King George III** refused to receive the emissary carrying the document and in turn issued his own proclamation declaring that he considered the American colonies in a state of rebellion. **John Adams** opposed the petition and some members of Congress supporting independence backed the Olive Branch Petition, correctly believing that the king would reject the petition and thus help swing other congressmen to the side of complete independence. *See also* DECLARATION OF THE CAUSES AND NECESSITIES FOR TAKING UP ARMS.

OLIVER, ANDREW (1731–1799). Andrew Oliver was a noted scientist during the period of Revolutionary America. He wrote important papers on many subjects including electricity, meteorology, and astronomy.

ORDERS IN COUNCIL OF 1783. The British Orders denied **trade** privileges that were in existence prior to the Revolution to the merchants of the newly independent United States. **Great Britain** chose to discuss trade with individual states and the new American federal government was too weak to intervene. At the same time, the British refused to negotiate a commercial treaty, using the lack of American compensation to **loyalists** as the official reason. Americans countercharged that British posts still existed in the area known as the **Northwest Territory**.

ORDINANCE OF 1784. **Thomas Jefferson** played a major role in developing this document as well as the **Land Ordinance of 1785** and the **Northwest Ordinance of 1787**. The Ordinance of 1785 called for dividing the **Northwest Territory** into 10 territorial units. When each unit reached a population of 20,000, it could prepare a constitution, develop its own government, and send a nonvoting representative to **Congress**. When the population reached the level of the least populous original state, the area could petition Congress for statehood. A call for eliminating **slavery** from the Northwest Territory after 1800 was rejected. The ordinance passed on April 23, 1784, but never became operational. It was replaced by the Northwest Ordinance of 1787.

ORDINANCE OF 1786. Congress passed the Ordinance of 1786 in an attempt to end the conflict with **Native American** groups in the Ohio area following the collapse of the **Treaty of Fort Finney**. The ordinance provided for an Indian Department within the national government. Superintendents would be appointed to protect the interests of Native Americans. This action did not end the violence between Native Americans and settlers in the Ohio region. *See also* FORT MCINTOSH, TREATY OF; FORT STANWIX, SECOND TREATY OF.

ORR, HUGH (1715–1798). Hugh Orr was an inventor and manufacturer during the periods of colonial and Revolutionary America. During the **Revolutionary War**, he manufactured cannon for the American cause, utilizing a new boring technique. He was also a major advocate of the use of machinery to replace hand labor in manufacturing.

OSGOOD, SAMUEL (1747 or 1748–1813). Samuel Osgood sat in the **Massachusetts** legislature and represented his state in the **Second Continental Congress** in 1781 and the **Congress of the Confederation** from 1781–1784. While in Congress, he was appointed a director of the **Bank of North America**. Osgood later served as U.S. postmaster general.

OSWEGO, TREATY OF. The Treaty of Oswego, signed on July 24, 1766, ended what is known as **Pontiac's War**. Despite the viciousness and length of the **Native American** uprising, **Pontiac** followed the Treaty of Oswego and became a British ally until his death in 1769.

OTIS, JAMES (1725–1783). James Otis, an attorney and early patriot, helped lead American opposition to the **Sugar Act of 1764** and the **Stamp Act of 1765**. As the King's Advocate General for the **Admiralty Court** in **Boston** in 1760, Otis chose to resign rather than argue on behalf of the British customs collectors who wanted **writs of assistance** to help them search for illegal goods being transported by Americans. Otis proved to be instrumental in the calling and formation of the **Stamp Act Congress** of 1765. His leadership of the patriot movement waned before the opening shot of the **Revolutionary War**. In 1769, a political opponent struck Otis in the head and he never fully recovered from the wound. Many friends reported that he would fly into irrational rages and often drank to excess. He died after being struck by lightning. *See also* ARMSTRONG, FREEBORN; HAMPDEN, JOHN.

OTTO, BODO (1711–1787). Bodo Otto was a prominent **Pennsylvania** physician and the senior surgeon of the **Continental Army** during the **Revolutionary War**.

OUTACITY (?–1777). Outacity was a **Cherokee** chief during the period of Revolutionary America and fought for **Great Britain** during the **Revolutionary War**.

– P –

PACA, WILLIAM (1740–1799). William Paca sat in the **Maryland** legislature and represented his colony and then state in the **First Continental Congress** in 1774 and **Second Continental Congress** from 1775–1779. He signed the **Declaration of Independence**. Paca held state and national posts for judges between 1779 and 1782 and was elected governor of Maryland in 1782, serving in this post until 1785. He represented Maryland at the **Constitution Convention** of 1787 and voted in favor of the U.S. **Constitution**. Later, Paca filled a post as a federal judge.

PAINE, ROBERT (1731–1814). Robert Paine served in the **Massachusetts** legislature and represented Massachusetts in the **First Continental Congress** in 1774 and **Second Continental Congress** from 1775–1776. He signed the **Declaration of Independence**. Although reelected to Congress in 1777, Paine chose not to attend. Paine signed the **Olive Branch Petition** and is one of the few individuals to have signed both this document and the Declaration of Independence when the British government refused to respond in terms acceptable to the American colonists. Paine became the first attorney general of Massachusetts in 1777 and later accepted a seat on the state supreme court.

PAINE, THOMAS (1737–1809). Thomas Paine arrived in **Philadelphia** from England in 1774 and quickly became an avid patriot. He wrote the successful pamphlet ***Common Sense*** and published it in January 1776. After enlisting in the **Continental Army**, he also authored ***Crisis***, first published on December 19, 1776, in Philadelphia. Paine's works were read to the American army prior to the Battles of

Trenton and Princeton to rekindle enthusiasm for the task of securing American independence. In 1780, he wrote ***Public Good***.

PAINTING. Painting as an American art form grew slowly during the colonial period due to the harshness of life and religious restrictions. As a result, most of the notable artists of the Revolutionary America period emerged late in the colonial history of the **colonies** or after independence. Artists who achieved notoriety during this period included **Mather Brown, John Copley**, **Ralph Earle**, **John Hesselius**, **Samuel King**, **Charles Willson Peale**, **Matthew Pratt**, **John Ramage**, **Gilbert Stuart**, **Jeremiah Theus**, and **Benjamin West**. *See also* CRAFTS; MUSIC; THEATER.

PANTON, WILLIAM (1742?–1801). William Panton, a **loyalist**, was a noted merchant and trader among the **Native Americans** in what is now Florida.

PAPER MONEY. *See* CURRENCY.

PARIS, TREATY OF, 1763. The Treaty of Paris of 1763 officially ended what is known as the Seven Years' War by Europeans and the **French and Indian War** by North Americans on February 10, 1763. The provisions of this treaty had a significant impact on the crisis that would erupt between the American **colonies** and **Great Britain** from 1763–1775 when the first shots were fired in the **Revolutionary War**. In the treaty, **France** surrendered **Canada** and the North American interior to Great Britain while **Spain** turned over West and East Florida in exchange for Cuba. Under a separate treaty, France transferred its land holdings west of the Mississippi River to Spain. The treaty thus eliminated France, the common opponent of Great Britain and the American colonies, and opened the way for a potential settlement of the western lands. The crises that led to the opening of hostilities between Great Britain and the colonies began almost immediately after the Treaty of Paris with the **Proclamation of 1763**.

PARIS, TREATY OF, 1783. The **Revolutionary War** ended officially with the Treaty of Paris, signed on September 3, 1783. The **Congress of the Confederation** ratified the document in January 1784 and exchanged ratified copies with **Great Britain** in May 1784. The treaty granted British recognition of American independence, established the boundaries of the new country, permitted American **fishing** rights off **Canada**, provided amnesty for actions during the war, encouraged states to restore confiscated property and the rights of **loyalists**, ordered the removal of all British forces from the United States, permitted free navigation along the Mississippi River, and restored seized territory. The British did not adhere to some of these points and reluctantly followed others.

PARKE, JOHN (1754–1789). John Parke, a **Revolutionary War** officer, is best known as a **poet** of the Revolutionary America period.

PAROLE. Parole involved releasing prisoners in exchange for their promise not to return to active hostilities. After capture, many **militia** and regular soldiers were paroled rather than shipped to prisoner-of-war camps. While on parole, an individual could remain at home and conduct his normal occupation, such as farming, but was prohibited from participating in military actions against those who had captured him. Those who broke their parole were subject to immediate arrest and, frequently, execution.

PARSON'S CAUSE. *See* TWO PENNY ACT OF 1758.

PARSONS, THEOPHILUS (1750–1813). Theophilus Parsons, a lawyer, sat in the 1788 **Massachusetts** convention to ratify the U.S. **Constitution**. Parsons later served in the state legislature and filled the post of chief justice of the Massachusetts Supreme Court.

PATERSON, WILLIAM (1745–1806). William Patterson sat in the **New Jersey** legislature but declined to accept a seat in the **Second Continental Congress** in 1780. In 1776, he became state attorney general and held that position until 1783. Patterson represented New Jersey in the **Constitutional Convention of 1787** and signed the U.S. **Constitution**. He introduced the **New Jersey Plan** of government during the convention. He later served in the U.S. Senate, played a significant role in drafting the Judiciary Act of 1789, and became an associate justice of the U.S. Supreme Court.

PAXTON BOYS. Many settlers in western **Pennsylvania** resented what they perceived as a lack of adequate protection from the government during **Pontiac's War** and attacked the peaceful Susquehannock **Native Americans**, killing six of them. When the survivors were moved for their safety to Lancaster, some settlers followed and killed another 14 Native Americans on December 27, 1763. The governor called for the arrest of 50 of these settlers, known as the Paxton Boys. However, locals refused to find the men guilty. Several hundred of these settlers initiated an armed march toward **Philadelphia** in January 1764. **Benjamin Franklin** played a significant role in persuading them to return to their homes. Similar discontent would lead to the **regulator** movement in **North Carolina**.

PEALE, CHARLES WILLSON (1741–1827). Charles Willson Peale emerged as one of the first American-born **painters** to earn distinction during Revolutionary America. Between 1766 and 1769, he studied art in London with **Benjamin West**. Peale established a portrait business in **Maryland** and **Philadelphia** after returning from London and later painted in **Boston**. He founded the Museum of Natural History of Philadelphia in 1784 and later the **Pennsylvania** Academy of Fine Arts.

PEERY, WILLIAM (1743–1800). William Peery represented **Delaware** in the **Congress of the Confederation** in 1786.

PENDLETON, EDMUND (1721–1803). Edmund Pendleton, a lawyer and early patriot, represented **Virginia** in the **First Continental Congress**. Pendleton played important roles in the formation of the new state government of Virginia until injured in an accident in 1777. He served as the president of the state convention to ratify the U.S. **Constitution**.

PENN, JOHN (1729–1795). John Penn, the grandson of William Penn and the brother of **Richard Penn**, served as lieutenant governor of **Pennsylvania** from 1763–1771 and then 1773–1776. He should not be confused with **John Penn** who signed the **Declaration of Independence** for **North Carolina**.

PENN, JOHN (1740–1788). John Penn, a lawyer, represented **North Carolina** in the **First Continental Congress** in 1774 and the **Second Continental Congress** from 1775–1777 and 1778–1780. He signed the **Declaration of Independence** and the **Articles of Confederation**. He should not be confused with **John Penn** the lieutenant governor of **Pennsylvania**.

PENN, RICHARD (1735–1811). Richard Penn, the grandson of William Penn and brother of **John Penn**, served as lieutenant governor of **Pennsylvania** from 1771–1773. Penn delivered the **Olive Branch Petition** to **King George III**. Penn remained in England for most of his life and served in Parliament on four different occasions.

PENNSYLVANIA. Pennsylvania, one of the **middle colonies**, was governed by **Great Britain** as a **proprietary colony** until the **Revolutionary War** and American independence. By the end of America's Revolutionary period in 1790, the state boasted 434,373 people (0.9% slaves). The governor of Pennsylvania also served as the chief executive of **Delaware**, which had been permitted to elect its own legislature since 1704. In June 1776, Delaware officially cut all ties with Pennsylvania. The **First Continental Congress**, **Second Continental Congress**, **Congress of the Confederation**, and the **Constitutional Convention of 1787** met in **Philadelphia**, the largest town in the state of Pennsylvania. While there were many individuals who supported the pre-Revolutionary War American position on **taxation** and eventual independence, there was little noteworthy anti-British political opposition compared to other colonies. Pennsylvania was the only **colony** that did not border the Atlantic Ocean and most opposition to British policies originated at ports and along the Atlantic seaboard, which were more directly affected by **trade** policies with Great Britain. After the American **Declaration of Independence**, Pennsylvania assumed a more active role in the struggle. The state ratified the U.S. **Constitution** on December 12, 1787. Philadelphia also served as the nation's capital from 1790 until 1800. Pennsylvania was the largest producer and exporter of flour, the second-largest producer and exporter of flax seed, and the fourth-largest producer and exporter of **wheat** in the United States during this period. Notable individuals from Pennsylvania during this period include **George Clymer**, **John Dickinson**, **Benjamin Franklin**, **Robert Morris**, **John Morton**, **Benjamin Rush**, and **James Wilson**.

PERSON, THOMAS (1733–1800). Thomas Person sat in the **North Carolina** legislature. Although elected to represent the state in the **Congress of the Confederation** in 1784, he declined to take his seat. Person opposed the U.S. **Constitution** in the **Hillsborough state convention** and the **Fayetteville state convention**.

PETERS, RICHARD (1744–1828). Richard Peters, a lawyer, represented **Pennsylvania** in the **Congress of the Confederation** from 1782–1783. Peters later served in the state legislature and as a federal judge.

PETERSHAM. *See* SHAYS'S REBELLION.

PETTIT, CHARLES (1736–1806). Charles Pettit, a merchant and **Revolutionary War** officer, sat in the **Pennsylvania** legislature. He represented his state in the **Congress of the Confederation** from 1785–1787. He supported the U.S. **Constitution** in the 1788 Pennsylvania state convention.

PHELPS, OLIVER (1749–1809). Oliver Phelps, a merchant, served in the **Connecticut** legislature and the state convention to ratify the U.S. **Constitution**.

PHILADELPHIA. At the time of Revolutionary America, Philadelphia, **Pennsylvania**, was the largest city in the American **colonies** and then the United States. The city served as the capital of the United States for most of the period of 1776–1789. The British occupied Philadelphia in September 1777 and departed in June 1778.

PICKERING, JOHN (c.1738–1805). John Pickering, a lawyer, sat in the **New Hampshire** legislature. He declined to serve as a delegate to the **Constitutional Convention of 1787** but did attend the New Hampshire state convention to ratify the U.S. **Constitution**. Pickering later served as a presidential elector and federal judge.

PICKERING, TIMOTHY (1745–1829). Timothy Pickering, a lawyer and **Revolutionary War** officer, sat as a delegate in the **Pennsylvania** convention that ratified the U.S. **Constitution**. He later served as the secretary of war and the secretary of state for the United States.

PIERCE, WILLIAM (c.1740–1789). William Pierce, a **Revolutionary War** officer, represented **Georgia** in the **Congress of the Confederation** in 1787 before accepting his state's selection as a delegate to the **Constitutional Convention of 1787**. He departed the convention prior to its completion but is known to have favored the new U.S. **Constitution**.

PILLORY. An individual convicted in the **criminal justice system** might be sentenced to the pillory. Under this rather common form of punishment, the criminal stood with his or her head and arms locked into holes cut into a piece of wood. He or she would have to stand there until completing the sentence, allowing others to throw rotting vegetables or fruit and scorn those being punished. *See also* STOCKS.

PINCKNEY, CHARLES (1757–1824). Charles Pinckney, a **Revolutionary War** officer and cousin of **Charles Cotesworth Pinckney** and **Thomas Pinckney**, sat in the **South Carolina** legislature. He represented South Carolina in the **Congress of the Confederation** from 1784–1787. Pinckney played a significant role in support of the U.S. **Constitution** as a delegate to the **Constitutional Convention of 1787**. He signed the U.S. Constitution. Pinckney later served as state governor, a member of the U.S. Senate, and minister to **Spain**.

PINCKNEY, CHARLES COTESWORTH (1746–1825). Charles Cotesworth Pinckney, a **Revolutionary War** officer, the cousin of **Charles Pinckney**, the brother of **Thomas Pinckney**, and the son of **Elizabeth Pinckney**, served in the **South Carolina** legislature and represented the state in the **Constitutional Convention of 1787**. He signed the U.S. **Constitution**. Pinckney later accepted the post of U.S. minister to **France**.

PINCKNEY, ELIZABETH (c.1722–1793). Elizabeth Pinckney, often known by her maiden name of Eliza Lucas, was the mother of

Charles Cotesworth Pinckney and **Thomas Pinckney**. She is best remembered for her experiments with **indigo** in South Carolina. Her patience and experimentation led to the development of indigo as a major export crop from the state.

PINCKNEY, THOMAS (1750–1828). Thomas Pinckney, the brother of **Charles Cotesworth Pinckney**, the son of **Elizabeth Pinckney**, and the cousin of **Charles Pinckney**, fought as a **Revolutionary War** officer. He became governor of **South Carolina** in 1787 and sat as the president of the 1788 state convention to ratify the U.S. **Constitution**. He served later as the U.S. minister to **Great Britain** and then **Spain**.

PINKNEY, WILLIAM (1764–1822). William Pinkney, a lawyer, sat as a delegate in the 1788 **Maryland** state convention to ratify the U.S. **Constitution**. He opposed ratification of the document. He later served in the Maryland legislature.

PISTOL. A short, single, handheld weapon that loaded and fired similarly to a musket. Pistols were generally carried by officers and members of the cavalry.

PITCHER, MOLLY. *See* HAYS, MARY LUDWIG.

PITT, FORT. Fort Pitt, located at the site of modern Pittsburgh, **Pennsylvania**, served as an important frontier post during **Pontiac's War** and the **Revolutionary War**.

PITT, WILLIAM (1708–1778). William Pitt, a member of the British Parliament, served as prime minister of his country from 1757–1761 and 1766–1768. He frequently defended the American **colonies** during Parliamentary debates on **taxation** issues. However, Pitt, also known as Lord Chatham, did not favor American independence. Pitt died in 1778 as he rose to deliver a speech in Parliament countering a colleague's proposal to make peace with the colonies before **France** could effectively enter the war. His son, known as **William Pitt the Younger**, later became the youngest prime minister in British history.

PITT, WILLIAM, THE YOUNGER (1759–1806). William Pitt, often known as "the Younger," was the son of **William Pitt**, twice prime minister of Britain. William Pitt, the Younger, became Britain's youngest prime minister after the **Revolutionary War**. He followed British business concerns and chose to continue the practice of **mercantilism** against the new United States.

PLAN OF 1776. The **Second Continental Congress** approved the Plan of 1776 on September 17, 1776. The plan, initiated by **Richard Henry Lee**, outlined the policies of the new country toward **trade** and foreign relations. The document included American views on neutral shipping between the ports of belligerent countries and a definition of contraband goods. Following these declarations, Congress appointed **commissioners** to negotiate trade agreements with other countries. *See also* COMMITTEE OF SECRET CORRESPONDENCE; COMMITTEE ON FOREIGN AFFAIRS; FRANCE AND REVOLUTIONARY AMERICA; NETHERLANDS AND REVOLUTIONARY AMERICA; SPAIN AND REVOLUTIONARY AMERICA.

PLAN OF UNION. *See* ALBANY PLAN OF UNION.

PLANTATION DUTY ACT OF 1673. Although originally issued before the Revolutionary America period, the Plantation Duty Act of 1673 remained one of the primary tariff bills applied to the American **colonies** for nearly 100 years. American colonists tended to ignore the act and the British collected few duties from it. After the conclusion of the **French and Indian War**, the British opted to replace the Plantation Duty Act and the **Molasses Act of 1733** with the highly controversial Grenville Plans. *See also* TAXATION.

PLANTATION DUTY ACT OF 1764. *See* SUGAR ACT OF 1764.

PLANTATION DUTY ACT OF 1766. *See* REVENUE ACT OF 1766.

PLATER, GEORGE (1735–1792). George Plater represented **Maryland** in the **Second Continental Congress** from 1778–1780. He presided over the state convention to ratify the U.S. **Constitution**.

Plater later served as a presidential elector and governor of Maryland.

PLIARNE, PENET, ET CIE. Pliarne, Penet, et Cie was a private French firm that purchased and shipped military supplies to the Americans prior to the signing of the **French Treaty of Amity and Commerce**. French officials quietly allowed the company to purchase weapons directly from government arsenals. *See also* FRANCE AND REVOLUTIONARY AMERICA; HORTALEZ ET CIE.

PLOMBARD, MONSIEUR (?). The French government appointed Plombard as its consul based in **Charleston, South Carolina**. Plombard played a major role in planning the disastrous attack on Savannah in 1779.

POETRY. **Philip Freneau** emerged as the first great poet of the Revolutionary period and is noted for his work on the **Revolutionary War**. One of the most famous female poets was **Phillis Wheatley**, an African American **slave** living in **Boston**. She was taken to London before the Revolution, where many of her poems were published as a collection. She returned to the United States as a free woman and continued to write poetry in the post-Revolution years. Other prominent poets of Revolutionary America included **Joel Barlow**, **Ann Bleeker**, **Nathaniel Evans**, **Elizabeth Ferguson**, **Jupiter Hammon**, **Joseph Ladd**, **Peter Markoe**, **Judith Murray**, and **John Parke**. *See also* LITERATURE.

POINT PLEASANT, BATTLE OF. The Battle of Point Pleasant ended what is known as **Lord Dunmore's War** against the **Shawnee** in 1774. Dunmore, the governor of **Virginia**, dispatched a military expedition into Shawnee country to counter attacks by the latter against settlers violating the **Proclamation of 1763**. After this military unit was ambushed, Dunmore called up 1,500 militia from western Virginia. The Shawnee chief **Cornstalk** ambushed the Virginians at Point Pleasant on October 10, 1774 (some historians mark the date as October 6, 1774). The fighting lasted all day and ended in a victory for the Virginia military unit. Subsequent negotiations resulted in the Shawnee withdrawing all claims to the area known today as **Kentucky**. *See also* LOGAN, JAMES.

POLICE. *See* CRIMINAL JUSTICE SYSTEM.

PONTIAC (1720?–1769). Pontiac, a chief of the Ottawa, led a **Native American** uprising against the British in 1763 known as **Pontiac's War**.

PONTIAC'S WAR. **Pontiac**, an Ottawa chief, led an uprising of his people and allies from the Chippewa, Huron, and other **Native American** groups in 1763. The uprising, known as Pontiac's War, resulted from many factors, including prodding by the French after the **French and Indian War**, ill treatment of Native Americans by many British traders, and the illegal movement of **land speculators** onto Native American land. Pontiac initiated his campaign on May 7, 1763, with an attack on the British fort at Detroit. The post had received a warning and managed to hold out against the assault. However, by the end of June, every British fort west of Niagara, except the garrisons at Detroit and Pitt, had fallen to Pontiac's warriors. **Fort Pitt** held out against a savage attack by the Delaware and a relief column from **Philadelphia** defeated the Delaware at the **Battle of Bushy Run**. An initial relief column sent to Fort Pitt received a sharp beating by Pontiac while a second group encountered tough resistance and was defeated at the Battle of Bloody Ridge on August 6, 1763.

By 1764, Pontiac's alliance was coming apart as some warriors questioned his leadership, others were discouraged after the Battle of Bushy Run, and some simply tired of the long siege of Detroit. The British turned to negotiations and slowly achieved an understanding with the various groups that had joined Pontiac. The **Treaty of Oswego**, on July 24, 1766, officially ended Pontiac's War. This conflict represented the most serious uprising by Native Americans during the Revolutionary period. However, it collapsed due to the inability of the various groups to remain united in an alliance for various reasons, the refusal of **France** to become involved in the war despite the assurances of many French traders to the Native Americans, and the refusal of the southern groups, who had agreed to the

Treaty of Augusta, to join the uprising. Pontiac's War was a significant event in Revolutionary America. The conflict helped persuade the British to maintain a permanent military presence within the 13 **colonies**, leading to future confrontations with the colonists who resented having to pay for them through various **taxation** schemes. *See also* BOUQUET, HENRY; EDGEHILL, BATTLE OF.

POOR RICHARD'S ALMANACK. *See* FRANKLIN, BENJAMIN; PUBLICATIONS.

POPLICOLA. Poplicola was the pen name assigned to rebuttals to the ***Alarm*** **newspaper** articles in **New York** attacking British tea policy in 1773. *See also* HAMPDEN.

PORTSMOUTH. American colonists in New England grew weary of the British **Intolerable Acts** imposed after the **Boston Tea Party**. In December 1774, patriot **militia** units seized cannon and ammunition at Fort William and Mary in Portsmouth, **New Hampshire**. Militia units throughout the **New England colonies** were removing weapons and powder from public arsenals and hiding them in case hostilities erupted with the British forces garrisoned in **Boston**. The tense relations between the colonists and the British would eventually result in open conflict at the **Battle of Lexington-Concord** the following spring. *See also* CAMBRIDGE; CHARLESTOWN; NEWPORT.

PORTUGAL AND REVOLUTIONARY AMERICA. Although neutral in the **Revolutionary War**, many military supplies destined for **smuggling** into the American **colonies** and later the United States were transshipped through Portugal. Goods would be moved to Portugal and then sold to American agents who arranged their shipment across the Atlantic Ocean on American or neutral vessels.

POST, CHRISTIAN (c.1710–1785). Christian Post was a prominent Moravian missionary among the **Native Americans** during the period of Revolutionary America.

POTASH PRODUCTION. Potash results from boiling the ashes produced by burning hardwood trees such as birch and oak and is utilized in the production of glass, soap, and some fertilizers. The American **colonies**, especially those in the north, produced considerable quantities of potash due to the abundance of hardwood trees. Potash was exported to **Great Britain** where it was also important for the production of wool cloth. The largest American producers at the opening of the Revolution were **New York** and the **New England colonies**.

POTTS, JONATHAN (1745–1781). Jonathan Potts served as a delegate in the **Pennsylvania** legislature and was a prominent physician within the **Continental Army**.

POTTS, RICHARD (1753–1808). Richard Potts, a lawyer, sat in the **Virginia** legislature and represented his state in the **Second Continental Congress** from 1781–1782. He served as a delegate in the 1788 state convention that ratified the U.S. **Constitution**. He later held posts as a federal attorney and judge.

POWNALL, THOMAS (1722–1805). Thomas Pownall, a member of the British Parliament, proposed legislation within that body in May 1780 calling for peace with the Americans. Parliament rejected the bill.

PRATT, MATTHEW (1734–1805). Matthew Pratt was a noted portrait **painter** during the period of Revolutionary America.

PRESCOTT, SAMUEL (1751–c.1777). Samuel Prescott, a physician, joined **Paul Revere** and **William Dawes** on their ride to warn the residents of Lexington and Concord of the British march from **Boston**. A British patrol captured Revere but Prescott managed to avoid them and rode ahead to warn the **Minutemen** of Concord. The **Battle of Lexington-Concord** would erupt the next morning as the local Minutemen confronted the British column.

PRESIDENT OF CONGRESS. The **First Continental Congress**, the **Second Continental Congress**, and the **Congress of the Confederation** selected an individual from its membership to serve as the president of Congress. Officially, the president who presided over the

First and Second Continental Congresses was known as the president of the Continental Congress and the individual who presided over the Congress of the Confederation was the president of the United States in Congress Assembled. The position was similar in many ways to the current Speaker of the House of Representatives in the sense that the individual presided over Congress when in session. Some individuals have attempted over the years to claim that these individuals were the first U.S. presidents but this is not the case. The presidents of Congress were not heads of an executive branch of government. Most sources state that **John Hanson** served as the first president of Congress under the **Articles of Confederation**. This is not precisely true. Hanson was the first president of Congress selected by a Congress that had been elected after the ratification of the Articles of Confederation on March 1, 1781. Between March 1, 1781, and the seating of the next Congress, **Samuel Huntington** and **Thomas McKean** served as presidents of Congress. A list with each president of Congress is included as appendix D of this book.

PRESIDENT OF THE CONTINENTAL CONGRESS. *See* PRESIDENT OF CONGRESS.

PRESIDENT OF THE UNITED STATES IN CONGRESS ASSEMBLED. *See* PRESIDENT OF CONGRESS.

PRESS. *See* NEWSPAPERS; PUBLICATIONS.

PRESS GANG. *See* IMPRESSMENT.

PRINGLE, JOHN (1753–1843). John Pringle, a lawyer, sat in the **South Carolina** legislature and the 1788 state convention to ratify the U.S. **Constitution**. He served later as a federal attorney and South Carolina attorney general.

PRINTING. Printing has a long tradition in the United States. By the Revolutionary period, most American cities had at least one printer. **Benjamin Franklin** is perhaps the most famous colonial American printer, among many other accomplishments. **Great Britain** attempted to control the printing industry in the American **colonies**

through the use of copyright laws. For example, colonists were forced to purchase Bibles printed in Great Britain because the British government upheld a copyright law that prevented the printing of Bibles by American printers. In 1782, Robert Aitken released the first Bible printed in the United States. The first recorded labor **strike** in the United States involved the printers of **Philadelphia**. The printers successfully received an increase in their weekly wages. Other prominent printers during Revolutionary America included **Robert Aitken**, **Francis Bailey**, **Robert Bell**, **Benjamin Edes**, **Hugh Gaine**, **John Gill**, **William Goddard**, **Jonas Green**, **Thomas Green**, **David Hall**, **Samuel Hall**, **George Kline**, **Samuel Loudon**, **James Rivington**, **Isaiah Thomas**, and **Benjamin Towne**. *See also* NEWSPAPERS; PUBLICATIONS.

PRISONS. *See* CRIMINAL JUSTICE SYSTEM.

PRIVATEER. The **Second Continental Congress** officially authorized privateering on March 23, 1776. Privateers were privately owned, armed merchant ships commissioned by **letters of marque** to attack enemy vessels. Most privateer crewmen were not in the military but were considered civilians. Crews, eager to earn quick money, were easy to recruit for the armed ships. If a captured ship was officially declared a legal **prize**, the crew shared in the proceeds from the sale of the captured vessel and its cargo. The purpose of a privateer was to seize unarmed or lightly armed enemy merchantmen while avoiding warships. Most privateers would flee at the sight of a warship. Although lightly armed, American privateers seized 560 British ships by the end of 1777. Approximately 2,000 privateer ships operated for the United States during the **Revolutionary War**.

With the introduction of **France** into the war, some American privateers sailed in larger and more heavily armed ships. The most successful of the larger privateers was the ***Marlborough***, the victor in 28 captures. The British navy attempted to counter the growing menace of American privateers by sailing in convoys. A large group of merchant ships would assemble and sail together, often with armed escort, to North America. Convoys failed to completely deter the privateers, who would follow the group of vessels waiting to capture any stragglers. At times, one privateer would lure the armed escorts from a convoy while other privateers rushed in to capture a merchantman.

PRIZE. A prize was a vessel, usually seized by a **privateer**, that had been sailed into a friendly port and sold, with all or part of the proceeds going to the crew of the capturing ship. A prize was considered legal if it was seized outside of neutral waters by a vessel carrying a **letter of marque** from a belligerent government.

PROCLAMATION OF 1763. The British government issued the Proclamation of 1763 on October 7, 1763. The document, based on information from the **Mohawk Valley Report**, dealt with three issues. First, the British utilized the document to officially establish governments in four regions (East Florida, Grenada, Quebec, and West Florida) transferred to the country following the **French and Indian War**. Second, the proclamation offered grants of land to veterans of the French and Indian War. However, those wanting to receive the grants had to apply in person. This is the reason several future **Revolutionary War** generals moved to the American **colonies** from England.

The third area addressed by the proclamation involves the boundary between colonial and **Native American** lands. Following the **Treaty of Paris in 1763**, ending the French and Indian War, the British moved to halt the migration of American colonists into the newly secured western lands. American **land speculators** had been acquiring land and encouraging the movement into the interior, but an uprising of the Ottawa known as **Pontiac's War** persuaded the British to initiate actions to stem the flow of colonists and pacify the Native American inhabitants who previously had been French allies.

The proclamation was intended as a temporary measure until a permanent plan could be developed that would provide more land for Americans wanting to move westward. However, most colonists did not understand this provision and only saw the proclamation as a restriction to their movement. The territory from the Mississippi River to the Allegheny Mountains and from Florida to 50 degrees north latitude was reserved for Native Americans. London forbade trade with the Native Americans and the acquisition of land west of the proclamation line that American veterans of the French and Indian War felt the British owed to them. The colonists resented the British policy and openly ignored it as they streamed westward. The proclamation can be seen as one of the many issues that drove a wedge between **Great Britain** and the American colonies, resulting in the Revolution. *See also* HARD LABOR, TREATY OF; LOCHABER, TREATY OF; FORT STANWIX, TREATY OF.

PROHIBITORY ACT OF 1775. *See* AMERICAN PROHIBITORY ACT OF 1775.

PROPRIETARY COLONY. A proprietary **colony** was an area of land granted to an individual or group by the Crown. The arrangement permitted the selection of the governor by the proprietor. Although a proprietary colony was granted the right to self-government, the Crown reserved the right to approve the selection of the governor. After 1760, proprietary colonies included **Delaware**, **Maryland,** and **Pennsylvania**. *See also* CHARTER COLONY; ROYAL COLONY.

PROUD, ROBERT (1728–1813). Robert Proud was a noted **educator** and historian during the period of Revolutionary America.

PROVINCIAL. Provincials were American **loyalists** who enlisted in special British military units during the **Revolutionary War**. The enlistments of the provincials were to last for the duration of the conflict, unlike **militia** members who served for short periods of time before returning home. Thus, the provincials were essentially enlisting in all-American units fighting alongside the British army. Provincials can be seen as the loyalist equivalents of **State Troops** in terms of enlistment durations. The British used provincials to supplement their hard-pressed regular military units and frequently based them outside of their home states to avoid possible problems when the soldiers might have to confront or fire upon neighbors, friends, or relatives supporting the patriot cause.

PRUSSIA AND REVOLUTIONARY AMERICA. **Congress** dispatched American diplomats after the Revolution to negotiate commercial treaties. **John Adams** met with Prussian leaders to discuss a commercial treaty. During the negotiations, Adams departed to assume his new post as ambassador to **Great Britain**. William Short replaced Adams and completed the negotiations in August 1786.

PUBLICATIONS. The relative freedom of the press in Revolutionary America promoted the publication of **newspapers**, magazines, almanacs, and books. Newspapers tended to be the most important items published within Revolutionary America while magazines were fewer in number. Americans produced numerous almanacs, including the famous *Poor Richard's Almanack* edited by **Benjamin Franklin**. Although publication of the latter ended in 1757, its importance to this topic in Revolutionary America should be noted. In May 1784, *Gentlemen and Ladies' Town and Country Magazine* became the first such American publication specifically written to include **women** as readers. *See also* LITERATURE.

PUBLIC GOOD. **Thomas Paine** wrote ***Public Good*** in 1780, four years after his famous pamphlet ***Common Sense***. In *Public Good*, Paine opposes the claims of **Virginia** to the lands between the Appalachian Mountains and the Mississippi River. *See also CRISIS*; KENTUCKY.

PUBLIUS. *See FEDERALIST PAPERS*.

PUNCH. Punch was the name given to a popular **alcoholic** beverage consisting of four or five ingredients, nearly all being a form of liquor. Punch was mixed and served from "punch bowls."

– Q –

QUARTERING ACT OF 1765. British Prime Minister **George Grenville** persuaded Parliament to pass the Quartering Act of 1765 on the heels of the **Sugar Act of 1764**. After the conclusion of the **French and Indian War**, the British opted to retain a permanent military presence in the American **colonies** to help maintain peace on the frontier and prevent the illegal migration of the colonists into **Native American** lands as guaranteed by the **Proclamation of 1763**. The

Quartering Act of 1765, also called the Mutiny and Quartering Act by some writers, required the American colonies to provide housing in taverns, inns, barns, or other uninhabited buildings if adequate barracks were not available. The Americans would pay for the quarters as well as certain supplies such as bedding, salt, candles, utensils, and alcohol rations for soldiers stationed on their territory.

The American colonists objected to the Quartering Act of 1765 because they viewed the primary mission of the British soldiers as enforcing the Sugar Act of 1764 and other **taxation** schemes. Others noted that it was not British custom to maintain a large standing army in times of peace. The earliest colonial protest originated in **Boston** where **James Otis** led the opposition and persuaded the **Massachusetts** Assembly not to approve the funding requested by British soldiers. The greatest objection to the Quartering Act of 1765 arose in **New York**, since this was the location of the majority of the British troops based in the American colonies. However, organized protest did not materialize among the colonies against the Quartering Act of 1765 as it did with the Sugar Act of 1764. New York did delay compliance with the act until June 1766 when its assembly agreed to provide all of the required items except the alcohol ration. At this time, the New York Assembly declared that it was honoring a request from the Crown and not fulfilling the Quartering Act of 1765. When Lord Shelburne, the secretary of state for the **Southern Department**, wrote to Governor Henry Moore of New York that it was the colonists' duty to obey all parliamentary acts, New York ceased complying with the Quartering Act of 1765. This was the first time the colonies had been asked to support a standing army and many saw it as a form of illegal taxation.

The **southern colonies** took longer to protest the Quartering Act of 1765. **Pennsylvania** became the only colony to completely abide by the provisions of the Quartering Act of 1765. Many colonial allies in **Great Britain** during the **Stamp Act of 1765** crisis felt betrayed by the American opposition to the Quartering Act of 1765. The British government later modified the original legislation by passing the **Quartering Act of 1774**.

QUARTERING ACT OF 1774. On June 2, 1774, the British Parliament passed the Quartering Act of 1774. After the **Boston Tea Party**, the British passed a series of legislative bills known collectively as the **Intolerable Acts**. Some writers refer to them as the Coercive Acts. The Quartering Act of 1774 is considered the fourth of the Intolerable Acts by the American colonists. However, it was actually a separate bill that happened to appear at the same time as the Intolerable Acts. The legislation served as an extension of the **Quartering Act of 1765** and extended to royal governors the authorization to requisition privately owned buildings to house British soldiers even if military barracks existed in the area. This new Quartering Act, along with the other Intolerable Acts, served to solidify colonial opposition to the British and led to the formation of the **First Continental Congress**.

QUEBEC ACT OF 1774. After the **Boston Tea Party**, the British government passed what are known as the **Intolerable Acts** aimed at the American **colonies**. The Quebec Act of 1774, while not one of the Intolerable Acts, had the misfortune of being passed only one month after them. The Quebec Act involved British relations with **Canada**. However, the American colonists saw it as driving another wedge between them and the British government. The Quebec Act of 1774 established the first civilian government for the province of Quebec following the conclusion of the **French and Indian War**. The British allowed the French inhabitants to maintain their traditions in government and provided a privileged position to the Roman Catholic Church. The bill also placed all territory north of the Ohio River into Quebec. The latter action alarmed **Connecticut**, **Massachusetts**, **Pennsylvania**, and **Virgini**a since these American colonies claimed much of this territory. In addition the American colonies, which were predominantly Protestant, mistrusted the British concessions to the Roman Catholic Church. The Quebec Act emerged at the same time as the Intolerable Acts and served to further anger the American colonies and push them closer to armed conflict the following year at **Boston**. On the other hand, the British concessions to the French in Quebec via this act helped to maintain their loyalty during the **Revolutionary War**. *See also* QUEBEC REVENUE ACT OF 1774.

QUEBEC REVENUE ACT OF 1774. The Quebec Revenue Act of 1774, passed by Parliament along with the **Quebec Act of 1774**, served to establish import duties for goods entering Quebec. The act also reaffirmed French revenue provisions. Although of minor concern to the American **colonies**, this act, along with the Quebec Act of 1774, tended to add lumps of coal to the growing fire within **Canada**'s southern neighbors and culminated in the armed conflict around **Boston** in 1775.

– R –

RAMAGE, JOHN (c.1748–1802). John Ramage, a **loyalist**, was a noted miniature **painter** during the period of Revolutionary America.

RAMSAY, DAVID (1749–1815). David Ramsay, a physician and the brother of **Nathaniel Ramsay**, sat in the **South Carolina** legislature. He was apprehended and held in Saint Augustine for a year after the siege of **Charleston**. He represented South Carolina in the **Congress of the Confederation** from 1782–1785.

RAMSAY, NATHANIEL (1741–1817). Nathaniel Ramsay, a **Revolutionary War** officer and the brother of **David Ramsay**, represented **Maryland** in the **Second Continental Congress** in 1775 and the **Congress of the Confederation** from 1785–1787.

RANDALL, BENJAMIN (1749–1808). Benjamin Randall, a clergyman, founded the Free Will Baptist Church in 1780.

RANDOLPH, EDMUND (1753–1813). Edmund Randolph was elected governor of **Virginia** in 1786. He sat as a delegate in the **Annapolis Convention** in 1786 and the **Constitutional Convention of 1787**. Randolph introduced the **Virginia Plan** in the latter convention. He opposed the U.S. **Constitution** while sitting in the Constitutional Convention of 1787 and did not sign the document. However, he did support its ratification in the 1788 Virginia state convention. Randolph later served as U.S. attorney general and secretary of state.

RANDOLPH, PEYTON (c.1721–1775). Peyton Randolph sat in the **Virginia** legislature and represented his colony in the **First Continental Congress** in 1774 and the **Second Continental Congress** in

1775. He was selected as **president of Congress** in 1774 and 1775 but died suddenly in 1775.

READ, DANIEL (1757–1836). Read was born in **Massachusetts** and became one of the greatest musicians of the Revolutionary America period. He wrote most of his **music** in the 1780s and 1790s. His most important work is possibly the 1785 *American Singing Book*.

READ, GEORGE (1733–1798). George Read, a lawyer and early patriot, sat in the **Delaware** legislature. He represented Delaware in the **First Continental Congress** in 1774 and the **Second Continental Congress** from 1775–1777. While a member of the latter body, Read signed the **Declaration of Independence**. Read attended the **Annapolis Convention** in 1786 and the **Constitutional Convention of 1787**. In the Constitutional Convention, Read proved to be very active in supporting the protection of small states in a new government. He signed the U.S. **Constitution** and was instrumental in ensuring that Delaware was the first state to ratify the document. Read later served as a U.S. senator.

READ, JACOB (1752–1816). Jacob Read, a **Revolutionary War** officer, represented **South Carolina** in the **Congress of the Confederation** from 1783–1786. Read sat as a delegate in the state convention to ratify the U.S. **Constitution**. He supported the document and later served as a U.S. senator.

REAL MERCHANTS. "Real Merchants" was a nickname for the group of merchants who called for the discontinuation of the **nonimportation agreement** in **Boston**. *See also* FANEUIL HALL FRIENDS; OLD IMPORTERS.

RECREATION. Recreation in Revolutionary America involved pastimes that would be recognized by Americans today. However, like today, the exact types of recreation could vary between **colonies** due to culture or religious restrictions. Billiards, bowling, cricket, shuffleboard, and ninepins were common pastimes for the aristocracy. Other games played by all social classes included cards and dice. Lotteries were also popular. However, all of these activities could be restricted by **religion**, depending on the area. Numerous social organizations and fraternities existed. Sideshows traveled between towns, offering their entertainment. Many individuals enjoyed spending evenings in the taverns or inns where they indulged in **alcoholic** beverages and traded the latest political gossip. Numerous formal and informal political organizations were born in America's taverns. Dancing was another favorite pastime that was, again, often restricted due to religion in some areas. Hunting and fishing were timeless sports for many Americans. In the rural countryside, individuals gathered for house raisings, barn raisings, and corn huskings. Horse racing and cock fighting were activities that were popular in the **southern colonies** and generally carried a decreased interest among the population as one traveled north. Americans throughout the colonies delighted in celebrating cultural and religious holidays such as Christmas. Children played with marbles and tops.

REDEMPTIONERS. Redemptioners were individuals, frequently from the area that became Germany, who traveled to the Americas on a type of credit. Ship captains permitted them passage and gave them two weeks to deliver the fare after arriving in America. If the individuals could not pay the captain, the latter was permitted to "sell" them as **indentured servants**. The numbers of redemptioners was on the decline just prior to the **Revolutionary War**.

RED JACKET (c.1758–1830). Red Jacket, an **Iroquois** chief and rival of **Cornplanter**, actively opposed American intrusions in **Native American** land during the period of Revolutionary America. However, he was known to play both sides and would secretly sign land treaties after they had been negotiated and signed by other Native American leaders.

REDMAN, JOHN (1722–1808). John Redman was a prominent physician and medical **educator** in Revolutionary America.

REED, JOSEPH (1741–1785). Joseph Reed, a lawyer and **Revolutionary War** officer, represented **Pennsylvania** in the **Second Continental Congress** in 1775 and 1778. Reed signed the **Articles of Confederation**. He declined election to the **Congress of the Confederation** in 1784 due to ill health and died the next year.

REGULATION, WAR OF THE. *See* REGULATORS.

REGULATIONS FOR THE ORDER AND DISCIPLINE OF THE TROOPS OF THE UNITED STATES. The *Regulations for the Order and Discipline of the Troops of the United States* is the title of the drill book written for the **Continental Army** by General von Steuben while at Valley Forge. This book remained the standard drill manual of the American army until 1812.

REGULATORS. The term *regulators* is applied to the farmers whose opposition to the royal government in **North Carolina** beginning in 1764 culminated in the **Battle of the Alamance** in 1771. This period has been referred to as the War of the Regulation by some scholars. The frontiersmen of western North Carolina harbored numerous grievances about the royal government in the eastern part of the state. They noted that many of their local governmental offices were sold rather than being democratically elected. They also complained about high **taxes**, underrepresentation in the colonial legislature, and dishonest sheriffs. The latter individuals often embezzled as much as and sometimes more than half of the taxes they were appointed to collect. In fact, many of the complaints by the settlers in western North Carolina about their colonial government in the east mirrored the ones issued by Americans about the British government. Governor **William Tryon** of North Carolina admitted that many of the problems existed but found them difficult to correct.

The frontiersmen felt isolated by the easterners but lacked a leader to organize them. Herman Husband emerged as an organizer of the movement but broke ranks when the frontiersmen, often known as the regulators, turned to armed revolt. The regulators initiated riots and other acts of violence during the collection of taxes in 1765. Between 1768 and 1771, the regulators continued to oppose their local governments with increasing tenacity. In 1769, Governor Tryon led a force of **militia** to Hillsborough in response to a plea by the Superior Court justices in the town. The justices claimed that they were not able to conduct business due to the regulators and feared for their lives. Tryon's force of 1,500 militiamen confronted a group of 3,700 regulators and persuaded them to disband. However, this show of force did nothing to alleviate the grievances of the frontiersmen. In

March 1771, following continued regulator violence, Governor Tryon and General Hugh Waddell led two militia groups into the western frontier. The resulting Battle of the Alamance left Governor Tryon in control of the area and effectively ended the resistance. After the battle, most of the regulators and their supporters swore an oath of allegiance to the government, but many others moved to **Tennessee** and **Kentucky** to avoid the process.

The regulator movement is a controversial topic in Revolutionary American history. Many scholars view the regulators and their movement as a prelude to the **Revolutionary War**, similar to revolts in the northern **colonies** such as the **Boston Tea Party**. These scholars tend to see the Battle of the Alamance as the first shooting engagement of the Revolutionary War. Other scholars hold that the regulators were a movement separate from the Revolutionary War and were instead related to the general East vs. West disagreements before and after the war. These east vs. west clashes include Bacon's Rebellion, **Shays's Rebellion**, and the Whiskey Rebellion. In support of the latter argument, one must consider that the regulators clashed with colonial militia and not British troops. *See also* JOHNSTON ACT.

RELIGION. Religion played a major role in the lives of colonial Americans and the Revolutionary period is not an exception. Many religious denominations could be found throughout the **colonies**. By the Revolution, the largest Christian denominations, in order based on the number of churches, were Congregational, Presbyterian, Baptist, Anglican, Quaker, German and Dutch Reformed, Lutheran, and Roman Catholic. Jewish synagogues were few in number and tended to be located in the larger cities along the eastern seaboard. Although converts were already in the colonies prior to the Revolution, the Methodist Church, a splinter from the Church of England, became officially organized in the United States after the war. After the Revolution, a movement to separate church and state emerged. In the years after the Revolution, states wrote "freedom of religion" clauses into constitutions and bills of rights to guarantee choice, and the elimination of compulsory church attendance and religious qualifications for public office. At the same time, religious denominations began severing ties with their church organizations in Great Britain. Prominent clergy and others associated with religion in Revolutionary America included **John Andrews**, **James Caldwell**, John Commerhoff, **John Carroll**, **Ezekiel Cooper**, **Nathaniel Evans**, **Abiel Foster**, **Richard Furman**, **Freeborn Garrettson**, **Pierre Gibault**, **Barnard Gratz**, **Jacob Green**, **Benjamin Griffith**, **Bernhard Grube**, **Jacob Hardenbergh**, **Gideon Hawley**, **Barbara Heck**, **John Heckewelder**, **John Helffenstein**, **John Hendel**, **Alexander Hewat**, **Henry Holcombe**, **John Jungman**, **Samuel Kirkland**, **John Kunze**, **Jeremiah Leaming**, **John Leland**, **Ann Lee**, **Alexander MacWhorter**, **James Madison** (not the president of the United States), **Daniel Marshall**, **Henry Muhlenberg**, **John Murray**, **Christian Newcomer**, **John Olgilvie**, **Christian Post**, **Benjamin Randall**, **David Rice**, **William Savery**, **Samuel Seabury**, **Gershom Seixas**, **Hezekiah Smith**, **Samuel Spring**, **Shubal Stearns**, **Samuel Stillman**, **Peter Thatcher**, **Noah Welles**, **Charles Wharton**, and **Eleazar Wheelock**. *See also* GREAT AWAKENING.

RESTRAINING ACTS. The Restraining Acts were a series of declarations issued by the British government in 1775 to counter growing opposition among the American colonists in the area around **Massachusetts**. Eventually, the acts applied to all of the American **colonies** except **Georgia**, **New York**, and **North Carolina**. *See also* FIRST RESTRAINING ACT; SECOND RESTRAINING ACT.

REVENUE. *See* CURRENCY; DEBT, PUBLIC; REVENUE ACT OF 1766; SUGAR ACT OF 1764; TAXATION; TRADE.

REVENUE ACT OF 1764. *See* SUGAR ACT OF 1764.

REVENUE ACT OF 1766. The Revenue Act of 1766 modified the **Sugar Act of 1764**. It repealed the duty on foreign sugar imported into the British colonies. The sugar would be duty-free if stored and re-exported to Britain within one year. If sold in Britain or the American **colonies**, the product faced the standard foreign sugar tax. The Revenue Act of 1766 also dropped the duty on coffee and pimento listed in the Sugar Act of 1764. Like sugar, these two products did not face duties if stored and re-exported to Britain within one year. Duties on foreign cotton and **indigo** were also modified. The American colonists opposed the imposition of the Revenue Act of 1766 because it served to prohibit them from carrying sugar and other goods in their ships. The colonists frequently accepted sugar in exchange for their goods in the West Indies and then resold the product in Britain to pay debts. The Revenue Act of 1766 did reduce the duty on molasses, to the delight of many **northern colonies**. *See also* WEST INDIES FREE PORT ACT OF 1766.

REVENUE ACT OF 1767. *See* TOWNSHEND REVENUE ACT OF 1767.

REVERE, PAUL (1735–1818). Paul Revere, an early patriot, helped plan the **Boston Tea Party** and performed courier duties for patriot leaders. He is best known, thanks to the Longfellow poem, for carrying the warning of the British march from **Boston** that would lead to the **Battle of Lexington-Concord**. However, few realize that he was apprehended on the journey and did not complete his mission. Revere also printed the first **Continental currency**. Revere was also a noted craftsman, especially known for his silversmith work. *See also* LIBERTY BOWL.

REVOLUTIONARY WAR. In April 1775, British forces marched from **Boston** to seize cannon and other items of military value, sparking the **Battle of Lexington-Concord**, and igniting the Revolutionary War. The British retreat from the Battle of Lexington-Concord prompted the arrival of thousands of colonial **militia**, who initiated a siege of Boston. The **Second Continental Congress** established the **Continental Army** with General **George Washington** as its commander in June 1775. During the same month, British troops attacked colonists who had entrenched themselves on Breed's Hill across Boston Harbor, resulting in the Battle of Bunker Hill. This engagement proved to be the bloodiest of the war and demonstrated that American militia could stand against the professional soldiers of **Great Britain**. American forces launched a two-pronged attack on **Canada** during the fall of 1775. Montreal fell quickly, but Quebec City proved to be more difficult. A desperate American attack failed to capture the city and resulted in the death or capture of over half of the assault force.

The year 1776 dawned with the Americans in retreat from Canada and a stalemate around Boston. The Battle of Moore's Creek, **North Carolina**, in February resulted in the crushing of **loyalist** resistance in that **colony** and persuaded the British to attack Fort Sullivan outside of **Charleston, South Carolina**. American forces stood firmly behind the palmetto log Fort Sullivan, however, and forced the British navy to retreat from the area. Cannon from Fort Ticonderoga were emplaced on Dorchester Heights above Boston, forcing the British to withdraw from the city. The British sailed to Canada and the Americans reveled in their victory.

The main body of the American army shifted to **New York City** to await the next move of the British. A flotilla of British ships arrived off New York City in June. The British army attacked the American forces at the Battle of Long Island in August and quickly won a series of small engagements around New York City. The Americans managed to check the British temporarily at the Battles of Harlem Heights and White Plains but were still forced to withdraw from the area. American Forts Washington and Lee fell, forcing General Washington to retreat across **New Jersey** at the end of the year. However, the retreat turned into one of the most memorable victories of the war as Washington surprised and defeated the **Hessians** garrisoned at Trenton on December 26, 1776. A British advance from Canada down the Hudson River Valley was slowed by American resistance at the Battle of Valcour Island, prompting the former to delay further movement until 1777.

The year 1777 opened with the American victory at the Battle of Princeton and a forced march to winter quarters at Morristown. In the spring of 1777, the British opted for a new strategy and moved their army around New Jersey by sea and drove for **Philadelphia** from **Delaware**. American defeats at the Battles of Brandywine, Germantown, and Fort Mercer slowed but did not prevent the British from capturing their objective and forcing the Continental Congress to evacuate the city. The American army spent a cold winter at Valley Forge, outside of Philadelphia, where the British enjoyed the winter months.

In **New York**, the British resumed their advance down the Hudson River in coordination with a second column marching east from Oswego. The latter force retired after the Battles of Oriskany and Fort

Stanwix. The main British column on the Hudson River met defeat at the Battle of Bennington before surrendering at the Battle of Saratoga. The latter engagement, along with the American performance at the Battle of Germantown, persuaded **France** to form an alliance with the United States and enter the war against Great Britain.

The British army departed Philadelphia in June 1778 and traveled overland toward New York City. A newly trained American army pursued and fought it to a draw at the Battle of Monmouth in New Jersey, which became the last major battle north of **Virginia** during the war. The British managed to get the majority of their force back to New York City before dispatching a large contingent to fight the French in the West Indies. The main Continental Army moved into winter quarters at Morristown at the end of the year. A combined French and American force failed to capture **Newport**, **Rhode Island**. In the south, Savannah fell to the British at the end of 1778 as they implemented a new strategy of subduing the southern states.

The year 1779 witnessed the American victories of George Rogers Clark in the west while John Paul Jones launched his famous naval raid into British waters. The Continental Army endured its worst winter of the war but did not fight any major open battles the following spring and summer. In the south, a combined French and American army failed to recapture Savannah and withdrew after heavy losses.

The year 1780 proved gloomy as the Americans suffered their worst battlefield defeat—the loss of an entire army and the capture of Charleston. American troops returned to the south and suffered a humiliating defeat at the Battle of Camden before retreating back to North Carolina and leaving resistance in South Carolina to the patriot guerrillas of Francis Marion and **Thomas Sumter**. Benedict Arnold turned traitor and defected to the British after being discovered. Again, a major open battle did not materialize in the north as the Continental Army continued to watch the British in New York City. The year ended on a high note for the Americans with a victory at King's Mountain in South Carolina.

The year 1781 opened with promise as the Americans inflicted a stunning defeat on the British at the Battle of Cowpens in South Carolina. The Americans began a hasty but coordinated retreat across North Carolina in order to avoid British pursuit. At the Battle of Guilford Courthouse, the Americans turned and fought the British army following them. Despite holding the field after the battle, the British, having suffered heavy casualties, withdrew to the coast and eventually marched into Virginia where they would become trapped at Yorktown. The American southern army returned to South Carolina and slowly forced the British to withdraw to Charleston, despite American losses at the Battles of Hobkirk's Hill and Ninety-Six. Augusta, **Georgia**, fell to the Americans who went on to achieve another tactical loss but strategic victory at the Battle of Eutaw Springs. A combined French and American force moved south to engage the British force at Yorktown, Virginia. The British surrender of an entire army at Yorktown signaled the end of their major military campaigns during the war. Until the signing of the **Treaty of Paris of 1783**, the two armies kept a close watch but did not engage in any further major operations. Skirmishing continued in the south.

Peace negotiations commenced in April 1782 and the final document was signed on September 3, 1783. This document officially ended the American Revolution and confirmed the independence of the United States of America. Congress ratified the agreement on January 14, 1784.

RHEA, JOHN (1753–1832). John Rhea sat in the **North Carolina** legislature and supported the U.S. **Constitution** at the **Fayetteville state convention**. Rhea later served in the U.S. House of Representatives for **Tennessee**.

RHODE ISLAND. Rhode Island, one of the **New England colonies**, was governed by **Great Britain** as a **charter colony** until the **Revolutionary War** and American independence. By the end of America's Revolutionary period in 1790, the state boasted 68,825 people (1.4% slaves). Rhode Islanders tended to be liberally minded during the period of Revolutionary America. They supported individual liberties, actions to end **slavery**, and colonial efforts to counter British **taxation** policies. A group of Rhode Islanders burned the British customs vessel ***Liberty*** in 1769. In 1774, Rhode Island became the first colony to prohibit the importation of slaves although the institution of slavery continued for many years. In that same year, Rhode Island **militia** seized British cannons in **Newport**. The state fielded a regular unit of **African American** soldiers during the Revolutionary War. The state ratified the U.S. **Con-**

stitution on May 29, 1790. Rhode Island was the last state to approve the document. It had been acting as a semi-autonomous political entity and had not been sending representatives to the **Congress of the Confederation** for several years. Residents of the state were concerned that the Constitution would grant the federal government too much power over the states and individual citizens. Therefore, the ratification of the document did not occur until after the **Bill of Rights** was added to the Constitution. Even then, ratification came by only a slim majority of 34 to 32. Rhode Island was a seafaring state with a comparatively large **fishing** and maritime industry during this period. Notable individuals from Rhode Island include **Benjamin Bourne**, **John Collins**, **William Ellery**, **Stephen Hopkins**, and **Henry Marchant**.

RICE. Rice, along with **indigo**, **wheat**, and **tobacco**, proved to be an important export crop during the period of Revolutionary America. Rice was the most important commercial crop in **South Carolina** during the period and was grown on plantations along the coast. The wetlands around **Charleston** were ideal for the cultivation of rice and the crop emerging from this area was noted to be the best in the world. By 1770, South Carolina exported over 125,000 barrels of rice annually. **Georgia** exported another 24,000 barrels of rice annually during this period. Rice production declined immediately after the Revolution due to **trade** restrictions placed on the United States by European countries. However, rice recovered within a few years following the conclusion of the **Revolutionary War** because **Great Britain** was not able to acquire the same quality product through alternative sources. *See also* AGRICULTURE.

RICE, DAVID (1733–1816). David Rice, a clergyman, was instrumental in establishing the Presbyterian Church in **Kentucky** during the period of Revolutionary America.

RICHARDSON, JOSEPH (1711–1784). Joseph Richardson was a prominent silversmith in Revolutionary America.

RIDGLEY, NICHOLAS (1762–1830). Nicholas Ridgley, a lawyer, served as a delegate in the 1787 **Delaware** convention to ratify the U.S. **Constitution**. He later sat in the U.S. House of Representatives.

RIFLE DRESS. Rifle dress is a nickname given to the clothing authorized by the **Second Continental Congress** to each soldier enlisting in the **Continental Army**. The articles included two linen hunting shirts, two pairs of stockings, two pairs of shoes, two pairs of overalls, a leather or woolen jacket, a pair of breeches, and a cap or hat. The British tended to associate linen hunting jackets with the expert riflemen from the **militia** units and thus the term rifle dress evolved as a nickname for this clothing issue. It should be noted that, especially early in the war, many soldiers did not receive their entire clothing issue.

RIGHTS OF THE COLONIES ASSERTED AND PROVED. **James Otis** published this pamphlet in **Boston** after passage of the **Sugar Act of 1764** by the British. The 1764 document seemed to ramble between support for the rights of the **colonies** and the right of Parliament to have its laws obeyed. However, Otis clearly indicated within the document that the colonies should not be taxed without consent. He also proposed a more formal means for colonial representation in Parliament. The idea of colonial representatives in Parliament alarmed the British. Many colonial politicians also did not want to support this idea since it would negate their defense against British **taxation**. The document is important in its declaration that the colonies should not be taxed without consent of their own legislatures, which were elected by the people and spoke for the people. This argument would be continued throughout the next decade as the colonies moved toward open war with **Great Britain**.

RIOT ACT. *See* JOHNSTON ACT.

RITTENHOUSE, DAVID (1732–1796). David Rittenhouse was a noted astronomer and mathematician in Revolutionary America.

RIVINGTON, JAMES (1724–1802). James Rivington was a prominent **printer** during the period of Revolutionary America.

ROBERDEAU, DANIEL (1727–1795). Daniel Roberdeau, a merchant and early patriot, represented **Pennsylvania** in the **Second**

Continental Congress from 1777–1779. He signed the **Articles of Confederation** for Pennsylvania.

ROBERTSON, JAMES (1742–1814). James Robertson was a noted pioneer in the lands now known as **Kentucky** and **Tennessee**. Robertson led settlers into Tennessee and later played an important role in the establishment of this area as a state. He also lived among the **Native Americans** of the area and worked as an agent between the **Cherokee** and the governments of **North Carolina** and **Virginia**.

ROCKINGHAM, MARQUIS OF (1730–1782). Charles Watson-Wentworth, the Marquis of Rockingham, served twice as British prime minister. His first administration lasted from 1765–1766 and his second was in 1782. A friend of the American colonists, Rockingham repealed the **Stamp Act of 1765** after he assumed office. **King George III** ensured that Rockingham was replaced in 1766 with **William Pitt** (Lord Chatham), who tended to take a harder line with the American colonists. Rockingham returned to power in 1782 and opened peace negotiations with the Americans. However, he died before the completion of these talks and the signing of the **Treaty of Paris of 1783**.

RODNEY, CAESAR (1728–1784). Caesar Rodney, the father of **Thomas Rodney**, sat in the **Delaware** legislature and represented Delaware in the **First Continental Congress** in 1774 and the **Second Continental Congress** from 1775–1776 and again in 1777. In July 1776, Rodney was not present in Congress and the other two delegates were divided on whether Delaware should support the **Declaration of Independence**. Rodney returned quickly by horseback in time to sign the document on July 2, 1776, and ensure Delaware's endorsement of the Declaration

RODNEY, THOMAS (1744–1811). Thomas Rodney, a farmer and the son of **Caesar Rodney**, sat in the **Delaware** legislature. He represented his state in the **Second Continental Congress** in 1781 and the **Congress of the Confederation** from 1781–1783 and 1785–1787. He served later as a federal judge in the Mississippi Territory.

ROMAYNE, NICHOLAS (1756–1817). Nicholas Romayne was a prominent physician and medical **educator** in Revolutionary America.

ROOT, JESSE (1736–1822). Jesse Root, a lawyer and **Revolutionary War** officer, represented **Connecticut** in the **Second Continental Congress** from 1778–1781 and the **Congress of the Confederation** from 1781–1782. He later served as a state judge and presidential elector.

ROSS, BETSY (1752–1836). Legend states that Betsy Ross sewed the first "**stars and stripes**" American flag at the request of General **George Washington**. However, evidence does not exist to support the claims, first made by her grandson in 1870.

ROSS, GEORGE (1730–1779). George Ross, a lawyer, sat in the **Pennsylvania** legislature. He represented Pennsylvania in the **First Continental Congress** in 1774 and the **Second Continental Congress** from 1775–1777. Ross signed the **Declaration of Independence** and later served as a state judge.

ROUND SHOT. Round shot is one name for a solid iron cannonball.

ROWSON, SUSANNA (c.1762–1824). Susanna Rowson was a prominent writer in Revolutionary America.

ROYAL COLONY. A royal colony was governed by a governor appointed by and responsible to the Crown, although popular assemblies with limited power did exist. After 1760, **Georgia**, **New Hampshire**, **New Jersey**, **Massachusetts**, **North Carolina**, **South Carolina**, and **Virginia** were royal colonies. *See also* CHARTER COLONY; PROPRIETARY COLONY.

ROYAL PROCLAMATION OF 1763. *See* PROCLAMATION OF 1763.

RULE OF 1756. American colonists illegally conducted business with the islands of the West Indies to avoid British **taxes** and restrictive

trade policies. During the **French and Indian War**, British authorities began to realize the magnitude of colonial **smuggling** to avoid duties and trade restrictions. The British cracked down on the American trade with French colonial holdings in the West Indies. However, the American response was to transport their cargo to Dutch islands and then transfer the goods to the French islands. The British government passed the Rule of 1756 in the attempt to halt this process. The legislation stated that neutral states could not conduct trade during wartime if it was prohibited to them during peace. British ships began seizing Dutch vessels conducting trade between the American colonists and the French. The Rule of 1756 angered American merchants, who saw the bill as interfering with their right to conduct trade and helped set the colonial mood when new forms of taxation were introduced after 1763.

RUSH, BENJAMIN (1746–1813). Benjamin Rush, a prominent physician, sat in the **Pennsylvania** legislature and represented his state in the **Second Continental Congress** from 1776–1777. He signed the **Declaration of Independence**. Rush emerged as a leader among anti-**slavery** groups in Pennsylvania and became a major figure in **education** and the founding of Dickinson College in 1783. He supported the U.S. **Constitution** and served as a delegate in the state convention to ratify the document.

RUSSIA AND REVOLUTIONARY AMERICA. In 1775, **King George III** of **Great Britain** requested Empress Catherine the Great of Russia to provide 20,000 men to help suppress the **Revolutionary War**. Catherine declined, realizing that assisting Great Britain could tip the balance of power in Europe to the British. **France** and **Spain** would probably enter the conflict at some point and this would drag Russia, as a British ally, into a European war at a time when she had to contend with her own rebellion in the south of Russia. Catherine was instrumental in forming the **League of Armed Neutrality** during the conflict. In response to the establishment of this league, the **Congress** dispatched **Francis Dana** to Russia as a commissioner in December 1780. Catherine did not receive or extend recognition to Dana. At one point in 1781, Catherine did offer to mediate a peace treaty between the United States and Great Britain but the British did not accept her offer.

RUSTICUS. **John Dickinson** used the pen name Rusticus when writing about his opposition to British tea policy in **Philadelphia** in November 1773. *See also* HAMDEN; HAMPDEN.

RUTLEDGE, EDWARD (1749–1800). Edward Rutledge, a lawyer and the brother of **John Rutledge**, represented **South Carolina** in the **First Continental Congress** in 1774 and the **Second Continental Congress** from 1775–1776 and then in 1782. He signed the **Declaration of Independence**. He was captured after the fall of **Charleston** and exchanged by the British immediately before serving his last term in Congress. Rutledge sat in the state legislature after 1782 and then as a delegate to the 1788 state convention to ratify the U.S. **Constitution**. He later served as a presidential elector and the governor of South Carolina.

RUTLEDGE, JOHN (1730–1800). John Rutledge, a lawyer and the brother of **Edward Rutledge**, sat in the **South Carolina** legislature and became governor in 1779. He represented South Carolina in the **First Continental Congress** in 1774, the **Second Continental Congress** from 1775–1776, and the **Congress of the Confederation** from 1782–1783. He escaped from **Charleston** prior to its fall to the British and established a government-in-exile in **North Carolin**a. He returned to South Carolina in 1781. Rutledge attended the **Constitutional Convention of 1787** and signed the U.S. **Constitution**. He later served as chief justice for the state of South Carolina.

– S –

SACKVILLE, GEORGE. *See* GERMAIN, GEORGE SACKVILLE.

ST. CLAIR, ARTHUR (1736–1818). Arthur St. Clair, a **Revolutionary War** officer, represented **Pennsylvania** in the **Congress of the Confederation** from 1785–1787. He was **president of Congress** in 1787. St. Clair became the first governor of the newly established **Northwest Territory** in 1787 and held that position until 1802. His long administration as governor was marked by considerable controversy.

SAINT CROIX AND REVOLUTIONARY AMERICA. Saint Croix, a Danish island in the Caribbean (currently one of the Virgin Islands of the United States), permitted American vessels to utilize its port facilities and acquire supplies destined for the **Continental Army**. **Denmark** remained neutral during the **Revolutionary War**. *See also* SAINT EUSTATIUS AND REVOLUTIONARY AMERICA; SAINT THOMAS AND REVOLUTIONARY AMERICA.

SAINT-ETIENNE MUSKET. The Saint-Etienne musket, like the Charleville musket, was a .69 caliber French weapon. Approximately 100,000 of these muskets were exported to the United States and it became the primary weapon of the **Continental Army** and many American **militia** units by the end of the **Revolutionary War**. The name derives from the arsenal where the muskets were produced.

SAINT EUSTATIUS AND REVOLUTIONARY AMERICA. Saint Eustatius, a small Dutch island in the Caribbean, allowed American vessels to utilize its port facilities and acquire supplies destined for the **Continental Army** early in the **Revolutionary War**. The first formal salute of the American flag occurred at this port with the arrival of the *Andrea Doria* on November 16, 1776. The island fell to the British in February 1781 after London's declaration of war against the **Netherlands** in December 1780. A French force then recaptured the small island in November 1781. *See also* SAINT CROIX AND REVOLUTIONARY AMERICA; SAINT THOMAS AND REVOLUTIONARY AMERICA.

SAINT JOHN. The American colonists viewed the **Sugar Act of 1764** with animosity. To avoid the **trade** restrictions placed on them by the Sugar Act of 1764 and earlier trade acts, many Americans smuggled goods. On June 30, 1764, the crew of the British vessel *Saint John* seized the cargo of a colonial ship suspected of **smuggling** in violation of the Sugar Act of 1764. Before the captain could escort the colonial captain to the **Admiralty Court** in Nova Scotia, a group of Americans arrested him under a charge of detaining an individual without the correct credentials. The British captain was released to return to **Boston** in order to acquire the proper credentials. On July 9, 1764, the same British captain and ship arrested a suspected deserter in **Newport**, **Rhode Island**. Locals rescued the man and forced the British sailors to retreat to their ship. As the *Saint John* sailed past a battery, the locals seized the guns and fired eight rounds at the ship, splitting the mainsail. Complaints to the colonial government in Rhode Island fell on deaf ears. These incidents, resulting from colonial resentment of the Sugar Act of 1764, helped set a precedent for future opposition to the British and to stir the coals leading to the **Revolutionary War**. *See also LIBERTY.*

SAINT THOMAS AND REVOLUTIONARY AMERICA. Saint Thomas, a Danish island in the Caribbean (currently one of the Virgin Islands of the United States), allowed American vessels to utilize its port facilities and acquire supplies destined for the **Continental Army**. **Denmark** remained neutral during the **Revolutionary War**. *See also* SAINT CROIX AND REVOLUTIONARY AMERICA; SAINT EUSTATIUS AND REVOLUTIONARY AMERICA.

SALEM. Tensions between the **New England colonies** and **Great Britain** were tense after the imposition of the **Intolerable Acts** in retaliation for the **Boston Tea Party** in 1774. **Militia** units throughout New England were seizing weapons and powder stored in public arsenals and hiding them in case hostilities erupted with the British forces garrisoned in **Boston**. British forces in the city sallied out on numerous occasion to capture weapons and powder before the militia could remove and hide them. One particular British foray nearly resulted in direct hostilities with the **Massachusetts** militia. On February 26, 1775, British forces marched to seize cannon at Salem. The local militia, under Colonel Thomas Pickering, confronted the British advance. Each side showed restraint and the colonists were able to remove the cannon during the stalemate, forcing the British to return to Boston empty-handed. The tensions displayed in these operations would lead to open conflict at the **Battle of Lexington-Concord** in April 1775. *See also* ALARM RIDERS; CAMBRIDGE; CHARLESTOWN; NEWPORT; PORTSMOUTH.

SALEM, PETER. Salem, an **African American** marksman, is credited with shooting British Marine Major Pitcairn at the Battle of Bunker Hill during the **Revolutionary War**.

SALUTARY NEGLECT. Salutary neglect is the policy of not enforcing a piece of legislation or executive order/act. The British applied salutary neglect to many of their **economic** policies directed at the American **colonies**. In order to stem American resistance, the British sometimes found it beneficial to leave the acts in place but not enforce or lightly enforce them. Such actions encouraged American **smuggling**, especially to and from the Caribbean area. However, when the British opted to clamp down on American noncompliance after the **French and Indian War**, American merchants and smugglers reacted aggressively, leading to many confrontations with the British government.

SAMPSON, DEBORAH (1760–1827). In 1782, Deborah Sampson enlisted and served as a soldier in the **Continental Army**. Her gender was discovered and she was released from service. However, she enlisted again under a different alias and was honorably discharged after being exposed a second time. At one point, Sampson received a leg wound in a skirmish with a **loyalist** unit, but she refused medical assistance out of concern that her identity would be discovered. She later married, had children, and received a military pension from **Massachusetts** for her war service. *See also* WOMEN IN REVOLUTIONARY AMERICA.

SAVERY, WILLIAM (1750–1804). William Savery was a prominent Quaker clergyman and missionary among the **Native Americans** during Revolutionary America.

SCAEVOLA. **Thomas Mifflin** utilized Scaevola as a pen name in a **Philadelphia** broadside attacking the 1773 British plans for importing tea into the American **colonies**. The announcement warned the tea consignees of the consequences of accepting and storing the shipment of tea in the port.

SCARBOROUGH. **Georgia** Royal Governor Sir **James Wright** took refuge on the British ship *Scarborough* after escaping from patriot forces on February 11, 1776.

SCHOONER. A schooner is a small sailing vessel with two masts.

SCHUYLER, PHILIP (1733–1804). Philip Schuyler, a **Revolutionary War** officer, represented **New York** in the **Second Continental Congress** from 1775–1777 and 1778–1781. He served later in the state senate and U.S. Senate.

SCIENCE. Many colonial Americans received recognition for their scientific research and inventions in the 17th and 18th centuries. Although the majority of his scientific work occurred prior to the Revolutionary period, **Benjamin Franklin** is perhaps the best-known American engaged in research during the last half of the 18th century. For example, Franklin developed his bifocal eyeglasses in 1783. Scientific developments made their way into American colleges. **Adam Kuhn** offered the first college course in botany in 1768 at what is now the University of **Pennsylvania**. Nautical scientific developments in the Revolutionary period included the construction of a working submarine, the ***Turtle***, in 1776 and the development of a **steamboat** in 1787. Other prominent American scientists included **John Bartram**, **William Bartram**, **Joseph Brown**, **David Bushnell**, **John Clayton**, **George Clymer**, **Cadwallader Colden**, **Jane Colden**, **Christopher Colles**, **Alexander Garden**, **Peter Harrison** (architect-building science), **John Jeffries**, **Ebenezer Kinnersley**, **John Leeds**, **William Longstreet**, **Humphrey Marshall**, **Samuel Morey**, **Andrew Oliver**, **David Rittenhouse**, **Thomas Walter**, **Pelatiah Webster** (political economist), and **John Winthrop**.

SCOTT, JOHN (c.1730–1784). John Scott, a lawyer and avid patriot, represented **New York** in the **Second Continental Congress** and **Congress of the Confederation** from 1779–1783.

SCUDDER, NATHANIEL (1733–1781). Nathaniel Scudder, a **Revolutionary War** officer, represented **New Jersey** in the **Second Continental Congress** from 1777–1779. He signed the **Articles of Confederation** for New Jersey.

SEABURY, SAMUEL (1729–1796). Samuel Seabury, a noted clergyman during the period of Revolutionary America, became the first bishop of the Episcopal Church in America in 1784.

SEARLE, JAMES (1733–1797). James Searle, a merchant, represented **Pennsylvania** in the **Second Continental Congress** from 1778–1780.

SEARS, ISAAC (c.1730–1786). Isaac Sears, a very active patriot, led the **Sons of Liberty** in their first 1774 confrontation against a British tea ship. Sears avidly pursued **loyalists**. He led a unit of **Connecticut** cavalry and launched a series of raids against **New York** loyalists in the fall of 1775. On November 23, 1775, Sears and his band, "bayonets fixed" according to sources, raided a loyalist **printing** press in **New York City**. Many patriots questioned the methods of Sears, and the **Congress** protested to Connecticut authorities about the tactics of the firebrand. From 1777–1783, Sears operated as a **privateer**.

SECOND CONTINENTAL CONGRESS. *See* CONTINENTAL CONGRESS, SECOND.

SECOND OHIO COMPANY. *See* OHIO COMPANY.

SECOND RESTRAINING ACT. In 1775, the British government enacted the Second Restraining Act to extend the **trading** and **fishing** restrictions of the **First Restraining Act**. The Second Act added **Delaware**, **Maryland**, **New Jersey**, **Pennsylvania**, **South Carolina**, and **Virginia** to the list of **New England colonies** forbidden to trade among themselves or with any areas other than **Great Britain**, Ireland, and the British West Indies. The act also forbade sailors from these states from fishing or **whaling** in the waters off Newfoundland or Nova Scotia.

SECOND TREATY OF FORT STANWIX. *See* FORT STANWIX, SECOND TREATY OF.

SECRET COMMITTEE. The **Second Continental Congress** established the Secret Committee on September 18, 1775, to coordinate **trade** and the importation of clandestine arms and ammunition shipments from allies and neutrals during the **Revolutionary War**. The organization also directed the operations of American **privateers**. In July 1777, Congress renamed the body as the **Committee of Commerce**.

The Secret Committee should not be confused with the **Committee of Secret Correspondence**. *See also* HORTALEZ ET CIE.

SECRETARY OF STATE FOR THE COLONIES. The British established the position of secretary of state for the colonies in 1768. This governmental office was charged with overseeing policy toward British colonies.

SEDGWICK, THEODORE (1746–1813). Theodore Sedgwick, a lawyer, served in the **Massachusetts** legislature and represented his state in the **Congress of the Confederation** from 1785–1788. Sedgwick supported the U.S. **Constitution** and sat in the 1788 Massachusetts convention to ratify the document. He later served in the U.S. House of Representatives and the U.S. Senate.

SEIXAS, GERSHOM (1746–1816). Gershom Seixas was a prominent Jewish rabbi during the period of Revolutionary America.

SELBY, WILLIAM (1739?–1798). William Selby was a noted musician and composer in Revolutionary America. *See also* MUSIC.

SEPARATION OF POWERS. Separation of powers is the concept that governmental power should not be concentrated in one person or one group of individuals. This term as it is known in the United States emerged from the various compromises developed during the **Constitutional Convention of 1787**. **James Madison** was the major architect of this concept as well as that of "**checks and balances**." The separation of powers within the U.S. **Constitution** is best seen as the division of political power between executive (president), legislative (Congress), and judicial (Supreme Court) branches of government. Many delegates at the convention wanted this division of power to ensure the federal government would not grow too despotic.

SERGEANT, JONATHAN (1746–1793). Jonathan Sergeant, a lawyer, sat in the **New Jersey** legislature and represented his colony in the **Second Continental Congress** from February to June 1776. He departed just prior to the debate on the **Declaration of Independence**. He returned to **Congress** from November 1776 to September 1777.

Hessian troops burned his New Jersey home in retaliation for his patriotic stance. Sergeant moved his home to **Philadelphia** and left Congress in 1777 to accept the post of **Pennsylvania** attorney general.

SERVANTS. *See* INDENTURED SERVANTS; REDEMPTIONERS; SLAVERY.

SHAYS, DANIEL (c.1747–1825). Daniel Shays, a **Revolutionary War** officer, led **Shays's Rebellion** in **Massachusetts** after the Revolutionary War.

SHAYS'S REBELLION. Many small farmers were in **debt** after the **Revolutionary War**. General **economic** conditions were poor, sound money was in short supply, and manufactured goods were very expensive. At the same time, farmers were receiving lower prices for their crops. In **Massachusetts** and other states, courts were ordering the foreclosure on farms and imprisonment of debtor farmers. A movement arose in Massachusetts in late summer 1786 to reverse this trend. Led by Daniel Shays, a former **Continental Army** officer, several hundred farmers marched on Springfield to force the state supreme court not to foreclose on more farms. The group also attempted to seize weapons from the Springfield armory. The governor ordered General **Benjamin Lincoln** to lead a force of 4,000 **militia** to suppress the uprising. After several small skirmishes, Lincoln forced an end to the movement on February 2, 1787. Shays escaped to **Vermont**. The uprising alarmed many individuals throughout the country, including **George Washington**. This type of farmers' movement could spread to other states and the national government was powerless to assist. Shays's Rebellion helped to persuade many leaders in the country that the **Articles of Confederation** was too weak and that a stronger document was needed to bind the states. The **Constitutional Convention of 1787** resulted from such concerns. *See also* HALL, PRINCE.

SHEATHE. Sheathing involved adding copper plating to the hulls of naval vessels. The sheathing prevented worms from boring into the wood and helped reduce the buildup of barnacles.

SHERMAN, ROGER (1722–1793). Roger Sherman sat in the **Connecticut** legislature and served as a delegate in the **First Continental**

Congress in 1774, the **Second Continental Congress** from 1775–1781, and the **Congress of the Confederation** from 1783–1784. Sherman signed the **Declaration of Independence**. He attended the **Constitutional Convention of 1787** and signed the U.S. **Constitution**. Sherman is the only person who signed the **Continental Association**, the Declaration of Independence, the **Articles of Confederation**, and the U.S. Constitution. He later served in the U.S. House of Representatives and the U.S. Senate.

SHIP OF THE LINE. A ship of the line was a large naval vessel with sufficient armament to participate with similar vessels in a battle line against opposing ships of the line. A ship of the line usually carried at least 74 guns and was the "battleship" of the 18th century.

SHIPBUILDING INDUSTRY. The abundance of forests throughout eastern North America led to a profitable **lumber industry** in Revolutionary America. Shipbuilding emerged as an important by-product of the North American forests. The **New England colonies** developed strong **fishing** and **whaling** industries, requiring the construction of many vessels throughout the period. Most shipbuilding occurred north of **Maryland**, in part to meet this domestic demand for vessels. Special sections of large vessels were produced from live oak trees growing in **North Carolina**, **South Carolina**, and **Georgia**. These trees have large, naturally crooked branches that provided natural bends for specialty pieces of wood fitted within vessel hulls. In 1775, New England boasted over 2,000 ships. This total did not include fishing vessels. At the same time, **Great Britain** needed considerable quantities of wood for its own shipbuilding industry. However, ships could be constructed in the American **colonies** at a 30% savings compared to building them in Great Britain. Therefore, many British ships were actually constructed in the American colonies and approximately one-third of the 7,700 British ships sailing on the eve of the Revolution were built by American colonists. During the Revolution, American shipbuilders constructed warships for the **Continental Navy**, including one **ship of the line**—the "battleship" of the 18th century. The latter was completed after the ending of hostilities and was given to the French as a gift. *See also* NAVAL CONSTRUCTION ACT OF 1776.

SHIPPEN, WILLIAM (1736–1801). William Shippen, a physician, was a prominent teacher of anatomy and midwifery during the period of Revolutionary America.

SHIRT MEN. "Shirt men" was a British slang term for American **militia** members who wore hunting shirts rather than uniforms.

SIX NATIONS. *See* IROQUOIS.

SIXTH OF ANNE. Sixth of Anne was the popular name for the law forbidding British **impressment** policies in the waters of the American **colonies**.

SKENANDOA (1706?–1816). Skenandoa was a noted Oneida chief. His influence over the Oneida and Tuscarora groups of **Native Americans** ensured their neutrality and then pro-American stance in the **Revolutionary War**.

SLAVERY. Slavery was a controversial institution as early as the Revolutionary period in American history. While there were free **African Americans** in the **colonies**, the vast majority of individuals with African origins were held as slaves. Although **Great Britain** outlawed slavery in 1771, she still tolerated the slave trade to the American colonies in support of the many British companies making profits from the commerce. Many British politicians even questioned the increasing anti-slavery sentiment in the American colonies. In 1776, there were approximately 500,000 slaves in the 13 colonies with 40 percent of this total (or 200,000) in **Virginia**. **New Hampshire** had the least number of slaves (approximately 700) in 1776. The first motions to eliminate slavery began with the African slave trade. Many individuals protested the African slave trade and the **Second Continental Congress** concluded a **nonimportation agreement** early in its history. **Delaware** initiated its own ban on the arrival of slave ships in 1776.

In 1775, **Lord John Dunmore**, the royal governor of Virginia, offered slaves the opportunity for freedom if they would fight for the British military. Dunmore did form a small unit, known as **Lord Dunmore's Ethiopian Regiment**. However, the British army treated most slaves as captured enemy property and did not free them. Instead, the British often transported them to the West Indies. Some were given passage and freedom to **Canada** or Africa. Approximately 5,000 African Americans served with the patriot forces during the Revolution and many of these were slaves. Some of the latter fought under a promise of eventual freedom. Although officially not a state, **Vermont** in 1777 became the first territorial entity in the United States to outlaw slavery within its constitution. **Pennsylvania** became the first state to abolish slavery on March 1, 1780. The new law stated that children born after the law's passage could not be slaves.

After 1783, the slave trade issue was essentially in the hands of the individual states. However, by 1786, every state except **Georgia** had either banned or restricted the importation of slaves from Africa. The ending of slavery itself followed in many states. By 1784, **Connecticut**, **Massachusetts**, New Hampshire, Pennsylvania, and **Rhode Island** had either eliminated slavery entirely or provided for gradual emancipation. The question of slavery arose again during the debate and preparation of the U.S. **Constitution**. In the new document, the states settled lingering questions of the slave trade by papering over their differences about the institution of slavery and the counting of slaves in the general population for the purpose of representation in Congress. Individuals who made an impact on Revolutionary American history despite their conditions under the slavery system included **Jupiter Hammon** and **Phillis Wheatley**. Prominent anti-slavery advocates during the Revolutionary Period included **Richard Allen, William Allen**, **Joshua Atherton**, **John Bartram**, **George Bedinger**, **Nathan Dane**, **Jacob Green**, **Prince Hall**, **Thomas Hazard**, **John Leland**, **Levi Lincoln**, **George Mason**, and **Benjamin Rush**. Significant supporters of slavery included **Pierce Butler** and **James Habersham**. *See also* CANVAS TOWN; CONSTITUTIONAL CONVENTION; GREAT AWAKENING; SOCIETY FOR THE PROMOTION OF MANUMISSION OF SLAVES AND PROTECTING SUCH OF THEM THAT HAVE BEEN OR MAY BE LIBERATED; THREE-FIFTHS COMPROMISE.

SLOOP. A sloop is a small sailing vessel with a single mast.

SMALLPOX. Smallpox proved to be a very resilient disease in Revolutionary America. It was very contagious and spread quickly when individuals within a large, confined group caught it. Smallpox, while dangerous to the American colonists, was very deadly to **Native Americans** who had little resistance to European diseases. The lifting of the Native American siege of Fort Pitt during **Pontiac's War** is credited in part to a smallpox outbreak among the Shawnee and Delaware outside the British fort. A rumor has persisted that the British spread the disease by giving smallpox infected blankets to the Native Americans during a period of negotiations. However, this event is not proven and evidence to the contrary does exist. In 1721, **Zabdiel Boylston** conducted the first inoculation for smallpox in America. This controversial program had not proven itself and caused fear among the locals. During the **Revolutionary War**, the **Continental Army** initiated a program of inoculating soldiers against smallpox. However, all civilians living around the military camps had to be inoculated as well, leading many to challenge the practice that could actually spread the disease it was meant to halt.

SMALLWOOD, WILLIAM (1732–1792). William Smallwood, a **Revolutionary War** officer, declined to represent **Maryland** in the **Congress of the Confederation** in 1784. He was elected governor of Maryland in 1785.

SMITH, DANIEL (1748–1818). Daniel Smith sat as a delegate in **North Carolina**'s **Fayetteville state convention** to ratify the U.S. **Constitution**. He later served as a U.S. senator from **Tennessee**.

SMITH, HEZEKIAH (1737–1805). Hezekiah Smith was a noted Baptist clergyman in Revolutionary America.

SMITH, JAMES (c.1719–1806). James Smith, a lawyer, represented **Pennsylvania** in the **Second Continental Congress** in 1776 and from 1777–1778. He signed the **Declaration of Independence**.

SMITH, JOHN (1756–1799). John Smith was a prominent Presbyterian clergyman during the period of Revolutionary America.

SMITH, JONATHAN (1742–1812). Jonathan Smith, a merchant, represented **Pennsylvania** in the **Second Continental Congress** from 1777–1778. He signed the **Articles of Confederation**.

SMITH, MELANCTON (1744–1798). Melancton Smith, a lawyer, sat in the **New York** legislature and represented his state in the **Congress of the Confederation** from 1785–1788. He attended the 1788 state convention to ratify the U.S. **Constitution**.

SMITH, MERIWETHER (1730–1794). Meriwether Smith sat in the **Virginia** legislature and represented his state in the **Second Continental Congress** from 1778–1782. He was also a delegate to the Virginia state convention to ratify the U.S. **Constitution**.

SMITH, RICHARD (1735–1803). Richard Smith represented **New Jersey** in the **First Continental Congress** in 1774 and the **Second Continental Congress** from 1775–1776.

SMITH, ROBERT (c.1722–1777). Robert Smith was a noted architect and builder in Revolutionary America.

SMUGGLING. **Great Britain** applied a policy of **mercantilism** to its **trade** relations with the American **colonies**. Americans resented these trade restrictions and turned to smuggling in order to avoid British duties. However, the British often practiced **salutary neglect** and tended to ignore many American actions to avoid trade regulations. After the **French and Indian War**, the British opted to enforce their trade restrictions, endangering the profits made by some Americans through smuggling. Other Americans viewed British trade restrictions as assaults upon individual liberties. Noted American smugglers included **Samuel Adams** and **John Hancock**. Their opposition to British trade restrictions and the crackdown on smuggling helped spur the American popular reaction against Great Britain, leading to the **Revolutionary War**. Important incidents with American smuggling vessels or British customs craft included confrontations involving the ***Gaspée***, the ***Liberty***, and the ***Lydia***. *See also* ECONOMY.

SOCIETY FOR THE PROMOTION OF ARTS, AGRICULTURE, AND ECONOMY. **New York City** residents formed the Society for the Promotion of Arts, Agriculture, and Economy to counter the impact of the **Sugar Act of 1764** on the local economy. The society emphasized the development of local industries in order to make local inhabitants more economically self-sufficient. The idea spread to other cities and **colonies**.

SOCIETY FOR THE PROMOTION OF MANUMISSION OF SLAVES AND PROTECTING SUCH OF THEM THAT HAVE BEEN OR MAY BE LIBERATED. Founders established the society in 1785 to promote the end of **slavery** in **New York**. **John Jay** led the society, which encouraged its members to boycott those who sold slaves and established a school for freed slaves.

SOCIETY OF THE CINCINNATI. The Society of the Cincinnati was an organization proposed by General **Henry Knox**. The title of the organization is taken from the name of the famous Roman general. Former officers of the **Continental Army** officially formed the organization on May 13, 1783, to continue their ties and friendships. Chapters were established in the United States and **France**. As the war's participants died, their heirs assumed the memberships in the society, which still exists and has its headquarters in Washington, D.C.

SOLEMN LEAGUE AND COVENANT. The Solemn League and Covenant was a pledge among **Bostonians** to maintain the **economic** boycott against British goods during the summer of 1774. **Samuel Adams** and many others viewed coercion as a method of enforcing the boycott via the covenant.

SONS OF LIBERTY. The term "Sons of Liberty," coined by **Isaac Barré** of **Great Britain**, referred to American colonists who had joined secret organizations to counter the British attempts at **taxation** after 1765. The members frequently carried out their activities using violence and coercion.

SOUTH CAROLINA. South Carolina, one of the **southern colonies**, was governed by **Great Britain** as a **royal colony** until the **Revolutionary War** and American independence. By the end of America's Revolutionary period in 1790, the state boasted 393,751 people (43%

slaves). South Carolinians were divided on the issue of independence. It has been estimated that one-third of the population were patriots, one-third were **loyalists**, and one-third just wanted to be left alone. Patriots and loyalists took strong stands on their beliefs within the state. Patriots seized British tea in **Charleston** and later helped drive the governor from the colony. The divisions among the populace led to many small battles within the state during the Revolutionary War. South Carolina can be accurately described as a state embroiled in a civil war between 1780 and 1782. Although there were several battles between **Continental** and British regular forces, most battles were between patriot and loyalist **militia** units. The state ratified the U.S. **Constitution** on May 23, 1788. South Carolina was the largest producer and exporter of **rice** and the fourth-largest producer and exporter of **tobacco** in the United States during this period. Notable individuals from South Carolina include **Thomas Heyward Jr.**, **Henry Laurens**, **Thomas Lynch Jr.**, **Thomas Lynch Sr.**, **Arthur Middleton**, **Henry Middleton**, **Charles Pinckney**, **Charles Cotesworth Pinckney**, **Thomas Pinckney**, **Edward Rutledge**, and **John Rutledge**.

SOUTH-END MOB. The South-End Mob was a loose organization of individuals living in southern **Boston**. The group was known for its rowdy confrontations with the **North-End Mob** every November 5th (the anniversary of Guy Fawkes's gunpowder plot). The **Loyal Nine** persuaded the two mobs to direct their activities against the British and their **taxation** schemes.

SOUTHERN COLONIES. The southern colonies included **Georgia**, **North Carolina**, **Maryland**, **South Carolina**, and **Virginia**. *See also* AGRICULTURE; RICE; SHIPBUILDING INDUSTRY; TOBACCO.

SOUTHERN DEPARTMENT. The **Second Continental Congress** established the Southern Department as a **military department** on February 27, 1776. The Southern Department consisted of **Georgia**, **North Carolina**, **South Carolina**, and **Virginia**.

SPAIGHT, RICHARD (1758–1802). Richard Spaight sat in the **North Carolina** legislature and represented his state in the **Congress of the**

Confederation from 1783–1785. He served as a delegate to the **Constitutional Convention of 1787** and signed the U.S. **Constitution**. He then attended North Carolina's **Hillsborough state convention** and **Fayetteville state convention** to ratify the Constitution. Spaight later served as governor, a presidential elector, and member of the U.S. House of Representatives.

SPAIN AND REVOLUTIONARY AMERICA. Spain authorized the secret shipment of munitions to the Americans on May 2, 1776, following a similar French decision. Spain did not fully support the American notion of independence from the British monarchy, but Madrid saw the **Revolutionary War** as a strategy for weakening her British rival and regaining Florida, Gibraltar, and Minorca. Spain negotiated the **Convention of Aranjuez** with **France** in April 1779 and officially entered the conflict in June 1779. The Spanish did not sign a formal treaty of alliance with the Americans, relying instead on renewing an older pact with France. Thus, in many eyes, Spain was joining France in a war against **Great Britain** rather than supporting the ideals of American independence. Spanish military units did not join their French counterparts in active operations with the **Continental Army**. However, Spanish forces were active in engaging British posts along the Mississippi River and in Florida.

Although Spain wanted to see a defeated Great Britain and the restoration of territory at the end of the Revolution, she did not trust the Americans. In 1779, **Congress** appointed **John Jay** as the U.S. commissioner to Spain. Jay's instructions included obtaining a treaty of alliance and another for **trade** with Spain, navigation rights along the Mississippi River, access to a port south of the 31st parallel, a loan, and recognition for the new country. In return, the United States pledged to back Spanish efforts to wrest Florida from the British. The Spanish government never granted a formal audience to Jay and never concluded a treaty of alliance with the United States despite fighting Great Britain as an American ally. Jay did obtain a small loan. Spain practiced **mercantilism** and did not have any intention of allowing the United States to trade with her colonies or spread ideas about revolution and democracy.

Spain informed the United States in 1784 that she would not abide by the **Treaty of Paris of 1783** concluded between the latter country and Great Britain. The treaty permitted free navigation of the Mississippi River to the Americans. However, Spain controlled the territory through which the mouth of the Mississippi River entered the Gulf of Mexico and did not have any intention of allowing the United States free navigation rights. Americans on the Mississippi River faced the seizure of their vessels and cargo. Spain worked to agitate the **Native Americans** living along the American western frontier and even tried to entice the settlers in the western areas to separate themselves from the United States. In 1785, the Spanish ambassador to the United States, Don Diego de Gardoqui, met with John Jay to discuss the Mississippi River issue and the question of demarcating the border between American territory and Spanish Florida. On the latter question, the United States insisted on the 31st parallel while Spain argued for a more northerly border. Spain also refused to permit free navigation of the Mississippi River by American vessels. Spain and the United States did conclude a commercial treaty. However, negotiations continued through 1787 on the other two points. *See also* GARDOQUI AND SONS.

SPECIE. *See* CURRENCY.

SPRING, SAMUEL (1746–1819). Samuel Spring was a noted Congregational clergyman in Revolutionary America.

SPRINGFIELD ARSENAL. *See* SHAYS'S REBELLION.

SPONTOON. A spontoon was a large metal blade on the end of a long (often seven-foot) pole used by commissioned officers as a symbol of rank as well as a weapon. *See also* HALBERD.

STAMP ACT CONGRESS. Following the British announcement of the **Stamp Act of 1765**, **James Otis** of **Massachusetts** called for a conference to discuss the colonial response to the **taxation** scheme. Some **colonies** proved to be wary of gathering to formally protest against the British act. However, general public debate and the **Virginia Resolutions** prompted many of the skeptics to move in favor of the congress. Delegates from nine colonies (**Connecticut**, **Delaware**, **Maryland**, Massachusetts, **New Jersey**, **New York**, **Pennsylvania**,

Rhode Island, and **South Carolina**) met in **New York City** from October 7 to 24, 1765. Governors in the other three colonies prevented their legislatures from appointing delegates. However, each of the three assemblies forwarded letters to the congress stating they would accept the resolutions approved by the delegates in attendance.

The representatives at the congress maintained that they remained loyal to the British Crown and Parliament but objected to the new taxes. Their arguments rested on the belief that they should only be taxed by their colonial assemblies. The colonists elected members to represent them in the colonial assemblies but did not have the same privilege in the British Parliament. Many Americans at this time quoted the early political philosopher **Edward Coke**. The congress demanded the repeal of the Stamp Act of 1765 and the **Sugar Act of 1764**. The delegates also prepared what is known as the **Declaration of Rights and Grievances**. Although not all of the delegates signed the declaration, the majority did pen their names to the document. The unity displayed by the delegates concerned the British, who preferred to prevent any political unity among the colonies.

STAMP ACT OF 1765. British Prime Minister **George Grenville** persuaded Parliament to pass the Stamp Act on March 22,1765, with an effective date for implementation of November 1, 1765. The settlement of the **French and Indian War** in 1763 left **Great Britain** in debt. At the same time, London realized that a standing army had to be maintained in the American **colonies** in order to watch the **Native American** frontier and provide positions for the officers and men of the large military force developed during the war. At the same time, Grenville wanted to reduce the land tax at home. In order to pay for a standing army in the American colonies and a reduction in local taxes, Grenville proposed that the American colonists should cover part of the costs of this permanent military force. As a result, Parliament passed the **Sugar Act of 1764**. Since this piece of legislation would not raise all of the revenue the British wanted from the American colonies, Grenville also proposed the Stamp Act of 1765.

The Stamp Act of 1765 involved the first attempt to directly tax the American colonies. Parliament approved the legislation despite colonial protests and the opposition of a few of its own members with connections in colonial **trade**. The act placed a tax on documents, other forms of printed matter, and gambling devices. Documents used in court, mortgages, shipping clearance certificates, newspapers, pamphlets, and liquor licenses were also included. Dice and playing cards were subject to a tax as well. The duties were to be paid in sterling, not local currency, and **Admiralty Courts** were given jurisdiction over violators.

Grenville originally suggested the legislation behind the act in March 1764. By December of that year, the **Board of Trade and Plantations** heard the complaints of the American colonies and dismissed them. As a result, **Benjamin Franklin** requested a personal meeting with Grenville, who offered to consider American **taxation** alternatives. However, he refused to abandon the general plan to have the Americans pay for their protection and other services. Between the March 1765 passage of the Stamp Act and its effective date in November 1765, the American colonies continued their protests. Grenville refused to alter his plan despite the petitions of several colonies to **King George III** and Parliament through their agents in London. **Patrick Henry** of **Virginia** addressed that colony's House of Burgesses on the issue and prompted the body to pass a series of resolutions against the measure. **Rhode Island** announced that it was not required to obey the Stamp Act of 1765 since the taxation legislation had not been passed by its own assembly. In June 1765, **James Otis** of **Massachusetts** proposed the formation of what became known as the **Stamp Act Congress**. The nine colonies in attendance prepared the **Declaration of Rights and Grievances**, which pledged support for the Crown but decreed that individuals should only be taxed by those chosen to represent them.

Many port cities established groups known as **Sons of Liberty** with the purpose of preventing the distribution of the stamps. Colonial protests led by the Sons of Liberty often became very violent and included the complete destruction of homes. Mobs turned on stamp distributors such as Andrew Oliver and Augustus Johnston as well as political figures including Massachusetts Lieutenant Governor **Thomas Hutchinson**. Many individuals in Britain, including **John Wilkes** and **William Pitt**, supported the colonial position with regard to the act. American merchants agreed to boycott British goods in protest of the Stamp Act. Although trade did not completely cease, the boycott had enough of an impact on British merchants to persuade them to petition for a repeal of the Stamp Act. The **Marquis of Rockingham** replaced Grenville as prime minister in late 1765. Under his leadership, Parliament opted to repeal the Stamp Act of 1765 due to the opposition at home and in the American colonies. **Georgia** was the only colony where the Stamp Act had been implemented prior to its repeal. After repealing the Stamp Act on March 17, 1766, Parliament passed the **Declaratory Act** stating that the body had the authority to make laws for the American colonies.

STARS AND STRIPES. The Stars and Stripes is the nickname for the American flag adopted after June 1777. The flag contained 13 horizontal alternating red and white stripes representing the 13 states. The upper corner of the flag contains a blue field with 13 stars in a circle representing a new constellation—the United States of America. The Stars and Stripes replaced the **Grand Union Flag**, originally adopted in 1775. *See also* ROSS, BETSY.

STATE DEPARTMENT. **Congress** established the State Department on July 27, 1789, to oversee U.S. **foreign policy**. **Thomas Jefferson** became the first secretary of state.

STATEMENT OF RIGHTS AND GRIEVANCES. The **Grand Committee** of the **First Continental Congress** drafted the Statement of Rights and Grievances, also known as the Declaration of Rights and Grievances, on October 14, 1774. The document highlighted 13 acts of Parliament passed since 1763 and described American colonial grievances with them. It is interesting to note that Congress omitted two important acts—the **Declaratory Act of 1766** and the **Tea Act of 1773** from the Statement of Rights and Grievances. By omitting the former, Congress acknowledged the right of Parliament to pass colonial legislation. However, the delegates declared that Parliament should have the consent of the American **colonies** on **taxation** and other **economic** issues. The statement included an announcement that the American colonies planned to economically boycott British goods. The delegates formed the **Continental Association** to manage this boycott.

STATEN ISLAND, PEACE CONFERENCE OF. The **Second Continental Congress** authorized a delegation consisting of **Benjamin**

Franklin, **John Adams**, and **Edward Rutledge** to discuss a settlement of the **Revolutionary War** with Admiral Lord Richard Howe on September 11, 1776. However, the talks collapsed because Howe did not have the authority to negotiate with the Americans and could only pass their proposals on to London.

STATE OF TRADE. In December 1763, **Boston** merchants wrote the *State of Trade* to protest the renewal of the **Molasses Act of 1733** as the **Sugar Act of 1764**. The document declared that the act would benefit British West Indies sugar growers and damage American colonial **trade**. Many American colonial goods could not be consumed by **Great Britain** and thus the merchants needed to conduct foreign trade. Copies of the document were distributed to other American **colonies** and to British merchants.

STATE TROOPS. State Troops were military units raised by the states but serving on a full-time basis rather than for short durations like the **militia**. Although full time, these units served their respective states and not the **Continental Army**, even though they frequently assisted the latter. Thus, late in the Revolution, the Americans were fielding three types of military units: the Continental Army, state militia units, and State Troops.

South Carolina offers a clear example behind the establishment of State Troops. **Thomas Sumter**, in the absence of the Continental Army and realizing that a militia force would not be able to remove the British forces from the state, proposed the establishment of State Troops in early 1781. The volunteers comprising these units would serve the state of South Carolina in a full-time capacity similar to regular soldiers in the Continental or British armies. Sumter, a guerrilla leader known as the Gamecock, essentially dictated the establishment of the force since the state did not have a patriot government located within its borders. Sumter proposed to pay the State Troops through the use of what is known as **Sumter's Law**, which involved looting the estates of **loyalists**. He also offered to equip each volunteer and provide his family with half a bushel of salt as a recruiting bonus. The excitement of acquiring loot led many North Carolinians to join the State Troops of South Carolina.

Governor **John Rutledge**, in exile, gave his approval to the plan. However, he would later denounce Sumter's Law as illegal. Sumter originally commanded the South Carolina State Troops. Later, Brigadier General William Henderson served as commander of State Troops until he was wounded at the Battle of Eutaw Springs. Sumter then returned from temporary retirement and assumed his old post with the State Troops.

STEAMBOAT. In 1763, **William Henry** constructed the first steamboat in what is now the United States. However, his tests were failures. **John Fitch** built the first successful steamboat in the United States. Fitch's craft was successfully tested for the first time on August 22, 1787.

STEARNS, SHUBAL (1706–1771). Shubal Stearns was a prominent Baptist clergyman during the period of Revolutionary America.

STEELE, JOHN (1764–1815). John Steele attended the North Carolina **Hillsborough state convention** and the **Fayetteville state convention** for the ratification of the U.S. **Constitution**. He later served in the U.S. House of Representatives.

STILLMAN, SAMUEL (1737–1807). Samuel Stillman, a Baptist clergyman, attended the **Massachusetts** state convention to ratify the U.S. **Constitution**. He unsuccessfully argued for the inclusion of a **Bill of Rights** before ratification of the document.

STOCKS. Individuals convicted in the **criminal justice system** might be sentenced to the stocks. The criminal would sit, normally on a stool, while his or her arms and legs were locked into the holes cut into a piece of wood. The individual would have to sit in this position until completing the sentence. Locals would often stop to publicly scorn or throw rotting fruit and vegetables at the convicted person. *See also* PILLORY.

STOCKTON, RICHARD (1730–1781). Richard Stockton, a lawyer, represented **New Jersey** in the **Second Continental Congress** in 1776 and signed the **Declaration of Independence**. The British captured Stockton in 1776. He received poor treatment while held by the

British and this ruined his health. Stockton died in 1781 after being exchanged.

STONE, THOMAS (1743–1787). Thomas Stone, a lawyer, represented **Maryland** in the **Second Continental Congress** from 1775–1778 and **Congress of the Confederation** from 1783–1784. Stone signed the **Declaration of Independence** and sat on the committee that drafted the **Articles of Confederation**. Maryland selected Stone to represent the state in the **Constitutional Convention of 1787** but he was too ill to attend and died before the end of the year.

STRONG, CALEB (1745–1819). Caleb Strong, a lawyer, declined the opportunity to represent **Massachusetts** in the **Continental Congress**. However, he did accept the offer to attend the **Constitutional Convention of 1787**. During the deliberations, Strong favored the preparation of a new constitution but was absent for its signing due to an illness in his family. Strong served in the U.S. Senate and as governor of his state later in life.

STUART, GILBERT (1755–1828). Gilbert Stuart emerged as one of the greatest early American **painters** and is known for his classic works on the **Revolutionary War** and **French and Indian War**. Many of his most famous paintings were actually completed after the Revolutionary period in American history. However, it was during the Revolutionary period that he traveled to **Great Britain** and studied art under another American, **Benjamin West**. His most famous paintings are portraits of **George Washington**.

SUFFERERS OF 1763. The Sufferers of 1763 is a term describing the **land speculators** and others who suffered financially as a result of **Pontiac's War**.

SUFFOLK RESOLVES. Suffolk County, **Massachusetts**, included the city of **Boston**. The county passed the Suffolk Resolves on September 9, 1774, in response to the British **Intolerable Acts**. The resolves were then dispatched to the **First Continental Congress** for consideration. The resolves declared that the people should preserve their liberties. They also noted that the inhabitants of Suffolk County should initiate a program of civil disobedience to the British in Boston. The document also announced weekly drills for the local **militia** units. **Paul Revere** carried the document to **Philadelphia**, where the First Continental Congress endorsed them on September 14, 1774.

SUFFRAGE. *See* FRANCHISE.

SUGAR ACT OF 1764. After the conclusion of the **French and Indian War**, the British government made the decision to maintain a standing army in the American **colonies**. Prime Minister **George Grenville** wanted the American colonies to pay a percentage of the costs associated with keeping an army in North America. At the same time, he wanted to lower the land taxes in **Great Britain**. In response to his request, Parliament passed the Sugar Act of 1764 in April 1764 in order to clamp down on the widespread bribery and **smuggling** of American colonists to avoid the **Molasses Act of 1733**. The Sugar Act of 1764, also known as the American Revenue Act or the Plantation Duties Act of 1764, actually reduced the tax on imported molasses from six to three pence per gallon, making bribery and smuggling less profitable for the American colonial merchants. The act also listed new duties for coffee, **indigo**, textiles that were not of British origin, and wine from Madeira. The American colonists were banned from importing French wines and foreign rum while American exports of **iron**, silk, and **potash** could only be shipped to Great Britain. The act also doubled the tax on foreign products shipped through Great Britain to the American colonies.

Violations of the Sugar Act would be tried in **Admiralty Courts** and not colonial courts. Prior to 1764, juries in the colonial courts tended to acquit or pass soft judgments on violators of the Molasses Act of 1733. Cases in Admiralty Courts would be heard by judges appointed in Great Britain and not the American colonies. The American colonists resisted the Sugar Act of 1764 for several reasons. First, the merchants resented the interference in their lucrative trade with non-British possessions in the Caribbean. Second, the tax represented the first time the British Parliament moved to actually exercise its perceived right to tax the American colonies for any purpose. Prior to 1764, customs taxes had been directed toward financing the regulation of **trade**. Third, the money collected from the tax was destined to support the stationing of regular British soldiers in the American colonies. The colonists did not trust a permanent British military presence on their territory. Fourth, many Americans viewed the **taxation** scheme as a violation of their natural rights. In their eyes, the colonial assemblies were the only bodies with the power to levy taxes on them. **James Otis** is noted for his eloquent speech attacking the provisions of the Sugar Act of 1764 on ideological grounds. Fifth, the British tightened the bonding laws associated with shipping cargo. In the past, a captain could load his ship and then acquire the bond prior to sailing. The Sugar Act of 1764 stated that all products must be bonded prior to loading. If an inspector discovered any unbonded goods on board, he had the authority to seize the goods and/or the ship. Many customs officials used this provision for private profit by seizing American cargoes. The incident involving the vessel ***Liberty***, owned by **John Hancock**, hinged on the issue of bonding.

Massachusetts appointed a **Committee of Correspondence** to coordinate responses to the tax with other colonies. **Boston**, **Philadelphia**, and **New York** implemented limited boycotts of British goods in retaliation. In **Rhode Island**, the crew of the British ship ***Saint John*** encountered public resentment and armed attack. The **southern colonies** offered little resistance since the vast majority of their trade was directly with Great Britain and not through the West Indies. **Charleston**, **South Carolina**, was one exception in the south. The British lowered the sugar tax to one pence two years later due to the American colonial opposition. However, other duties remained in place. The Sugar Act of 1764 can be seen as the first of a series of new taxes that would draw the colonists into the **Revolutionary War**. *See also* CURRENCY ACT OF 1764; STAMP ACT OF 1765.

SULLIVAN, JOHN (1740–1795). John Sullivan briefly represented **New Hampshire** in the **Second Continental Congress** in 1775 before accepting a commission as a brigadier general in the **Continental Army**. He resigned in 1779 due to ill health and returned to the Second Continental Congress from 1780–1781. Sullivan served as the governor of New Hampshire from 1786–1789 and the chair of the 1788 state convention to ratify the U.S. **Constitution**. Later he was a federal district judge.

***SUMMARY VIEW OF THE RIGHTS OF BRITISH AMERICA*.** **Thomas Jefferson** wrote *A Summary View of the Rights of British America* in 1774 in response to the imposition of the **Boston Port Act**. Jefferson's pamphlet became one of the most widely distributed documents protesting the act and reaffirming individual rights.

SUMNER, INCREASE (1746–1799). Increase Sumner, a judge, attended the 1788 **Massachusetts** state convention to ratify the U.S. **Constitution**. He later served as governor of Massachusetts.

SUMTER, THOMAS (1734–1832). Thomas Sumter served as a **Continental Army** officer and later a **militia** brigadier general while leading a group of partisans in **South Carolina** between 1780 and 1782. Sumter is known for the implementation of what became known as **Sumter's Law**. He utilized this controversial program to justify seizing **loyalist** property in order to pay his troops. Sumter sat in the **Congress of the Confederation** from 1783–1784 and later represented South Carolina in the U.S. Congress and Senate.

SUMTER'S LAW. Sumter's Law is the term often applied to the policies of **Thomas Sumter** for paying his partisan forces and **State Troops** in **South Carolina**. The imposition of Sumter's Law also indicates the serious nature of the civil conflict in many states between patriots and **loyalists**. In a highly controversial move denounced by leaders of both sides of the **Revolutionary War**, Sumter's Law involved the seizure of property from loyalist South Carolinians and its distribution as payment to South Carolina State Troops. In particular, Francis Marion, another guerrilla leader in South Carolina, actively opposed Sumter's Law and complained to Major General Nathanael Greene as well as South Carolina civilian officials. South Carolina Governor **John Rutledge** did outlaw the practice in August 1781. The controversy over Sumter's Law stretched into the postwar years as the South Carolina Assembly finally decided to pass a law exempting all officers from liabilities for the seizure of private property during the **Revolutionary War**.

SWEDEN AND REVOLUTIONARY AMERICA. After the Revolution, **Congress** dispatched American diplomats to secure commercial treaties with European states. **Benjamin Franklin** and **John Adams** negotiated the first U.S. commercial treaty with Sweden in 1783.

SYCAMORE SHOALS, TREATY OF. **Richard Henderson**, president of the **Transylvania Company**, concluded the Treaty of Sycamore Shoals with the **Cherokee** in 1775. Under the terms of the treaty, Henderson acquired the land between the Ohio and Cumberland Rivers for settlement by his company. The Transylvania Company was never able to settle the land based on its claims from the treaty.

SYMES, JOHN (1742–1814). John Symes, a **Revolutionary War** officer, represented **New Jersey** in the **Congress of the Confederation** from 1785–1786.

– T –

TAHGAHJUTE. *See* LOGAN, JAMES.

TANNENBERGER, DAVID (1728–1804). David Tannenberger was a well-known organ builder in Revolutionary America.

TAR AND FEATHERS. Patriots and **loyalists** turned to tarring and feathering each other as a form of public insult and punishment. Individuals would strip the victim and literally cover him or her with hot tar and then feathers. At one point, a book was published explaining how to properly tar and feather an individual.

TAXATION. The British attempts to tax the American **colonies** after the **French and Indian War** greatly strained relations between the two parties and helped lead to the opening hostilities of the **Revolutionary War**. British taxes and **trade** restrictions, including the **Molasses Act of 1733**, existed before the French and Indian War. However, the American colonists utilized various means, including **smuggling**, to avoid trade restrictions and taxes while the British made only half-hearted attempts to enforce them. At the conclusion of the French and Indian War, Prime Minister **George Grenville**

looked to the American colonists to pay a percentage of the costs for maintaining a standing British army in North America. The American colonists resented the long arm of London reaching across the Atlantic Ocean to tax and restrict their trade. The taxes were seen as parliamentary interference in colonial affairs since each American colony viewed its assembly as the only legitimate source of taxation. Taxing a man without his consent (via representative government) involved stripping him of his "natural rights" as espoused by **John Locke**. It is ironic to note that many of the taxes, such as the **Sugar Act of 1764**, actually involved a lowering of the existing tax but increased enforcement. Many early American patriots were businessmen accustomed to smuggling and would lose money under the new British policies.

Calls of "no taxation without representation" emerged from the colonists. But this often carried little weight with the Crown and even ordinary Englishmen. The British Parliament consisted of members based on "virtual representation." Many areas of **Great Britain** did not select parliamentary members but were represented by everyone seated in the legislature. Thus, the British saw nothing wrong with not having directly elected American representatives in Parliament. However, the American colonists declared that people should have the right to choose the individuals who represented them in Parliament.

After the declaration of American independence, the American colonies organized themselves under the **Articles of Confederation**. However, this document did not permit **Congress** to tax as the national government. When Congress proposed a 5% duty on imports, the states fought the measure in order to maintain their own individual import taxes. The inability to tax proved to be one of the major weaknesses of the Articles of Confederation and helped lead to the **Constitutional Convention of 1787**. On July 4, 1789, Congress established its national first tariff bill, taxing 30 different items imported into the United States. *See also* BANK OF NORTH AMERICA; INTOLERABLE ACTS; STAMP ACT OF 1765; TEA ACT OF 1773; TOWNSHEND ACTS OF 1767.

TAYLOR, GEORGE (1716–1781). George Taylor, an ironmaster, served in the **Pennsylvania** legislature. He represented the state in the **Second Continental Congress** from 1776–1777 and signed the **Declaration of Independence**.

TEA ACT OF 1773. The **East India Company** faced an economic crisis due to mismanagement, corruption, British wars in the Far East, and the declining American demand for British tea. Supporters of the company persuaded the British Parliament to pass the Tea Act on May 10, 1773, to allow the sale of a half-million pounds of tea directly to the American **colonies** without the previous requirement to transship the product through England. The price set for the tea was so low that it would cut heavily into the profits of those individuals smuggling Dutch tea and even those importing legal tea from **Great Britain**. Consignees for the tea were selected in **Boston**, **Charleston**, **New York City** and **Philadelphia**. However, considerable American opposition arose after the passage of the Tea Act. Locals, often led by the **Sons of Liberty**, forced many of the consignees to resign and prevented the transfer of the tea from some of the ships. Consignee defiance of the local opposition led to the **Boston Tea Party** in December 1773. *See also* BODY, THE; HAMPDEN; RUSTICUS; SCAEVOLA.

TELFAIR, EDWARD (1735–1807). Edward Telfair, a merchant, arrived in **Georgia** from Scotland in 1766 and became a member of the **Sons of Liberty**. He represented Georgia in the **Second Continental Congress** from 1777–1781 and the **Congress of the Confederation** from 1781–1783. He signed the **Articles of Confederation**. Telfair served as the governor of Georgia later in life.

TENNESSEE. **North Carolina** claimed most of the area known today as Tennessee during the Revolutionary period. **South Carolina** claimed a small strip of land running west toward the Mississippi River that today is part of southern Tennessee. **Georgia** also made some claims on land that now is part of Tennessee. At the end of the **French and Indian War**, the British implemented the **Proclamation of 1763** to protect **Native American** lands by prohibiting the westward movement of American settlers. The movement of Americans to the Watauga area of Tennessee began as early as 1768 in defiance of the British. In 1771, **James Robertson** (sometimes known as the "father of Tennessee") led a group of North Carolinians into the same area. The settlers in the area, under the leadership of Robertson, formed the **Watauga Association** in 1772. The independent stance of the settlers changed during the Revolution as Native Americans increased their raids on the settlements. The settlers petitioned North Carolina to annex them, which occurred in 1777.

In 1783, an economically drained North Carolina offered land in what is now Tennessee for low sums in order to raise cash. Residents of eastern North Carolina viewed the area as a drain on state taxes and **land speculators** wanted access to large tracts of cheap land. As a result, the two groups were allied in working to persuade North Carolina to cede the area to the national government. An offer by North Carolina was withdrawn when it met opposition from the settlers. Further discussions led to a division among the settlers and a pro-statehood faction achieved the upper hand in the area and declared the formation of the state of Franklin. The national government rejected Franklin's bid for statehood. Divisions within the self-proclaimed state evolved into civil war and the defeat of the statehood faction in 1788. South Carolina withdrew its claims on land in the region in 1787 and Georgia in 1802. Tennessee received statehood within the United States in 1796. *See also* DUMPLIN CREEK, TREATY OF; KENTUCKY; WHITE, JAMES.

THATCHER, GEORGE (1754–1824). George Thatcher represented **Massachusetts** in the **Congress of the Confederation** from 1787–1789. He later served in the U.S. House of Representatives and as a state judge.

THATCHER, PETER (1752–1802). Peter Thatcher was a prominent Congregational clergyman in Revolutionary America.

THAYENDANEGEA. Thayendanegea is the **Native American** name for **Joseph Brandt**, a Mohawk who led numerous raids against patriot settlements during the **Revolutionary War**.

THEATER. The development of theater in the American **colonies** did not begin until after 1700 and grew slowly due to the scattered population and cultural belief that it was a shameful or sinful profession. By the beginning of the Revolutionary period, several large theaters existed in the colonies. Politics crept into the theater as it did into other aspects of colonial life. The first permanent commercial theater in what is now the United States was built in **Philadelphia**. In 1766, a theater in **New York** was destroyed in reaction to British players participating in a production. Noted playwrights during the Revolutionary Period included **Hugh Brackenridge**, **Thomas Godfrey**, and **Royall Tyler**. Tyler staged the first American comedy in New York on April 16, 1787. Other writers and actors associated with the theater during the period of Revolutionary America included **Lewis Hallman**, **Elizabeth Morris**, and **Thomas Wignell**.

THEUS, JEREMIAH (1716–1774). Jeremiah Theus, born in Switzerland, arrived in **South Carolina** in 1735. He emerged as one of the great **painters** of Revolutionary America and was the most renowned artist in **Charleston**, South Carolina, between 1740 and his death in 1774.

THOMAS, ISAIAH (1749–1831). Isaiah Thomas was a noted **printer** in Revolutionary America.

THOMSON, CHARLES (1729–1824). Charles Thomson served as the secretary to Congress from 1774–1789, which included every session of the **First Continental Congress**, the **Second Continental Congress**, and the **Congress of the Confederation**.

THOMSON, WILLIAM (1727–1796). William Thomson, a **Revolutionary War** officer, sat in the **South Carolina** legislature. In 1788, he was a delegate to the state convention to ratify the U.S. **Constitution**.

THORNTON, MATTHEW (1714–1803). Matthew Thornton, a physician, represented **New Hampshire** in the **Second Continental Congress** from 1776–1777 and signed the **Declaration of Independence**. He served in the state senate later in life.

THREE DRUNKS. This was a nickname for military payday during the period of Revolutionary America. The term implies a statement about how little the soldier earned for his service.

THREE-FIFTHS COMPROMISE. During the **Constitutional Convention of 1787**, delegates hotly debated the issue of representation in a new national legislature and the basis for direct **taxation** of the states by the same body. States supporting **slavery** called for each slave to be counted toward representation in the legislature. Non-slave states argued that representation should be based on only free population. A compromise emerged that permitted the slave states to count three-fifths of the slave population for representation in the new national legislature and direct taxation by the national government. *See also* CONNECTICUT COMPROMISE.

TILGHMAN, MATTHEW (1718–1790). Matthew Tilghman, a patriot and the uncle of **William Tilghman**, sat in the **Maryland** legislature and represented Maryland in the **First Continental Congress** in 1774 and the **Second Continental Congress** from 1775–1776.

TILGHMAN, WILLIAM (1756–1827). William Tilghman, a **loyalist** and the nephew of **Matthew Tilghman**, sat in the **Maryland** legislature and the state convention to ratify the U.S. **Constitution**. He later served as a federal judge and a state judge for **Pennsylvania**.

TOBACCO. Tobacco, along with **indigo**, **rice**, and **wheat**, proved to be an important **agricultural** export from Revolutionary America. **Virginia** and other **southern colonies** produced the majority of the American tobacco crop. Within the area, many Americans utilized tobacco as form of currency and even salaries were paid in tobacco leaves. Just prior to the Revolution, **Great Britain** imported nearly 75 million pounds of tobacco annually from the southern colonies. Despite the hostilities associated with the Revolution, up to one-third of the prewar tobacco exports still found their way to Great Britain via neutral ports. In 1781, British raids in eastern Virginia included the targeting and burning of the area's tobacco crop as a form of **economic** warfare. The export of tobacco immediately after the Revolution continued to suffer due to the refusal of the British to negotiate a commercial treaty with the United States. However, both tobacco and rice found their way to Great Britain via commercial deals developed directly with individual states. Tobacco and rice were the only American export products wanted by the French after the Revolution. By 1786, southern commercial exports, including tobacco, had either recovered or nearly recovered to their pre-Revolution numbers due to the inability of Great Britain to acquire products of the same quality from alternative sources. *See also* TRADE.

TOMAHAWK. A tomahawk is a flat-bladed weapon on the end of a short handle. The tomahawk looks like a hatchet and was a favorite weapon of **Native Americans** and Americans during the **Revolutionary War**.

TONYN, PATRICK (1725–1804). Patrick Tonyn served as the British governor and military commander of East Florida between 1774 and 1783.

TORY. Tory is a name often applied to American **loyalists** who opposed the struggle for independence from **Great Britain**. The name derives from the British political party that supported the policies of the king and Parliament on issues relating to the American **colonies**. For example, Tories would have supported the imposition of **taxation** on the American colonies.

TOWNE, BENJAMIN (?–1793). Benjamin Towne, a noted **printer** in **Philadelphia**, is an example of an American who wanted to get on with his life and not be bothered by the **Revolutionary War**. Patriot and **loyalist** Americans took their political stances very seriously and have been known to persecute their opposite number by threats or even house burnings and the use of **tar and feathers**. Towne, originally a self-proclaimed patriot **newspaper** printer, became pro-loyalist in his writings during the British occupation of his city when other patriot printers chose to flee. When the British evacuated the city, Towne quickly switched to printing pro-patriot material in his newspaper.

TOWNSHEND, CHARLES (1725–1767). Charles Townshend served as Chancellor of the Exchequer in the cabinet of Prime Minister **William Pitt**. In 1767, he managed to persuade the British government to pass the bills that became known collectively as the **Townshend Acts of 1767**. These measures increased the tension between the American colonists and the British government.

TOWNSHEND ACTS OF 1767. **Charles Townshend** persuaded the British Parliament to enact the Townshend Acts in 1767. The legislation known as the Townshend Acts actually consisted of two documents—the **Townshend Revenue Act of 1767** and the **New York Restraining Act of 1767**. The latter is technically not a piece of legislation introduced by Townshend but was lumped into the same category with the former by the American colonists. Both measures added more fuel to the growing flames of resistance demonstrated by the American colonists.

TOWNSHEND REVENUE ACT OF 1767. Charles Townshend, the Chancellor of the Exchequer in the cabinet of Prime Minister **William Pitt**, required additional funds for the British budget. He studied the colonial arguments against **taxation** and believed that the Americans only opposed internally based taxes. If presented with externally based taxes (taxes to regulate **trade**), he assumed the colonists would accept them. This belief led Townshend to persuade Parliament to pass the Townshend Revenue Act of 1767, one of the **Townshend Acts of 1767**, with an effective date of November 20, 1767. Townshend died before the Revenue Act became effective in the American **colonies**.

The Townshend Revenue Act of 1767 placed duties on lead, paint, paper, glass, and tea imported from **Great Britain**. It reaffirmed the legitimacy of **writs of assistance** and placed jurisdiction with the **Admiralty Courts**. Fines collected by the Admiralty Courts would be used to pay the customs officials enforcing the legislation. Officials paid in this manner would be financially independent of the colonial assemblies, which normally allocated funds for civil authorities. The legislation also included the establishment of the **American Board of Customs Commissioners** in **Boston** to enforce compliance by the American colonists.

American colonial merchants, greatly affected by the new round of duties, renewed their boycott of British goods. The **Sons of Liberty** helped persuade boycott violators to cease importing British goods. In addition, the Sons of Liberty initiated a campaign aimed at reducing the average colonist's desire for imported products and encouraging a return to a form of self-reliance. Colonial opposition via the boycott led to the repeal of the Townshend Revenue Act of 1767 on

April 12, 1770. The Townshend Revenue Act of 1767 can be seen as another taxation scheme aimed at the American colonists that paved the way for the opening of hostilities in 1775 and the complete declaration of independence the next year.

TRACY, NATHANIEL (1751–1796). Nathaniel Tracy, a merchant, was a major financier of the American cause during the **Revolutionary War**.

TRADE. There are two types of trade: commerce among the 13 **colonies**/states and external commerce with **Great Britain** and other countries. Intercolonial **trade** and commerce between the new colonies/states proved to be minor since most **manufactured** goods and **agricultural** crops were utilized in the immediate area of their production. The most important American exports included **indigo**, **fish**, **lumber**, **naval stores**, **rice**, **tobacco**, **whaling** products, and **wheat**. Great Britain applied a policy of **mercantilism** in its trade relations with the American colonies. London enacted various pre-**French and Indian War** trade restrictions on the colonies including the **Woolens Act of 1699**, **Hat Act of 1732**, **Molasses Act of 1733**, and the **Iron Act of 1750**. British duties and trade restrictions were often ignored by the colonists and not enforced by the Crown and its representatives through **salutary neglect**. Many Americans turned to **smuggling** to move goods in and out of the colonies without paying duties. Much of this illegal American trade was conducted with European colonies in the Caribbean area. However, after the war, the British opted to strengthen the enforcement of its trade restrictions and duties through the **Sugar Act of 1764**, the **Revenue Act of 1766**, and the **West Indies Free Port Act of 1766**.

Many Americans resented this new policy and viewed it as an assault upon their liberties as well as smuggling profits. American protests continued to harden colonial attitudes against British policies, eventually leading to the **Revolutionary War**.

After the Revolution, the United States found itself officially freed from mercantilism but still under the economic domination of Great Britain and other European states. Despite the British refusal to negotiate a commerce agreement with the United States, she continued to deal with individual states. On July 2, 1783, the British issued an Order in Council that officially closed that country's West Indies possessions to American products. Even **France** and **Spain** limited

American trade in the initial years after the Revolution. The trade in indigo, naval stores, rice, and tobacco recovered within a couple years of the war's conclusion because Great Britain could not acquire these products from other areas. As a result, the south tended to recover economically from the Revolution faster than the other areas of United States. The end of the war permitted France to export directly to the new country without having to go through Great Britain. France was interested in importing American rice and tobacco. **Thomas Jefferson** negotiated with the French to permit American vessels to trade with her possessions in the West Indies. British West Indies ports, while officially under orders to not admit American trading vessels, would frequently ignore the British government and allow the ships to arrive by claiming they were "in distress."

In 1784, American trade took a new twist as **Robert Morris** and other merchants constructed the *Empress of China* and dispatched her to **China** to initiate commerce with that country. Trade with China allowed Americans to deal directly with a non-European country and attempt to bypass some of the trade restrictions encountered immediately after the Revolution. Imports from China included nankeen cloth, porcelain, silk, and tea. However, Americans needed to find products, other than gold and silver (which were scarce), that the Chinese were willing to exchange for these goods. A system developed where American vessels would sail around South America to the Vancouver area of the northwest and trade trinkets and **iron** tools for otter fur, which was prized by the Chinese. The vessels would then sail to Hawaii and acquire sandalwood and proceed to China, returning around Africa. Other American vessels conducted trade with China in the opposite direction rounding Africa first. See also CURRENCY; NETHERLANDS AND REVOLUTIONARY AMERICA; PITT, WILLIAM.

TRANSYLVANIA COMPANY. **Richard Henderson** formed the Transylvania Company (originally known as the Louisa Company) and became its president. The purpose of the company was to acquire land west of the Appalachian Mountains for settlement. In 1775, the company concluded the **Treaty of Sycamore Shoals** with the **Cherokee** in order to obtain the land between the Ohio and Cumberland Rivers. Henderson hired **Daniel Boone** to cut a road north from the Cumberland Gap to the Ohio River. In 1776, Boonesborough was founded to provide a base for the anticipated settlers arriving to buy land from the Transylvania Company. **North Carolina** and **Virginia**, which claimed the territory, did not recognize the Treaty of Sycamore Shoals or the Transylvania Company as the legitimate owner of the land. Virginia, at the urging of George Rogers Clark organized the area as an official county under its government. Henderson appealed to **Congress**, which refused to interfere with the Virginia decision. In compensation, North Carolina and Virginia did grant Henderson land in the Cumberland Valley. *See also* CUMBERLAND AGREEMENT; LAND SPECULATORS; OHIO COMPANY.

TREASON ACT. In June 1768, the **Massachusetts** legislature refused to rescind the **Circular Letter of Massachusetts**, written to unite colonial opposition to the **Townshend Acts**. In response, the British government ordered two additional regiments of British soldiers to embark for **Boston** and extended the 16th-century Treason Act to the American **colonies**. The Treason Act stated that any individual suspected of treason against the Crown could be sent to England for trial.

TREASURY DEPARTMENT. **Congress** established the Treasury Department on September 2, 1789. **Alexander Hamilton** became the first secretary of the treasury and one of three executive branch cabinet leaders authorized by the **Constitution**.

TREATY OF AMITY AND COMMERCE. *See* DUTCH TREATY OF AMITY AND COMMERCE; FRENCH TREATY OF AMITY AND COMMERCE.

TREATY OF AUGUSTA. *See* AUGUSTA, TREATY OF.

TREATY OF DUMPLIN CREEK. *See* DUMPLIN CREEK, TREATY OF.

TREATY OF EASTON. *See* EASTON, TREATY OF.

TREATY OF FORT FINNEY. *See* FORT FINNEY, TREATY OF.

TREATY OF FORT MCINTOSH. *See* FORT MCINTOSH, TREATY OF.

TREATY OF FORT STANWIX. *See* FORT STANWIX, TREATY OF.

TREATY OF GALPHINTON. *See* GALPHINTON, TREATY OF.

TREATY OF HARD LABOR. *See* HARD LABOR, TREATY OF.

TREATY OF LOCHABER. *See* LOCHABER, TREATY OF.

TREATY OF OSWEGO. *See* OSWEGO, TREATY OF.

TREATY OF PARIS, 1763. *See* PARIS, TREATY OF, 1763.

TREATY OF PARIS, 1783. *See* PARIS, TREATY OF, 1783.

TREATY OF SYCAMORE SHOALS. *See* SYCAMORE SHOALS, TREATY OF.

TRENCHARD, JOHN (1662–1723). American colonists quoted John Trenchard and his friend **Thomas Gordon** during protests over British **taxation** following the conclusion of the **French and Indian War**. Trenchard, borrowing ideas from **John Locke**, believed that the role of government should be to protect individual liberties. However, when abusive rulers threatened individual liberties, Trenchard declared, the people had the right to check their power.

TRIPOLI AND REVOLUTIONARY AMERICA. *See* BARBARY STATES AND REVOLUTIONARY AMERICA.

TRUMBULL, JOHN (1756–1843). John Trumbull, the brother of **Joseph Trumbull** and **Jonathan Trumbull**, became one of America's greatest **painters**. Although Trumbull's best-known works emerged after the Revolutionary period, it was during this time that he studied art under **Benjamin West**, another American living in **Great Britain**.

TRUMBULL, JONATHAN (1710–1785). Jonathan Trumbull, governor of **Connecticut** between 1769 and 1784, was the father of **John Trumbull**, **Jonathan Trumbull**, and **Joseph Trumbull**. He helped to coordinate the acquisition of military supplies from his state for the

Continental Army. Connecticut supplied a large percentage of all supplies destined for the Continental Army.

TRUMBULL, JONATHAN (1740–1809). Jonathan Trumbull, the son of **Jonathan Trumbull** and brother of **John Trumbull** and **Joseph Trumbull**, served in the **Connecticut** legislature. He represented Connecticut in the **Second Continental Congress** from 1775–1779 but did not sign either the **Declaration of Independence** or the **Articles of Confederation**. Trumbull became a U.S. senator and the governor of Connecticut later in life.

TRUMBULL, JOSEPH (1738–1778). Joseph Trumbull, the son of **Jonathan Trumbull** and the brother of **John Trumbull** and **Jonathan Trumbull**, served as the commissary general for the **Continental Army**. He resigned in 1777 after a controversy with **Congress** and other American officers. Trumbull briefly sat on the **Board of War** but resigned in 1778 and died four months later.

TRYON, WILLIAM (1729–1788). William Tryon served as the royal governor of **North Carolina** between 1765 and 1771. During this period, Tryon dispatched the **militia**, which challenged the **regulators** at the **Battle of the Alamance**. Tryon became the royal governor of **New York** after leaving North Carolina in 1771. After being forced out of office in New York by the patriots in 1775, Tryon returned to the British army. Tryon was promoted to lieutenant general in 1782.

TUCKER, GEORGE (1752–1827). George Tucker sat as a delegate for **Virginia** in the 1786 **Annapolis Convention**. He later served as a state and federal judge.

TUCKEY, WILLIAM (1708–1781). William Tuckey was an accomplished organist and choirmaster during the period of Revolutionary America. In 1770, he directed the first American performance of Handel's *Messiah*. *See also* MUSIC.

TUFTS, COTTON (1732–1815). Cotton Tufts was a prominent physician in Revolutionary America.

TUNIS AND REVOLUTIONARY AMERICA. *See* BARBARY STATES AND REVOLUTIONARY AMERICA.

TURTLE. The *Turtle* is often hailed as the world's first operational submarine and is an example of the budding development of American **science** and technology. **David Bushnell** developed the idea for the *Turtle* after pondering the problem of forcing the British to leave **Boston** in 1775. If he could attach and explode kegs of powder underneath British ships, he thought they would have to withdraw from Boston in order to preserve their fleet. The submarine was shaped like a child's toy top. It measured six feet in width and seven-and-a-half feet in length. The construction of the submarine utilized a hull of six-inch oak bound with iron bands. Bushnell included a brass hatch and six small portholes that allowed light to illuminate the interior. During submerged travel, the navigation instruments were illuminated by phosphorescent seaweed. A coating of tar made the vessel watertight and preserved a half-hour supply of air. Bushnell named it the *Turtle* because it resembled two upper tortoise shells joined together.

The British departed Boston before the *Turtle* became operational. Therefore, Bushnell transported his submarine to **New York City**, where he persuaded General **George Washington** to allow a submerged attack on Admiral Richard Howe's flagship, the *Eagle*. On the night of September 6, 1776, Bushnell, along with the pilot, Sergeant Ezra Lee, attempted an attack on the British ship *Eagle*. Two whaleboats towed the submarine into close proximity of the target and released her. The tides played havoc with the small craft and it took Lee over two hours to get close enough to the target for a submerged attack. When Lee tried to screw a hole into the hull and attach the gunpowder, he hit an iron bar that held the rudder hinge with the stern of the vessel. Frustrated and running out of time, Lee withdrew and fought the currents back to a location where he could be recovered by the American whaleboats. The *Turtle* would later go to the bottom of the Hudson River when its transport, the *Crane*, was sunk by the British fleet.

Although the attack failed, the *Turtle* demonstrated that the principle was sound. Lee could have succeeded with his attack if he had simply attempted to drill a few inches away from the bar. However, he thought that the problem lay with the copper sheathe on the ship. Alternatively, Lee could have surfaced and attached the gunpowder to the side of the ship's hull. Further submarine attacks were not attempted during the **Revolutionary War**.

TUSCANY AND REVOLUTIONARY AMERICA. **Congress** appointed Ralph Izard as a **Commissioner** to Tuscany and dispatched him to seek aid from that country during the **Revolutionary War**. Izard made little progress with Tuscany. *See also* PLAN OF 1776.

TWO PENNY ACT OF 1758. Although the Two Penny Act was passed in 1758, the American colonial opposition to it helped pave the way for more direct challenges of the British government after 1763 and the opening of Revolutionary America. Anglican clergy in America received a salary paid in **tobacco** (17,000 pounds) in the mid-18th century. However, a drought reduced the tobacco crop and drove prices up for the product. The **Virginia** Assembly passed the Two Penny Act of 1758 to halt the practice of paying the clergy in tobacco. The act authorized a reimbursement to the clergy at a rate of two pennies per pound of tobacco. This measure actually reduced the salaries of the clergy. Reverend James Maury sued to stop the practice in an action often described as the Parson's Cause. Since the British government had recently vetoed the Virginia Two Penny Act, the question under consideration dealt with back pay.

Patrick Henry represented the defendants in the case. Henry delivered an eloquent speech to the jury that was highlighted by his denunciation of **King George III** and British colonial policy. The jury awarded Maury back pay of one penny per pound of tobacco. However, the significance of the case can be seen in Patrick Henry's verbal attack on the king and British colonial policy. The speech brought instant fame to Henry and set the stage for future questioning of the right of the king and his government to challenge colonial laws.

TYLER, JOHN (1747–1813). John Tyler sat in the **Virginia** legislature and was the member who presented the 1785 resolution calling for the formation of the **Annapolis Convention**. He served as a delegate in the 1788 state convention to ratify the U.S. **Constitution**. Tyler was also governor of Virginia.

TYLER, ROYALL (1757–1826). Royall Tyler emerged as one of the greatest American playwrights during the Revolutionary period. In

1787, Tyler's *The Contrast* became the first American comedy to be staged. *See also* THEATER.

– U –

UNION JACK. The Union Jack is the nickname for the flag of **Great Britain**. The flag is a combination of the banners of England and Scotland to form a single banner. The Union Jack, flown by British forces during the **Revolutionary War**, was incorporated into the **Grand Union Flag** of the American **colonies** prior to declaring independence.

UNITED COLONIES. United Colonies is a term for the unification of the American **colonies** for the purpose of common defense against **Great Britain**. The **Declaration of Independence** changed the United Colonies to the United States as the new country opted for complete independence from Great Britain. On September 9, 1776, the **Second Continental Congress** passed a resolution that officially changed "United Colonies" to "United States."

UNITED PROVINCES AND REVOLUTIONARY AMERICA. *See* NETHERLANDS AND REVOLUTIONARY AMERICA.

UNITED STATES IN CONGRESS ASSEMBLED. The **Second Continental Congress** transformed itself into the United States in Congress Assembled on March 3, 1781. The body remained the government of the **United States of America** under the **Articles of Confederation** until March 2, 1789. *See also* CONGRESS OF THE CONFEDERATION.

UNITED STATES OF AMERICA. With the signing of the **Declaration of Independence** on July 4, 1776, the **United Colonies** evolved into a single country based upon a confederation of the 13 member states. The name chosen for the new country was the United States of America to emphasize the unification of the 13 new states into a single confederation (later federation)-based government. On September 9, 1776, the **Second Continental Congress** passed a resolution that the term "United States" should officially replace "United Colonies."

– V –

VAN DYKE, NICHOLAS (1738–1789). Nicholas Van Dyke, a lawyer, represented **Delaware** in the **Second Continental Congress** from 1777–1781 and the **Congress of the Confederation** from 1781–1782. He signed the **Articles of Confederation** and later served as the president of Delaware from 1783–1786.

VANDALIA. A number of individuals, including **Benjamin Franklin**, petitioned the British government for the establishment of a 14th **colony** to be named Vandalia. The proposed colony would consist of modern West Virginia and part of **Kentucky**. The **Board of Trade** approved this request just prior to the Revolution. However, hostilities occurred before the king could sign the document and the issue was dropped and forgotten.

VARNUM, JAMES (1748–1789). James Varnum, a **Revolutionary War** officer and the brother of **Joseph Varnum**, represented **Rhode Island** in the **Second Continental Congress** from 1780–1781 and the **Congress of Confederation** from 1781–1782 and then 1786–1787.

VARNUM, JOSEPH (1750 or 1751–1821). Joseph Varnum, a **Revolutionary War** officer and the brother of **James Varnum,** sat in the **Massachusetts** legislature and the state convention to ratify the U.S. **Constitution**. He later served in the U.S. House of Representatives and the U.S. Senate.

VERGENNES, CHARLES GRAVIER DE (1717–1787). The Count of Vergennes served as the foreign minister of **France** during the period of the **Revolutionary War**. He assumed his duties in 1774 and quickly reintroduced the **Duke of Choiseul's** strategy of maintaining French spies in the American **colonies**. Vergennes viewed the Revolution as an opportunity to obtain revenge on **Great Britain** for the **French and Indian War** and the loss of **Canada**. He agreed to supply covert aid but waited until the American victory at the Battle of Saratoga in 1777 to bring France into the war as an active belligerent.

VERMONT. **New Hampshire** and **New York** claimed the area now comprising the state of Vermont during the period of Revolutionary America. **Ethan Allen** and the Green Mountain Boys helped seize Fort Ticonderoga and supported the patriot cause early in the **Revolutionary War**. However, they expected an offer of statehood in return for this support. A divided **Second Continental Congress** rejected Vermont's appeal due to the territorial claims of New Hampshire and New York. In defiance, some Vermont residents declared the establishment of an independent state in 1777. Although not officially a state at the time, Vermont became the first territory to outlaw **slavery** within its constitution in 1777. Others, including Ethan Allen, opened negotiations with the British in Quebec for absorption of Vermont in exchange for liberal political freedoms. These discussions collapsed at the end of the Revolution but others continued until New Hampshire and New York finally withdrew their claims. In 1791, Vermont became the first state to join the United States after the original founding of the country in 1776. *See also* FAY, JONAS.

***VIPER* INCIDENT**. The crew of the British ship *Viper* seized three American colonial ships attempting to enter Brunswick, **North Carolina**, in January 1766 for failing to have the proper document stamps as prescribed by the **Stamp Act of 1765**. Before the ships could be sent to the **Admiralty Court** in Nova Scotia, a mob gathered and demanded of Governor **William Tryon** that the crews should not be prosecuted. The mob then persuaded the local customs officials to drop the charges and agree not to enforce the Stamp Act of 1765. This action served as an example of the resistance offered by the American colonists to the Stamp Act of 1765.

VIRGINIA. Virginia, one of the **southern colonies**, was governed by **Great Britain** as a **royal colony** until the **Revolutionary War** and American independence. By the end of America's Revolutionary period in 1790, the state boasted 747,610 people (39% slaves). Virginians were leaders in the opposition to British policies of **taxation** as demonstrated by the **Virginia Resolves** of 1765 and the **Virginia Association** of 1774. After the Revolutionary War, Virginia was one of the organizers of the **Alexandria Convention** and the **Annapolis**

Convention to discuss the problems with the **Articles of Confederation**. Delegates from the state were instrumental in developing the **Virginia Plan** at the **Constitutional Convention of 1787**. These men wanted to ensure that states held power in the new federal government based on their population size. A compromise with the proponents of the **New Jersey Plan** led to the **Connecticut Compromise**. Virginians also played important roles in the development of the **Bill of Rights** as the first 10 amendments to the U.S. **Constitution**. The state ratified the Constitution on June 25, 1788. Virginia was the largest producer and exporter of **tobacco**, **wheat**, corn, lead, and coal and the third-largest producer and exporter of flour in the United States during this period. Notable individuals from Virginia include **Carter Braxton**, **Cyrus Griffin**, **Benjamin Harrison**, **Patrick Henry**, **Thomas Jefferson**, **Francis Lee**, **Richard Henry Lee**, **James Madison**, **George Mason**, **James Monroe**, **Thomas Nelson Jr.**, **George Washington**, and **George Wythe**.

VIRGINIA ASSOCIATION. The **Virginia** Association was the model for the 1774 agreement of the **First Continental Congress** known as the **Continental Association**. The Virginia Association, adopted on May 18, 1769, called for a ban on European luxury items, **slaves**, and all British imports carrying a duty or tax. *See also* TRADE.

VIRGINIA PLAN. **Edmund Randolph** proposed the **Virginia** Plan during the **Constitutional Convention** of 1787. **James Madison** played a significant role in helping to develop the Virginia Plan. The plan, designed to maximize the power of the larger population states in a newly proposed government for the United States, can be seen as being at odds with the **New Jersey Plan** of the smaller states. The Virginia Plan, introduced only four days after the convention convened, included numerous proposed changes from the current **Articles of Confederation** for a new constitution. It included the following:

1. A two-house legislature with the lower chamber elected directly by the people and the upper chamber selected by the lower.
2. The legislature should have broad powers, including the right to veto the laws of state governments.

3. The national executive should consist of a single president with a cabinet elected by the national legislature.
4. The national judiciary should consist of justices elected by the national legislature.

Delegates to the Constitutional Convention reached an agreement, known as the **Connecticut Compromise**, that incorporated elements of both the Virginia Plan and the New Jersey Plan into the **Constitution** of the United States.

VIRGINIA RESOLUTIONS. *See* VIRGINIA RESOLVES.

VIRGINIA RESOLVES. The **Virginia** House of Burgesses passed what is known as the Virginia Resolves on May 31, 1765. The resolves were introduced into the House of Burgesses by **Patrick Henry** in response to the **Stamp Act of 1765**. The resolves, approved by the delegates following hot debate and close votes, included the point that Americans were entitled to the same liberties as individuals living within **Great Britain**; two specific charters issued under James I had verified the belief listed in the first point; **taxation** should not be imposed on the people unless issued by those selected to represent them in government; the American colonists have always enjoyed the right to be governed by laws based on their own consent; and the Virginia House of Burgesses is the only body that has the right to levy taxes on Virginians and any attempt by another body destroys freedom. The latter point was later removed after additional discussion. Americans in other **colonies** debated the Virginia Resolves, which became instrumental in influencing other colonies to send delegates to the **Stamp Act Congress**.

VOLUNTEER COMPANY. Volunteer companies began forming in some of the American **colonies** in late 1774 and early 1775. These **militia** units consisted of men who had volunteered to march where needed to counter the British military. In contrast, most militia units were only called upon to defend their local communities. Very few volunteer companies were ever formed and they became unnecessary after the **Battle of Lexington-Concord** when an army gathered outside of **Boston**.

– W –

WADSWORTH, JEREMIAH (1743–1804). Jeremiah Wadsworth, a **Revolutionary War** officer, represented **Connecticut** in the **Congress of the Confederation** from 1787–1788. However, he only attended during 1788. He sat as a delegate in the 1788 Connecticut state convention to ratify the U.S. **Constitution**.

WALTER, THOMAS (c.1740–1789). Thomas Walter was a noted botanist in Revolutionary America.

WALTON, GEORGE (1741–1804). George Walton represented **Georgia** in the **Second Continental Congress** from 1776–1778 and 1780–1781. He signed the **Declaration of Independence** and **Articles of Confederation**. Walton also fought as a **militia** officer in the Battle of Savannah. He sat as a delegate in the 1788 state convention to ratify the U.S. **Constitution**. Later Walton served in the U.S. Senate and as a presidential elector and the chief justice of Georgia.

WANTON, JOSEPH (1705–1780). Joseph Wanton served as the governor of **Rhode Island** from 1769–1775.

WAR DEPARTMENT. **Congress** established the War Department on August 7, 1789. General **Henry Knox** became the first secretary of war and one of three executive branch cabinet leaders authorized by the U.S. **Constitution**.

WAR OF THE REGULATION. *See* REGULATORS.

WARD, ARTEMUS (1727–1800). Aretmus Ward, a **Revolutionary War** officer, represented **Massachusetts** in the **Second Continental Congress** from 1780–1781. He later served in the U.S. House of Representatives.

WARD, NANCY (?–1781). Nancy Ward, a leader among the **Cherokee**, was a well-known peace advocate among her people and the Americans of European background.

WARD, SAMUEL (1725–1776). Samuel Ward, the father of **Samuel Ward**, was the governor of **Rhode Island** in 1761 and from 1765–1766. He represented Rhode Island in the **First Continental Congress** in 1774 and the **Second Continental Congress** from 1775–1776.

WARD, SAMUEL (1756–1832). Samuel Ward, the **Revolutionary War** officer and the son of **Samuel Ward** the governor, represented **Rhode Island** at the 1786 **Annapolis Convention**.

WARREN, JOSEPH (1741–1775). Joseph Warren, an early supporter of anti-British activity, wrote the **Suffolk Resolves** and dispatched **Paul Revere** on his famous ride to warn patriots of the approaching British army from **Boston**. He died in the Battle of Bunker Hill.

WASHINGTON, GEORGE (1732–1799). George Washington is one of the best-known leaders from the period of Revolutionary America. A farmer, military officer during the **French and Indian War**, and early patriot, he represented **Virginia** in the **First Continental Congress** in 1774 and **Second Continental Congress** in 1775. In the First Continental Congress, he supported the move to apply a **trade** boycott against **Great Britain**. Delegates at the Second Continental Congress discussed the requirements of the 13 American **colonies** if the situation around **Boston** after the **Battle Lexington-Concord** devolved into full-scale warfare with Great Britain. The members of Congress appointed Washington to several military-related committees and **John Adams** raised the issue of selecting a commander in chief of the colonial forces gathered around Boston. Adams praised Washington, who was unanimously elected the next day to the position. He accepted the call from Congress and refused a salary, asking only that his expenses be reimbursed.

During the **Revolutionary War**, Washington's character held together the **Continental Army** despite numerous tactical defeats and the hazards of winter. The newly declared United States would have collapsed if Washington had not been able to keep his army in the field despite the shortages of food and clothing. In May 1782, several officers of the Continental Army complained to him about the treatment the military had received from Congress during the war and offered to establish him as king of the United States. Washington refused to consider the suggestion. In 1783, he returned to his plantation where he introduced numerous innovations in farming.

Washington emerged again in national politics in 1786. He actively supported reforming the **Articles of Confederation** or the preparation of a new constitution to allay the many weaknesses of the former document, including the inability of the national government to counter **Shays's Rebellion** in **Massachusetts**. He invited the delegates to the **Alexandria Convention** to his home. A call for another gathering, the **Annapolis Convention**, resulted from this meeting. The delegates at the Annapolis Convention proposed a meeting of all 13 states to discuss reforming the Articles of Confederation. The **Constitutional Convention of 1787** resulted from this call. Virginia selected Washington to head its delegation to the national convention. Upon arriving in **Philadelphia**, the representatives of the other states chose Washington to serve as president of the convention. Washington, frustrated at times by the considerable disagreement among the delegates, did not actively participate in the debate. However, as president of the convention, he worked to keep the delegates together and in the meeting. In 1789, presidential electors unanimously elected Washington as the first president of the United States. He served two terms before retiring in 1797.

WATAUGA ASSOCIATION. The individuals living in the **Watauga Settlements** in what is now eastern **Tennessee** opted to form their own government since they were so far from other inhabited areas. The resulting Watauga Association offered religious freedom and manhood suffrage to residents. The area became Washington County, **North Carolina**, in 1777. This move negated the Watauga Association.

WATAUGA SETTLEMENTS. Settlers pushing west from **North Carolina** moved into what is now eastern **Tennessee** and established homes at what is known as Watauga after the **French and Indian War**. In 1771, hundreds of North Carolinians moved into the area after the **Battle of Alamance** and the failure of the **regulator** movement. The settlers established their own government under the auspices of the **Watauga Association**. In 1776, the settlers requested annexation by North Carolina. The North Carolina legislature agreed and annexed the region in 1777 as the new county of Washington.

WATSON-WENTWORTH, CHARLES. *See* ROCKINGHAM, MARQUIS OF.

WATERHOUSE, BENJAMIN (1754–1846). Benjamin Waterhouse was a prominent physician in Revolutionary America. He later became a leading pioneer in the use of inoculations.

WEBSTER, NOAH (1758–1843). Noah Webster, born in **Connecticut**, emerged as one of the most famous writers in the Revolutionary period. Webster desired to revolutionize **education** in America and in 1783 introduced his popular speller *A Grammatical Institute of the English Language*, which was utilized for over 100 years. He later helped "Americanize" the English language through the publication of his now famous dictionary.

WEBSTER, PELATIAH (1726–1795). Pelatiah Webster was a noted political economist during the period of Revolutionary America.

WELLES, NOAH (1718–1776). Noah Welles was a prominent Congregational clergyman in Revolutionary America.

WENTWORTH, JOHN, JR. (1745–1787). John Wentworth Jr. represented **New Hampshire** in the **Second Continental Congress** in 1778 and signed the **Articles of Confederation**.

WEST, BENJAMIN (1738–1820). Benjamin West was the first American-born **painter** to earn a renowned reputation in Europe. He was born in **Pennsylvania** but spent most of his adult life in Europe where he helped train other American artists, including **Charles Willson Peale**, **Gilbert Stuart**, and **Jonathan Trumbull**. One of West's more famous works is the incomplete painting of the American and British peace negotiators discussing the 1783 **Treaty of Paris**. The painting was never completed because the British negotiators refused to sit for West. He died in London.

WEST, SAMUEL (1730–1807). Samuel West, a clergyman, served as a **Massachusetts** delegate to the **Constitutional Convention of 1787**.

WEST INDIES FREE PORT ACT OF 1766. The British Parliament passed the West Indies Free Port Act of 1766 at the same time as the **Revenue Act of 1766**. The former opened Dominica as a free port for **trade**. While encouraging the importation of cheap sugar into Dominica for British refineries, it would also serve to protect British sugar interests on Jamaica. The act failed in its purpose and served to anger the American colonists by limiting their ability to conduct a profitable trade in the area.

WESTERN DEPARTMENT. The **Second Continental Congress** established the Western Department as a **military department** in 1777. The Western Department consisted of the territory north of the Ohio River and portions of modern **West Virginia**, **Pennsylvani**a, and the southwest corner of **New York**.

WHALING. Whaling proved to be one of the most profitable industries within pre-Revolutionary America and supported numerous other industries, including **shipbuilding**, **lumbering**, the manufacturing of candles, and the export of oil for lamps. Coastal **New England** (including Nantucket, Martha's Vineyard, **Boston**, New Bedford, and Cape Cod) emerged as the hub of the American whaling industry due to the proximity of the mammals to shore in the area. By the mid-18th century, whalers had to sail further from home to find the animals. The period 1770–1775 was the height of the early American whaling industry during the 18th century. Nantucket boasted 80 whaling vessels in 1768 and this total increased to 100 in 1770 and 150 in 1775 at the opening of the Revolution. Estimates place the total American whaling fleet at 300 vessels in 1775. American whalers dominated the industry during this period. In 1770, the total British whaling fleet consisted of only 50 vessels, as London preferred to import American oil.

On the eve of the Revolution, the British government grew concerned about the country's heavy reliance on American oil imports. To counter this reliance and encourage the growth of the domestic whaling fleet, the British Parliament passed the **First Restraining Act** (sometimes known as the Fisheries Act) in 1775. The act restricted the trade of New England to Great Britain, the British West Indies, and Ireland and denied New England sailors the right to hunt whales and fish off Newfoundland and Nova Scotia. The **Second Restraining Act** imposed these restrictions on every **colony** except **Georgia**, **New York**, and **South Carolina**. In return, many American areas vowed to not supply British vessels with provisions, resulting in an estimated cost of half a million pounds to the British economy as partially filled ships had to return home for resupply. The British also offered heavy bounties to develop their domestic whaling industry and placed stiff duties on American oil. These actions and naval hostilities associated with the Revolution devastated the American whaling industry. Throughout the Revolution, the British offered captured American whalers the choice between imprisonment or sailing under the British flag. Many whalers chose the latter rather than face the deathly conditions aboard British prison ships. The importance of the whaling industry can also be seen in the 1778 and 1779 British raids on fishing and whaling towns in New England. During the raids, a British priority included destroying any vessels in the ports.

At the conclusion of the Revolution, American negotiators demanded the right of New England sailors to fish off the waters of Newfoundland and Nova Scotia. Despite considerable British opposition, London finally granted that demand as part of the final peace treaty. However, the American whaling industry did not make a turnaround in the years immediately after the conclusion of the Revolution. In 1784, London placed a stiff duty on American oil and again encouraged the growth of its own whaling industry. The British offered bounties for **loyalist** Americans to move to Nova Scotia or Wales in order to whale. **France** also attempted to persuade American whalers to emigrate to that country but was not very successful. British whaling vessels increased from 50 in 1775 to 200 by 1790. In 1784, Nantucket could muster only 60 whaling vessels. In 1786, France closed its ports to foreign oil imports, hurting the American whaling industry, until persuaded by **Thomas Jefferson** to exclude the United States from this ban. The American whaling industry did not recover its pre-Revolutionary strength until the 19th century.

WHARTON, CHARLES (1748–1833). Charles Wharton was a noted Episcopal clergyman in Revolutionary America.

WHARTON, THOMAS (1735–1778). Thomas Wharton served as the president (governor) of **Pennsylvania** from 1776 until his death in 1778.

WHEAT. Wheat, grown in the **middle colonies**, was an important export crop, along with **indigo**, **rice**, and **tobacco**, during the period of Revolutionary America. Wheat was traded with other **colonies** and exported to **Great Britain** and the British West Indies. The export of wheat suffered during the Revolution and recovered very slowly after the war due to British **trade** restrictions. *See also* AGRICULTURE.

WHEATLEY, PHILLIS (1753–1784). Phillis Wheatley, born in Africa, emerged as one of most famous **poets** during the Revolutionary period. John Wheatley purchased her as a **slave** in 1761. She learned to read and write very quickly and published her first poem in 1767. John Wheatley took her to London where a collection of her poems was published under the title *Poems on Various Subjects, Religious and Moral* in 1773. Phillis Wheatley returned to North America in 1773 and was freed after John's death in 1778. She is also noted for writing a poem in support of General **George Washington** in 1776.

WHEELOCK, ELEAZAR (1711–1779). Eleazar Wheelock, a Congregational clergyman, was a prominent educator and the founder and first president of Dartmouth College in 1769.

WHIG. Whig was a term applied to Americans supporting the cause of independence from **Great Britain**. The name comes from the British political party that opposed many of the policies of the king and Parliament on issues related to the **Revolutionary War**. For example, British Whigs tended to speak out against the **taxation** policies imposed on the American **colonies**. *See also* TORY.

WHIPPLE, WILLIAM (1730–1785). William Whipple represented **New Hampshire** in the **Second Continental Congress** from 1776–1779 and signed the **Declaration of Independence**. Whipple briefly held a commission as a brigadier general and fought at the Battles of Saratoga and **Newport**. He later served as a judge.

WHITE, JAMES (1747–1821). James White sat as a delegate in the **North Carolina Fayetteville state convention** to ratify the U.S. **Constitution**. He also worked diligently in the attempt to establish a new state known as Franklin and was later prominent in **Tennessee** politics.

WHITE EYES (?–1778). White Eyes, a Delaware chief, was instrumental in keeping his **Native American** group neutral in **Lord Dunmore's War** and the **Revolutionary War**. In 1778, he was murdered by American troops that he was helping to guide.

WHITEHILL, ROBERT (1738–1813). Robert Whitehill sat in the **Pennsylvania** legislature and attended the 1787 state convention to ratify the U.S. **Constitution**. He later served in the U.S. House of Representatives.

WIGGLESWORTH, EDWARD (1732–1794). Edward Wigglesworth was a prominent **educator** during the period of Revolutionary America.

WIGNELL, THOMAS (c.1753–1803). Thomas Wignell was a well-known comedian in Revolutionary America.

WILKES, JOHN (1727–1797). John Wilkes, a British parliamentarian, became an avid opponent of the British government. He was jailed and declared an outlaw but was supported by his constituents, who continued to elect him to Parliament despite that body's refusal to recognize the election results. Many Americans viewed him as a hero for his stand against the British government. *See also* WILKES AND LIBERTY.

WILKES AND LIBERTY. This was a common colonial rallying cry during the crisis period ignited by the **Stamp Act of 1765**. **John Wilkes**, a British parliamentarian and political agitator, supported the American colonial causes during this period. The American colonists made Wilkes a popular hero of their struggle and borrowed the phrase "Wilkes and Liberty" to rally support against British policies. *See also* 45; TAXATION.

WILLARD, JOSEPH (1738–1804). Joseph Willard became the president of Harvard College in 1781.

WILLIAMS, JOHN (1731–1799). John Williams, a lawyer, represented **North Carolina** in the **Second Continental Congress** from 1778–1779 and signed the **Articles of Confederation**. He later served as a state judge.

WILLIAMS, WILLIAM (1731–1811). William Williams represented **Connecticut** in the **Second Continental Congress** from 1776–1778 and the **Congress of the Confederation** from 1783–1784. He signed the **Declaration of Independence** and helped frame the **Articles of Confederation**. Williams sat as a delegate in the 1788 Connecticut state convention to ratify the U.S. **Constitution** and later served as a state judge.

WILLIAMSON, HUGH (1735–1819). Hugh Williamson represented **North Carolina** in the **Constitutional Convention of 1787** and signed the U.S. **Constitution**. He also sat as a delegate in the **Fayetteville state convention** to ratify the document.

WILLING, THOMAS (1731–1821). Thomas Willing, a banker, represented **Pennsylvania** in the **Second Continental Congress** from 1775–1776. He became the president of the **Bank of North America** in 1781.

WILSON, JAMES (1742–1798). James Wilson represented **Pennsylvania** in the **Second Continental Congress** from 1775–1777 and the **Congress of the Confederation** in 1782 and from 1785–1787. He signed the **Declaration of Independence**. Wilson attended the **Constitutional Convention of 1787** and signed the U.S. **Constitution**. He also sat in the Pennsylvania state convention to ratify the U.S. Constitution. He later became an associate justice of the U.S. Supreme Court.

WINTHROP, JOHN (1714–1779). John Winthrop was a noted astronomer and mathematician in Revolutionary America.

WISNER, HENRY (1720–1790). Henry Wisner sat in the **New York** legislature and represented New York in the **Second Continental Congress** from 1775–1777. He also sat as a delegate in the state convention to ratify the U.S. **Constitution**.

WITHERSPOON, JOHN (1723–1794). John Witherspoon represented **New Jersey** in the **Second Continental Congress** from 1776–1781 and the **Congress of the Confederation** from 1781–1782. He signed the **Declaration of Independence** and **Articles of Confederation**. He served as a delegate to the 1787 New Jersey state convention to ratify the U.S. **Constitution**.

WOLCOTT, OLIVER (1726–1797). Oliver Wolcott represented **Connecticut** in the **Second Continental Congress** from 1775–1778 and 1780–1781 and then the **Congress of the Confederation** from 1781–1783. He signed the **Declaration of Independence** and **Articles of Confederation**. He also sat as a delegate in the state convention to ratify the U.S. **Constitution**. He was later governor of Connecticut and a presidential elector.

WOMEN AND REVOLUTIONARY AMERICA. In Revolutionary America, women tended to fulfill the housewife and mother roles although there are many documented incidents of women becoming the chief administrators of plantations and businesses during the absence of their husbands. Older unmarried women, known as spinsters, were often the subject of jokes due to being outside the expected social order. Up to this period, women had few rights but this began to change in the Revolutionary period as Enlightenment principles slowly began to expand in scope. Husbands exercised corporal punishment over wives they considered disobedient. It was very common for a much older man to wed a young girl. Although divorces were rare and hard to obtain, after the Revolution American women began to have slightly fewer difficulties in obtaining divorces.

In 1775, the first article published in support of women's rights, written by **Thomas Paine**, appeared in *Pennsylvania Magazine*. In 1776, **Abigail Adams** reminded her husband, **John Adams**, not to forget the ladies when working with other **Founding Fathers** to change the social and political structure of America. During the Revolution, there were several documented cases of women, including **Deborah Sampson** and **Mary Ludwig Hays**, fighting in disguise as men or even taking to the battlefield during times of need without disguise. Many women accompanied their husbands' units as **camp followers**, performing various cooking and cleaning tasks for all of the men.

Literacy among women began to increase after the Revolution. However, approximately half of all white women still could not read by the end of the 1780s. Some publishers did see women as a potential source of readers. In 1784, *Gentlemen and Ladies' Town and Country Magazine* became the first magazine specifically written to attract women readers. In 1787, the publication of *Thoughts on Female Education* spurred debate on the issue of **education** for women. The book argued that educated mothers are important for the education of children.

The vast majority of **African American** women were **slaves** during this period, although there are some examples of free African American women. Educational opportunities for women held as slaves were practically nonexistent. **Phillis Wheatley** was one of the most well-known free African American women during this period. However, she learned to read and write while a slave. Her **poetry** earned international recognition and played a factor in her receiving freedom from slavery. Other prominent women in Revolutionary America included **Hannah Adams**, **Ann Bailey**, **Ann Bleeker**, **Jane Colden**, **Elizabeth Ferguson**, **Isabella Graham**, **Barbara Heck**, **Ann Lee**, **Charlotte Lennox**, **Elizabeth Morris**, **Judith Murray**, **Betsy Ross**, **Susanna Rowson**, and **Nancy Ward**. *See also* LLOYD, JAMES.

WOOD PRODUCTS. *See* LUMBER INDUSTRY; NAVAL STORES INDUSTRY; SHIPBUILDING INDUSTRY.

WOOLENS ACT OF 1699. The Woolens Act, although implemented prior to the Revolutionary Period of American history, added early fuel to the fire of protest in the American **colonies** against British economic policies. It placed restrictions on the production and **trade** of wool and woolen products in order to protect the English woolen industry. Trade of wool and woolen goods between the American **colonies** or to foreign countries was prohibited under the Act. Americans viewed the Woolens Act as a restraint on individual rights. *See also* HAT ACT OF 1732; IRON ACT OF 1750.

"**WORLD TURNED UPSIDE DOWN**." The name of the song reportedly played by the British army while it surrendered after the Battle of Yorktown. The exact tune played by the British, if the story is valid, is not known, since more than one song bore this name.

WRIGHT, JAMES (1714–1785). James Wright served as the British governor of **Georgia** during the **Revolutionary War**. He departed Georgia during 1776 and was restored to his position in 1779 by the British authorities.

WRITS OF ASSISTANCE. Writs of assistance provided British customs collectors with the authority to search for **smuggled** cargo with the assistance of local peace enforcement officers. The writs had to be renewed when **George III** ascended the British throne. **James Otis**, a Bostonian, challenged the writs in court in 1761, basing his argument on the ideals of **John Locke**. The case was referred to the courts of England where a decision was rendered in favor of issuing the writs of assistance. Although Otis lost the case and general knowledge of the actual proceedings were not well known by the public for several years, the eloquent argument he offered set a precedent for opposing British policies with ideals of Locke.

WYTHE, GEORGE (1726–1806). George Wythe sat in the **Virginia** legislature and represented Virginia in the **Second Continental Congress** from 1775–1776. He signed the **Declaration of Independence**. He attended the **Constitutional Convention of 1787** for Virginia. Although absent for the signing, he did support the new U.S. **Constitution**. He also attended the Virginia state convention for the ratification of the Constitution.

– Y –

"**YANKEE DOODLE**." Historians are not clear as to the origins of this song but believe it was written as an insult to the colonial soldiers besieging the British in **Boston**. The British army played the song as they marched from the surrender field at the Battle of Yorktown. However, it is not believed to have been played as an insult against the victors. It later became very popular among the American soldiers and people in general.

YATES, ABRAHAM (1724–1796). Abraham Yates sat in the **New York** legislature and represented his state in the **Congress of the Confederation** from 1787–1788.

YATES, ROBERT (1738–1801). Robert Yates, a judge, sat as a delegate for **New York** in the **Constitutional Convention of 1787**. He left early, saying that the delegates had exceeded their mandate to amend the **Articles of Confederation**. He opposed ratification of the U.S. **Constitution** in the 1788 state convention.

YEATES, JASPER (1745–1817). Jasper Yeates, a lawyer, sat as a delegate in the **Pennsylvania** state convention to ratify the U.S. **Constitution**.

YORK. The **Second Continental Congress** convened in York, **Pennsylvania**, on September 30, 1777, after the withdrawal from **Philadelphia**. Congress returned to Philadelphia on July 2, 1778, after the British withdrawal to **New York City**.

– Z –

Z. "Z" was the pen name used by Richard Clarke, one of the **Boston** tea consignees, in October 1773. Clarke used the pseudonym when rebutting the series of articles and letters protesting British tea policy and threatening the consignees.

ZUBLY, JOHN (1724–1781). John Zubly, a clergyman, sat in the **Georgia** legislature and represented Georgia in the **Second Continental Congress** in 1775. He opposed complete American independence and left Congress. Georgia banished him from the state.

Appendix A
Signers of the Articles of Confederation

CONNECTICUT

Andrew Adams
Titus Hosmer
Samuel Huntington
Roger Sherman
Oliver Wolcott

DELAWARE

John Dickinson
Thomas McKean
Nicholas Van Dyke

GEORGIA

Edward Langworthy
Edward Telfair
John Walton

MARYLAND

Daniel Carroll
John Hanson

MASSACHUSETTS

Samuel Adams
Francis Dana
Elbridge Gerry
John Hancock
Samuel Holten
James Lovell

NEW HAMPSHIRE

Josiah Bartlett
John Wentworth Jr.

NEW JERSEY

Nathaniel Scudder
John Witherspoon

NEW YORK

James Duane
William Duer
Francis Lewis
Gouverneur Morris

NORTH CAROLINA

Cornelius Harnett
John Penn
John Williams

PENNSYLVANIA

William Clingan
Robert Morris
Joseph Reed
Daniel Roberdeau
Jonathan Bayard Smith

RHODE ISLAND

John Collins
William Ellery
Henry Marchant

SOUTH CAROLINA

William Henry Drayton
Thomas Heyward Jr.
Richard Hutson
Henry Laurens
John Mathews

VIRGINIA

Thomas Adams
John Banister
John Harvie
Francis Lightfoot Lee
Richard Henry Lee

Appendix B
Constitutional Convention of 1787 Attendees

I. VOTED IN FAVOR OF THE CONSTITUTION

Connecticut

William Johnson
Roger Sherman

Delaware

Richard Bassett
Gunning Bedford Jr.
Jacob Broom
John Dickinson
George Read

Georgia

Abraham Baldwin
William Few

Maryland

Daniel Carroll
Daniel of St. Thomas Jenifer
James McHenry

Massachusetts

Nathaniel Gorham
Rufus King

New Hampshire

John Langdon
Nicholas Gilman

New Jersey

David Brearley
Jonathan Dayton
William Livingston
William Paterson

New York

Alexander Hamilton

North Carolina

William Blount
Richard Spaight
Hugh Williamson

Pennsylvania

George Clymer
Thomas FitzSimons
Benjamin Franklin
Jared Ingersoll

Thomas Mifflin
Gouverneur Morris
Robert Morris
James Wilson

South Carolina

Pierce Butler
Charles Pinckney
Charles Cotesworth Pinckney
John Rutledge

Virginia

John Blair
James Madison
George Washington

II. VOTED AGAINST THE CONSTITUTION

Massachusetts

Elbridge Gerry

Virginia

George Mason
Edmund Randolph

III. ABSENT BUT FAVORED THE CONSTITUTION

Connecticut

Oliver Ellsworth

Georgia

William Pierce
William Houstoun

Massachusetts

Caleb Strong

New Jersey

William Houston

North Carolina

William Davie

Virginia

James McClurg
George Wythe

IV. ABSENT BUT AGAINST THE CONSTITUTION

Maryland

Luther Martin
John Mercer

New York

John Lansing
Robert Yates

North Carolina

Alexander Martin

Appendix C
Signers of the Declaration of Independence

CONNECTICUT

Samuel Huntington
Roger Sherman
William Williams
Oliver Wolcott

DELAWARE

Thomas McKean
George Read
Caesar Rodney

GEORGIA

Button Gwinnett
Lyman Hall
George Walton

MARYLAND

Charles Carroll
Samuel Chase
William Paca
Thomas Stone

MASSACHUSETTS

John Adams
Samuel Adams
Elbridge Gerry
John Hancock
Robert T. Paine

NEW HAMPSHIRE

Josiah Bartlett
Matthew Thornton
William Whipple

NEW JERSEY

Abraham Clark
John Hart
Francis Hopkinson
Richard Stockton
John Witherspoon

NEW YORK

William Floyd
Francis Lewis

Philip Livingston
Lewis Morris

NORTH CAROLINA

Joseph Hewes
William Hooper
John Penn

PENNSYLVANIA

George Clymer
Benjamin Franklin
Robert Morris
John Morton
George Ross
Benjamin Rush
James Smith
George Taylor
James Wilson

RHODE ISLAND

William Ellery
Stephen Hopkins

SOUTH CAROLINA

Thomas Heyward Jr.
Thomas Lynch Jr.
Arthur Middleton
Edward Rutledge

VIRGINIA

Carter Braxton
Benjamin Harrison
Thomas Jefferson
Francis Lightfoot Lee
Richard Henry Lee
Thomas Nelson Jr.
George Wythe

Appendix D
Presidents of Congress

PRESIDENT OF THE CONTINENTAL CONGRESS

First Continental Congress

September 1774–October 1774	Peyton Randolph
October 1774	Henry Middleton

Second Continental Congress

May 1775	Peyton Randolph
May 1775–October 1777	John Hancock
November 1777–December 1778	Henry Laurens
December 1778–September 1779	John Jay
September 1779–March 1781	Samuel Huntington

PRESIDENT OF THE UNITED STATES IN CONGRESS ASSEMBLED

March 1781–July 1781	Samuel Huntington
July 1781–November 1781	Thomas McKean
November 1781–November 1782	John Hanson
November 1782–November 1783	Elias Boudinot
November 1783–October 1784	Thomas Mifflin
November 1784–November 1785	Richard Henry Lee
November 1785–June 1786	John Hancock
June 1786–November 1786	Nathaniel Gorham
February 1787–November 1787	Arthur St. Clair
January 1788–November 1788	Cyrus Griffin

Bibliography

INTRODUCTORY NOTE

An extensive—and constantly expanding—amount of literature exists on the Revolutionary period of American history between 1763 and 1789. The purpose of this introductory note is to highlight some of the better books and Web-based sources for those seeking to conduct additional research on issues in the field. Websites can and do change their URLs; therefore, each website highlighted here includes the name of the sponsoring organization. If a Web address has changed, readers can perform an Internet search for the sponsoring organization.

There are several excellent general surveys of American history between 1763 and 1789. Individuals wanting a greater understanding of this pivotal period can consult *The Birth of the Republic, 1763–1789* by Edmund S. Morgan; *The Glorious Cause: The American Revolution, 1763–1789* by Robert Middlekauf; *The Colonial Period of American History* by Charles M. Andrews; and *The Ideological Origins of the American Revolution* by Bernard Bailyn. A good Web source for general information on the period is maintained by Primedia History Group (www.thehistorynet.com).

Many worthy books detailing the entire Revolutionary War exist. However, some of the better volumes include *The Glorious Cause: The American Revolution, 1763–1789* by Robert Middlekauf; *The War of Independence* by Claude H. Van Tyne; and *Liberty: The American Revolution* by Thomas Fleming. The latter book is the companion volume to the Public Broadcasting Service television series by the same name (www.pbs.org/ktca/liberty). Excellent works on individual campaigns or battles include *Beat the Last Drum* by Thomas Fleming and *The Road to Guilford Courthouse* by John Buchanan. Richard M. Ketchum has written three well-received studies, including *Decisive*

Day: The Battle for Bunker Hill, *The Winter Soldiers*, and *Saratoga*, while David H. Fischer has produced *Washington's Crossing* and *Paul Revere's Ride*. All are classics or destined to become classic studies in their particular areas. A handy guide to the war is provided by Terry M. Mays in *The Historical Dictionary of the American Revolution*. The latter book includes an extensive bibliography on the Revolutionary War, thus, only a select list of material on the conflict is included in this volume.

The Forging of the Union, 1781–1789 by Richard B. Morris stands out as a good source on the United States under the Articles of Confederation. *Original Meanings: Politics and Ideas in the Making of the Constitution* by Jack N. Rakove is an excellent place to start when working with the U.S. Constitution. The Constitution Society maintains a website (www.constitution.org) that holds digital versions of the speeches and letters of many individuals (Federalist and anti-Federalist) associated with the Constitution and its ratification.

Worthwhile general studies on important political figures of Revolutionary America include *Patriots: The Men Who Started the Revolution* by A. J. Langguth, *Founding Fathers* by Charles W. Meister, and *Founding Brothers: The Revolutionary Generation* by Joseph J. Ellis. The Library of Congress (www.loc.gov) holds the papers of many prominent Americans associated with the Revolutionary period of history. Most are not in digital form and must be utilized at the library.

John Adams, written by David McCullough, is one of the best biographies on this important Founding Father. Other excellent surveys on the life of Adams include *Honest John Adams* by Gilbert Chinard, *John Adams: A Life* by John Ferling, and *John Adams* by Page Smith. The Massachusetts Historical Society (www.masshist.org) maintains the papers of John Adams and offers some digital documents on its site, including the texts of his autobiography, diaries, and correspondence with his wife, Abigail. The microfilm format of the society's collection consists of over 600 reels. Digital copies of his papers can also be found at the Yale University law library's Avalon project website (www.yale.edu/lawweb/avalon/president/adamspap.htm).

A comprehensive study of Thomas Jefferson can be found in *Jefferson and His Times*, vols. 1–5 by Dumas Malone. Princeton University is producing the *Papers of Thomas Jefferson*, a projected 60-volume series. The official Monticello website (www.monticello.org) holds considerable information on Thomas Jefferson. However, one of the best sites for documents related to Jefferson's life is located at the University of Virginia (http://etext.virginia.edu/jefferson/). This site contains 1,700 digital documents on Jefferson as well as a 9,000-entry encyclopedia on his life. Many of Jefferson's papers can also be found online at the Manuscript Division of the Library of Congress (www.loc.gov), the Yale University law library's Avalon project (www.yale.edu/lawweb/avalon/president/jeffpap.htm), and Princeton University (www.princeton.edu/~tjpapers/). The Public Broadcasting Service (www.pbs.org/jefferson/) maintains the official companion site to the Ken Burns documentary on Jefferson.

Excellent reviews of George Washington's life include *George Washington*, vols. 1–6, edited by Douglas S. Freeman and vol. 7 edited by John A. Carroll and Mary W. Ashworth, and *George Washington*, vols. 1–3 by James T. Flexner. The documents and correspondence of George Washington can be found in the multiple volumes of *The Papers of George Washington* edited by the University of Virginia. The editors maintain their own website (www.gwpapers.virginia.edu/). The Manuscript Division of the Library of Congress holds approximately 65,000 documents associated with the life of Washington. A limited number of digital documents are available through the Library of Congress (www.memory.loc.gov/ammem/gwhtml/gwhome.html).

Numerous authors have written well-researched books on the life of Benjamin Franklin. Classic biographies of Franklin include *Benjamin Franklin: Self Revealed* by William C. Bruce, *Benjamin Franklin* by Carl Van Doren, and *The First American: The Life and Times of Benjamin Franklin* by H. W. Brands. Franklin wrote his own autobiography, appropriately titled *The Autobiography of Benjamin Franklin*. Yale University edits Franklin's documents in a series known as *The Papers of Benjamin Franklin*. The Public Broadcasting Service produced a television show on Franklin's life and it maintains an associated website on him (www.pbs.org/benfranklin).

James Madison: A Biography, by Ralph Ketcham, is an outstanding work on the Father of the Constitution. The University of Virginia currently edits the series of books known as *The Papers of James Madison*. The Constitution Society (www.constitution.org/jm/jm.htm) is a good source for digital versions of documents and correspondence related to the Constitution written by Madison.

Several books on Alexander Hamilton have emerged since 1982 and include *Alexander Hamilton* by Jacob E. Cooke, *Alexander Hamilton* by Ron Chernnow, *Alexander Hamilton* by Richard Brookhiser, and *Odd Destiny: The Life of Alexander Hamilton* by Marie B. Hecht.

Good works on the lives of women during the Revolutionary period include *Abigail Adams: An American Woman* by Charles W. Akers, *Portia: The World of Abigail Adams* by Edith Gelles, *The Women of the American Revolution* by Elizabeth F. Ellet, *Liberty's Daughters: The Revolutionary Experience of American Women* by Mary B. Norton, and *Founding Mothers* by Cokie Roberts. Books that discuss the roles of African Americans during this era include *Blacks in the American Revolution* by Philip S. Foner and *Slavery and Servitude in North America, 1607–1800* by Kenneth Morgan. Native American studies include *The Revolutionary Frontier, 1763–1783* by Jack M. Sosin, *The American Revolution in Indian Country: Crisis and Diversity in Native American Communities* by Colin Calloway, and *Contact Points: American Frontiers from the Mohawk Valley to the Mississippi, 1750–1830* edited by Andrew Cayton and Fredrika Teute.

While numerous books contain important documents from American history, *Sources and Documents Illustrating the American Revolution and the Formation of the Federal Constitution, 1764–1788*, is devoted entirely to Revolutionary America and contains 62 documents. Several websites are excellent sources as well as helpful in locating documents from Revolutionary America. Perhaps the best website for reading historical documents of this period is the Yale University law library's Avalon Project (www.yale.edu/lawweb/avalon/). The site contains transcripts from dozens of documents and diaries from the era between 1763 and 1789. Many of these documents are difficult to find through other sources. The National Archives website (www.archives.gov) holds the basic documents of American government. However, an affiliated site on the 100 milestone documents of American history (www.ourdocuments.gov) is even better for research; 12 of the 100 documents are from the Revolutionary America period. The site allows researchers to see and read actual scanned copies of the documents as well as transcripts that can be printed. The website of Congress (www.congress.gov) contains information on the Continental Congress and the Constitutional Convention of 1787 as well as links to the National Archives. Extensive collections of Revolutionary era newspapers can be found at many locations including the Library of Congress and Duke University as well as other universities.

CONTENTS

7. Silas Deane
8. John Dickinson
9. John Murray Dunmore (Lord Dunmore)
10. Benjamin Franklin
11. Christopher Gadsden
12. Thomas Gage
13. King George III
14. George Germain
15. Elbridge Gerry
16. George Grenville
17. Nathan Hale
18. Alexander Hamilton
19. John Hancock
20. Patrick Henry
21. Thomas Hutchinson
22. John Jay
23. Thomas Jefferson
24. Henry Laurens
25. Richard Henry Lee
26. William Legge (Lord Dartmouth)
27. Robert Livingston
28. James Madison
29. Gouverneur Morris
30. Robert Morris
31. Frederick North
32. Thomas Paine
33. Charles Willson Peale
34. Edmund Randolph
35. Paul Revere
36. Charles Rockingham (Marquis of Rockingham)
37. Benjamin Rush
38. John Rutledge
39. William Tryon
40. Joseph Warren
41. George Washington
42. Noah Webster
43. Benjamin West

I. REFERENCE WORKS AND BIBLIOGRAPHIES

Blanco, Richard. L. *The War of the American Revolution: A Selected Annotated Bibliography of Published Sources*. New York: Garland, 1984.

Cappon, Lester J., et al., eds. *Atlas of Early American History: The Revolutionary Era, 1760–1790*. Princeton: Princeton University Press, 1976.

Coakley, Robert W. *The War of the American Revolution: Narrative, Chronology, and Bibliography*. Washington, D.C.: Center of Military History, 1975.

Davies, K. G., ed. *Documents of the American Revolution, 1770–1783*. 21 vols. Shannon, Ireland: Irish University Press, 1972–1981.

Gephart, Ronald M., comp., *Revolutionary America, 1763–1789: A Bibliography*. 2 vols. Washington, D.C.: Library of Congress, 1984.

Greene, Jack P., ed. *Colonies to Nation, 1763–1789*. New York: McGraw-Hill, 1967.

Harley, J. B., et al. *Mapping the American Revolutionary War*. Chicago: University of Chicago Press, 1978.

Jenson, Merrill, ed. *English Historical Documents: American Colonial Documents to 1776*. New York: Oxford University Press, 1955.

Mays, Terry M. *The Historical Dictionary of the American Revolution*. Lanham, Md.: Scarecrow Press, 1999.

Morison, Samuel E., ed. *Sources and Documents Illustrating the American Revolution, 1764–1788, and the Formation of the Federal Constitution*. 2nd ed. Oxford: Oxford University Press, 1929.

Shy, John, comp. *The American Revolution. Goldentree Bibliographies in American History*. Northbrook, Ill.: AHM, 1973.

Smith, Dwight L., ed. *Era of the American Revolution: A Bibliography*. Santa Barbara, Calif.: ABC-Clio, 1975.

Smith, Dwight L., and Terry Simmerman, eds. *Era of the American Revolution: A Bibliography*. Santa Barbara, Calif.: ABC-Clio, 1975.

Smith, Myron J. *Navies in the American Revolution: A Bibliography*. Metuchen, N.J.: Scarecrow Press, 1973.

II. BRITISH COLONIAL ACTS AND THE AMERICAN REACTION

1. General Works

Allison, Robert J., ed. *The Revolutionary Era, 1754–1783*. Detroit: Gale Research, 1998.

Andrews, Charles M. *The Colonial Background of the American Revolution*. New Haven, Conn.: Yale University Press, 1924.

Bailyn, Bernard. *The Ideological Origins of the American Revolution*. Cambridge, Mass.: Harvard University Press, 1967.

Beer, George L. *British Colonial Policy, 1754–1765*. New York: Macmillan, 1907.

Christie, Ian, and Benjamin W. Labaree. *Empire or Independence, 1760–1887: A British-American Dialogue on the Coming of the American Revolution*. New York: Norton, 1976.

Clark, Dora M. *The Rise of the British Treasury: Colonial Administration in the Eighteenth Century*. New Haven, Conn.: Yale University Press, 1960.

Crowley, John E. *The Privileges of Independence: Neomercantilism and the American Revolution*. Baltimore, Md.: Johns Hopkins University Press, 1993.

Donoughue, Bernard. *British Politics and the American Revolution: The Path to War, 1773–1775*. New York: St. Martin's Press, 1964.

Egnal, Marc. *A Mighty Empire: The Origins of the American Revolution*. Ithaca, N.Y.: Cornell University Press, 1988.

Gipson, Lawrence H. *The British Empire before the American Revolution*. 15 vols. New York: Alfred A. Knopf, 1939–1970.

———. *The Coming of the Revolution, 1763–1775*. New York: Harper and Brothers, 1954.

Greene, Jack P. *Interpreting Early America: Historiographical Essays*. Charlottesville: University Press of Virginia, 1996.

Jensen, Merrill. *The Founding of a Nation: A History of the American Revolution*. New York: Oxford University Press, 1968.

Kammen, Michael G. *A Rope of Sand: The Colonial Agents, British Politics, and the American Revolution*. Ithaca, New York: Cornell University Press, 1968.

Knollenberg, Bernhard. *Origins of the American Revolution, 1759–1776*. New York: Macmillan, 1960.

Maier, Pauline. *From Resistance to Revolution: Colonial Radicals and the Development of American Opposition to Britain, 1765–1776*. New York: Alfred A. Knopf, 1972.

Martin, James K. *Men in Rebellion: Higher Governmental Leaders and the Coming of the American Revolution*. New Brunswick, N.J.: Rutgers University Press, 1973.

Miller, John C. *Origins of the American Revolution*. New York: Atlantic Monthly Press, 1943.

Morgan, Edmund S. *The Birth of the Republic, 1763–1789*. Chicago: University of Chicago Press, 1956.

Nash, Gary B. *The Urban Crucible: The Northern Seaports and the Origins of the American Revolution*. Cambridge, Mass.: Harvard University Press, 1986.

Purvis, Thomas L. *Revolutionary America, 1763 to 1800*. New York: Facts on File, 1995.

Ritcheson, Charles R. *British Policies and the American Revolution*. Norman: University of Oklahoma Press, 1954.

Rogers, Alan. *Empire and Liberty: American Resistance to British Authority, 1755–1763*. Berkeley: University of California Press, 1974.

Rossiter, Clinton L. *Seedtime of the Republic, The Origins of the American Tradition of Political Liberty*. New York: Harcourt, Brace, 1953.

Savelle, Max. *Seeds of Liberty: The Genesis of the American Mind*. Seattle: University of Washington Press, 1965.

Schlesinger, Arthur M. *The Colonial Merchants and the American Revolution, 1763–1776*. New York: Columbia University Press, 1918.

Sosin, Jack M. *Agents and Merchants: British Colonial Policy and the Origins of the American Revolution, 1763–1775*. Lincoln: University of Nebraska Press, 1965.

Spector, Margaret M. *The American Department of the British Government, 1768–1782*. New York: Columbia University Press, 1940.

Thomas, Peter D. *Tea Party to Independence: The Third Phase of the American Revolution, 1773–1776*. Oxford: Clarendon Press, 1991.

———. *The Townshend Duties Crisis: The Second Phase of the American Revolution, 1767–1773*. Oxford: Clarendon Press, 1987.

Tyler, John W. *Smugglers and Patriots: Boston Merchants and the Advent of the American Revolution*. Boston: Northeastern University Press, 1986.

Wickwire, Franklin B. *British Subministers and Colonial America, 1763–1783*. Princeton, N.J.: Princeton University Press, 1966.

2. Boston Massacre

Adams, Randolph G. "New Light on the Boston Massacre." *American Antiquarian Society Proceedings* 47 (1937): 259–354.

Blood in the Streets: The Boston Massacre, 5 March 1770. Boston: Revolutionary War Bicentennial Commission, 1970.

David, Leon T. "The Trial of Corporal William Wemms and Seven Others." *Los Angeles Bar Bulletin* 33 (1958): 323–31.

Dickerson, Oliver M. "The Commissioners of Customs and the 'Boston Massacre.'" *New England Quarterly* 27 (1954): 307–25.

Fleming, Thomas J. "Verdicts of History: The Boston Massacre." *American Heritage* 18, no. 12 (1966): 6–10.

Knollenberg, Bernhard. *Origins of the American Revolution, 1759–1776*. New York: Macmillan, 1960.

Wroth, L. Kinvin, and Hiller B. Zobel. "The Boston Massacre Trials." *American Bar Association Journal* 55 (1969): 329–33.

Zobel, Hiller B. *The Boston Massacre*. New York: W. W. Norton, 1970.

3. Boston Tea Party

Boston Citizens. "Minutes of the Tea Meetings in 1773." *Massachusetts Historical Society Proceedings* 20 (1882/1883): 10–17.

Cecil, Robert. "The Famous Tax Included, Tea Was Still Cheaper Here." *American Heritage* 12, no. 3 (1961): 8–11.

Dickerson, Oliver M. "Use Made of the Revenue from the Tax on Tea." *New England Quarterly* 31 (1958): 232–43.

Farrand, Max. "The Taxation of Tea, 1767–1773." *American Historical Review* 3 (1898): 266–69.

Frothingham, Richard. "The Destruction of the Tea in Boston on the 16th of December, 1773." *Massachusetts Historical Society Proceedings* 13 (1873/1875): 155–84.

Griswold, Wesley S. *The Night the Revolution Began: The Boston Tea Party, 1773*. Brattleboro, Vt.: S. Greene Press, 1972.

Knollenberg, Bernhard. *Origins of the American Revolution, 1759–1776*. New York: Macmillan, 1960.

Labaree, Benjamin W. *The Boston Tea Party*. New York: Oxford University Press, 1964.

———. "The Boston Tea Party and the American Revolution." *Cambridge Historical Society Publications* 39 (1961/1963): 144–64.

Schlesinger, Arthur M. "The Uprising against the East India Company." *Political Science Quarterly* 32 (1917): 60–79.

Strickland, Jacqueline. "Three Ships Attended the Boston Tea Party." *Daughters of the American Revolution Magazine* 128 (1994).

Thomas, Peter D. *Tea Party to Independence: The Third Phase of the American Revolution, 1773–1776*. Oxford: Clarendon Press, 1991.

Upton, Leslie F. S., ed. "Proceedings of Ye Body Representing the Tea." *William and Mary Quarterly* 22 (1967): 287–300.

4. Sons of Liberty and Other Revolutionary Protestors

Boyer, Lee R. "Lobster Backs, Liberty Boys, and Laborers in the Streets: New York's Golden Hill and Nassau Street Riots." *New York Historical Society Quarterly Bulletin* 57 (1973): 281–308.

Champagne, Roger J. "Liberty Boys and Mechanics of New York City, 1764–1774." *Labor History* 8 (1967): 115–35.

——. "The Military Association of the Sons of Liberty." *New York Historical Society Quarterly* 41 (1957): 338–50.

——. "New York's Radicals and the Coming of Independence." *Journal of American History* 51 (1964): 21–40.

Davidson, Philip G. "Sons of Liberty and Stamp Men." *North Carolina Historical Review* 9 (1932): 38–56.

Dawson, Henry B. "The First Blood Shed in the American Revolution. The Battle of Golden-Hill." *Historical Magazine* 5 (1869): 1–28.

——. *The Sons of Liberty in New York*. New York: Arno Press, 1969.

Haywood, C. Robert. "Economic Sanctions: Use of the Threat of Manufacturers by the Southern Colonies." *Journal of Southern History* 25 (1959): 207–19.

Knollenberg, Bernhard. *Origins of the American Revolution, 1759–1776*. New York: Macmillan, 1960.

Lemisch, Jesse. "Jack Tar in the Streets: Merchant Seamen in the Politics of Revolutionary America." *William and Mary Quarterly* 25 (1968): 371–407.

Longley, R. S. "Mob Acts in Revolutionary Massachusetts." *New England Quarterly* 6 (1933): 98–130.

Maier, Pauline. "The Charleston Mob and the Evolution of Popular Politics in Revolutionary South Carolina, 1765–1784." *Perspectives in American History* 4 (1970): 173–96.

——. *From Resistance to Revolution: Colonial Radicals and the Development of American Opposition to Britain, 1765–1776*. New York: Alfred A. Knopf, 1972.

Peabody, Andrew P. "Boston Mobs before the Revolution." *Atlantic Monthly* 62 (1888): 321–33.

Schlesinger, Arthur M. "Political Mobs and the American Revolution, 1765–1776." *American Philosophical Society Proceedings* 99 (1955): 244–50.

Wood, Gordon S. "A Note on the Mobs in the American Revolution." *William and Mary Quarterly* 23 (1966): 635–42.

5. Customs Incidents

A. General Works

Barrow, Thomas C. *Trade and Empire: The British Customs Service in Colonial America, 1660–1775*. Cambridge, Mass.: Harvard University Press, 1967.

Clark, Dora M. "The American Board of Customs, 1767–1783." *American Historical Review* 45 (1940): 777–806.

Dickerson, Oliver M. "England's Most Fateful Decision [1767]." *New England Quarterly* 22 (1949): 388–94.

Frese, Joseph R. "Some Observations on the American Board of Customs Commissioners." *Massachusetts Historical Society Proceedings* 81 (1969): 3–30.

Martin, Alfred S. "The King's Customs: Philadelphia, 1763–1774." *William and Mary Quarterly* 5 (1948): 201–16.

Morris, Richard B. "Then and There the Child Independence Was Born." *American Heritage* 13, no. 2 (1962): 36–39, 82–84.

Tyler, John W. *Smugglers and Patriots: Boston Merchants and the Advent of the American Revolution*. Boston: Northeastern University Press, 1986.

B. The Gaspée *Affair*

Bryant, Samuel W. "*HMS Gaspée:* The Court Martial of Lieutenant William Dudingston." *Rhode Island History* 25 (1966): 65–72.

———. "Rhode Island Justice—1772 Vintage." *Rhode Island History* 26 (1967): 65–71.

Kitchin, Frederick H. "The Burning of the *Gaspée*." *Blackwood's Magazine* 219 (1926): 256–64.

Staples, William R., comp. *The Documentary History of the Destruction of the 'Gaspée.'* Providence, R.I.: Knowles, Vose, and Anthony York, 1845.

Wulsin, Eugene. "The Political Consequences of the Burning of the *Gaspée*." *Rhode Island History* 3 (1944): 1–11, 55–64.

C. The Liberty *Affair*

Harrison, Joseph. "Joseph Harrison and the *Liberty* Incident." *William and Mary Quarterly* 20 (1963): 585–95.

Wolkins, George C. "The Seizure of John Hancock's Sloop *Liberty*." *Massachusetts Historical Society Proceedings* 55 (1921/1922): 239–84.

6. Currency Act

Ernst, Joseph A. "The Currency Act Repeal Movement: A Study of Imperial Policies and Revolutionary Crisis, 1764–1767." *William and Mary Quarterly* 25 (1968): 177–211.

———. "Genesis of the Currency Act of 1764: Virginia Paper Money and the Protection of British Investments." *William and Mary Quarterly* 22 (1965): 33–74.

———. *Money and Politics in America, 1755–1775: A Study in the Currency Act of 1768 and the Political Economy of Revolution*. Chapel Hill: University of North Carolina Press, 1976.

Gipson, Lawrence H. *The Coming of the Revolution, 1763–1775*. New York: Harper and Brothers, 1954.

Greene, Jack P., and Richard M. Jellison. "The Currency Act of 1764 in Imperial-Colonial Relations, 1764–1776." *William and Mary Quarterly* 18 (1961): 485–518.

Knollenberg, Bernhard. *Origins of the American Revolution, 1759–1776*. New York: Macmillan, 1960.

Ritcheson, Charles R. *British Policies and the American Revolution*. Norman: University of Oklahoma Press, 1954.

Sosin, Jack M. "Imperial Regulation of Colonial Paper Money, 1764–1773." *Pennsylvania Magazine of History and Biography* 88 (1964): 174–98.

7. Quartering Act

Gerlach, Don R. "A Note on the Quartering Act of 1774." *New England Quarterly* 39 (1966): 80–88.

Gipson, Lawrence H. *The Coming of the Revolution, 1763–1775*. New York: Harper and Brothers, 1954.

Knollenberg, Bernhard. *Origins of the American Revolution, 1759–1776*. New York: Macmillan, 1960.

Miller, Helen H. *The Case of Liberty*. Chapel Hill: University of North Carolina Press, 1965.

Ritcheson, Charles R. *British Policies and the American Revolution*. Norman: University of Oklahoma Press, 1954.

8. Stamp Act

Baker, William. "William Baker's Account of the Debate on the Repeal of the Stamp Act." *William and Mary Quarterly* 26 (1969): 259–65.

Chroust, Anton-Herman. "The Lawyers of New Jersey and the Stamp Act." *American Journal of Legal History* 6 (1942): 286–97.

Connolly, James C. "The Stamp Act and New Jersey's Opposition to It." *New Jersey Historical Society Proceedings* 9 (1924): 137–50.

Crane, Verner W. "Benjamin Franklin and the Stamp Act." *Colonial Society of Massachusetts Publications* 32 (1933/1937): 55–77.

Crouse, Maurice A. "Cautious Rebellion: South Carolina's Opposition to the Stamp Act." *South Carolina Historical Magazine* 73 (1972): 59–71.

"Debates on the Declaratory Act and the Repeal of the Stamp Act, 1766." *American Historical Review* 17 (1912): 563–86.

Ellefson, Clinton A. "The Stamp Act in Georgia." *Georgia Historical Quarterly* 46 (1962): 1–19.

Giddens, Paul H. "Maryland and the Stamp Act Controversy." *Maryland Historical Magazine* 27 (1932): 79–98.

Gipson, Henry H. "The Great Debate in the Committee of the Whole House of Commons on the Stamp Act, 1766, as Reported by Nathaniel Ryder." *Pennsylvania Magazine of History and Biography* 86 (1962): 10–41.

Gipson, Lawrence H. *The Coming of the Revolution, 1763–1775*. New York: Harper and Brothers, 1954.

Grager, Bruce I. "The Stamp Act in Satire." *American Quarterly* 8 (1956): 368–84.

Haywood, Clarence R. "The Mind of the North Carolina Opponents of the Stamp Act." *North Carolina Historical Review* 29 (1952): 317–43.

Hodge, Helen H. "The Repeal of the Stamp Act." *Political Science Quarterly* 19 (1904): 252–76.

Hughes, Edward. "The English Stamp Duties, 1664–1764." *English Historical Review* 56 (1941): 234–64.

Johnson, Allen S. "British Politics and the Repeal of the Stamp Act." *South Atlantic Quarterly* 62 (1963): 169–88.

Knollenberg, Bernhard. *Origins of the American Revolution, 1759–1776*. New York: Macmillan, 1960.

Laprade, William T. "The Stamp Act in British Politics." *American Historical Review* 35 (1930): 735–57.

"London Merchants on the Stamp Act Repeal." *Massachusetts Historical Society Proceedings* 55 (1923): 215–23.

McAnear, Beverly. "The Albany York Stamp Act Riots." *William and Mary Quarterly* 4 (1947): 486–98.

Miller, Elmer I. "The Virginia Legislature and the Stamp Act." *William and Mary Quarterly* 21 (1913): 233–48.

Miller, Randall M. "The Stamp Act in Colonial Georgia." *Georgia Historical Quarterly* 56 (1972): 318–31.

Morgan, Edmund S. "The Postponement of the Stamp Act." *William and Mary Quarterly* 7 (1950): 353–92.

Morgan, Edmund S., and Helen M. Morgan. *The Stamp Act Crisis: Prologue to Revolution*. Chapel Hill: University of North Carolina Press, 1953.

"Resistance to Stamp Act." *Maryland Historical Magazine* 4 (1909): 134–39.

Richards, David A. "New Haven and the Stamp Act Crisis of 1765–1766." *Yale University Library Gazette* 46 (1971): 67–85.

Ritcheson, Charles R. *British Policies and the American Revolution*. Norman: University of Oklahoma Press, 1954.

———. "The Preparation of the Stamp Act." *William and Mary Quarterly* 10 (1953): 543–59.

Sosin, Jack M. "A Postscript to the Stamp Act. George Grenville's Revenue Measures: A Drain on Colonial Specie?" *American Historical Review* 63 (1958): 918–23.

Stevens, John A. "The Stamp Act in New York." *Magazine of American History* 1 (1877): 337–69.

Thomas, P. D. G. *British Politics and the Stamp Act Crisis: The First Phase of the American Revolution, 1763–1767*. New York: Oxford University Press, 1967.

Young, Henry J. "Agrarian Reactions to the Stamp Act in Pennsylvania." *Pennsylvania History* 34 (1967): 25–30.

9. Sugar Act

Dickerson, Oliver M. *The Navigation Act and the American Revolution*. Philadelphia: University of Pennsylvania Press, 1951.

Gipson, Lawrence H. *The Coming of the Revolution, 1763–1775*. New York: Harper and Brothers, 1954.

Johnson, Allen S. "The Passage of the Sugar Act." *William and Mary Quarterly* 15 (1959): 507–14.

Knollenberg, Bernhard. *Origins of the American Revolution, 1759–1776*. New York: Macmillan, 1960.

Ritcheson, Charles R. *British Policies and the American Revolution*. Norman: University of Oklahoma Press, 1954.

Wierner, Frederick B. "The Rhode Island Merchants and the Sugar Act." *New England Quarterly* 3 (1930): 465–500.

10. Navigation Acts

Barrow, Thomas C. *Trade and Empire: The British Customs Service in Colonial America, 1660–1775*. Cambridge, Mass.: Harvard University Press, 1967.

Broeze, Frank, et al. "The New Economic Theory, the Navigation Acts, and the Continental Tobacco Market, 1770–1790." *Economic History Review* 26 (1973): 668–78.

Dickerson, Oliver M. *The Navigation Act and the American Revolution*. Philadelphia: University of Pennsylvania Press, 1951.

Gipson, Lawrence H. *The Coming of the Revolution, 1763–1775*. New York: Harper and Brothers, 1954.

Harper, Lawrence A. "The Effect of the Navigation Acts on the Thirteen Colonies." In *The Era of the American Revolution: Studies Inscribed to Evarts B. Greene*, edited by Richard B. Morris, 3–33. New York: Columbia University Press, 1939.

——. *The English Navigation Laws: A Seventeenth-Century Experiment in Social Engineering*. New York: Oxford University Press, 1940.

Knollenberg, Bernhard. *Origins of the American Revolution, 1759–1776*. New York: Macmillan, 1960.

McClelland, Peter D. "The Cost to America of British Imperial Policy." *American Economic Review* 59 (1969): 370–81.

Nettels, Curtis P. "British Mercantilism and the Economic Development of the Thirteen Colonies." *Journal of Economic History* 12 (1952): 105–14.

Ramson, Roger L. "British Policy and Colonial Growth: Some Implications of the Burden from the Navigation Acts." *Journal of Economic History* 28 (1968): 427–35.

Ritcheson, Charles R. *British Policies and the American Revolution*. Norman: University of Oklahoma Press, 1954.

Thomas, Robert P. "British Imperial Policy and the Economic Interpretation of the American Revolution." *Journal of Economic History* 28 (1968): 436–40.

Willon, Gary M. "The New Economic History and the Burden of the Navigation Acts." *Economic History Review* 24 (1971): 553–42.

11. Townshend Acts

Brooke, John. *The Chatham Administration, 1766–1768*. New York: St. Martin's Press, 1956.

Brunhouse, Robert L. "The Effects of the Townshend Acts on Pennsylvania." *Pennsylvania Magazine of History and Biography* 54 (1930): 353–73.

Chaffin, Robert J. "The Townshend Acts of 1767." *William and Mary Quarterly* 27 (1970): 90–121.

Dickerson, Oliver M. *The Navigation Act and the American Revolution*. Philadelphia: University of Pennsylvania Press, 1951.

Gipson, Lawrence H. *The Coming of the Revolution, 1763–1775*. New York: Harper and Brothers, 1954.

Knight, Carol L. *The American Colonial Press and the Townshend Crisis, 1766–1770: A Study in Political Imagery*. Lewiston: E. Mellen Press, 1990.

Knollenberg, Bernhard. *Origins of the American Revolution, 1759–1776*. New York: Macmillan, 1960.

Ritcheson, Charles R. *British Policies and the American Revolution*. Norman: University of Oklahoma Press, 1954.

Smith, Glen C. "An Era of Non-Importation Associations, 1768–1773." *William and Mary Quarterly* 20 (1945): 84–98.

Thomas, P. D. G. "Charles Townshend and American Taxation in 1767." *English Historical Review* 83 (1968): 33–51.

——. *The Townshend Duties Crisis: The Second Phase of the American Revolution, 1767–1773*. Oxford: Clarendon Press, 1987.

Watson, Derek H. "The Rockingham Whigs and the Townshend Duties." *English Historical Review* 84 (1969): 561–65.

12. Coercive Acts

Ammerman, David. *In the Common Cause: American Response to the Coercive Acts of 1774*. Charlottesville: University of Virginia Press, 1974.

Gipson, Lawrence H. *The Coming of the Revolution, 1763–1775*. New York: Harper and Brothers, 1954.

Knollenberg, Bernhard. *Origins of the American Revolution, 1759–1776*. New York: Macmillan, 1960.

13. British Politics and American Diplomacy

Barrow, Thomas C. "Background to the Grenville Program, 1757–1763." *William and Mary Quarterly* 22 (1965): 93–104.

Beer, George L. *British Colonial Policy, 1754–1765*. New York: Macmillan, 1907.

Cook, Don. *The Long Fuse: How England Lost the American Colonies, 1760–1785*. New York: Atlantic Monthly Press, 1995.

Eldridge, C. C., ed. *Kith and Kin: Canada, Britain, and the United States from the Revolution to the Cold War*. Cardiff: University of Wales Press, 1997.

Fagerstrom, D. I. "Scottish Opinion and the American Revolution." *William and Mary Quarterly* 11 (1954): 252–75.

Fortescue, Sir John, ed. *The Correspondence of King George from 1760 to December 1783*. London: Macmillan, 1928.

Great Britain Colonial Office. *Documents of the American Revolution, 1770–1783*. Edited by K. G. Davies. Shannon, Ireland: Irish University Press, 1972.

Hall, Hubert. "Chatham's Colonial Policy." *American Historical Review* 5 (1900): 659–75.

Johnson, Richard R. "'Parliamentary Egotisms': The Clash of Legislatures in the Making of the American Revolution." *Journal of American History* 74 (1987): 338–62.

King-Hall, Stephen. "The Parting of the Ways." *Parliamentary Affairs* 8 (1955): 192–204, 318–33.

Mullett, Charles F. "English Imperial Thinking, 1764–1783." *Political Science Quarterly* 45 (1930): 548–79.

Perry, K. R. *British Politics and the American Revolution*. New York: St. Martin's Press, 1990.

Ritcheson, Charles R. *Aftermath of Revolution: British Policy towards the United States, 1783–1795*. New York: Norton, 1969.

Scott, H. M. *British Foreign Policy in the Age of the American Revolution*. New York: Oxford University Press, 1991.

Stout, Neil R. "Goals and Enforcement of British Colonial Policy, 1763–1775." *American Neptune* 27 (1967): 211–20.

Temperley, Harold W. V. "Chatham, North, and North America." *Quarterly Review* 221 (1914): 295–319.

Thomas, P. D. G. "George III and the American Revolution." *History* 70 (1985): 16–31.

Van Alstyne, Richard W. "Great Britain, the War for Independence, and the Gathering Storm in Europe." *Huntington Library Quarterly* 27 (1964): 311–45.

Wead, Eunice. "British Public Opinion of the Peace with America, 1782." *American Historical Review* 34 (1929): 513–31.

III. AMERICAN DIPLOMACY

1. General Works

Auger, Helen. *The Secret War of Independence*. New York: Duell, Sloan, and Pierce, 1955.

Bemis, Samuel F. *The Diplomacy of the American Revolution*. New York: D. Appleton-Century, 1935.

Burnette, Edmund C. "Note on American Negotiations for Commercial Treaties, 1776–1786." *American Historical Review* 16 (1911): 579–87.

Callinor, Joan R., and Robert L. Beisner. *Arms at Rest: Peacemaking and Peacekeeping in American History*. New York: Greenwood Press, 1987.

Cook, Don. *The Long Fuse: How England Lost the American Colonies, 1760–1785*. New York: Atlantic Monthly Press, 1995.

Corwin, Edward. *French Policy and the American Alliance of 1778*. Princeton, N.J.: Princeton University Press, 1916.

Darling, Arthur B. *Our Rising Empire, 1763–1803*. New Haven, Conn.: Yale University Press, 1940.

Hoffman, Ronald, and Peter J. Albert, eds. *Peace and the Peacemakers: The Treaty of 1783*. Charlottesville: University Press of Virginia, 1986.

Hutson, James. H. *John Adams and the Diplomacy of the American Revolution*. Lexington: University Press of Kentucky, 1980.

Johnson, Emory R. "The Early History of the United States Consular Service, 1776–1792." *Political Science Quarterly* 13 (1898): 19–40.

Kaplan, Lawrence S. *The American Revolution and "A Candid World."* Kent, Ohio: Kent State University Press, 1977.

——. *Colonies into Nation: American Diplomacy, 1763–1801*. New York: Macmillan, 1972.

Kimball, Marie. *Jefferson: The Scene of Europe, 1784–1789*. New York: Coward-McCann, 1950.

Kite, Elizabeth. *Beaumarchais and the War of American Independence*. 2 vols. Boston: R. G. Badger, 1918.

——. *Conrad Alexandre Gerard and American Independence*. Philadelphia: Publisher unknown, 1921.

Meng, John J. *The Comte de Vergennes: European Phases of His American Diplomacy (1774–1780)*. Washington, D.C.: Catholic University Press, 1932.

——. *Dispatches and Instructions of Conrad Alexandre Gerard, 1778–1780: Correspondence of the First French Minister to the United States with the Comte de Vergennes*. Baltimore, Md.: Johns Hopkins University Press, 1939.

Morris, Richard B. *The Great Powers and the American Independence*. New York: Harper and Row, 1965.

——. "The West in Peace Negotiations." In *The Old Northwest in the American Revolution, An Anthology*. Edited by David C. Skaggs Jr. Madison: State Historical Society of Wisconsin, 1977: 269–304.

Morris, Richard B. *The Peacemakers: The Great Powers and American Independence*. New York: Harper and Row, 1965.

Nuxoll, Elizabeth M. *Congress and the Munitions Merchants: The Secret Committee of Trade during the American Revolution, 1775–1777*. New York: Garland, 1985.

Savelle, Max. "Colonial Origins of American Diplomatic Principles." *Pacific Historical Review* 3 (1934): 334–50.

Stinchombe, William C. *The American Revolution and the French Alliance*. Syracuse, N.Y.: Syracuse University Press, 1969.

Stourzh, Gerald. *Benjamin Franklin and American Foreign Policy.* Chicago: University of Chicago Press, 1954.

Trescott, William H. *The Diplomacy of the Revolution: A Historical Study*. New York: D. Appleton, 1852.

Tuchman, Barbara W. *The First Salute*. New York: Knopf, 1988.

Van Tyne, C. H. "French Aid before the Alliance of 1778." *American Historical Review* 31 (1925): 20–40.

Varg, Paul A. *Foreign Policies of the Founding Fathers*. East Lansing: Michigan State University Press, 1963.

Wood, George C. *Congressional Control of Foreign Relations during the American Revolution, 1774–1789*. Allentown, Pa.: H. R. Haas, 1919.

2. Denmark

Fodgall, Soren J. M. P. *Danish-American Diplomacy, 1776–1920*. Iowa City: University of Iowa, 1922.

Rinehard, Robert. "Denmark Gets the News of '76." *Scandinavian Review* 64 (1976): 5–14.

3. France

Abernathy, Thomas P. "Commercial Acts of Silas Deane in France." *American Historical Review* 39 (1934): 477–85.

Allaben, Winthrop G. "Why the Alliance of 1778?" *Journal of American History* 22 (1928): 197–205.

Auger, Helen. "Benjamin Franklin and the French Alliance." *American Heritage* 7, no. 3 (1956): 65–88.

——. *The Secret War of Independence*. New York: Duell, Sloane, and Pearce, 1955.

Bamford, Paul W. "France and the American Market in Naval Timber and Masts, 1776–1786." *Journal of Economic History* 12 (1952): 21–34.

Beaumarchais, Pierre A. C. de. "Early American Diplomacy: Beaumarchais' Opinion of Silas Deane and Arthur Lee." *Magazine of American History* 3 (1879): 631–35.

Bemis, Samuel F. *The Diplomacy of the American Revolution*. New York: D. Appleton-Century Co., 1935.

Buron, Edmund. "Statistics on Franco–American Trade, 1778–1806." *Journal of Economic and Business History* 4 (1932): 571–86.

Chinard, Gilbert, ed. *The Treaties of 1778, and Allied Documents*. Baltimore, Md.: Johns Hopkins University Press, 1928.

Clarke, Richard H. "France's Aid to America in the War of Independence." *American Catholic Quarterly Review* 22 (1897): 399–423.

Corwin, Edward S. "The French Objective in the American Revolution." *American Historical Review* 21 (1915): 35–61.

——. *French Policy and the American Alliance of 1778*. Princeton, N.J.: Princeton University Press, 1916.

Dull, Jonathan R. *The French Navy and American Independence: A Study of Arms and Diplomacy, 1774–1787*. Princeton, N.J.: Princeton University Press, 1975.

Harris, Robert D. "French Finances and the American War, 1777–1783." *Journal of Modern History* 48 (1970): 233–58.

Kaplan, Lawrence S. *The American Revolution and "A Candid World."* Kent, Ohio: Kent State University Press, 1977.

Ketchum, Ralph L. "France and American Politics, 1763–1793." *Political Science Quarterly* 78 (1963): 198–223.

Kimball, Marie. *Jefferson: The Scene of Europe, 1784–1789*. New York: Coward-McCann, 1950.

Kite, Elizabeth. *Beaumarchais and the War of American Independence*. 2 vols. Boston: R. G. Badger, 1918.

——. *Conrad Alexandre Gerard and American Independence*. Philadelphia: Publisher unknown, 1921.

——. "Early Secret Diplomacy of France and America, 1775–1778." *Legion d'honneur* 7 (1936): 31–41.

——. "French 'Secret Aid': Precursor to the Franco-American Alliance, 1776–1777." *Franco-American Review* 1 (1948): 143–52.

Meng, John J. "A Foot-note to Secret Aid in the American Revolution." *American Historical Review* 43 (1938): 791–95.

——. *The Comte de Vergennes: European Phases of His American Diplomacy (1774–1780)*. Washington, D.C.: Catholic University Press, 1932.

——. *Dispatches and Instructions of Conrad Alexandre Gerard, 1778–1780: Correspondence of the First French Minister to the United States with the Comte de Vergennes*. Baltimore, Md.: Johns Hopkins University Press, 1939.

——. "French Diplomacy in Philadelphia: 1778–1779." *Catholic Historical Review* 24 (1938): 39–57.

Morris, Richard B. *The Great Powers and the American Independence*. New York: Harper and Row, 1965.

——. "The West in Peace Negotiations." In *The Old Northwest in the American Revolution, An Anthology*. Edited by David C. Skaggs Jr. Madison: State Historical Society of Wisconsin, 1977: 269–304.

Pleasants, Henry J. "Contraband from L'orient." *Military Affairs* 7 (1943): 123–32.

Plumb, J. H. "The French Connection." *American Heritage* 26, no. 4 (1974): 26–57, 86–87.

Schaeper, Thomas J. *France and America in the Revolutionary Era: The Life of Jacques-Donatien Leray de Chaumont, 1725–1803*. Providence, R.I.: Berghahn Books, 1995.

Schoebrun, David. *Triumph in Paris: The Exploits of Benjamin Franklin*. New York: Harper and Row, 1976.

Sheldon, Laura C. *France and the American Revolution, 1763–1778*. Ithaca, N.Y.: Andrus and Church, 1900.

Stincombe, William C. *The American Revolution and the French Alliance*. Syracuse, N.Y.: Syracuse University Press, 1969.

Stourzh, Gerald. *Benjamin Franklin and American Foreign Policy*. Chicago: University of Chicago Press, 1954.

Van Alstyne, Richard W. *Empire and Independence: The International History of the American Revolution*. New York: John Wiley and Sons, 1966.

Van Tyne, Claude F. "French Aid before the Alliance of 1778." *American Historical Review* 31 (1925): 20–40.

———. "Influences Which Determined the French Government to Make a Treaty with America, 1778." *American Historical Review* 21 (1916): 528–41.

Whitridge, Arnold. "Beaumarchais and the American Revolution." *History Today* 17 (1967): 98–105.

4. German States

Adams, Henry M. *Prussian-American Relations, 1775–1871*. Cleveland, Ohio: Press of Western Reserve University, 1960.

Brown, Marvin L., Jr. "American Independence through Prussian Eyes: A Neutral View of the Negotiations of 1782." *Historian* 18 (1955–1956): 189–201.

Burnett, Edmund C. "Notes on American Negotiations for Commercial Treaties." *American Historical Review* 16 (1910–1911): 579–87.

Graewe, Richard. "The American Revolution Comes to Hannover." *William and Mary Quarterly* 20 (1963): 246–50.

Gunther, Hans K. "Frederick the Great, the Bavarian War of Succession, and the American Revolution." *Duquesne Review* 16 (1971): 59–74.

Haworth, P. I. "Frederick the Great and the American Revolution." *American History Review* 9 (1904): 460–78.

Lingelbach, William E. "Saxon-American Relations, 1778–1828." *American Historical Review* 17 (1912): 517–39.

5. Netherlands

Auger, Helen. *The Secret War of Independence*. New York: Duell, Sloane, and Pearce, 1955.

Elder, Friedrich. *The Dutch Republic and the American Revolution*. Baltimore, Md.: Johns Hopkins Press, 1911.

Morris, Richard B. *The Great Powers and the American Independence*. New York: Harper and Row, 1965.

Hunninghen, Benjamin. "Dutch–American Relations during the Revolution." *New York Historical Society Quarterly* 37 (1953): 170–184.

Jameson, J. Franklin. "St. Eustatius in the American Revolution." *American History Review* 8 (1903): 683–708.

Morice, Joseph. "The Contribution of Charles W. F. Dumas to the Cause of American Independence." *Duquesne Review* 7 (1961): 17–28.

Rubincam, Milton. "Samuel Witham Stockton, of New Jersey, and the Secret Treaty with Amsterdam in 1778." *New Jersey Historical Society Proceedings* 60 (1942): 98–116.

Van Alstyne, Richard W. *Empire and Independence: The International History of the American Revolution*. New York: John Wiley and Sons, 1966.
Van Oosten, F. C. "Some Notes Concerning the Dutch West Indies during the American Revolutionary War." *American Neptune* 36 (1976): 155–69.
Young, Philip. "The Netherlands and the United States." *Halve Maen* 40 (1966): 7–8, 14.

6. Portugal

Alden, Dauril. "The Marquis of Pompal and the American Revolution." *Americas* 17 (1960): 369–82.

7. Russia

Bolkovitinov, Nicholai N. *Russia and the American Revolution*. Translated and edited by C. Jay Smith. Tallahassee, Fla.: Diplomat Press, 1967.
Golden, Frank A. "Catherine II and the American Revolution." *American History Review* 21 (1915): 92–96.
Griffiths, David M. "American Commercial Diplomacy in Russia, 1780–1783." *William and Mary Quarterly* 27 (1970): 279–410.
———. "An American Contribution to the Armed Neutrality of 1780." *Russian Review* 30 (1971): 164–72.
———. "Nikita Panin, Russian Diplomacy, and the Other Revolution." *Slavic Review* 28 (1969): 1–24.
Kaplan, Lawrence S. *The American Revolution and "A Candid World."* Kent, Ohio: Kent State University Press, 1977.

8. Spain

Auger, Helen. *The Secret War of Independence*. New York: Duell, Sloane, and Pearce, 1955.
Boyd, Mark F., and Jose Navarro Latorre. "Spanish Interest in British Florida, and in the Progress of the American Revolution." *Florida Historical Quarterly* 32 (1954): 92–130.
Chavez, Thomas E. "Spain and the Independence of the United States." *Daughters of the American Revolution Magazine* 126 (1992).
Cummins, Light T. *Spanish Observers and the American Revolution, 1775–1783*. Baton Rouge: Louisiana State University Press, 1991.
Fernandez-Show, Carlos M. "Spain's Aid in the Independence of the United States." *Inter-American Review of Bibliography* 26 (1976): 456–508.
Klotz, Edwin F. "An American Patriot in Spain: 1781." *Social Studies* 57 (1960): 124–26.

Lawson, Katherine S. "Luciano de Herrera, Spanish Spy in British St. Augustine." *Florida Historical Quarterly* 23 (1945): 170–76.
McCarthy, Charles H. "The Attitude of Spain during the American Revolution." *Catholic Historical Review* 2 (1916): 47–65.
Morales Padron, Francisco. *Spanish Help in American Independence*. Madrid: Publicaciones Espanolas, 1952.
Morris, Richard B. *The Great Powers and the American Independence*. New York: Harper and Row, 1965.
——. "The Jay Papers: Mission to Spain." *American Heritage* 19, no. 2 (1968): 8–21, 85–96.
Rousseau, Francois. "La participation de l'Espagne à la guerre d'Amerique, 1779–1783." *Revue des questions historiques* 72 (1902): 444–89.
Thonhoff, Robert H. "Texas and the American Revolution." *Southwestern Historical Quarterly* 98 (1995): 511–17.
Van Alstyne, Richard W. *Empire and Independence: The International History of the American Revolution*. New York: John Wiley and Sons, 1966.
Wright, J. Leitch, Jr. *Anglo-Spanish Rivalry in North America*. Athens: University of Georgia Press, 1971.

9. Sweden

Barton, H. A. "Sweden and the War of American Independence." *William and Mary Quarterly* 23 (1966): 408–30.
Benson, Adolph B. *Sweden and the American Revolution*. New Haven, Conn.: Tuttle, Morehouse, and Taylor, 1926.
Carlson, Knute E. *Relations of the United States with Sweden*. Allentown, Pa.: H. R. Haas, 1921.
Johnson, Amandus. "The American–Swedish Treaty of 1783." *American Scandinavian Review* 46 (1958): 152–56.
Rosland-Mercurio, Carol. "Sweden and the American Revolution." *Scandinavian Review* 64 (1976): 45–51.

IV. THE POLITICS OF THE AMERICAN REVOLUTION

1. First Continental Congress

Anderson, Thomas. *Creating the Constitution: The Convention of 1787 and the First Congress*. University Park: Pennsylvania State University Press, 1993.
Becker, Carl L. "The Nomination and Election of Delegates from New York to the First Continental Congress, 1774." *Political Science Quarterly* 18 (1906): 17–46.

Collier, Christopher. *Connecticut in the Continental Congress*. Chester, Conn.: Pequot Press, 1973.

Davis, Derek. *Religion and the Continental Congress, 1774–1789: Contributions to Original Intent*. New York: Oxford University Press, 2000.

Fiske, John. "First Year of the Continental Congress." *Atlantic Monthly* 62 (1888): 358–77.

Ford, Paul L. "The Association of the First Congress." *Political Science Quarterly* 6 (1891): 613–24.

Ford, Worthington C., et al. *Journals of the Continental Congress, 1774–1789*. Washington, D.C.: Government Printing Office, 1905.

Garver, Frank H. "Attendance at the First Continental Congress." *American Historical Association Proceedings* 25 (1929): 21–40.

Meigs, Cornelia L. *The Violent Men, A Study of Human Relations in the First American Congress*. New York: Macmillan, 1949.

Montross, Lynn. *The Reluctant Rebels: The Story of the Continental Congress, 1774–1789*. New York: Barnes and Noble, 1950.

Mullet, Charles F. "Imperial Ideas at the First Continental Congress." *Southwestern Social Science Quarterly* 12 (1931): 238–44.

"The Original Petition to the King by the Continental Congress of 1774." *Magazine of American History* 9 (1883): 377–83.

Reed, William B. "The Congress of 1774." *New York Review* 4 (1839): 324–51.

Ryan, Frank W. "The Role of South Carolina in the First Continental Congress." *South Carolina Historical Magazine* 60 (1959): 147–53.

Sanders, Jennings B. *Evolution of Executive Departments of the Continental Congress, 1774–1789*. Chapel Hill: University of North Carolina Press, 1935.

———. *The Presidency of the Continental Congress, 1774–1789*. Gloucester, Mass.: P. Smith, 1971.

Smeall, J. F. S. "Revolutionary Process: The Publication of the Association, 1774–1775." *North Dakota Quarterly* 30 (1962): 89–98.

Smith, Paul H., ed. *Letters of Delegates to Congress, 1774–1789*. Vols. 1–8. Washington, D.C.: Library of Congress, 1976–1981.

Wolf, Edwin. "The Authorship of the 1774 Address to the King Restudied." *William and Mary Quarterly* 22 (1965): 189–224.

2. Second Continental Congress

Becker, Carl L. "Election of Delegates from New York to the Second Continental Congress." *American Historical Review* 9 (1903): 66–85.

Burnett, Edmund Cody. *The Continental Congress*. New York: Macmillan, 1941.

Collier, Christopher. *Connecticut in the Continental Congress*. Chester, Conn.: Pequot Press, 1973.

Davis, Derek. *Religion and the Continental Congress, 1774–1789: Contributions to Original Intent*. New York: Oxford University Press, 2000.

Ford, Worthington C., et al. *Journals of the Continental Congress, 1774–1789*. Washington, D.C.: Government Printing Office, 1905.

Horgan, Lucille E. *Forged in War: The Continental Congress and the Origin of Military Supply and Acquisition Policy*. Westport, Conn.: Greenwood Press, 2002.

Knollenberg, Bernhard. *Washington and the Revolution, a Reappraisal: Gates, Conway, and the Continental Congress*. New York: Macmillan, 1940.

Meigs, Corneila L. *The Violent Men: A Study of Human Relations in the First American Congress*. New York: Macmillan, 1949.

Montross, Lynn. *The Reluctant Rebels: The Story of the Continental Congress, 1774–1789*. New York: Barnes and Noble, 1950.

Morgan, David T., and William J. Schmidt. *North Carolinians in the Continental Congress*. Winston-Salem, N.C.: J. F. Blair, 1976.

Nuxoll, Elizabeth M. *Congress and the Munitions Merchants: The Secret Committee of Trade during the American Revolution, 1775–1777*. New York: Garland, 1985.

Rakove, Jack N. *The Beginnings of National Politics: An Interpretive History of the Continental Congress*. New York: Knopf, 1979.

Sanders, Jennings B. *Evolution of Executive Departments of the Continental Congress, 1774–1789*. Chapel Hill: University of North Carolina Press, 1935.

——. *The Presidency of the Continental Congress, 1774–1789*. Gloucester, Mass.: P. Smith, 1971.

Smith, Paul H., ed. *Letters of Delegates to Congress, 1774–1789*. Vols. 1–8. Washington, D.C.: Library of Congress, 1976–1981.

Ward, John. "The Continental Congress before the Declaration of Independence." *Magazine of American History* 2 (1878): 193–220.

3. Declaration of Independence

Bakeless, John E., and Katherine L. Bakeless. *Signers of the Declaration of Independence*. Boston: Houghton-Mifflin, 1969.

Becker, Carl L. *The Declaration of Independence, a Study in the History of Political Ideas*. New York: Harcourt Brace, 1922.

Beveride, Albert J. "Sources of the Declaration of Independence." *Pennsylvania Magazine of History and Biography* 50 (1926): 289–315.

Boyd, Julian P. *The Declaration of Independence: The Evolution of the Text as Shown in Facsimiles of Various Drafts by Its Author, Thomas Jefferson*. Princeton, N.J.: Princeton University Press, 1945.

Dana, William F. "The Declaration of Independence." *Harvard Law Review* 13 (1900): 319–43.

Darling, Arthur B. *A Historical Introduction to the Declaration of Independence*. New Haven, Conn.: Quinnipiack Press, 1932.

Ferris, Robert G., and Richard E. Morris. *The Signers of the Declaration of Independence*. Interpretative Publications, 1982.

Fisher, Sydney G. "The Twenty-eight Charges against the King in the Declaration of Independence." *Pennsylvania Magazine of History and Biography* 31 (1907): 257–303.

Friedenwald, Herbert. *The Declaration of Independence: An Interpretation and an Analysis*. New York: Macmillan, 1904.

Hazelton, John H. *The Declaration of Independence, Its History*. New York: Dodd, Mead, 1906.

Malone, Dumas. *The Story of the Declaration of Independence*. New York: Oxford University Press, 1954.

Schlesinger, Arthur M. "The Lost Meaning of 'the Pursuit of Happiness.'" *William and Mary Quarterly* 21 (1964): 325–27.

V. THE REVOLUTIONARY WAR

1. General Works

Carrington, Henry B. *Battles of the American Revolution, 1775–1781*. New York: Promontory Press, 1974.

Fleming, Thomas. *Liberty!: The American Revolution*. New York: Viking, 1997.

Jensen, Merrill. *The Founding of a Nation: A History of the American Revolution*. New York: Oxford University Press, 1968.

Middlekauf, Robert. *The Glorious Cause: The American Revolution, 1763–1789*. New York: Oxford University Press, 1982.

Van Tyne, Claude H. *The War of Independence*. New York: Houghton-Mifflin, 1929.

Ward, Christopher. *The War of the Revolution*. New York: Macmillan, 1952.

2. Battles and Campaigns

Buchanan, John. *The Road to Guilford Courthouse*. New York: Wiley, 1997.

Fischer, David H. *Paul Revere's Ride*. New York: Oxford University Press, 1994.

———. *Washington's Crossing*. New York: Oxford University Press, 2004.

Fleming, Thomas. *Beat the Last Drum*. New York: St. Martins, 1963.
French, Allen. *The First Year of the American Revolution*. Boston: Houghton-Mifflin, 1934.
Harrison, Lowell H. *George Rogers Clark and the War in the West*. Lexington: University Press of Kentucky, 1976.
Ketchum, Richard M. *Decisive Day: The Battle for Bunker Hill*. Garden City, N.Y.: Doubleday, 1974.
———. *Saratoga*. New York: Henry Holt, 1997.
———. *The Winter Soldiers*. Garden City, N.Y.: Doubleday, 1973.
Lumpkin, Henry. *From Savannah to Yorktown: The American Revolution in the South*. New York: Paragon House, 1981.
Smith, Samuel S. *The Battle of Monmouth*. Monmouth Beach, N.J.: Philip Freneau Press, 1964.

VI. POST-REVOLUTIONARY AMERICA

1. America under the Articles of Confederation

Bailyn, Bernard. *To Begin the World Anew: The Genius and Ambiguities of the American Founders*. New York: Alfred A. Knopf, 2003.
Brown, Richard D. "Shay's Rebellion and Its Aftermath: A View from Springfield, Massachusetts 1787." *William and Mary Quarterly*. October (1983).
Fiske, John. *The Critical Period of American History, 1783–1789*. Boston: Houghton-Mifflin, 1888.
Gianta, Mary A. *The Emerging Nation: A Documentary History of the U.S. under the Articles of Confederation*. Washington, D.C.: Publisher unknown, 1996.
Greene, Jack P. *Interpreting Early America: Historiographical Essays*. Charlottesville: University Press of Virginia, 1996.
Hoffert, Robert W. *A Politics of Tensions: The Articles of Confederation and American Political Ideas*. Niwot: University Press of Colorado, 1992.
Morgan, Edmund S. *The Birth of the Republic, 1763–1789*. Chicago: University of Chicago Press, 1992.
Morris, Richard B. *The Forging of the Union, 1781–1789*. New York: Harper and Row, 1987.
Pleasants, Samuel A. *The Articles of Confederation*. Columbus, Ohio: C. E. Merrill, 1968.
Sharp, James Roger. *American Politics in the Early Republic: The New Nation in Crisis*. New Haven, Conn.: Yale University Press, 1993.
Szatmary, David P. *Shays' Rebellion*. Amherst: University of Massachusetts Press, 1980.

Wood, Gordon S. *The Creation of the American Republic: 1776–1787*. Chapel Hill: University of North Carolina Press, 1969.

2. Congress of the Confederation

Davis, Derek. *Religion and the Continental Congress, 1774–1789: Contributions to Original Intent*. New York: Oxford University Press, 2000.

Josephy, Alvin, Jr. *On the Hill: A History of the American Congress*. New York: Simon and Schuster, 1979.

Montross, Lynn. *The Reluctant Rebels: The Story of the Continental Congress, 1774–1789*. New York: Barnes and Noble, 1950.

Sanders, Jennings B. *Evolution of Executive Departments of the Continental Congress, 1774–1789*. Chapel Hill: University of North Carolina Press, 1935.

———. *The Presidency of the Continental Congress, 1774–1789*. Gloucester, Mass.: P. Smith, 1971

Smith, Paul H., ed. *Letters of Delegates to Congress, 1774–1789*. Vols. 1–8. Washington, D.C.: Library of Congress, 1976–1981.

3. Economic Issues

Buel, Richard, Jr. *In Irons: Britain's Naval Supremacy and the American Revolutionary Economy*. New Haven, Conn.: Yale University Press, 1998.

Ernst, Joseph Albert. *Money and Politics in America, 1755–1775: A Study in the Currency Act of 1764 and the Political Economy of Revolution*. Chapel Hill: University of North Carolina Press, 1973.

Gilje, Paul A., ed. *Wages of Independence: Capitalism in the Early American Republic*. Madison, Wis.: Madison House, 1997.

Haseltine, John W. *Description of the Paper Money Issues by the Continental Congress of the United States and the Several Colonies*. Philadelphia: J. W. Haseltine, 1872.

Hoffman, Ronald, ed. *The Economy of Early America: The Revolutionary Period, 1763–1790*. Charlottesville: University Press of Virginia. 1988.

Koistinen, Paul A. C. *Beating Plowshares into Swords: The Political Economy of American Warfare, 1606–1865*. Lawrence: University Press of Kansas, 1996.

Rappaport, George David. *Stability and Change in Revolutionary Pennsylvania: Banking, Politics, and Social Structure*. University Park: Pennsylvania State University Press, 1996.

Spannaus, Nancy B., and Christopher White, eds. *The Political Economy of the American Revolution*. New York: Campaigner Publications, 1977.

Wright, Robert E. *Origins of Commercial Banking in America, 1750–1800*. Lanham, Md.: Rowman and Littlefield, 2001.

4. Social Issues

Andrews, Dee. *The Methodists and Revolutionary America, 1760–1800*. Princeton, N.J.: Princeton University Press, 2000.

Barker, Hannah, and Simon Burrows. *Press, Politics, and the Public Sphere in Europe and North America, 1760–1820*. Cambridge: Cambridge University Press, 2002.

Bjelajac, David. *American Art: A Cultural History*. New York: Abrams, 2001.

Blake, John B. *Public Health in the Town of Boston, 1630–1822*. Cambridge, Mass.: Harvard University Press, 1959.

Brown, Richard. *Knowledge Is Power: The Diffusion of Information in Early America, 1700–1865*. New York: Oxford University Press, 1989.

———. *The Strength of a People: The Idea of an Informed Citizenry in America, 1650–1870*. Chapel Hill: University of North Carolina Press, 1996.

Brown, Walt. *John Adams and the American Press*. Jefferson, N.C.: McFarland, 1995.

Cohen, I. Bernard. *Science and the Founding Fathers*. New York: Norton, 1995.

Hawes, Joseph M., and Elizabeth I. Nybakken, eds. *Family and Society in American History*. Urbana: University of Illinois Press, 2001.

Hawke, David Freeman. *Everyday Life in Early America*. New York: Harper and Row, 1988.

Higginbotham, Don. *War and Society in Revolutionary America: The Wider Dimensions of Conflict*. Columbia: University of South Carolina Press, 1998.

Hopkins, Donald R. *Princes and Peasants: Smallpox in History*. Chicago: University of Chicago Press, 1983.

Howe, John. *Language and Political Meaning in Revolutionary America*. Amherst: University of Massachusetts Press, 2004.

Leder, Lawrence H., ed. *The Meaning of the American Revolution*. Chicago: Quadrangle Books, 1969.

Pasley, Jeffrey L. *The Tyranny of Printers: Newspaper Politics in the Early American Republic*. Charlottesville: University of Virginia Press, 2001.

Rhoden, Nancy, and Ian. K. Steele, eds. *The Human Tradition in the American Revolution*. Wilmington, Del.: Scholarly Resources, 2000.

Schmidt, Klaus H., and Fritz Fleischmann, eds. *Early America Re-Explored: New Readings in Colonial, Early National, and Antebellum Culture*. New York: P. Lang, 2000.

5. Constitutional Convention, Ratification, and the Bill of Rights

Allen, William B. *Let the Advice Be Good: A Defense of Madison's Nationalism*. Lanham, Md.: University Press of America, 1993.

Amar, Akhl Reed. *The Bill of Rights: Creation and Reconstruction*. New Haven, Conn.: Yale University Press, 1998.

Anderson, Thomas. *Creating the Constitution: The Convention of 1787 and the First Congress*. University Park: Pennsylvania State University Press, 1993.

Bailyn, Bernard. *To Begin the World Anew: The Genius and Ambiguities of the American Founders*. New York: Alfred A. Knopf, 2003.

Barlow, J. Jackson, Leonard W. Levy, and Ken Masugi, eds. *The American Founding: Essays on the Formation of the Constitution*. New York: Greenwood Press, 1988.

Benton, Wilbourn E., ed. *1787: Drafting the U.S. Constitution*. College Station: Texas A&M Press, 1986.

Berkin, Carol. *A Brilliant Solution: Inventing the American Constitution*. New York: Harcourt: 2002.

Cogan, Neil H., ed. *The Complete Bill of Rights: The Drafts, Debates, Sources, and Origins*. New York: Oxford University Press, 1997.

Cornell, Saul. *The Other Founders: Anti-Federalism and the Dissenting Tradition in America, 1788–1828*. Chapel Hill: North Carolina University Press, 1999.

Eidelberg, Paul. *The Philosophy of the American Constitution: A Reinterpretation of the Intentions of the Founding Fathers*. New York: Free Press, 1968.

Engeman, Thomas S., Edward J. Erler, and Thomas B. Hofeller, eds. *The Federalist Concordance*. Chicago: University of Chicago Press, 1988.

Epstein, David F. *The Political Theory of the Federalist*. Chicago: University of Chicago Press, 1984.

Freedman, Russell. *In Defense of Liberty: The Story of America's Bill of Rights*. New York: Holiday House, 2003.

Furtwangler, Albert. *The Authority of Publius: A Reading of the Federalist Papers*. Ithaca, N.Y.: Cornell University Press, 1984.

Harding, Samuel Bannister. *The Contest Over the Ratification of the Federal Constitution in the State of Massachusetts*. New York: Longmans, Green, 1896.

Kesler, Charles, ed. *Saving the Revolution: The Federalist Papers and the American Founding*. New York: Free Press, 1987.

Ketcham, Ralph, ed. *The Anti-Federalist Papers and the Constitutional Convention Debates*. New York: New American Library, 1986.

Kramnick, Isaac. *James Madison, Alexander Hamilton, and John Jay: The Federalist Papers*. London: Penguin, 1987.

Levy, Leonard W. *Origins of the Bill of Rights*. New Haven, Conn.: Yale University Press, 1999.

Lyon, Hasting. *The Constitution and the Men Who Made It: The Story of the Constitutional Convention, 1787*. Boston: Houghton-Mifflin Company, 1936.

Mace, George. *Locke, Hobbes, and the Federalist Papers*. Carbondale: Southern Illinois University Press, 1979.

McWilliams, Wilson Carey, and Michael T. Gibbons, eds. *The Federalists, the Anti-Federalists, and the American Political Tradition*. New York: Greenwood Press, 1992.

Meister, Charles W. *The Founding Fathers*. Jefferson City, N.C.: McFarland, 1987.

Millican, Edward. *One United People: The Federalist Papers and the National Idea*. Lexington: University Press of Kentucky, 1990.

Miner, Clarence E. *The Ratification of the Federal Constitution by the State of New York*. New York: Columbia University, 1921.

Rutland, Robert Allen. *The Ordeal of the Constitution: The Anti-Federalists and the Ratification Struggle of 1787–1788*. Norman: University of Oklahoma Press, 1966.

Schrag, Peter. *The Ratification of the Constitution and the Bill of Rights*. Boston: D.C. Heath, 1964.

Trenholme, Louise Irby. *The Ratification of the Federal Constitution in North Carolina*. New York: AMS Press, 1967.

Van Doren, Carl. *The Great Rehearsal: The Story of the Making and Ratifying of the Constitution of the United States*. Westport, Conn.: Greenwood Press, 1982.

White, Morton. *Philosophy, The Federalist, and the Constitution*. New York: Oxford University Press, 1987.

Willis, Garry. *Explaining America: The Federalist*. Garden City, N.J.: Doubleday, 1981.

VII. THE PEOPLE OF REVOLUTIONARY AMERICA

1. Native Americans

Buckley, Thomas J., ed. "Attempt on Oswego, 1783." *Historical Magazine* 3 (1859): 186–87.

Calloway, Colin G. *The American Revolution in Indian Country: Crisis and Diversity in Native American Communities*. Cambridge: Cambridge University Press, 1995.

———. "'We Have Always Been the Frontier': The American Revolution in Shawnee Country." *American Indian Quarterly* 16 (1992): 39–52.

Cayton, Andrew R. L., and Fredrika J. Teute, eds. *Contact Points: American Frontiers from the Mohawk Valley to the Mississippi, 1750–1830*. Chapel Hill: University of North Carolina Press, 1998.

Dowd, Gregory Evans. *War under Heaven: Pontiac, the Indian Nations, and the British Empire*. Baltimore, Md.: Johns Hopkins University Press, 2002.

Downes, Randolph G. "Cherokee-American Relations in the Upper Tennessee Valley, 1776–1791." *East Tennessee Historical Society Publication*, no. 8 (1936): 35–53.

———. "Indian War on the Upper Ohio, 1779–1782." *West Pennsylvania History Magazine* 17 (1934): 93–115.

Gibb, Harky L. "Colonel Guy Johnson, Superintendent-General of Indian Affairs, 1774–1782." *Papers of the Michigan Academy of Science, Arts, and Letters*, no. 37 (1943): 596–613.

Graymont, Barbara. *The Iroquois in the American Revolution*. Syracuse, N.Y.: Syracuse University Press, 1972.

Hamer, Philip M. "John Stuart's Indian Policy during the Early Months of the American Revolution." *Journal of American History* 17 (1930): 351–66.

Holton, Woody. "The Ohio Indians and the Coming of the American Revolution in Virginia." *Journal of Southern History* 60 (1994): 453–79.

Hoxie, Frederick E., Ronald Huffman, and Peter J. Albert. *Native Americans and the Early Republic*. Charlottesville: University Press of Virginia. 1999.

James, James A. "The Northwest: Gift or Conquest?" *Indiana Magazine of History* 30 (1934): 1–15.

Langston, Donna Hightower. *The Native American World*. Hoboken, N.J.: Wiley, 2003.

Lyons, David. "The Balance of Injustice and the War for Independence." *Monthly Review* 45 (1994): 17–26.

Mancall, Peter C., and James H. Merrell, eds. *American Encounters: Natives and Newcomers from European Contact to Indian Removal, 1500–1850*. New York: Routledge, 2000.

O'Donnell, James H. *Southern Indians in the American Revolution*. Knoxville: University of Tennessee Press, 1973.

Pastore, Ralph T. "Congress and the Six Nations, 1775–1778." *Niagara Frontier* 20 (1973): 80–95.

Prucha, Francis Paul. *The Indians in American Society: From the Revolutionary War to the Present*. Berkeley: University of California Press, 1985.

Sosin, Jack M. *The Revolutionary Frontier, 1763–1783*. New York: Holt, Rinehart, and Winston, 1976.

White, Richard. *The Middle Ground: Indians, Empires, and Republics in the Great Lakes Region, 1650–1815*. Cambridge: Cambridge University Press, 1991.

Williams, Edward G., ed. "The Journal of Richard Butler, 1775. Continental Congress Envoy to the Western Indians." *West Pennsylvania History Magazine* 47 (1964): 31–46, 141–56.

2. African Americans

Adrien, Claude. "The Forgotten Heroes of Savannah." *Americas* 30, nos. 11–12 (1978): 55–57.

Barnett, Paul. "The Black Continentals." *Negro History Bulletin* 33 (1970): 6–10.

Boatner, Mark M., III. "The Negro in the Revolution." *American History Illustrated* 4, no. 2 (1969): 36–44.

Brown, Wallace. "Negroes and the American Revolution." *History Today* 14 (1964): 556–63.

Cresto, Kathleen M. "The Negro: Symbol and Participant in the Revolution." *Negro History Bulletin* 39 (1976): 628–31.

Davis, Burke. *Black Heroes of the American Revolution*. New York: Harcourt, Brace, and Jovanovich, 1976.

Dearden, Paul F. *The Rhode Island Campaign of 1778*. Providence: Rhode Island Publications Society, 1980.

Farley, M. Foster. "The South Carolina Negro in the American Revolution." *South Carolina History Magazine* 79 (1978): 75–80.

Finkleman, Paul, ed. *Slavery, Revolutionary America, and the New Nation*. New York: Garland, 1989.

Foner, Philip S. *Blacks in the American Revolution*. Westport, Conn.: Greenwood Press, 1976.

Franklin, John Hope, and Alfred A. Moss Jr. *From Slavery to Freedom: A History of Negro Americans*. New York: McGraw-Hill, 1988.

Glasrud, Bruce A., and Alan M. Smith, ed. *Race Relations in British North America, 1607–1783*. Chicago: Nelson-Hall, 1982.

Gordon-Reed, Annette. *Thomas Jefferson and Sally Hemings: An American Controversy*. Charlottesville: University Press of Virginia, 1997.

Gough, Robert J. "Black Men and the Early New Jersey Militia." *New Jersey History* 88 (1970): 227–38.

Greene, Lorenzo J. "Some Observations on the Black Regiment of Rhode Island in the American Revolution." *Journal of Negro History* 37 (April 1952): 142–72.

Hargrove, W. B. "The Negro Soldier in the American Revolution." *Journal of Negro History* 1 (1916): 110–37.

Hertzog, Keith P. "Naval Operations in West Africa and the Disruption of the Slave Trade during the American Revolution." *American Neptune* 55 (1995).

Jackson, Luther P. "Virginia Negro Soldiers and Seamen in the American Revolution." *Journal of Negro History* 27 (1942): 247–67.

Jones, Jacqueline. *Race, Sex, and Self-Evident Truths: The Status of Slave Women during the Era of the American Revolution*. Wellesley, Mass.: Wellesley College, 1986.

Kaplan, Sidney. *The Black Presence in the Era of the American Revolution, 1770–1800*. Greenwich, Conn.: New York Graphic Society, 1973.
Kolchin, Peter. *American Slavery, 1619–1877*. New York: Hill and Wang, 1994.
Lewis, Jan Ellen, and Peter S. Onuf, eds. *Sally Hemings and Thomas Jefferson*. Charlottesville: University Press of Virginia, 1999.
Maslowski, Pete. "National Policy toward the Use of Black Troops in the Revolution." *South Carolina History Magazine* 73 (1972): 1–17.
Moore, George H. "Historical Notes on the Employment of Negroes in the American Army of the Revolution." *Magazine of History* 1 (1907).
Morgan, Kenneth. *Slavery and Servitude in North America, 1607–1800*. Edinburgh: Edinburgh University Press, 2000.
Nash, Gary B. *Race and Revolution*. Madison, Wis.: Madison House, 1990.
———. "Slavery, Black Resistance, and the American Revolution." *Georgia Historical Quarterly* 77 (1993).
Nell, William C. *The Colored Patriots of the American Revolution*. New York: Arno Press, 1968.
Newman, Debra. L. "Black Women in the Era of the American Revolution of Pennsylvania." *Journal of Negro History* 61 (1978): 275–89.
Quarles, Benjamin. "Crispus Attucks." *American History Illustrated* 5, no. 4 (1970): 38–42.
———. *The Negro in the American Revolution*. Chapel Hill: University of North Carolina Press, 1961.
Walker, James St. G. "Blacks as American Loyalists: The Slave War for Independence." *Historical Reflections* 2 (1975): 51–67.
White, David O. *Connecticut's Black Soldiers, 1775–1783*. Chester, Conn.: Pequot Press, 1973.

3. Women

Benson, Mary S. *Women in Eighteenth-Century America*. New York: Columbia University Press, 1935.
Bloch, Ruth H. *Gender and Morality in Anglo-American Culture, 1650–1800*. Berkeley: University of California Press, 2003.
Blumenthal, Walter H. *Women Camp Followers of the American Revolution*. Philadelphia: George S. MacManus, 1952.
Bohrer, Melissa Lukeman. *Glory, Passion, and Principle: The Story of Eight Remarkable Women at the Core of the American Revolution*. New York: Atria Books, 2003.
Booth, Sally S. *The Women of '76*. New York: Hastings House, 1973.
Bruce, Henry A. *Women in the Making of America*. Boston: Little, Brown, 1933.

Buel, Richard, Jr., and Joy D. Buel. *The Way of Duty: A Woman and Her Family in Revolutionary America*. New York: Norton, 1980.

Bushnell, Charles I., ed. "Women of the Revolution." *Historical Magazine* 5 (1869): 105–12.

Campbell, Amelia D. "Women of New York State in the Revolution." *New York State Historical Association Quarterly Journal* 3 (1922): 155–68.

Cole, Adelaide M. "Anne Bailey: Woman of Courage." *Daughters of the American Revolution Magazine* 114 (1980): 322–25.

Cometti, Elizabeth. "Women in the Revolution." *New England Quarterly* 20 (1947): 329–46.

Copeland, Edna A. "Nancy Hart: A Revolutionary Heroine." *Georgia Magazine* 8 (1965): 30–31.

DePauw, Linda G. *Four Traditions: Women of New York during the American Revolution*. Albany: New York State Revolutionary Bicentennial Commission, 1974.

Downey, Fairfax. "Girls behind the Guns." *American Heritage* 8, no. 1 (1956): 46–48.

Edgerton, Samuel Y., Jr. "The Murder of Jane McCrae." *Early American Literature* 8 (1973): 28–30.

Ellet, Elizabeth F. *The Women of the American Revolution*. 3 vols. New York: Haskell House, 1969.

Engle, Paul. *Women in the American Revolution*. New York: Follett, 1976.

Evans, Elizabeth. *Weathering the Storm: Women of the American Revolution*. New York: Charles Scribner's Sons, 1975.

Freeman, Lucy. *America's First Woman Warrior: The Courage of Deborah Sampson*. New York: Paragon House, 1992.

Gudersen, Joan R. *To Be Useful to the World: Women in Revolutionary America, 1740–1790*. New York: Twayne, 1996.

Hoffman, Ronald, and Peter J. Albert, eds. *Women in the Age of the American Revolution*. Charlottesville: University of Virginia Press, 1989.

Jones, Jacqueline. *Race, Sex, and Self-Evident Truths: The Status of Slave Women during the Era of the American Revolution*. Wellesley, Mass.: Wellesley College, 1986.

Keller, Allan. "'Private' Deborah Sampson." *American History Illustrated* 11, no. 4 (1976): 30–33.

Kerber, Linda. *Women of the Republic: Intellectual Ideologies in Revolutionary America*. Chapel Hill: University of North Carolina Press, 1980.

Kovalenko, Charlotte. "Patriotic Female Ancestry of the American Revolution." *Daughters of the American Revolution Magazine* 126 (1992).

Lewis, Jan. "Women and the American Revolution." *Magazine of History* 8 (1994).

Logan, Mary S. *The Part Taken by Women in American History*. New York: Arno Press, 1972.

Lutz, Paul V. "An Army Wife in the Revolution." *Manuscripts* 23 (1971): 124–30.

Lyman, Susan E. "Three New Women of the Revolution." *New York Historical Society Quarterly* 29 (1945): 77–82.

Mann, Herman. *The Female Soldier: Life of Deborah Sampson, the Female Soldier in the War of the Revolution*. New York: Arno Press, 1972.

Martin, Wendy. "Women and the American Revolution." *Early American Literature* 11 (1976–1977): 322–35.

Miller, William C. "The Betsy Ross Legend." *Social Studies* 37 (1946): 317–23.

Newman, Debra. L. "Black Women in the Era of the American Revolution of Pennsylvania." *Journal of Negro History* 61 (1978): 275–89.

Norton, Mary B. *Liberty's Daughters: The Revolutionary Experience of American Women*. New York: Little, Brown, 1980.

Parry, Edward O. "Mary Frazer: Heroine of the American Revolution." *Daughters of the American Revolution Magazine* 113 (1979): 766–75.

Roberts, Cokie. *Founding Mothers*. New York: Harper Collins, 2004.

Ross, Betty. "Betsy Ross." *Daughters of the American Revolution Magazine* 127 (1993).

Schultz, Constance B. "Daughters of Liberty: The History of Women in the Revolutionary War Pension Records." *Prologue* 16 (1984): 139–53.

Stryker-Roda, Harriet. "Militia Women of 1780." *Daughters of the American Revolution Magazine* 113 (1979): 308–12.

White, John T. "The Truth about Molly Pitcher." In *The American Revolution: Whose Revolution*, edited by James K. Martin, 40–48. Huntington, N.Y.: Robert E. Krieger, 1977.

Whitton, Mary O. *These Were the Women*. New York: Hastings House, 1954.

4. Loyalists

Barger, B. D., ed. "Charles Town Loyalism in 1775: The Secret Reports of Alexander Innes," *South Carolina Historical Magazine* 63 (July 1962).

Bass, Robert D. "The South Carolina Regiment: A Forgotten Loyalist Regiment." *South Carolina Historical Association Proceedings* 19 (1977): 64–71.

Brown, Wallace. *The Good Americans: The Loyalists in the American Revolution*. New York: William Morrow, 1969.

——. *The King's Friends: The Composition and Motives of the American Loyalist Claimants*. Providence, R.I.: Brown University Press, 1965.

——. "The View at Two Hundred Years: The Loyalists of the American Revolution." *American Antiquarian Society Proceedings* 80 (1970): 25–47.

Callahan, North. *Royal Raiders: The Tories of the American Revolution*. New York: Bobbs-Merrill, 1963.

Chidsey, Donald B. *The Loyalists: The Story of Those Americans Who Fought against Independence*. New York: Crown, 1973.

Cruikshank, Ernest A. "The King's Royal Regiment of New York." *Ontario Historical Society Papers* 27 (1931): 293–324.

Cuneo, John R. "The Early Days of the Queen's Rangers, August 1776–February 1777." *Military Affairs* 22 (1958): 65–74.

East, Robert A., and Jacob Judd, eds. *The Loyalist Americans: A Focus on Greater New York*. Tarrytown, N.Y.: Sleepy Hollow Restorations, 1975.

Fergusson, Clyde R. "Carolina and Georgia Patriot and Loyalist Militia in Action, 1778–1783." In *The Southern Experience in the American Revolution*, edited by Jeffrey Crowe and Larry E. Tise, 174–99. Chapel Hill: University of North Carolina Press, 1978.

Godfrey, Carlos E. "Muster Rolls of Three Troops of Loyalist Light Dragoons Raised in Pennsylvania, 1777–1778." *Pennsylvania Magazine of History and Biography* 34 (1910): 1–8.

Haarman, Albert W. "American Provisional Corps Authorized by Lord Dunmore, 1775." *Journal of the Society for Army Historical Research* 52 (1974): 254–55.

Honeyman, A. Van Doren. "Concerning the New Jersey Loyalists in the Revolution." *New Jersey Historical Society Proceedings* 51 (1933): 117–33.

Katcher, Philip. "Loyalist Militia in the War of Independence." *Journal of the Society for Army Historical Research* 54 (1976): 136–41.

Kelby, William, ed. *Orderly Book of the Three Battalions of Loyalists Commanded by Brigadier-General Oliver DeLancey, 1776–1778*. New York: New York Historical Society, 1917.

Lampert, Robert S. *South Carolina Loyalists in the American Revolution*. Columbia: University of South Carolina Press, 1987.

Meyer, Mary K., and Virginia B. Bachman. "The First Battalion of Maryland Loyalists." *Maryland Historical Magazine* 68 (1973): 199–210.

Nelson, William H. *The American Tory*. Oxford: Oxford University Press, 1961.

Olson, Gary D. "Loyalists and the American Revolution: Thomas Brown and the South Carolina Backcountry, 1775–1776." *South Carolina Historical Magazine* 68 (1967): 201–19.

Sabine, Lorenzo. "The Tory Contingent in the British Army in America in 1781." *Historical Magazine* 8 (1864): 321–26, 354–59, 389–92.

Simcoe, John G. *Simcoes' Military Journal: A History of the Operations of a Partisan Corps, Called the Queen's Rangers, Commanded by Lieutenant-Colonel J. G. Simcoe, during the War of the American Revolution*. New York: Bartlett and Welford, 1844.

Smith, Paul H. "The American Loyalists: Notes on Their Organization and Numerical Strength." *William and Mary Quarterly* 25 (1968): 259–77.

——. *Loyalists and Redcoats: A Study in British Revolutionary Policy*. Chapel Hill: University of North Carolina Press, 1964.

Stryker, William S. *The New Jersey Volunteers (Loyalists) in the Revolutionary War*. Trenton, N.J.: Naar, Day, and Naar, 1887.

Tebbenhoff, Edward H. "The Associated Loyalists: An Aspect of Militant Loyalism." *New York Historical Society Quarterly* 63 (1979): 115–44.

Van Tyne, Claude. *The Loyalists in the American Revolution*. Gloucester, MA: P. Smith, 1959.

Villers, David H. "The British Army and the Connecticut Loyalists during the War of Independence, 1775–1783." *Connecticut Historical Society* 43 (1978): 65–80.

Wright, Edmond. "A Patriot for Whom? Benedict Arnold and the Loyalists." *History Today* 36 (1986): 29–35.

VIII. STATES

1. Connecticut

Buel, Richard, Jr. *Dear Liberty: Connecticut's Mobilization for the Revolutionary War*. Middletown, Conn.: Wesleyan University Press, 1980.

Collier, Christopher. *Connecticut in the Continental Congress*. Chester, Conn.: Pequot Press, 1973.

Roth, David M. "Connecticut and the Coming of the Revolution." *Connecticut Review* 7 (1973): 47–65.

——. "Connecticut in the American Revolution." *Connecticut Review* 9 (1975): 10–20.

2. Delaware

Munroe, John. *Federalist Delaware, 1775–1815*. New Brunswick, N.J.: Rutgers University Press, 1954.

——. "Non-Resident Representatives in the Continental Congress: The Delaware Delegation of 1782." *William and Mary Quarterly* 9 (1952): 166–90.

3. Georgia

Abbot, William. "The Structure of Politics in Georgia, 1782–1789." *William and Mary Quarterly* 14 (1957): 47–65.

Davis, Harold. *The Fledgling Province: Social and Cultural Life in Colonial Georgia, 1773–1776*. Chapel Hill: University of North Carolina Press, 1976.

Ellefson, Clinton. "Loyalists and Patriots in Georgia during the American Revolution." *Historian* 24 (1962): 347–56.

Johnson, Amanda. "A State in the Making: Georgia (1783–1798)." *Georgia Historical Quarterly* 15 (1931): 1–27.

4. Maryland

Bond, Beverly. *State Government in Maryland, 1777–1781*. Baltimore, Md.: Johns Hopkins University Press, 1905.

Crowl, Philip. *Maryland during and after the Revolution: A Political and Economic Study*. Baltimore, Md.: Johns Hopkins University Press, 1943.

Main, Jackson T. "Political Parties in Revolutionary Maryland, 1780–1787." *Maryland Historical Magazine* 52 (1967): 1–27.

5. Massachusetts

A. General Works

Brown, Richard D. *Revolutionary Politics in Massachusetts: The Boston Committee of Correspondence and the Towns, 1772–1774*. Cambridge, Mass.: Harvard University Press, 1970.

Hall, Van Beck. *Politics without Parties: Massachusetts 1780–1791*. Pittsburgh, Pa.: University of Pittsburgh Press, 1972.

Harlow, Ralph V. "Economic Conditions in Massachusetts during the American Revolution." *Colonial Society of Massachusetts Publications* 20 (1920): 163–93.

Knollenberg, Bernhard. "Did Samuel Adams Provoke the Boston Tea Party and the Clash at Lexington?" *American Antiquarian Society Proceedings* 70 (1961): 493–503.

Longley, R. S. "Mob Activities in Revolutionary Massachusetts." *New England Quarterly* 6 (1933): 98–130.

Massachusetts Bay Provincial Congress. *A Narrative of the Excisions and Ravages of the King's Troops under the Command of General Gage on the Nineteenth of April, 1775*. Boston: Arno Press, 1968.

Patterson, Stephen E. *Political Parties in Revolutionary Massachusetts*. Madison: University of Wisconsin Press, 1973.

B. Boston

Blake, John B. *Public Health in the Town of Boston, 1630–1822*. Cambridge, Mass.: Harvard University Press, 1959.

Rogers, George V. "Springtime in Boston, 1775." *New England Galaxy* 16 (1975): 49–57.

6. New Jersey

Gerlach, Larry R. *Prologue to Independence: New Jersey in the Coming of the American Revolution*. New Brunswick, N.J.: Rutgers University Press, 1976.

Levitt, James H. *New Jersey's Revolutionary Economy*. Trenton: New Jersey Historical Commission, 1975.

McCormick, Richard. *Experiment in Independence: New Jersey in the Critical Period, 1781–1789*. New Brunswick, N.J.: Rutgers University Press, 1950.

7. New Hampshire

Daniell, Jere. *Experiment in Republicanism: New Hampshire Politics and the American Revolution, 1741–1794*. Cambridge, Mass.: Harvard University Press, 1970.

Gemmill, John K. "The Problems of Power: New Hampshire Government during the Revolution." *Historical New Hampshire* 22 (1967): 27–38.

8. New York

A. General Works

Becker, Carl L. "The Growth of Revolutionary Parties and Methods in New York Province, 1765–1774." *American Historical Review* 7 (1901): 56–76.

———. *History of Political Parties in the Province of New York: 1766–1776*. Madison: University of Wisconsin Press, 1909.

Decker, Malcolm. *Brink of Revolution: New York in Crisis, 1765–1776*. New York: Argosy Antiquarian, 1964.

Flick, Alexander C., ed. *The American Revolution in New York: Its Political, Social, and Economic Significance*. Port Washington, N.Y.: Ira J. Friedman, 1967.

Jones, Thomas. *History of New York during the Revolutionary War, and of the Leading Events in the Other Colonies at that Period*. New York: New York Historical Society, 1879.

Mason, Bernard. *The Road to Independence: The Revolutionary Movement in New York, 1773–1777*. Lexington: University of Kentucky Press, 1966.

Wermuth, Thomas S. *Rip Van Winkle's Neighbors: The Transformation of Rural Society in the Hudson River Valley, 1720–1850*. Albany: State University of New York Press, 2002.

B. New York City

Barck, Oscar T. *New York City during the War for Independence*. Port Washington, N.Y.: Kennikat Press, 1966.

——. "The Occupation of New York City by the British." In *History of the State of New York*, vol. 4. New York: Columbia University Press, 1934.

Schaukirk, Ewald G. "Occupation of New York City by the British." *Pennsylvania Magazine of History and Biography* 10 (1886): 418–45.

9. North Carolina

A. General Works

Butler, Lindley S. *North Carolina and the Coming of the Revolution, 1763–1776*. Raleigh: North Carolina Department of Cultural Resources, 1976.

Demond, Robert O. *The Loyalists in North Carolina during the Revolution*. Durham, N.C.: Duke University Press, 1940.

Ganyard, Robert L. *The Emergence of North Carolina's Revolutionary State Government*. Raleigh: North Carolina Department of Cultural Resources, 1978.

Lefler, Hugh T., and William S. Powell. *Colonial North Carolina*. New York: Charles Scribner's Sons, 1973.

Sanders, William R., ed. *The Colonial Records of North Carolina*. 10 vols. Raleigh: State of North Carolina, 1886–1898.

B. Battle of the Alamance

Bailey, William H., Sr. "The Regulators of North Carolina." *The American Historical Register* (November 1895, December 1895, and January 1896): 313–34, 464–71, and 554–67.

Bassett, John S. "The Regulators of North Carolina (1765–1771)." *Annual Report of the American Historical Association for the Year of 1894*. Washington, D.C.: American Historical Association, 1895.

Henderson, Archibald. "The Origin of the Regulation in North Carolina." *American Historical Review* 21, no. 2 (January 1916): 320–32.

Hudson, Arthur P. "Songs of the North Carolina Regulators." *William and Mary Quarterly* 4, no. 4 (October 1947): 470–85.

Powell, William S. *The War of Regulation and the Battle of Alamance, May 16, 1771*. Raleigh: North Carolina Department of Cultural Resources, 1976.

Powell, William S., et al. *The Regulators in North Carolina: A Documentary History, 1759–1776*. Raleigh: Publisher unknown, 1971.

10. Pennsylvania

A. General Works

Brunhouse, Robert L. *The Counter-Revolution in Pennsylvania, 1776–1780*. New York: Octagon Books, 1971.

Lucas, Stanley E. *Portents of Rebellion: Rhetoric and Revolution in Philadelphia, 1765–1776*. Philadelphia: Temple University Press, 1976.

Pancake, John S. *1777: The Year of the Hangman*. Tuscaloosa: University of Alabama Press, 1977.

Rappaport, George David. *Stability and Change in Revolutionary Pennsylvania: Banking, Politics, and Social Structure*. University Park: Pennsylvania State University Press, 1996.

Thayer, Theodore. *Pennsylvania Politics and the Growth of Democracy, 1746–1776*. Harrisburg; Pennsylvania Historical and Museum Commission, 1953.

Young, Henry J. "Treason and Its Punishment in Revolutionary Pennsylvania." *Pennsylvania Magazine of History and Biography* 90 (1966): 287–313.

B. Philadelphia

Smith, Billy, ed. *Life in Early Philadelphia*. University Park: Pennsylvania State University Press, 1995.

Wierner, Frederick B. "The Military Occupation of Philadelphia in 1777–1778." *American Philosophical Society Proceedings* 111 (1967): 310–13.

11. Rhode Island

Chudacoff, Nancy F. "The Revolution and the Town: Providence, 1775–1783." *Rhode Island History* 35 (1976): 71–89.

Conley, Patrick T. *Democracy in Decline: Rhode Island's Constitutional Development, 1776–1841*. Providence: Rhode Island Publications Society, date unknown.

Lovejoy, David S. *Rhode Island Politics and the American Revolution, 1760–1776*. Providence, R.I.: Brown University Press, 1958.

Polishook, Irwin W. *1774–1795: Rhode Island and the Union*. Evanston, Ill.: Northwestern University Press, 1969.

Simister, Florence Parker. *The Fire's Center: Rhode Island in the Revolutionary Era, 1763–1790*. Providence: Rhode Island Bicentennial Foundation, 1978.

12. South Carolina

A. General Works

Barger, B. D., ed. "Charles Town Loyalism in 1775: The Secret Reports of Alexander Innes," *South Carolina Historical and Genealogical Magazine* 63 (July 1962): 125–37.

Hemphill, William Edwin, and Wylma Anne Wates, eds. *Extracts from the Journals of the Provincial Congresses of South Carolina, 1775–1776*. Columbia: South Carolina Archives Department, 1960.

Johnson, George Lloyd, Jr. *The Frontier in the Colonial South: South Carolina Backcountry, 1736–1800*. Westport, Conn.: Greenwood Press, 1997.

Landrum, J. B. O. *Colonial and Revolutionary History of Upper South Carolina*. Spartanburg, S.C.: Reprint Co., 1959.

McCrady, Edward. *The History of South Carolina in the Revolution, 1775–1783*. New York: Macmillan, 1901.

———. *The History of South Carolina under the Royal Government, 1719–1776*. New York: Macmillan, 1899.

Olson, Gary D. "Loyalists and the American Revolution: Thomas Brown and the South Carolina Backcountry, 1775–1776." *South Carolina Historical Magazine* 68 (1967): 201–19.

B. Charleston

Barnwell, Joseph W. "The Evacuation of Charleston by the British in 1782." *South Carolina Historical and Genealogical Magazine* 11 (1910): 1–26.

McCowen, George S., Jr. *The British Occupation of Charleston, 1780–1782*. Columbia: University of South Carolina Press, 1972.

Stoessen, Alexander L. "The British Occupation of Charleston, 1780–1782." *South Carolina History Magazine* 63 (1962): 71–82.

13. Virginia

Eckenrode, H. J. *The Revolution in Virginia*. Boston: Houghton-Mifflin, 1916.

Selby, John E. *A Chronology of Virginia and the War of Independence, 1763–1783*. Charlottesville: University of Virginia Press, 1973.

Tate, Thad W. "The Coming of the Revolution in Virginia: Britain's Challenge to Virginia's Ruling Class, 1773–1776." *William and Mary Quarterly* 19 (1962): 325–43.

IX. AUTOBIOGRAPHIES AND BIOGRAPHIES

1. Abigail Adams

Akers, Charles W. *Abigail Adams: An American Woman*. Boston: Little, Brown, 1980.

Gelles, Edith. *Portia: The World of Abigail Adams*. Bloomington: Indiana University Press, 1992.

Levin, Phyllis Lee. *Abigail Adams*. New York: St. Martin's Press, 1987.
Osborne, Angela. *Abigail Adams*. New York: Chelsea House, 1989.
Withey, Lynne. *Dearest Friend: A Life of Abigail Adams*. New York: Free Press, 1981.

2. John Adams

Adams, Charles F., ed. *Familiar Letters of John Adams and His Wife Abigail Adams, during the Revolution*. New York: Hurd and Houghton, 1876.
Adams, John. *Diary and Autobiography of John Adams*. 4 vols. Edited by L. H. Butterfield. New York: Atheneum, 1964.
——. *John Adams: A Biography in His Own Words*. New York: Harper and Row, 1973.
Bowen, Catherine D. *John Adams and the American Revolution*. Boston: Little, Brown, 1950.
Brown, Walt. *John Adams and the American Press*. Jefferson, N.C.: McFarland, 1995.
Burleigh, Anne H. *John Adams*. New Rochelle, N.Y.: Arlington House, 1969.
Chamberlain, Mellen. *John Adams: The Statesman of the American Revolution*. Boston: Houghton-Mifflin, 1899.
East, Robert A. *John Adams*. Boston: Twayne Publications, 1979.
Ferling, John. *John Adams: A Life*. Knoxville: University of Tennessee Press, 1992.
——. "John Adams, Diplomat." *William and Mary Quarterly* 51 (1994): 227–52.
Hayes, Frederic H. "John Adams and American Sea Power." *American Neptune* 15 (1965): 35–45.
Hutson, James H. *John Adams and the Diplomacy of the American Revolution*. Lexington: University of Kentucky Press, 1980.
Knollenberg, Bernard. "John Dickinson vs. John Adams, 1774–1776." *American Philosophical Society Proceedings* 107 (1963): 134–44.
Lint, Gregg L. "John Adams on the Drafting of the Treaty Plan of 1776." *Diplomatic History* 2 (1978): 313–20.
McCullough, David. *John Adams*. New York: Simon and Schuster, 2001.
Merrill, D. Peterson *Adams and Jefferson: A Revolutionary Dialogue*. Athens: University of Georgia Press, 1976.
Morgan, Edmund S. *The Meaning of Independence: John Adams, George Washington, and Thomas Jefferson*. Charlottesville: University of Virginia Press, 1976.
Morse, John T. *John Adams*. Boston: Houghton-Mifflin, 1884.

Ripley, Randell B. "Adams, Burke, and Eighteenth-Century Conservatism." *Political Science Quarterly* 80 (1965): 216–35.

Smith, Page. *John Adams*. 2 vols. Garden City, N.Y.: Doubleday, 1962.

3. Samuel Adams

Alexander, John J. *Samuel Adams: America's Revolutionary Politician*. Lanham, Md.: Rowman and Littlefield, 2002.

Beach, Stewart. *Samuel Adams: The Fateful Years, 1764–1775*. New York: Dodd, Mead, 1965.

Harlow, Ralph V. *Samuel Adams: Promoter of the American Revolution*. New York: Octagon Books, 1975.

——. *Samuel Adams' Revolution: 1765–1776*. New York: Harper and Row, 1976.

Harlow, Ralph V., and John R. Green. *Three Men of Boston*. New York: Crowell, 1976.

Hosmer, James K. *Samuel Adams*. Boston: Houghton-Mifflin, 1898.

Knollenberg, Bernhard. "Did Samuel Adams Provoke the Boston Tea Party and the Clash at Lexington?" *American Antiquarian Society Proceedings* 70 (1960): 493–503.

Maier, Pauline. "Coming to Terms with Samuel Adams." *American History Review* 81 (1946): 12–37.

Miller, John C. *Sam Adams: Pioneer in Propaganda*. Boston: Little, Brown, 1936.

Winston, Alexander. "Firebrand of the Revolution." *American Heritage* 18, no. 3 (1967): 60–64, 105–8.

4. Joseph Brandt

Kelsay, Isabel T. *Joseph Brandt, 1743, 1807, Man of Two Worlds*. Syracuse, N.Y.: Syracuse University Press, 1984.

5. Edmund Burke

Brooke, John. "Burke in the 1700s." *South Atlantic Quarterly* 68 (1959): 548–55.

Burke, Edmund. *Memoirs of the Right Honorable Edmund Burke*. Edited by Charles McCormick. London: Lee and Hurst, 1798.

Cone, Carl B. *Burke and the Nature of American Politics*. 2 vols. Lexington: University of Kentucky Press, 1957.

Crowe, Ian, ed. *Edmund Burke: His Life and Legacy*. Dublin, Ireland: Four Courts Press, 1997.

Ripley, Randell B. "Adams, Burke, and Eighteenth Century Conservatism." *Political Science Quarterly* 80 (1965): 216–35.

Ritcheson, Charles R. *British Policies and the American Revolution*. Norman: University of Oklahoma Press, 1954.

6. William Pitt Chatam (Lord Chatam)

Brooke, John. *The Chatham Administration, 1766–1768*. New York: St. Martin's Press, 1956.

Hall, Hubert. "Chatham's Colonial Policy." *American Historical Review* 5 (1900): 659–75.

Temperley, Harold W. V. "Chatham, North, and North America." *Quarterly Review* 221 (1914): 295–319.

7. Silas Deane

Abernethy, Thomas P. "Commercial Activities of Silas Deane in France." *American Historical Review* 39 (1934): 477–85.

Deane, Silas. "Correspondence of Silas Deane, Delegate to the First and Second Congresses at Philadelphia, 1774–1776." *Connecticut Historical Society Collection* 2 (1870): 127–368.

——. *The Deane Papers. Correspondence between Silas Deane, His Brothers, and Their Business and Political Associates, 1771–1795*. Vol. 23. Collections of the Connecticut Historical Society. Hartford, Conn.: Connecticut Historical Society, 1930.

James, Coy H. *Silas Deane: Patriot or Traitor?* East Lansing: Michigan State University Press, 1975.

8. John Dickinson

Flower, Milton E. *John Dickinson: Conservative Revolutionary*. Charlottesville: University Press of Virginia, 1983.

——. "John Dickinson, Delawarean." *Delaware History* 17 (1976): 12–20.

Jacobson, David L. *John Dickinson and the Revolution in Pennsylvania, 1764–1776*. Berkeley: University of California Press, 1965.

Knollenberg, Bernard. "John Dickinson vs. John Adams, 1774–1776." *American Philosophical Society Proceedings* 107 (1963): 134–44.

Powell, John H. "John Dickinson, President of the Delaware State, 1781–1782." *Delaware History* (1940): 111–34.

Stille, Charles J. *The Life and Times of John Dickinson, 1732–1808*. New York: B. Franklin, 1969.

9. John Murray Dunmore (Lord Dunmore)

Quarles, Benjamin. "Lord Dunmore as Liberator." *William and Mary Quarterly* 15 (1958): 494–507.

10. Benjamin Franklin

Auger, Helen. "Benjamin Franklin and the French Alliance." *American Heritage* 7, no. 3 (1956): 65–88.

——. *Secret War of Independence*. New York: Dull, Sloan, and Peace, 1955.

Bowen, Catherine D. *The Most Dangerous Man in America: Scenes from the Life of Benjamin Franklin*. Boston: Little, Brown, 1974.

Brands, H. W. *The First American: The Life and Times of Benjamin Franklin*. New York: Doubleday, 2000.

Burlingame, Roger. *Benjamin Franklin: Envoy Extraordinary*. New York: Coward-McCann, 1967.

Currey, Cecil B. *Road to Revolution: Benjamin Franklin in England 1765–1775*. Garden City, N.Y.: Doubleday, 1968.

Franklin, Benjamin. *Autobiography of Benjamin Franklin*. Boston: Bedford Books, 1993.

——. *Benjamin Franklin: A Biography in His Own Words*. Edited by Thomas Fleming. New York: Newsweek, 1972.

Hales, Edward E. *Franklin in France*. Boston: Roberts Brothers, 1888.

Isaacson, Walter. *Benjamin Franklin: An American Life*. New York: Simon and Schuster, 2003.

Labaree, Leonard E., ed. *The Autobiography of Benjamin Franklin*. New Haven, Conn.: Yale University Press, 2003.

Matthews, Lois K. "Benjamin Franklin's Plan for a Colonial Union, 1750–1775." *American Political Science Review* 8 (1914): 393–412.

Middlekauf, Robert. *Benjamin Franklin and His Enemies*. Berkeley: University of California Press, 1996.

Morgan, Edmund S. *Benjamin Franklin*. New Haven, Conn.: Yale University Press, 2002.

Morris, Richard B. "Meet Dr. Franklin." *American Heritage* 23, no. 1 (1971): 80–91.

Oberg, Barbara B. ed. *The Papers of Benjamin Franklin*. New Haven, Conn.: Yale University Press, 1997.

Prelinger, Catherine M. "Benjamin Franklin and the American Prisoners of War in England during the American Revolution." *William and Mary Quarterly* 32 (1975): 281–94.

Russell, Phillips. *Benjamin Franklin: The First Civilized American*. Chicago: University of Chicago Press, 1954.

Schoenbrun, David. *Triumph in Paris: The Exploits of Benjamin Franklin*. New York: Harper and Row, 1976.

Srodes, James. *Franklin: The Essential Founding Father*. Washington, D.C.: Regnery, 2002.

Stourzh, Gerald. "Reason and Power in Benjamin Franklin's Political Thought." *American Political Science Review* 47 (1953): 1092–1115.

——. *Benjamin Franklin and American Foreign Policy*. Chicago: University of Chicago Press, 1954.

Van Doren, Carl C. *Benjamin Franklin*. New York: Viking Press, 1938.

11. Christopher Gadsden

Gadsden, Christopher. *The Writings of Christopher Gadsden, 1746–1805*. Edited by Richard Walsh. Columbia: University of South Carolina Press, 1966.

Godbold, E. Stanley. *Christopher Gadsden and the American Revolution*. Knoxville: University of Tennessee Press, 1982.

Walsh, Richard. "Christopher Gadsden: Radical or Conservative Revolutionary?" *South Carolina Historical and Genealogical Magazine* 63 (1962): 195–203.

12. Thomas Gage

Alden, John Richard. *General Gage in America*. Baton Rouge: Louisiana State University Press, 1948.

Carter, Clarence E., ed. *The Correspondence of General Thomas Gage with the Secretaries of State, 1763–1770*. 2 vols. New Haven, Conn.: Yale University Press, 1931–1933.

Clarfield, Gerard H. "The Short Unhappy Civil Administration of Thomas Gage." *Essex Institute Historical Collections* 109 (1973): 138–51.

13. King George III

Ayling, Stanley. *George the Third*. New York: Alfred C. Knopf, 1972.

Brooke, John. *King George III*. New York: McGraw-Hill, 1972.

Fortescue, Sir John, ed. *The Correspondence of King George from 1760 to December 1783*. London: Macmillan, 1928.

Hibbert, Christopher. *George III: A Personal History*. New York: Viking Press, 1998.
Lloyd, Alan. *The King Who Lost America: A Portrait of the Life and Times of George III*. Garden City, N.Y.: Doubleday, 1971.
Numby, Frank A. *George III and the American Revolution*. New York: Kraus Reprint Co., 1970.
Ritcheson, Charles R. *British Policies and the American Revolution*. Norman: University of Oklahoma Press, 1954.
Thomas, P. D. G. "George III and the American Revolution." *History* 70 (1985): 16–31.

14. George Germain

Brown, Gerald S. *The American Secretary: The Colonial Policy of Lord George Germain, 1775–1778*. Ann Arbor: University of Michigan Press, 1963.
Burt, A. L. "The Quarrel between Germain and Carleton: An Invented Story." *Canadian History Review* 11 (1938): 202–30.
Gruber, Ira D. "Lord Howe and Lord George Germain: British Politics and the Winning of American Independence." *William and Mary Quarterly* 22 (1965): 225–43.
Guttridge, George H. "Lord Germain in Office, 1775–1782." *American Historical Review* 33 (1927): 23–43.
Kyte, George W. "Plans for the Reconquest of the Rebellious Colonies in America, 1775–1783." *Historian* 10 (1948): 101–17.
Valentine, Alan. *Lord George Germain*. New York: Oxford University Press, 1962.

15. Elbridge Gerry

Austin, James T. *The Life of Elbridge Gerry*. Vols. 1–2. New York: DaCapo Press, 1970.
Billias, George A. *Elbridge Gerry: Founding Father and Republican Statesman*. New York: McGraw-Hill, 1976.
Morison, Samuel Eliot. "Elbridge Gerry: Gentleman-Democrat." *New England Quarterly* (January 1929): 6–33.

16. George Grenville

Bullion, John L. *A Great Necessary Measure: George Grenville and the Genesis of the Stamp Act, 1763–1765*. Columbia: University of Missouri Press, 1982.

Christie, Ian R. "The Cabinet during the Grenville Administration, 1763–1765." *English Historical Review* 73 (1958): 86–92.

Lawson, Philip. *George Grenville: A Political Life*. Oxford: Clarendon Press, 1984.

Ritcheson, Charles R. *British Policies and the American Revolution*. Norman: University of Oklahoma Press, 1954.

Temple, Richard, ed. *The Grenville Papers*. London: J. Murray, 1853.

17. Nathan Hale

Byrne, Leonard. "Nathan Hale: A Testament to Courage." *New England Galaxy* 16 (1975): 13–22.

Darrow, Jane. *Nathan Hale: A Story of Loyalties*. New York: Century, 1922.

Seymour, G. D. "The Last Days and Valiant Death of Nathan Hale." *American Heritage* 15, no. 4 (1964): 50–51.

Stigall-Wright, Mary. "Nathan Hale, Martyr, Hero, Patriot." *Daughters of the American Revolution Magazine* 139 (1996).

18. Alexander Hamilton

Brookhiser, Richard. *Alexander Hamilton*. New York: Free Press, 1999.

Brown, Stuart G. *Alexander Hamilton*. New York: Washington Square Press, 1967.

Cooks, Jacob E. *Alexander Hamilton*. New York: Charles Scribner's Sons, 1982.

Lodge, Henry C. *Alexander Hamilton*. New York: Chelsea House, 1980.

Hamilton, Alexander. *The Papers of Alexander Hamilton*. Edited by Harold C. Syrett and Jacob E. Cook. 26 vols. New York: Columbia University Press, 1961–1979.

Mitchell, Broadus. *Alexander Hamilton*. New York: Macmillan, 1957.

——. *Alexander Hamilton: The Revolutionary Years*. New York: Crowell, 1970.

——. "The Battle of Monmouth through Alexander Hamilton's Eyes." *New Jersey Historical Society Proceedings* 73 (1955): 239–57.

Randall, Willard Sterne. *Alexander Hamilton: A Life*. New York: Harper Collins, 2003.

Schachner, Nathan. *Alexander Hamilton*. New York: A. S. Barnes, 1957.

19. John Hancock

Alan, Herbert S. *John Hancock: Patriot in Purple*. New York: Macmillan, 1948.

Fowler, William M. *The Baron of Beacon Hill: A Biography of John Hancock*. Boston: Houghton-Mifflin, 1980.

Ketchum, Richard M. "Men of the Revolution–John Hancock." *American Heritage* 26, no. 2 (1976): 64–65, 81–82.

Proctor, Donald J. "John Hancock: New Soundings on an Old Board." *Journal of American History* 64 (1977): 652–77.

Wolkins, George C. "The Seizure of John Hancock's Sloop *Liberty*." *Massachusetts Historical Society Proceedings* 55 (1931–1932): 239–84.

20. Patrick Henry

Beeman, Richard R. *Patrick Henry: A Biography*. New York: McGraw Hill, 1974.

Campbell, Norine D. *Patrick Henry: Patriot and Statesman*. New York: Devin-Adair, 1969.

Henry, William W. *Patrick Henry: Life, Correspondence, and Speeches*. New York: Charles Scribner's Sons, 1891.

Meade, Robert D. *Patrick Henry*. 2 vols. Philadelphia: J. B. Lippincott, 1957.

Wirt, William. *Patrick Henry: Firebrand of the Revolution*. Boston: Little, Brown, 1961.

21. Thomas Hutchinson

Bailyn, Bernard. *The Ordeal of Thomas Hutchinson*. Cambridge, Mass.: Belknap Press of Harvard University Press, 1974.

22. John Jay

Morris, Richard B. "The Jay Papers: Mission to Spain." *American Heritage* 19, no. 2 (1968): 8–21, 85–96.

———. *The Peacemakers: The Great Powers and American Independence*. New York: Harper and Row, 1965.

Smith, Donald C. *John Jay: Founder of a State and Nation*. New York: Columbia University Press, 1968.

23. Thomas Jefferson

Appleby, Joyce. *Thomas Jefferson*. New York: Times Books, 2003.

Chinard, Gilbert. *Thomas Jefferson: The Apostle of Americanism*. New York: Little, Brown, 1929.

Ellis, Joseph J. *American Sphinx: The Character of Thomas Jefferson*. New York: Knopf, 1997.

Fleming, Thomas. *The Man from Monticello: An Intimate Life of Thomas Jefferson*. New York: William Morrow, 1969.

Gordon-Reed, Annette. *Thomas Jefferson and Sally Hemings: An American Controversy*. Charlottesville: University Press of Virginia, 1997.

Kimball, Marie G. *Jefferson: War and Peace, 1776–1784*. New York: Coward-McCann, 1947.

Lewis, Jan Ellen, and Peter S. Onuf, eds. *Sally Hemings and Thomas Jefferson*. Charlottesville: University Press of Virginia, 1999.

Malone, Dumas. *Jefferson and His Times*. 4 vols. Boston: Little, Brown, 1948–1963.

Merrill, D. Peterson. *Adams and Jefferson: A Revolutionary Dialogue*. Athens: University of Georgia Press, 1976.

Morgan, Edmund S. *The Meaning of Independence: John Adams, George Washington, and Thomas Jefferson*. Charlottesville: University of Virginia Press, 1976.

Onuf, Peter. "Thomas Jefferson's Legacy." *Daughters of the American Revolution Magazine* 127 (1993).

Padover, Saul K. *Jefferson*. New York: New American Library, 1970.

Randall, Willard. *Thomas Jefferson: A Life*. New York: H. Holt, 1993.

Risjord, Norman K. *Thomas Jefferson*. Madison, Wis.: Madison House, 1994.

Smith, Page. *Jefferson: A Revealing Biography*. New York: McGraw Hill, 1976.

Wills, Garry. *Inventing America: Jefferson's Declaration of Independence*. Garden City, N.Y.: Doubleday, 1978.

24. Henry Laurens

Fetch, Laura P. *The Career of Henry Laurens in the Continental Congress, 1777–1779*. Chapel Hill: University of North Carolina Press, 1972.

Hamer, Philip M., et al. *The Papers of Henry Laurens*. Columbia: University of South Carolina Press, 1968.

Lamb, Martha J. *Henry Laurens in the Tower of London*. New York: Publisher unknown, 1987.

Lauren, Henry. "Narrative of His Capture, of His Confinement in the Tower of London, Etc., 1780, 1781, 1782." *South Carolina Historical Society Collections* 1 (1857): 18–83.

25. Richard Henry Lee

Ballagh, James, C., ed. *The Letters of Richard Henry Lee*. Vols. 1–2. New York: DaCapo Press, 1970.

Chitwood, Oliver P. *Richard Henry Lee: Statesman of the Revolution*. Morgantown: University of West Virginia Press, 1967.

Lee, Richard H. L. *Memoir of the Life of Richard Henry Lee*. Philadelphia: H. C. Carey and I. Lea, 1825.

McGaughy, J. Kent. *Richard Henry Lee of Virginia: A Portrait of an American Revolutionary*. Lanham, Md.: Rowman and Littlefield, 2003.

26. William Legge (Lord Dartmouth)

Bargar, B. D. *Lord Dartmouth and the American Revolution*. Columbia: University of South Carolina Press, 1965.

27. Robert Livingston

Dangerfield, George. *Chancellor Robert Livingston of New York, 1746–1813*. New York: Harcourt Brace, 1960.

28. James Madison

Ketcham, Ralph. *James Madison: A Biography*. Charlottesville: University Press of Virginia, 1990.

Mason, Joseph, ed. *The Papers of James Madison*. Charlottesville: University Press of Virginia, 1985.

29. Gouverneur Morris

Adams, William Howard. *Gouverneur Morris: An Independent Life*. New Haven, Conn.: Yale University Press, 2003.

Brookhiser, Richard. *Gentleman Revolutionary: Gouverneur Morris: The Rake Who Wrote the Constitution*. New York: Free Press, 2003.

Walther, Daniel. *Gouverneur Morris: Witness of Two Revolutions*. New York: Funk and Wagnalls, 1970.

30. Robert Morris

Summer, William G. *The Financier and the Finances of the American Revolution*. New York: B. Franklin, 1970.

Young, Eleanor M. *Forgotten Patriot: Robert Morris*. New York: Macmillan, 1950.

31. Frederick North

Christie, Ian R. *The End of North's Ministry, 1780–1782*. London: Macmillan, 1958.

Ketchum, Richard M. "Men of the Revolution–Lord North." *American Heritage* 23, no. 2 (1972): 18–19.

Ritcheson, Charles R. *British Policies and the American Revolution*. Norman: University of Oklahoma Press, 1954.

Robinson, Eric. "Lord North." *History Today* 2 (1952): 532–38.

Temperley, Harold W. V. "Chatham, North, and North America." *Quarterly Review* 221 (1914): 295–319.

Thomas, Peter D. *Lord North*. New York: St. Martins Press, 1976.

Valentine, Alan. *Lord North*. 2 vols. Norman: University of Oklahoma Press, 1967.

32. Thomas Paine

Aldridge, Alfred O. *Man of Reason: The Life of Tom Paine*. Philadelphia: J. B. Lippincott, 1957.

Conway, Moncure D. *The Life of Thomas Paine*. New York: B. Blom, 1969.

Foner, Eric. *Thomas Paine and Revolutionary America*. New York: Oxford University Press, 1976.

Gerson, Noel B. *Rebel! A Biography of Thomas Paine*. New York: Praeger, 1974.

Hawke, David F. *Paine*. New York: Harper and Row, 1974.

Paine, Thomas. *The Life and Works of Thomas Paine*. New Rochelle, N.Y.: Thomas Paine National Historical Association, 1925.

Philip, Mark. *Paine*. Oxford: Oxford University Press, 1989.

Wilson, Jerome D. *Thomas Paine*. Boston: Twayne Publications, 1989.

33. Charles Willson Peale

Richardson, Edgar P., Brooke Hindel, and Lillian B. Miller. *Charles Willson Peale and His World*. New York: Abrams, 1982.

34. Edmund Randolph

Reardon, John J. *Edmund Randolph: A Biography*. New York: Macmillan, 1974.

35. Paul Revere

Fischer, David H. *Paul Revere's Ride*. New York: Oxford University Press, 1994.

Forbes, Esther. *Paul Revere and the World He Lived In*. Boston: Houghton-Mifflin, 1942.
Goss, Elbridge H. *The Life of Colonel Paul Revere*. Boston: Howard W. Spurr, 1891.
Weisberger, Bernard. "Paul Revere: The Man, the Myth, and Midnight Ride." *American Heritage* 28, no. 2 (1977): 24–37.
Wright, Esmond. "An Artisan of the Revolution: Paul Revere." *History Today* 25 (1975): 401–9.
———. *Paul Revere: Artisan, Businessman, and Patriot: The Man behind the Myth*. Boston: Paul Revere Memorial Association, 1988.

36. Charles Rockingham (Marquis of Rockingham)

Hoffman, Ross J. *The Marquis: A Study of Lord Rockingham, 1730–1782*. New York: Fordham Press, 1973.
Longford, Paul. *The First Rockingham Administration, 1765–1766*. London: Oxford University Press, 1973.

37. Benjamin Rush

Butterfield, L. H., ed. *Letters of Benjamin Rush*. Vols. 1–2. Princeton, N.J.: American Philosophical Society, 1951.
Corner, George W., ed. *The Autobiography of Benjamin Rush*. Westport, Conn.: Greenwood Press, 1948.
Goodman, Nathan. *Benjamin Rush: Physician and Citizen, 1746–1813*. Philadelphia: University of Pennsylvania Press, 1934.
Hawke, David Freeman. *Benjamin Rush: Revolutionary Gadfly*. Indianapolis, Ind.: Bobbs-Merrill, 1971.

38. John Rutledge

Barnwell, Joseph W. "Letters of John Rutledge." *South Carolina Historical and Genealogical Magazine* 17 (1916): 131–46; vol. 18 (1917): 43–49, 56–69, 131–42, 155–67.
Barry, Richard H. *Mr. Rutledge of South Carolina*. Freeport, N.Y.: Books for Libraries Press, 1942.
Hartley, Cecil B. *Heroes and Patriots of the South: Comprising Lives of General Francis Marion, General William Moultrie, General Andrew Pickens, and Governor John Rutledge, with Sketches of Other Distinguished Heroes and Patriots Who Served in the Revolutionary War in the Southern States*. Philadelphia: G. G. Evans, 1860.

39. William Tryon

Haywood, Marshall D. *Governor William Tryon and His Administration in the Province of North Carolina, 1765–1771*. Raleigh: Publisher unknown, 1903.

Nelson, Paul D. *William Tryon and the Course of Empire: A Life in British Imperial Service*. Chapel Hill: University of North Carolina Press, 1990.

40. Joseph Warren

Cary, John H. *Joseph Warren: Physician, Politician, Patriot*. Urbana: University of Illinois Press, 1961.

Frothingham, Richard. *Life the Times of Joseph Warren*. New York: DaCapo Press, 1971.

41. George Washington

Abbot, W. W. *The Papers of George Washington*. Charlottesville: University of Virginia Press, 1991.

Baker, William S., comp. *Itinerary of General Washington from June 15, 1775 to December 23, 1783*. Philadelphia: J. B. Lippincott, 1892.

Bernath, Stuart L. "George Washington and the Genesis of American Discipline." *Mid-America* 49 (1967): 83–100.

Billias, George A., ed. *George Washington's Generals*. New York: W. Morrow, 1964.

Boller, Paul F. "Washington and Civilian Supremacy." *Southwest Review* 39 (1954): 9–23.

Burns, James MacGregor, and Susan Dunn. *George Washington*. New York: Times Books, 2004.

Carrington, Henry B. "Washington as a Strategist." *North American Review* 133 (1881): 405–15.

———. *Washington, the Soldier*. New York: C. Scribner's Sons, 1899.

Clark, E. Harrison. *All Cloudless Glory: The Life of George Washington*. Washington, D.C.: Regnery, 1995.

Cunliffe, Marcus. *George Washington: Man and Monument*. Boston: Little, Brown, 1957.

Davis, Burke. *George Washington and the American Revolution*. New York: Random House, 1975.

Ferling, John E. *First of Men: A Life of George Washington*. Knoxville: University of Tennessee Press, 1988.

Fitzpatrick, John C. *George Washington Himself: A Common-sense Biography Written from His Manuscripts*. Indianapolis: Bobbs-Merrill, 1933.

Flexner, James T. *George Washington*. 4 vols. Boston: Little, Brown, 1965–1972.

Freeman, Douglas S. *George Washington: A Biography*. 7 vols. New York: Charles Scribner's Sons, 1948–1957.

Frothingham, Thomas G. *Washington: Commander in Chief*. Boston: Houghton-Mifflin, 1930.

Grizzard, Frank E., Jr. *George Washington: A Biographical Companion*. Santa Barbara, Calif.: ABC-Clio, 2002.

Headley, Joel T. *Washington and His Generals*. 2 vols. New York: Baker and Scribner, 1847.

Higginbotham, Don. *George Washington Reconsidered*. Charlottesville: University Press of Virginia, 2001.

Irving, Washington. *The Life of George Washington*. Boston: Twayne, 1982.

Jones, Robert F. *George Washington: Ordinary Man, Extraordinary Leader*. New York: Fordham University Press, 2002.

Knollenberg, Bernhard. *Washington and the Revolution. A Reappraisal: Gates, Conway, and the Continental Congress*. New York: Macmillan, 1940.

Knox, Dudley W. *The Naval Genius of George Washington*. Boston: Houghton-Mifflin, 1932.

Morgan, Edmund S. *The Meaning of Independence: John Adams, George Washington, and Thomas Jefferson*. Charlottesville: University of Virginia Press, 1976.

Nettles, Curtis P. *George Washington and American Independence*. Boston: Little, Brown, 1951.

Rothenberg, Gunter E. "Steuben, Washington, and the Question of 'Revolutionary' War." *Indiana Military History Journal* 3 (1978): 5–11.

Schwartz, B. *George Washington: The Making of an American Symbol*. New York: Free Press, 1987.

Spaulding, Oliver L. "The Military Studies of George Washington." *American Historical Review* 29 (1924): 675–80.

Wall, Charles C. *George Washington: Citizen Soldier*. Charlottesville: University of Virginia Press, 1980.

Washington, George. *The Writings of George Washington*. 12 vols. Edited by Jared Sparks. Boston: Charles C. Little and James Brown, 1834–1837.

———. *The Writings of George Washington from the Original Manuscript Sources, 1745–1799*. 39 vols. Edited by John C. Fitzpatrick. Washington, D.C.: Government Printing Office, 1931–1944.

Wiencek, Henry. *An Imperfect God: George Washington, His Slaves, and the Creation of America*. New York: Farrar, Straus, and Giroux, 2003.

Wright, Esmond. *Washington and the American Revolution*. New York: Macmillan, 1957.

Young, Norwood. *George Washington: The Soul of the Revolution*. New York: R. M. McBride, 1932.

42. Noah Webster

Unger, Harlow Giles. *The Life and Times of Noah Webster: An American Patriot*. New York: Wiley, 1998.

43. Benjamin West

Alberts, Robert C. *Benjamin West: A Biography*. Boston: Houghton-Mifflin, 1978.

About the Author

Terry M. Mays (B.A., Auburn University; M.A., University of Southern California; Ph.D., University of South Carolina) is an associate professor at the Citadel in Charleston, South Carolina. He frequently writes in the fields of history and political science. Dr. Mays regularly investigates sites related to the military, political, and social history of Revolutionary America.

On a personal note, one of his ancestors was the wife of General Nathanael Greene. His publications include *Historical Dictionary of the American Revolution* (Scarecrow, 1999); *Historical Dictionary of Multinational Peacekeeping* (Scarecrow, 2003); *Historical Dictionary of International Organizations in Sub-Saharan Africa* (Scarecrow, 2002), cowritten with Dr. Mark DeLancey; and numerous articles and book chapters.